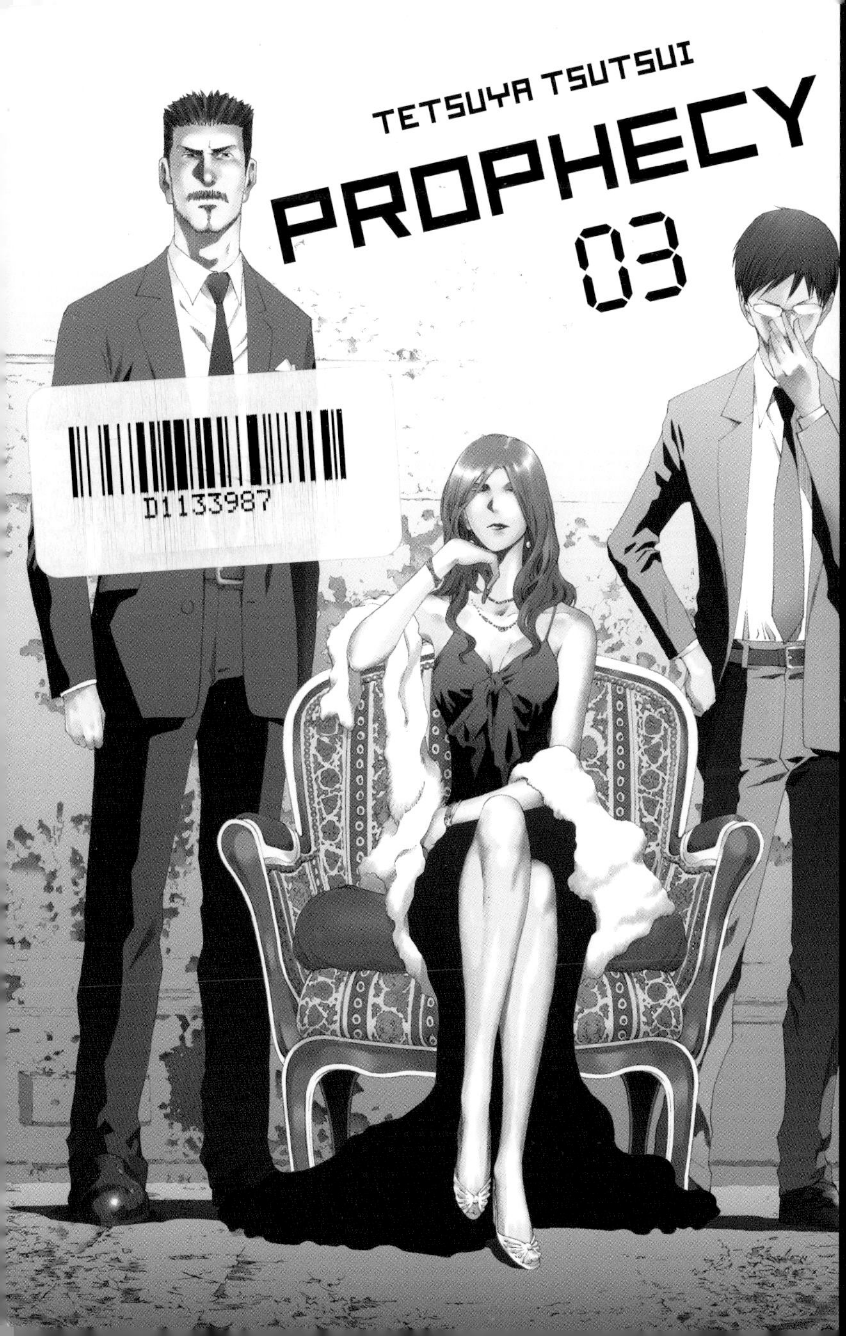
TETSUYA TSUTSUI
PROPHECY
03

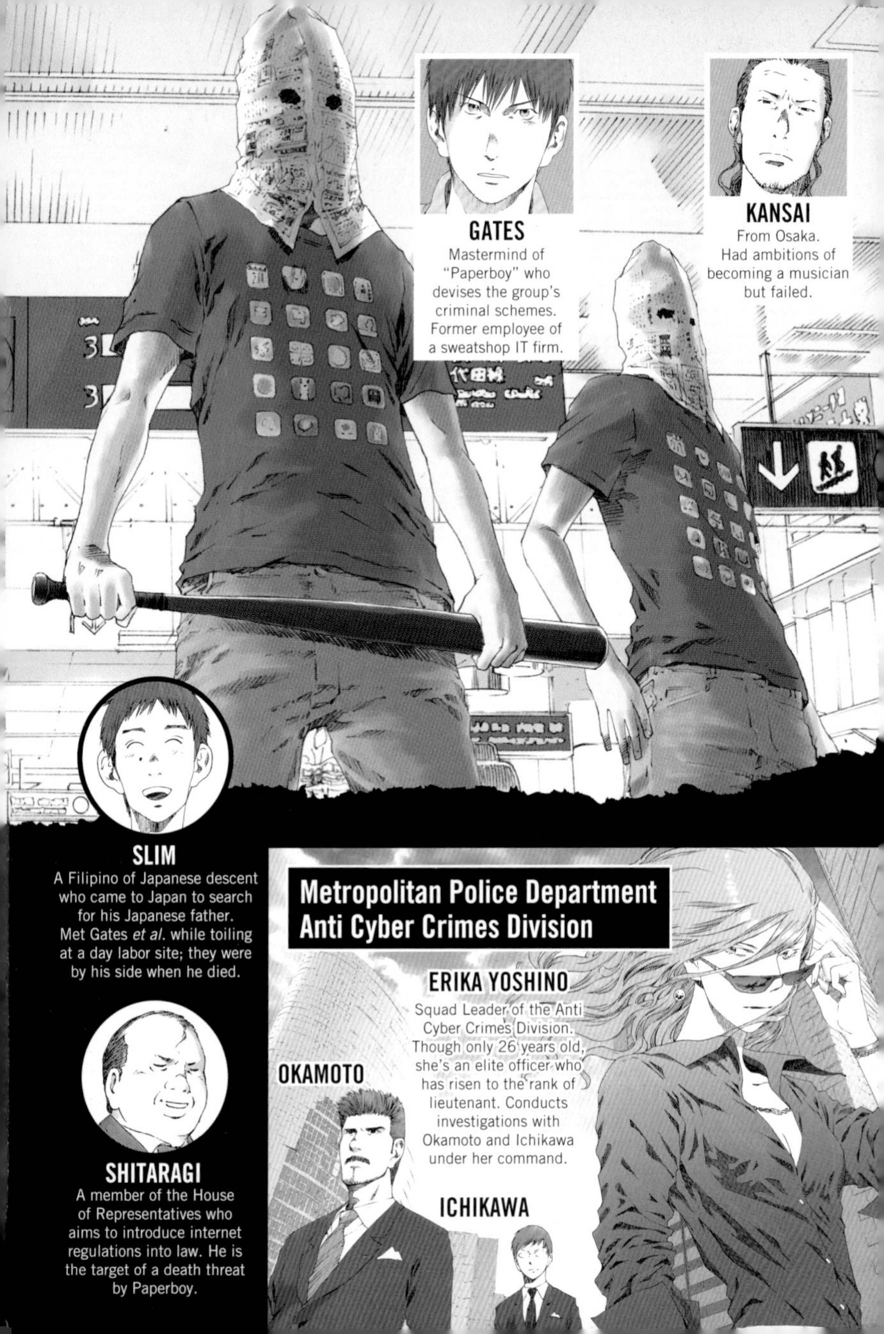

GATES
Mastermind of "Paperboy" who devises the group's criminal schemes. Former employee of a sweatshop IT firm.
KANSAI
From Osaka. Had ambitions of becoming a musician but failed.
SLIM
A Filipino of Japanese descent who came to Japan to search for his Japanese father. Met Gates *et al.* while toiling at a day labor site; they were by his side when he died.
SHITARAGI
A member of the House of Representatives who aims to introduce internet regulations into law. He is the target of a death threat by Paperboy.
Metropolitan Police Department
Anti Cyber Crimes Division
ERIKA YOSHINO
Squad Leader of the Anti Cyber Crimes Division. Though only 26 years old, she's an elite officer who has risen to the rank of lieutenant. Conducts investigations with Okamoto and Ichikawa under her command.
OKAMOTO
ICHIKAWA

Characters

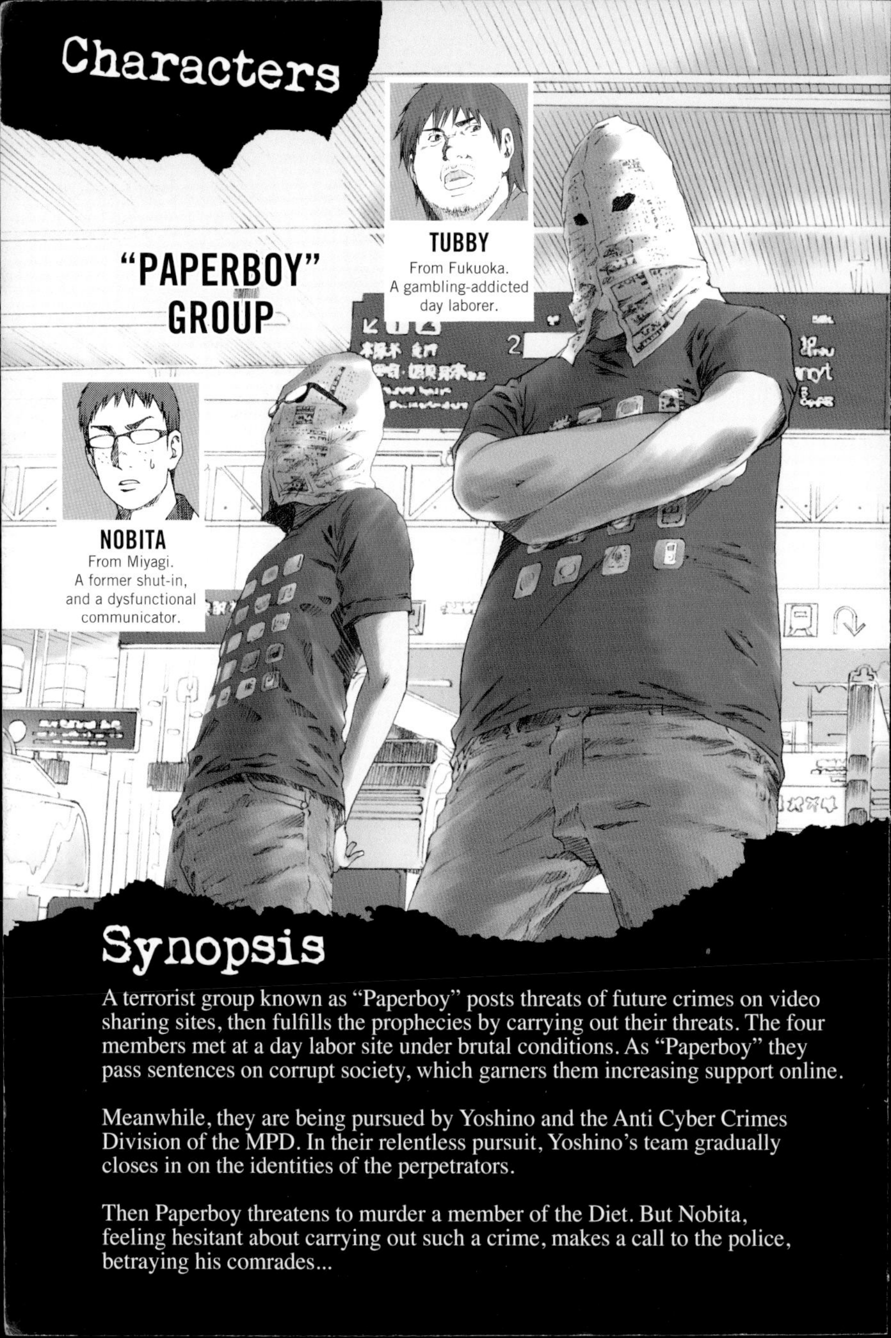

"PAPERBOY" GROUP

TUBBY
From Fukuoka.
A gambling-addicted day laborer.

NOBITA
From Miyagi.
A former shut-in, and a dysfunctional communicator.

Synopsis

A terrorist group known as "Paperboy" posts threats of future crimes on video sharing sites, then fulfills the prophecies by carrying out their threats. The four members met at a day labor site under brutal conditions. As "Paperboy" they pass sentences on corrupt society, which garners them increasing support online.

Meanwhile, they are being pursued by Yoshino and the Anti Cyber Crimes Division of the MPD. In their relentless pursuit, Yoshino's team gradually closes in on the identities of the perpetrators.

Then Paperboy threatens to murder a member of the Diet. But Nobita, feeling hesitant about carrying out such a crime, makes a call to the police, betraying his comrades...

CONTENTS

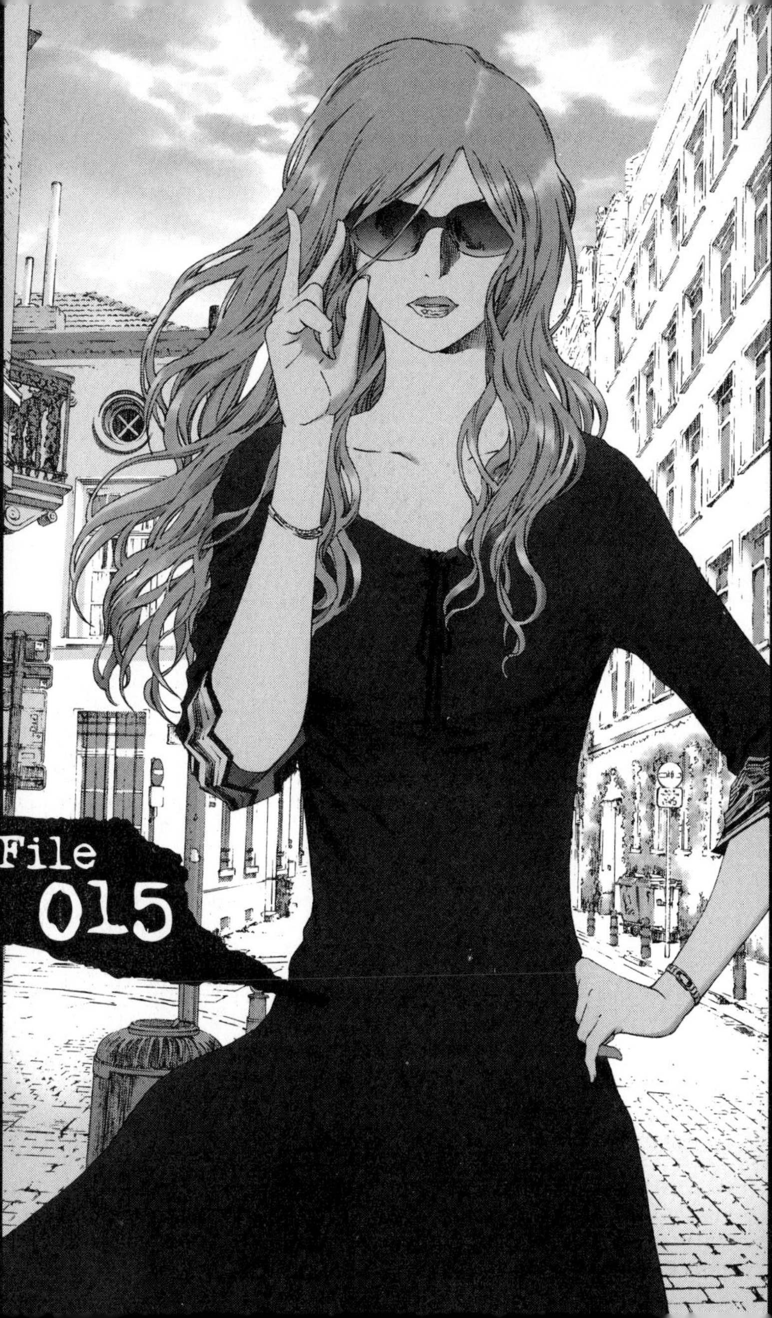
File
015

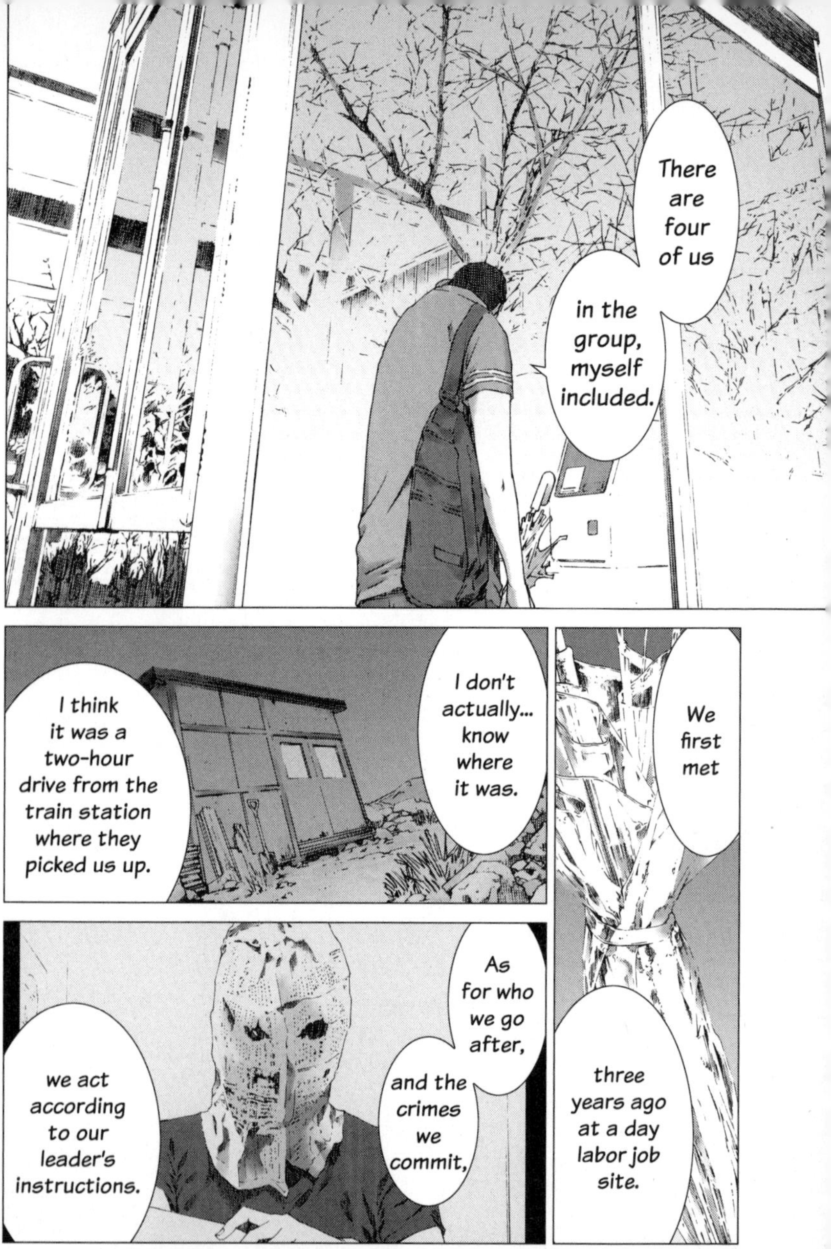
There are four of us
in the group, myself included.
We first met
three years ago at a day labor job site.
I don't actually... know where it was.
I think it was a two-hour drive from the train station where they picked us up.
As for who we go after,
and the crimes we commit,
we act according to our leader's instructions.

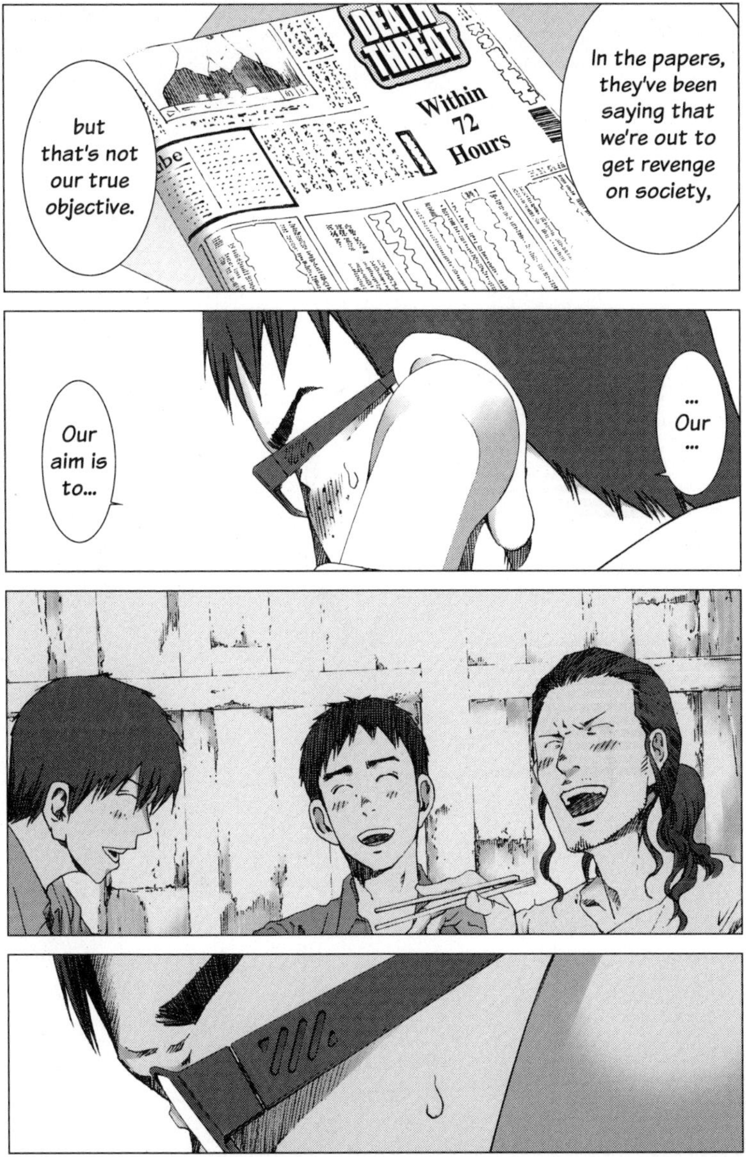

In the papers, they've been saying that we're out to get revenge on society,
DEATH THREAT
Within 72 Hours
but that's not our true objective.
... Our ...
Our aim is to...

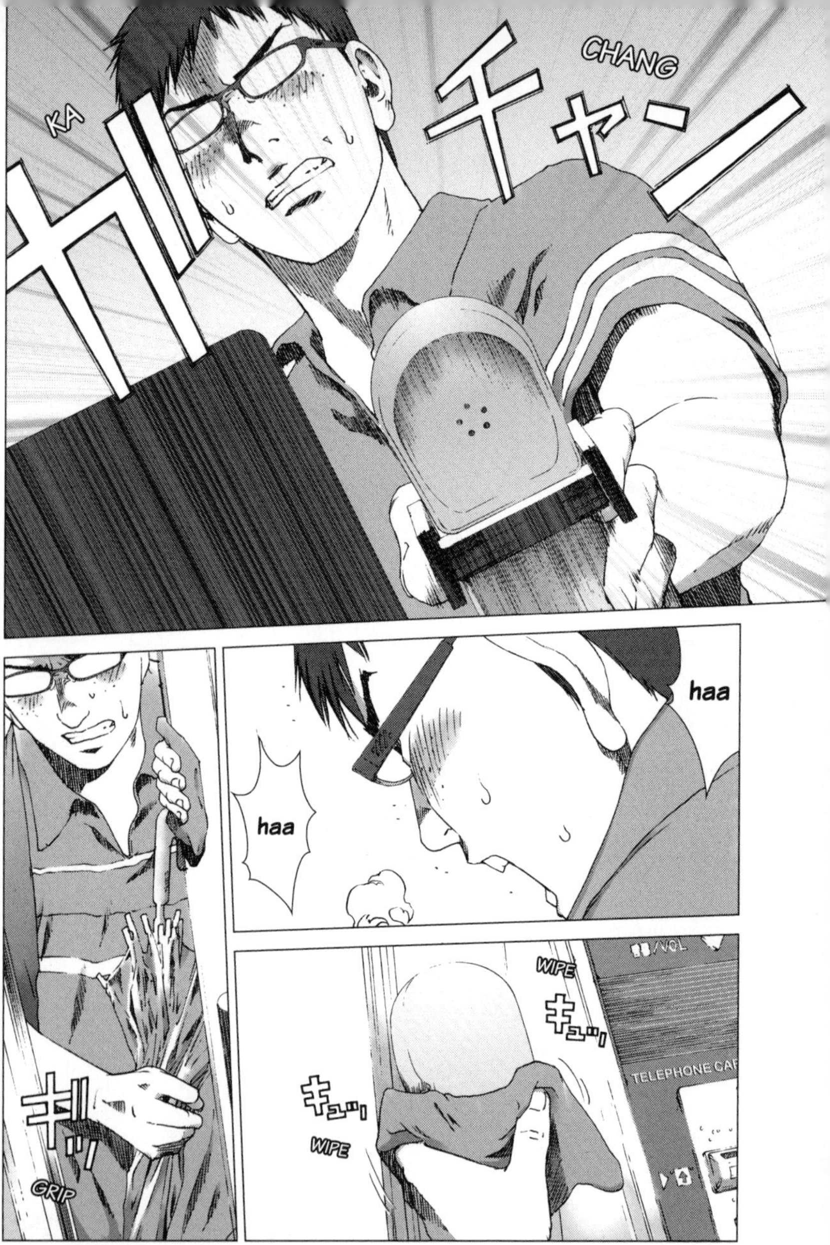

チャーン
CHANG
KA
haa
haa
WIPE
キュッ
キュッ
WIPE
ギュッ
GRIP

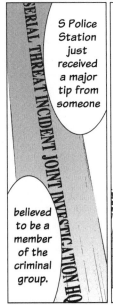

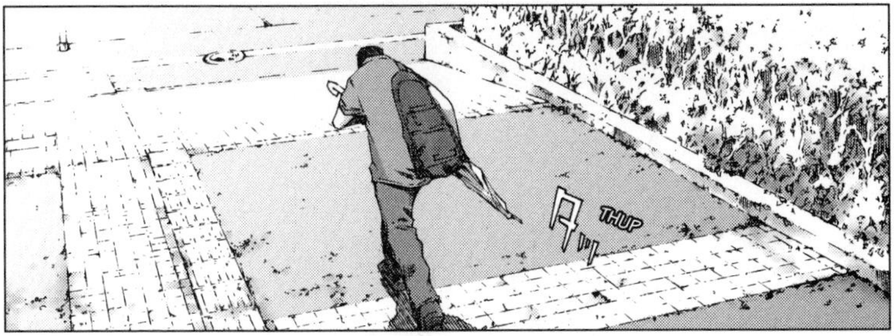
タッ
THUP

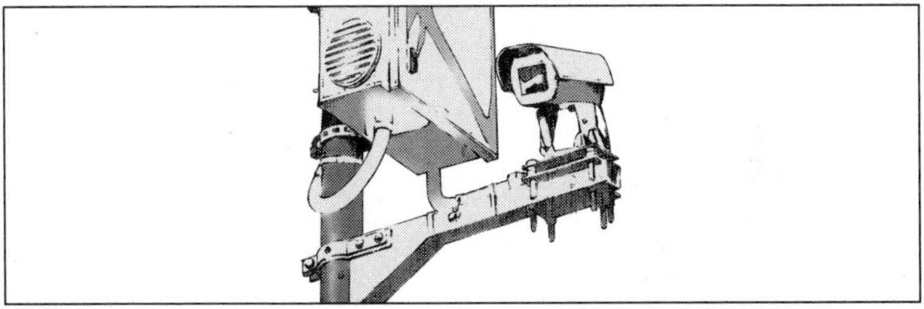

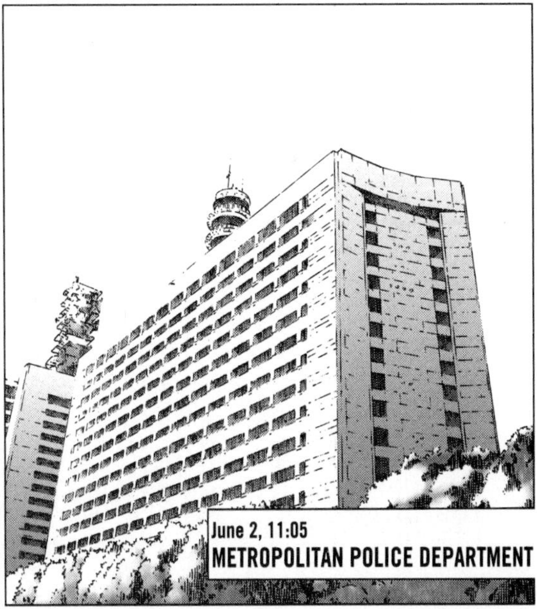
June 2, 11:05
METROPOLITAN POLICE DEPARTMENT

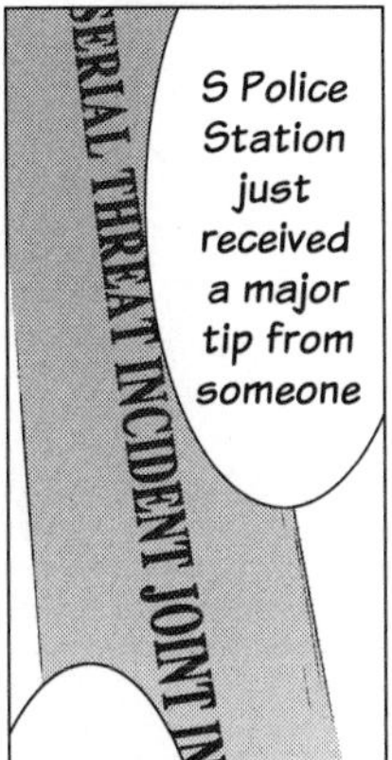
S Police Station just received a major tip from someone
believed to be a member of the criminal group.
SERIAL THREAT INCIDENT JOINT INVESTIGATION HQ

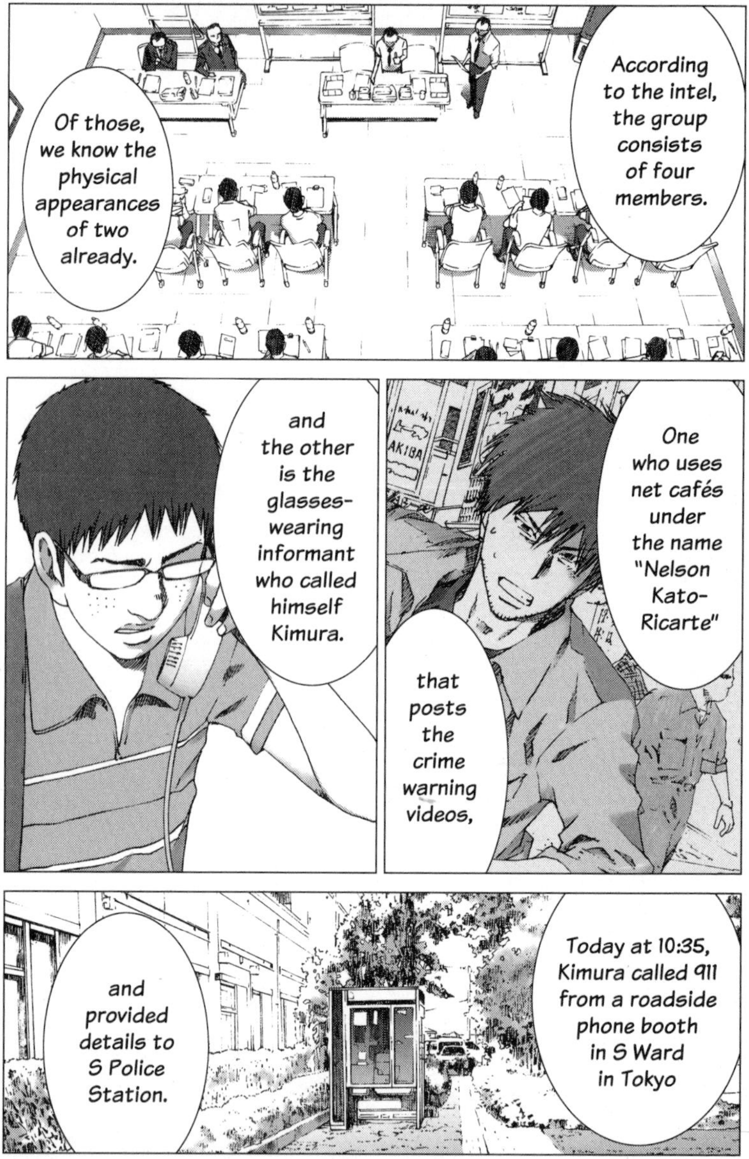
According to the intel, the group consists of four members.
Of those, we know the physical appearances of two already.
One who uses net cafés under the name "Nelson Kato-Ricarte"
that posts the crime warning videos,
and the other is the glasses-wearing informant who called himself Kimura.
Today at 10:35, Kimura called 911 from a roadside phone booth in S Ward in Tokyo
and provided details to S Police Station.

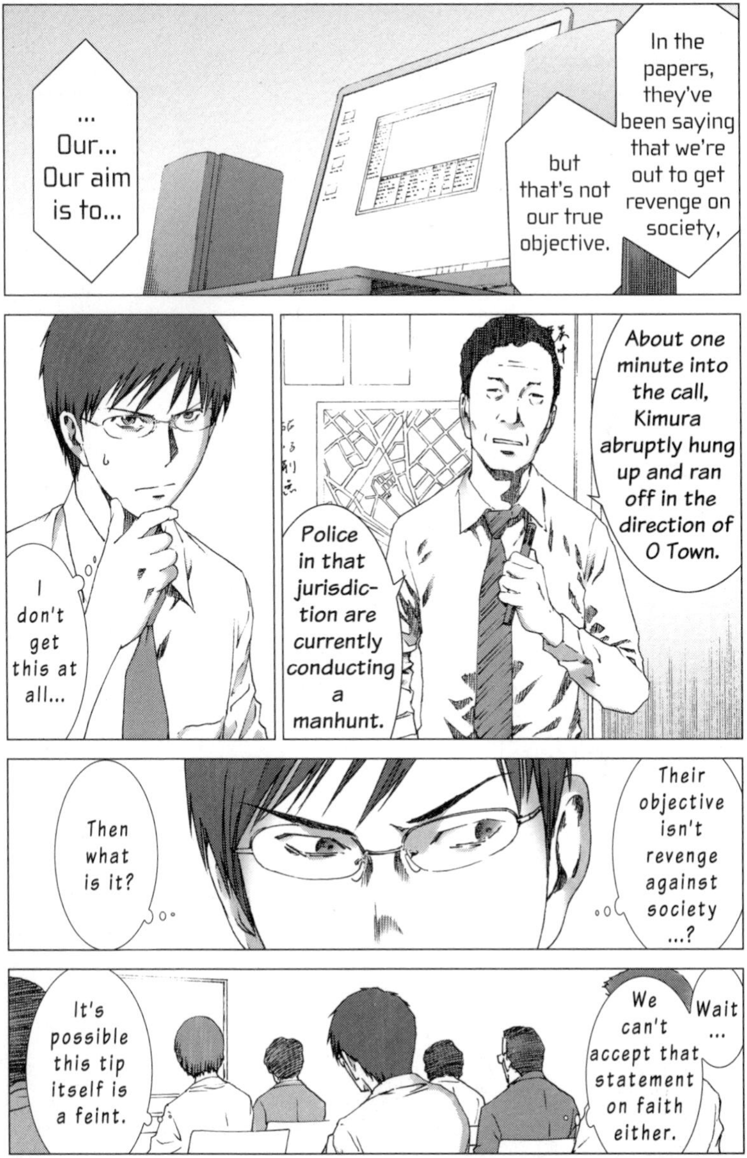
In the papers, they've been saying that we're out to get revenge on society,
but that's not our true objective.
... Our... Our aim is to...
About one minute into the call, Kimura abruptly hung up and ran off in the direction of O Town.
Police in that jurisdiction are currently conducting a manhunt.
I don't get this at all...
Their objective isn't revenge against society ...?
Then what is it?
Wait ...
We can't accept that statement on faith either.
It's possible this tip itself is a feint.

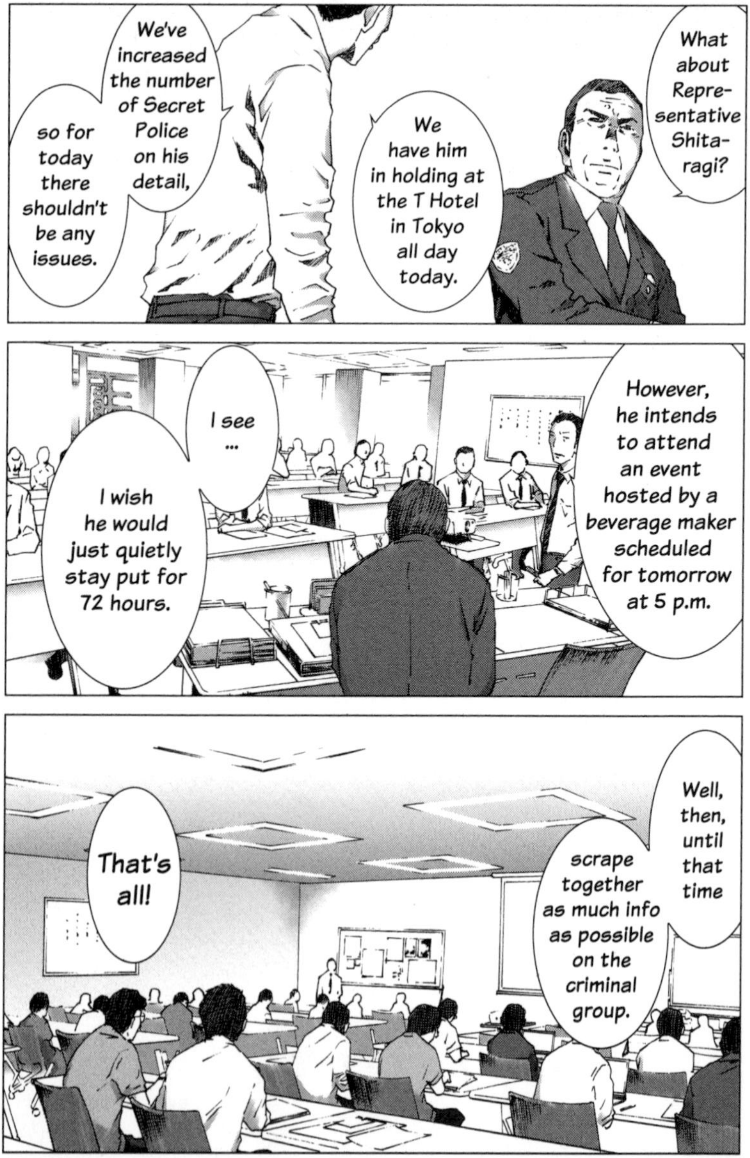
What about Representative Shitaragi?
We have him in holding at the T Hotel in Tokyo all day today.
We've increased the number of Secret Police on his detail,
so for today there shouldn't be any issues.
However, he intends to attend an event hosted by a beverage maker scheduled for tomorrow at 5 p.m.
I see ...
I wish he would just quietly stay put for 72 hours.
Well, then, until that time
scrape together as much info as possible on the criminal group.
That's all!

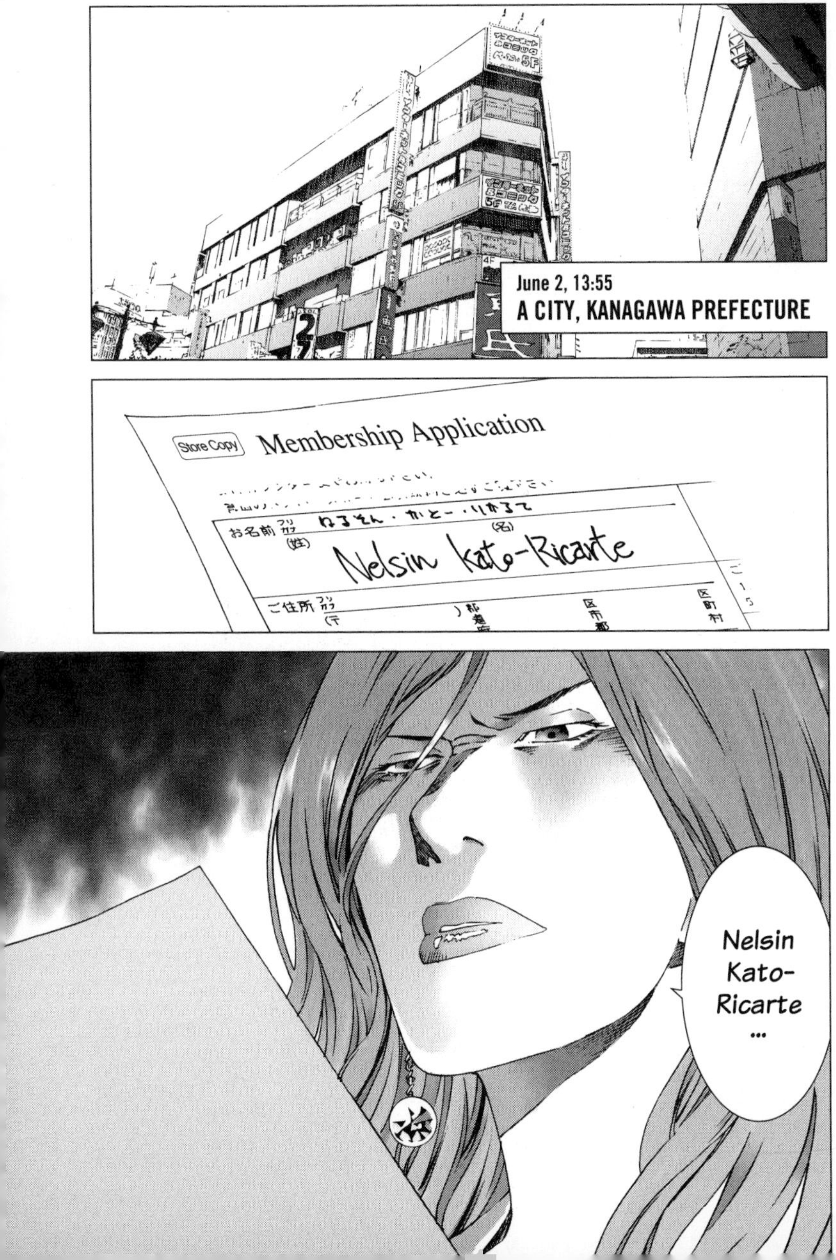

June 2, 13:55
A CITY, KANAGAWA PREFECTURE
Store Copy
Membership Application
お名前
ねるそん・かとー・りかるて
(姓)
(名)
Nelsin Kato-Ricarte
ご住所
Nelsin Kato-Ricarte ...

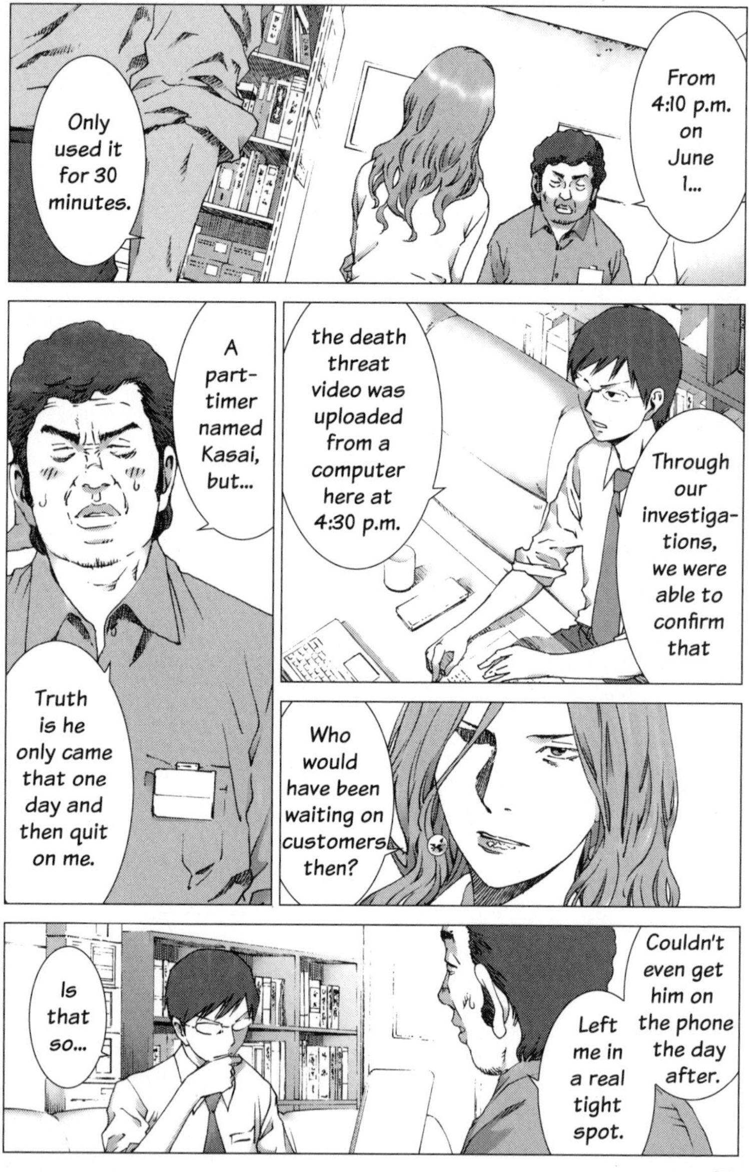
From 4:10 p.m. on June 1...
Only used it for 30 minutes.
Through our investigations, we were able to confirm that
the death threat video was uploaded from a computer here at 4:30 p.m.
Who would have been waiting on customers then?
A part-timer named Kasai, but...
Truth is he only came that one day and then quit on me.
Couldn't even get him on the phone the day after.
Left me in a real tight spot.
Is that so...

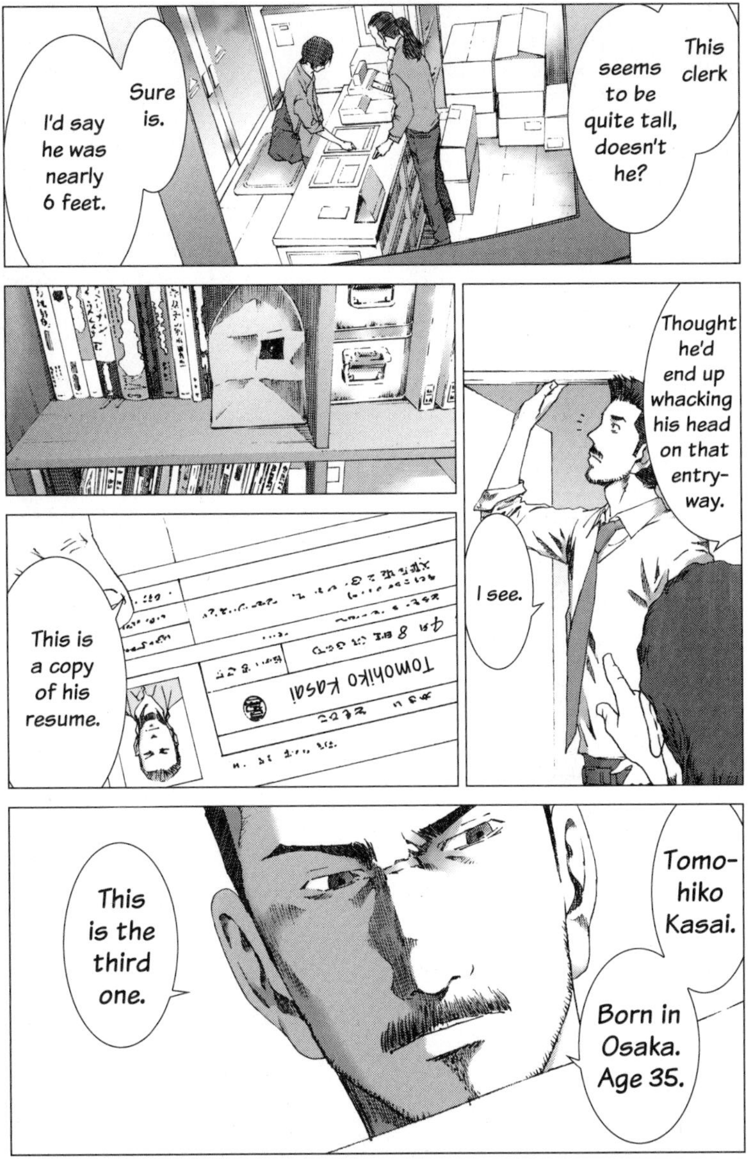
This clerk seems to be quite tall, doesn't he?
Sure is. I'd say he was nearly 6 feet.
Thought he'd end up whacking his head on that entryway.
I see.
This is a copy of his resume.
Tomohiko Kasai
Tomohiko Kasai.
Born in Osaka. Age 35.
This is the third one.

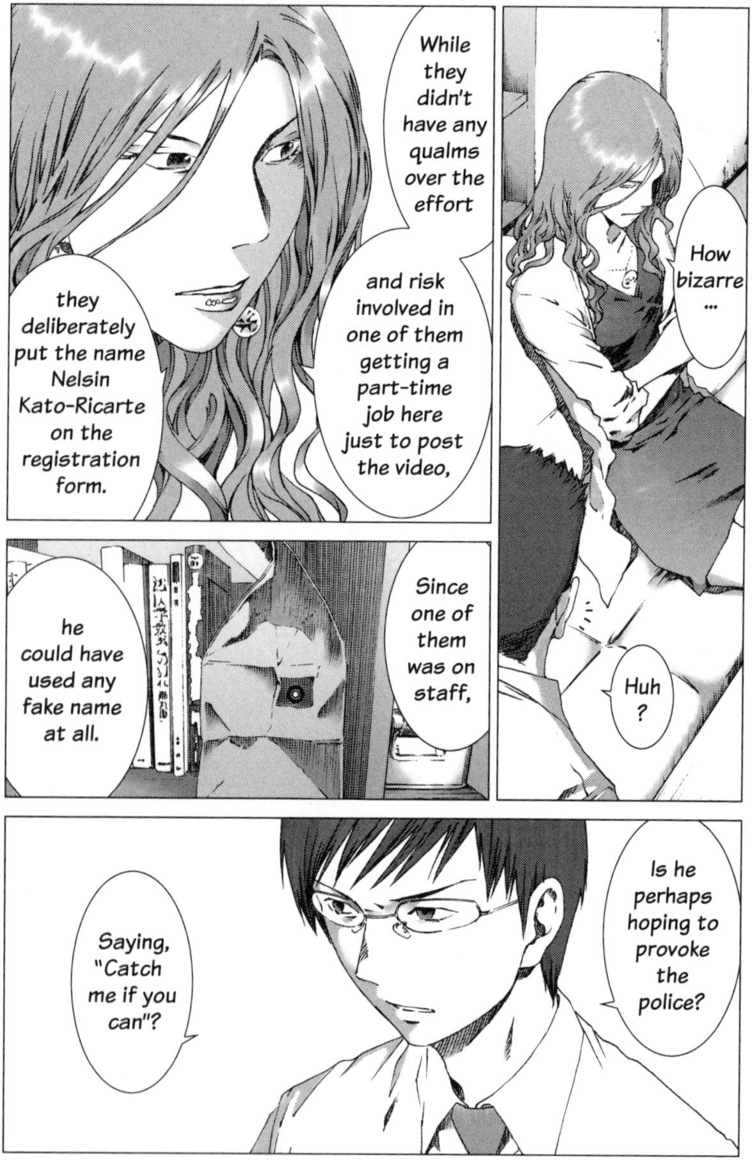
How bizarre ...
Huh?
While they didn't have any qualms over the effort
and risk involved in one of them getting a part-time job here just to post the video,
they deliberately put the name Nelsin Kato-Ricarte on the registration form.
Since one of them was on staff,
he could have used any fake name at all.
Is he perhaps hoping to provoke the police?
Saying, "Catch me if you can"?

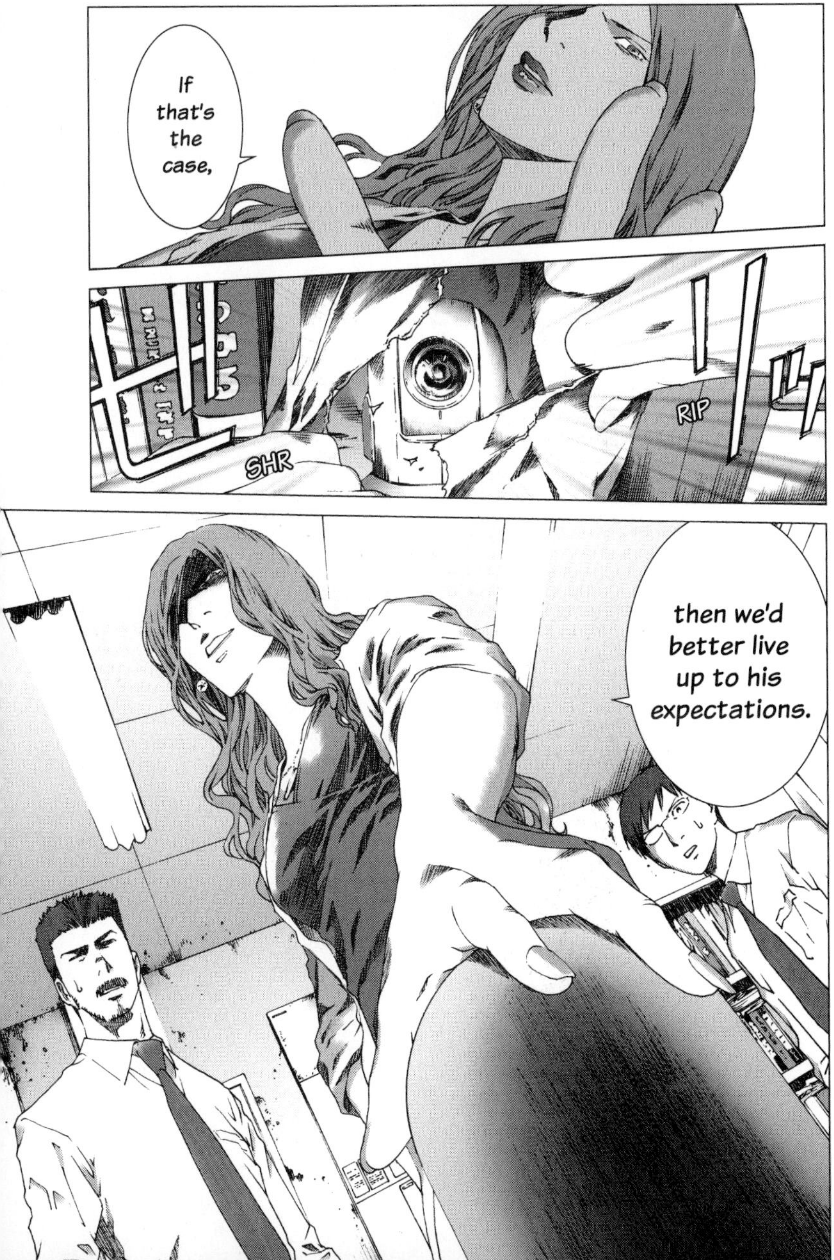
If that's the case,
RIP
SHR
then we'd better live up to his expectations.

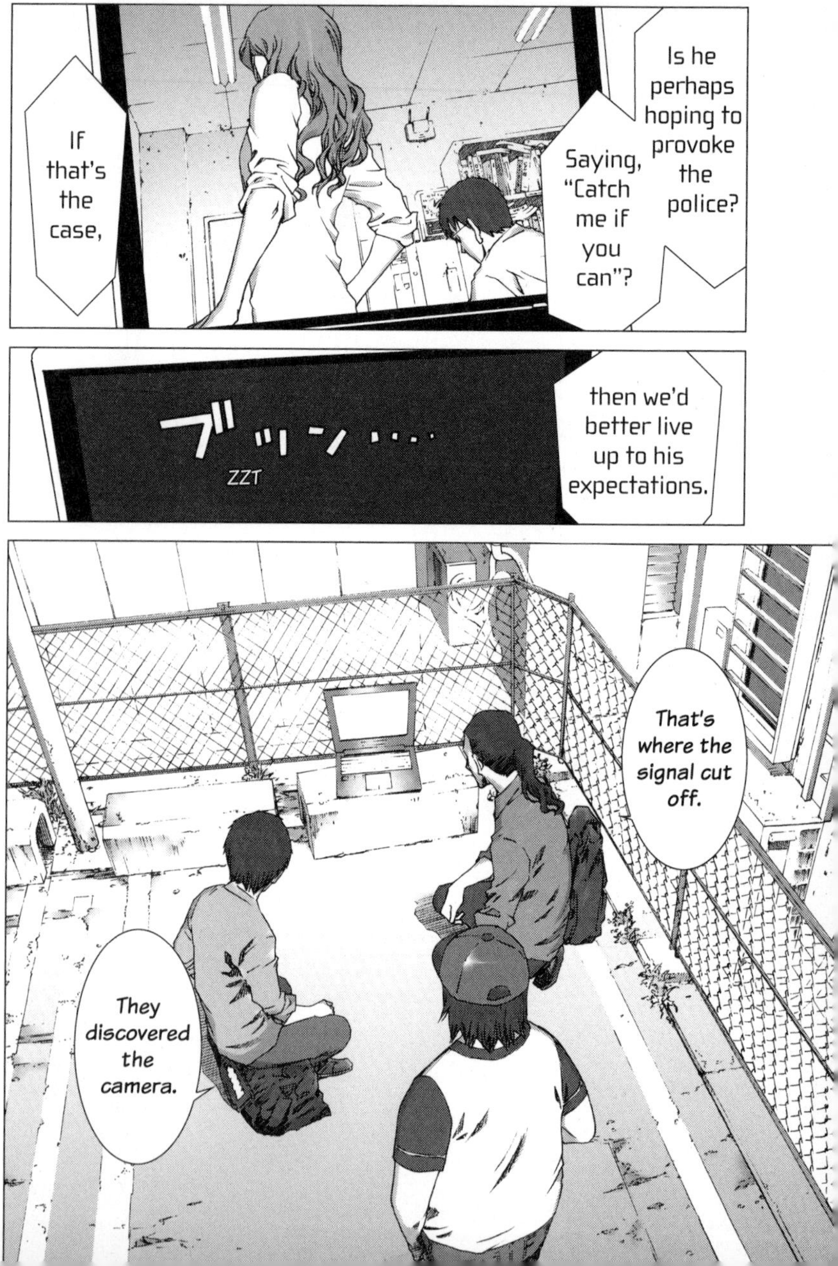
Is he perhaps hoping to provoke the police?
Saying, "Catch me if you can"?
If that's the case,
then we'd better live up to his expectations.
ブツン・・・・
ZZT
That's where the signal cut off.
They discovered the camera.

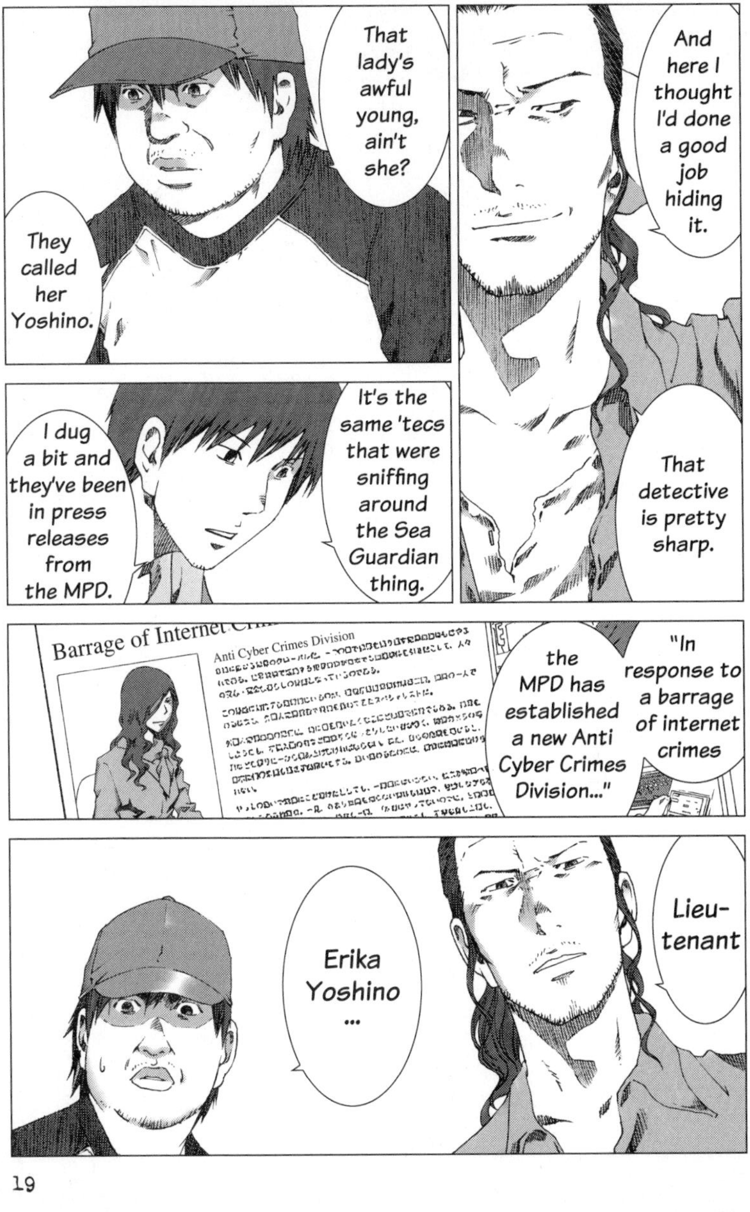

And here I thought I'd done a good job hiding it.
That detective is pretty sharp.
That lady's awful young, ain't she?
They called her Yoshino.
It's the same 'tecs that were sniffing around the Sea Guardian thing.
I dug a bit and they've been in press releases from the MPD.
"In response to a barrage of internet crimes
the MPD has established a new Anti Cyber Crimes Division..."
Barrage of Internet
Anti Cyber Crimes Division
Lieu-tenant
Erika Yoshino ...

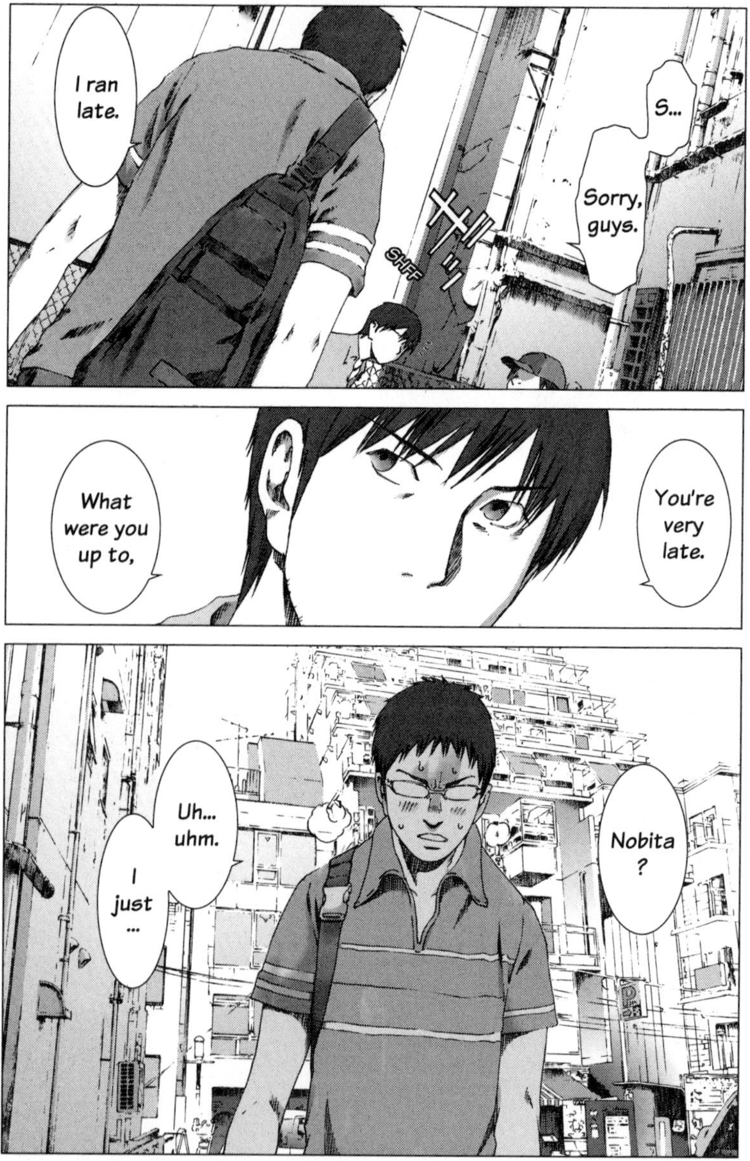
S...
Sorry, guys.
SHFF
I ran late.
You're very late.
What were you up to,
Nobita?
Uh... uhm.
I just ...

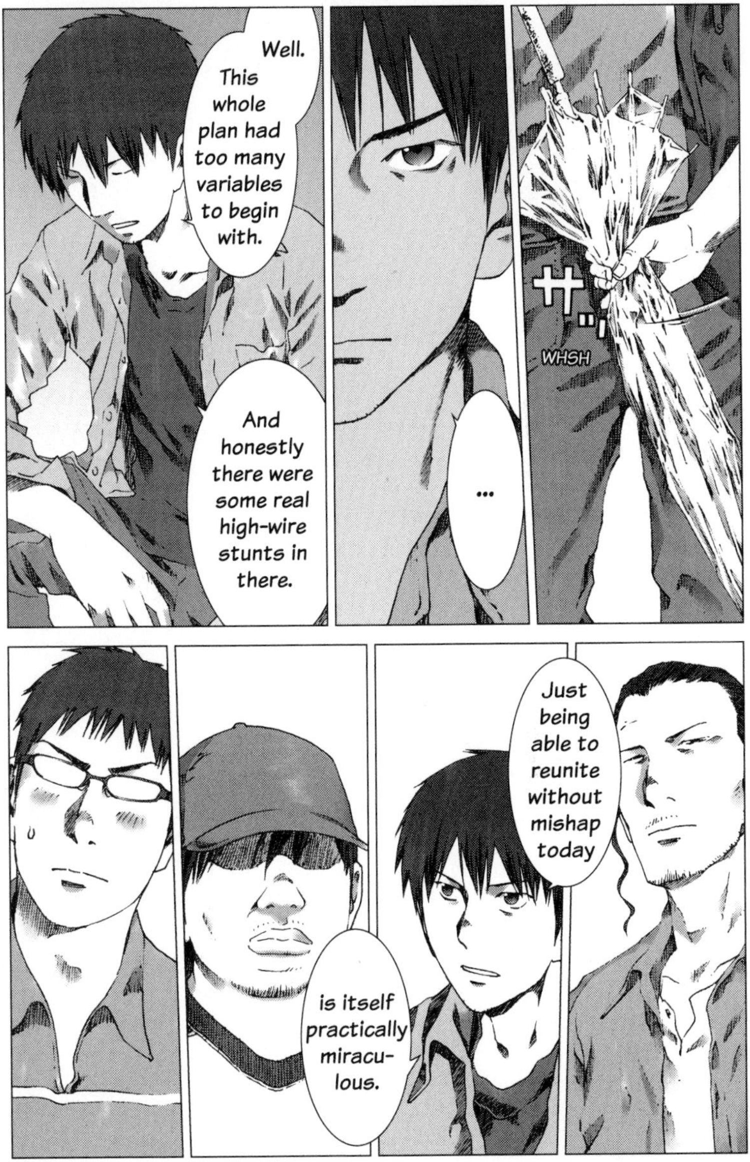
サッ
WHSH
...
Well. This whole plan had too many variables to begin with.
And honestly there were some real high-wire stunts in there.
Just being able to reunite without mishap today
is itself practically miracu-lous.

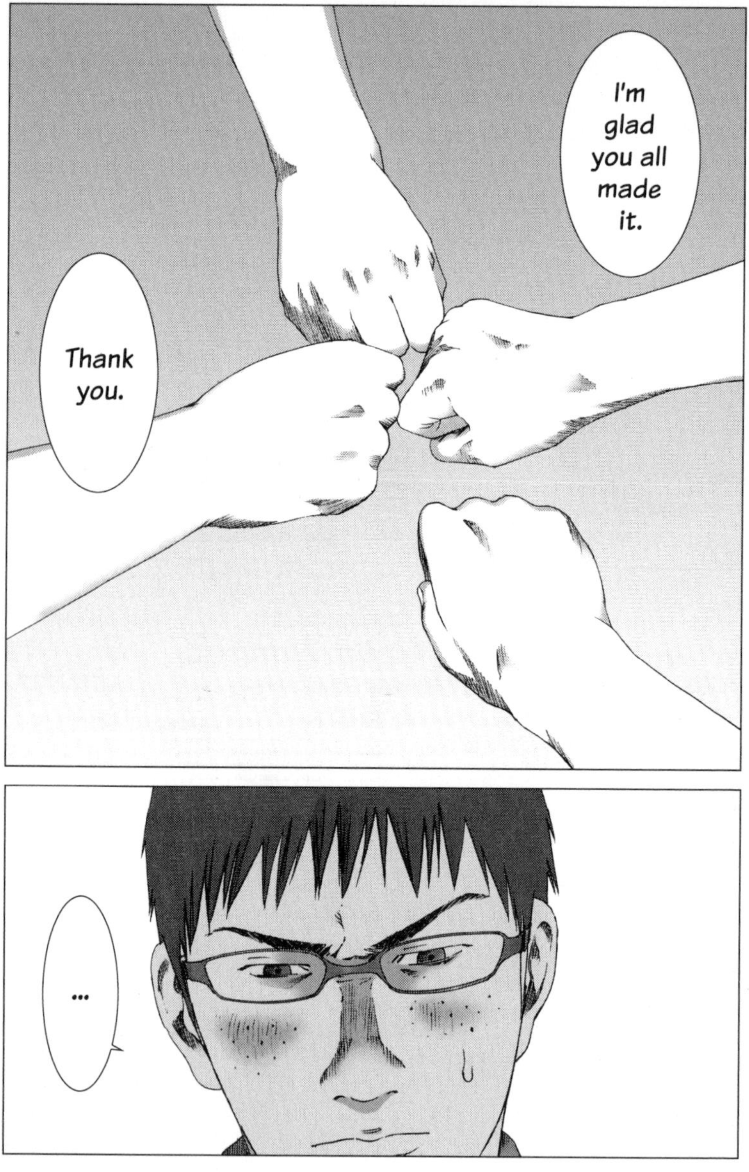
I'm glad you all made it.
Thank you.
...

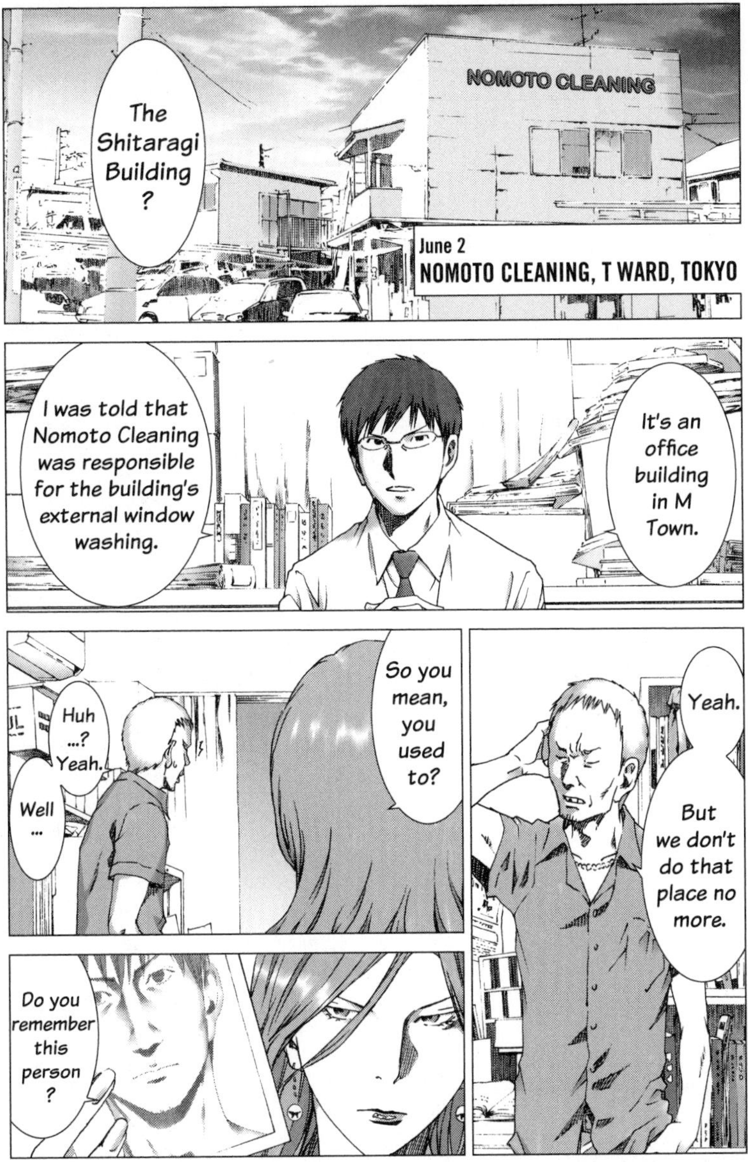
NOMOTO CLEANING
June 2
NOMOTO CLEANING, T WARD, TOKYO
The Shitaragi Building?
It's an office building in M Town.
I was told that Nomoto Cleaning was responsible for the building's external window washing.
Yeah.
But we don't do that place no more.
So you mean, you used to?
Huh ...? Yeah.
Well ...
Do you remember this person?

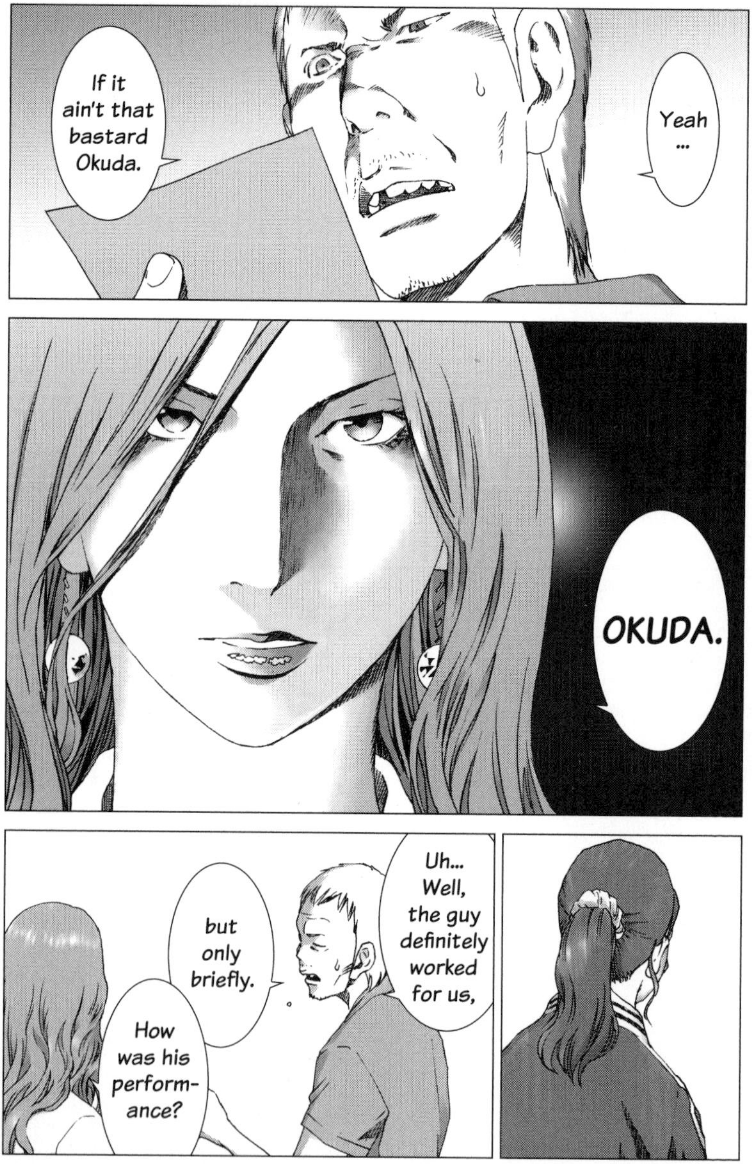
Yeah ...
If it ain't that bastard Okuda.
OKUDA.
Uh... Well, the guy definitely worked for us,
but only briefly.
How was his performance?

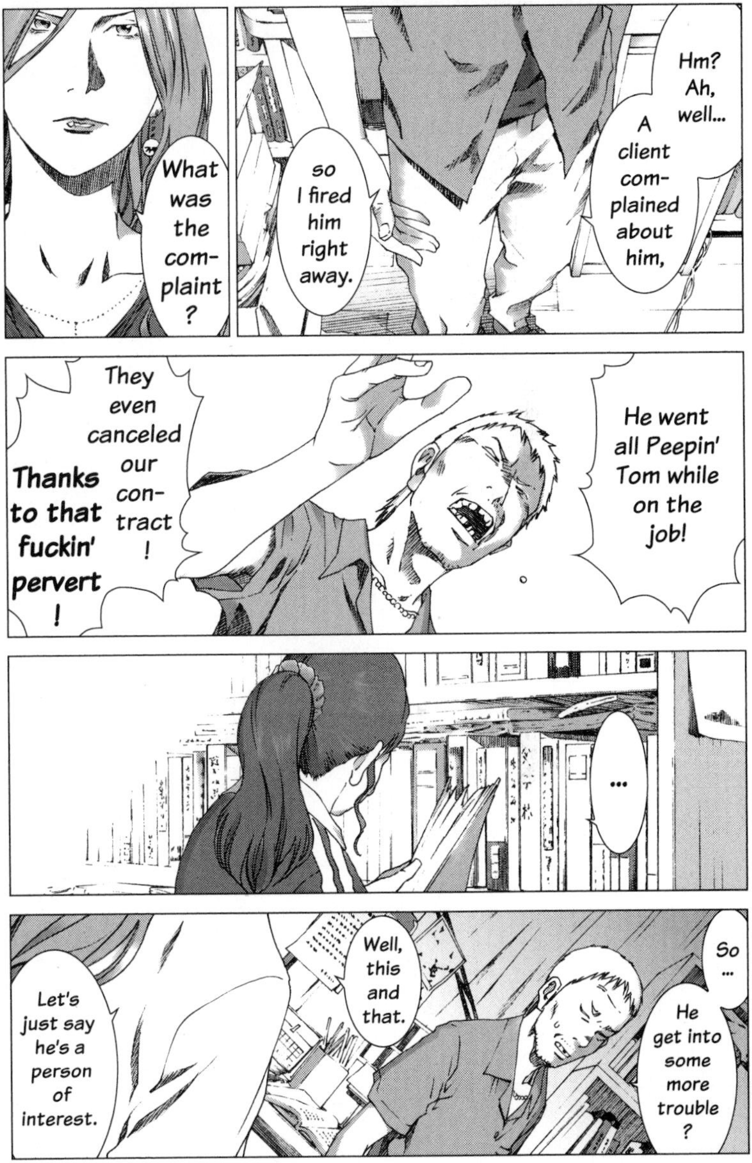
Hm? Ah, well...
A client com-plained about him,
so I fired him right away.
What was the com-plaint?
He went all Peepin' Tom while on the job!
They even canceled our con-tract!
Thanks to that fuckin' pervert!
...
So ... He get into some more trouble?
Well, this and that.
Let's just say he's a person of interest.

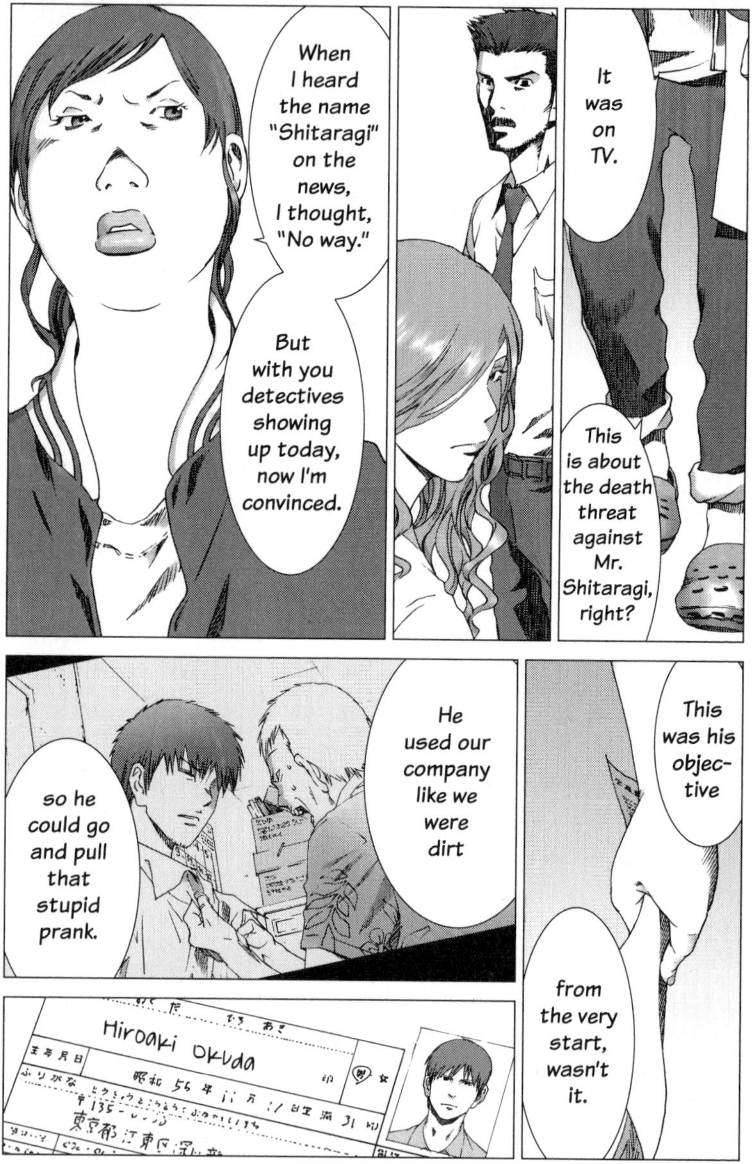
It was on TV.
This is about the death threat against Mr. Shitaragi, right?
When I heard the name "Shitaragi" on the news, I thought, "No way."
But with you detectives showing up today, now I'm convinced.
This was his objective
from the very start, wasn't it.
He used our company like we were dirt
so he could go and pull that stupid prank.
Hiroaki Okuda

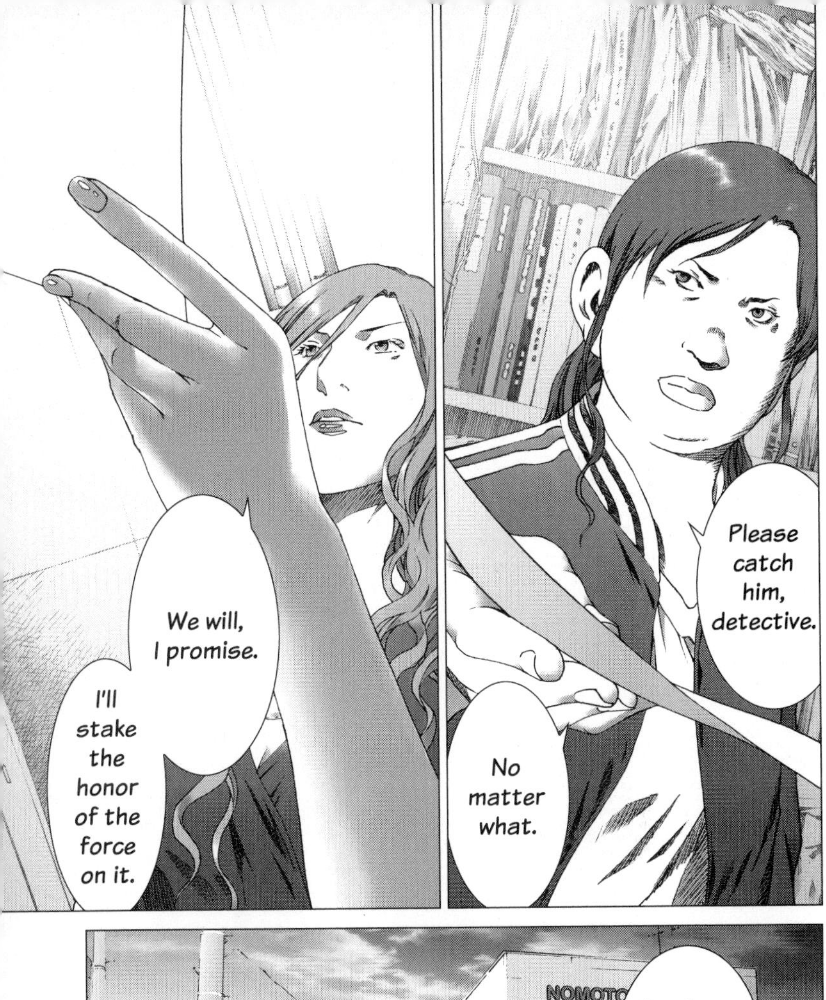
Please catch him, detective.
No matter what.
We will, I promise.
I'll stake the honor of the force on it.
NOMOTO
Thank you very much for your cooperation.

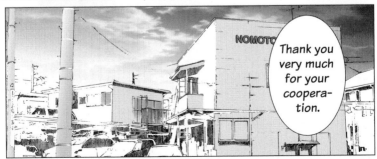

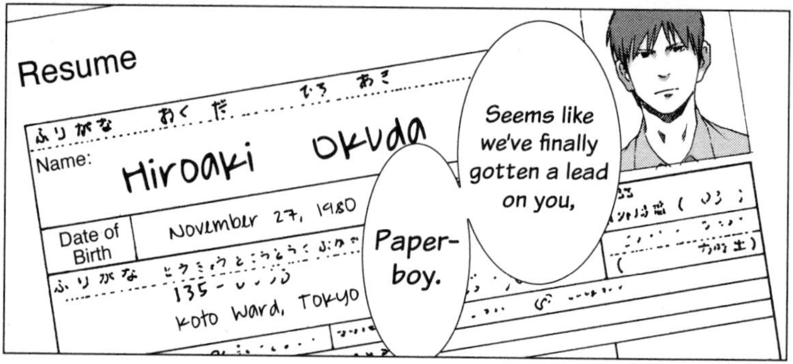
Resume
ふりがな おくだ ひろあき
Name: Hiroaki Okuda
Date of Birth
November 27, 1980
135-
Koto Ward, Tokyo
Seems like we've finally gotten a lead on you,
Paper-boy.

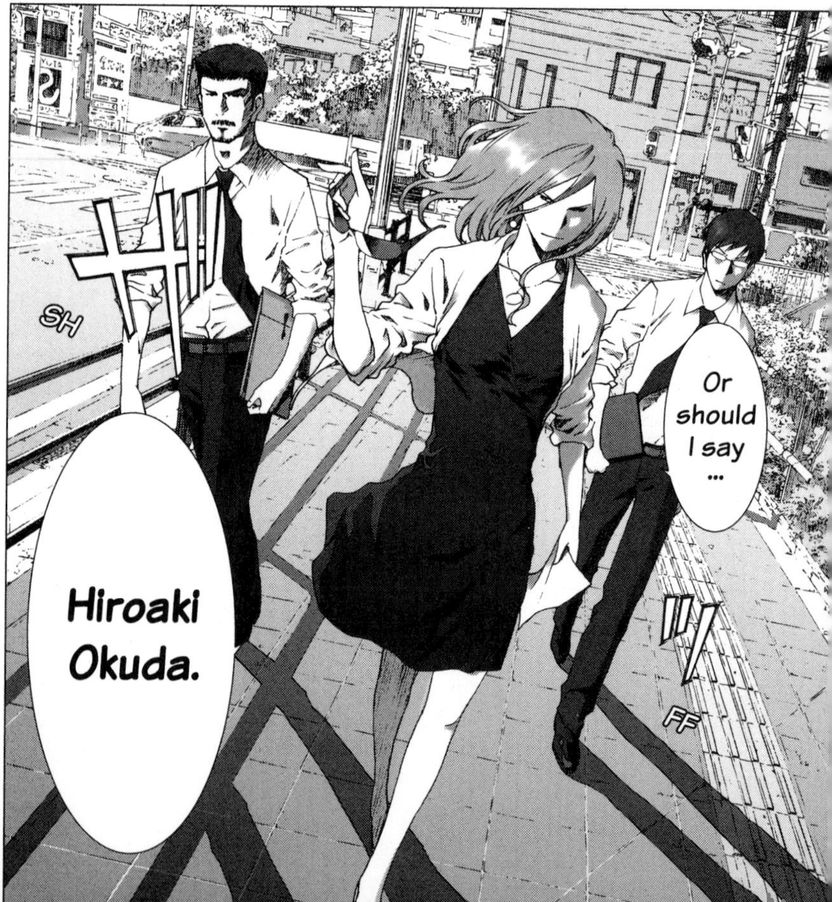
Or should I say ...
Hiroaki Okuda.
SH
FF

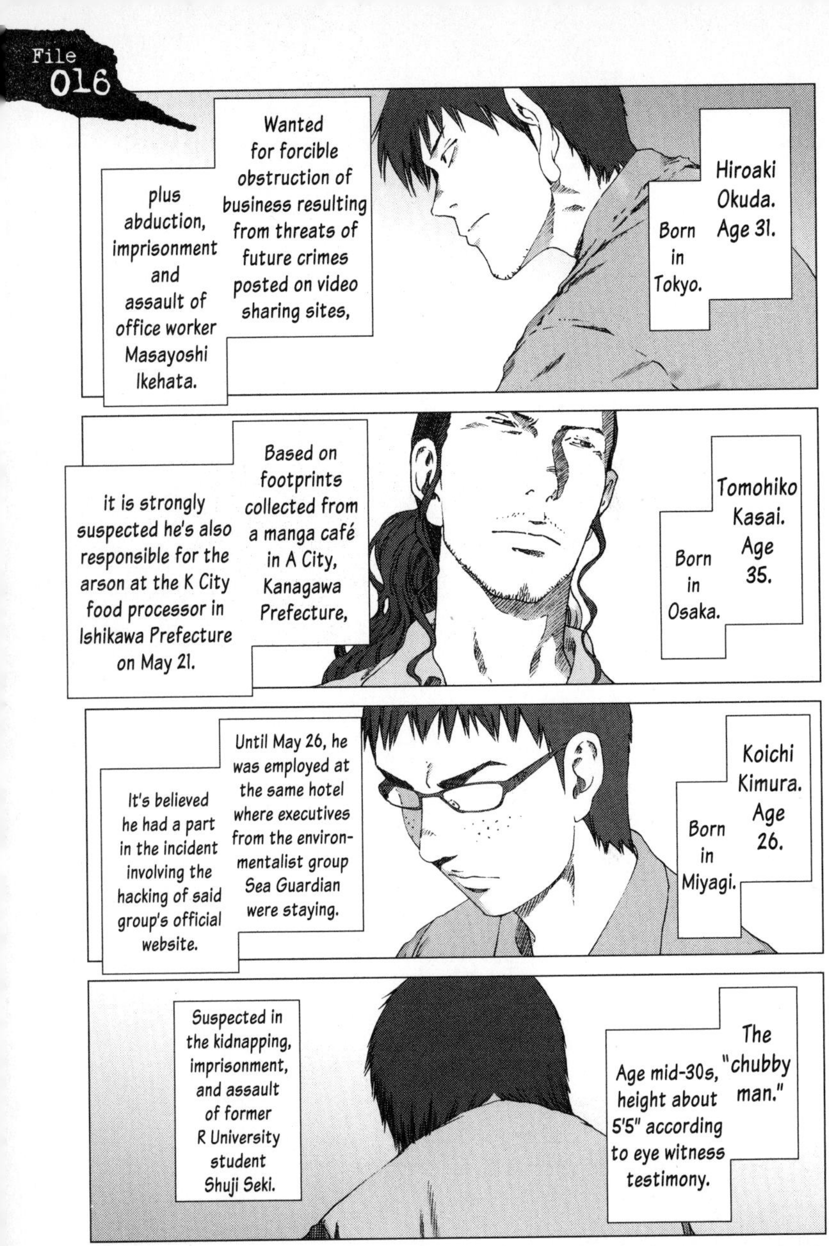
File 016
Hiroaki Okuda. Age 31.
Born in Tokyo.
Wanted for forcible obstruction of business resulting from threats of future crimes posted on video sharing sites,
plus abduction, imprisonment and assault of office worker Masayoshi Ikehata.
Tomohiko Kasai. Age 35.
Born in Osaka.
Based on footprints collected from a manga café in A City, Kanagawa Prefecture,
it is strongly suspected he's also responsible for the arson at the K City food processor in Ishikawa Prefecture on May 21.
Koichi Kimura. Age 26.
Born in Miyagi.
Until May 26, he was employed at the same hotel where executives from the environmentalist group Sea Guardian were staying.
It's believed he had a part in the incident involving the hacking of said group's official website.
The "chubby man."
Age mid-30s, height about 5'5" according to eye witness testimony.
Suspected in the kidnapping, imprisonment, and assault of former R University student Shuji Seki.

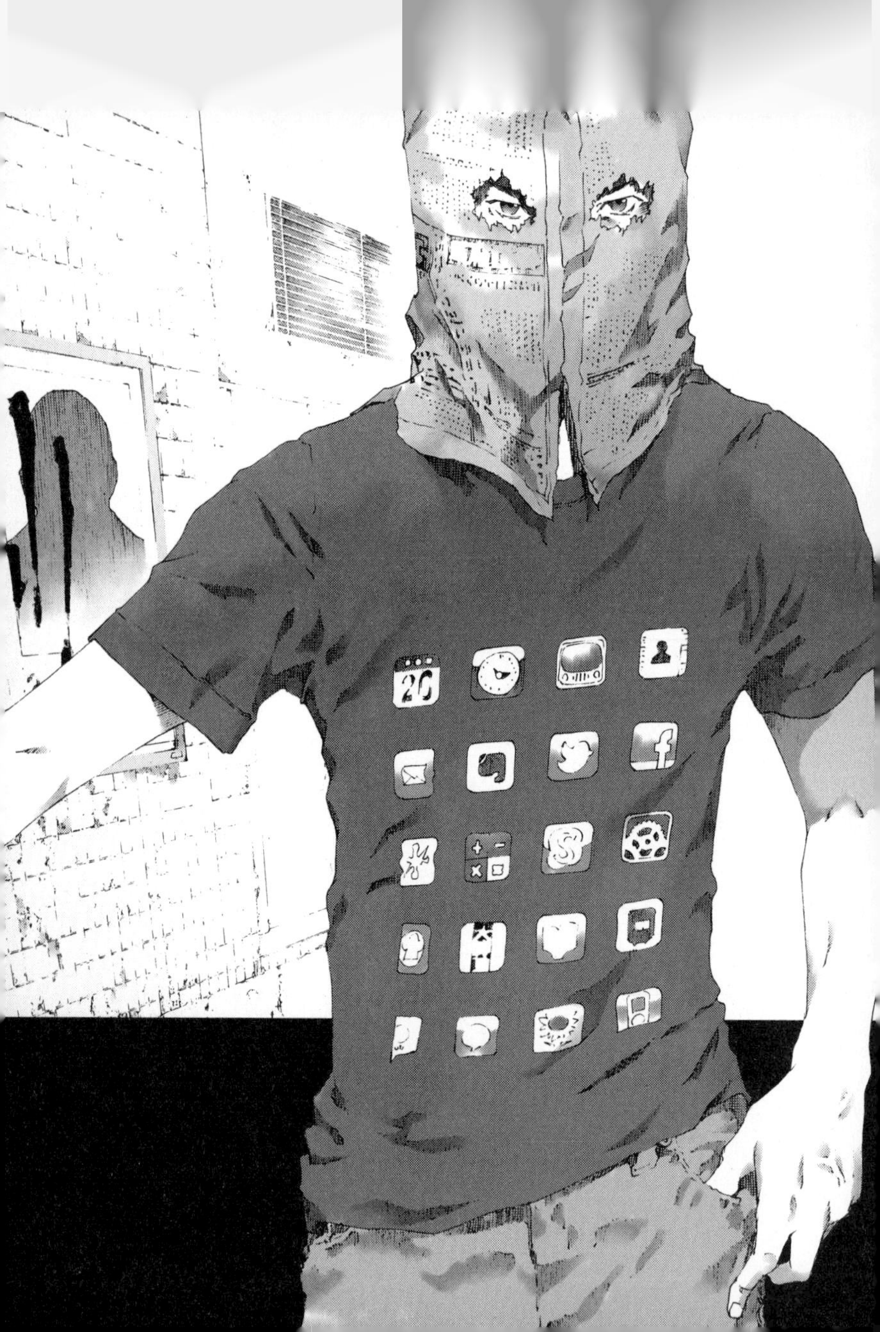

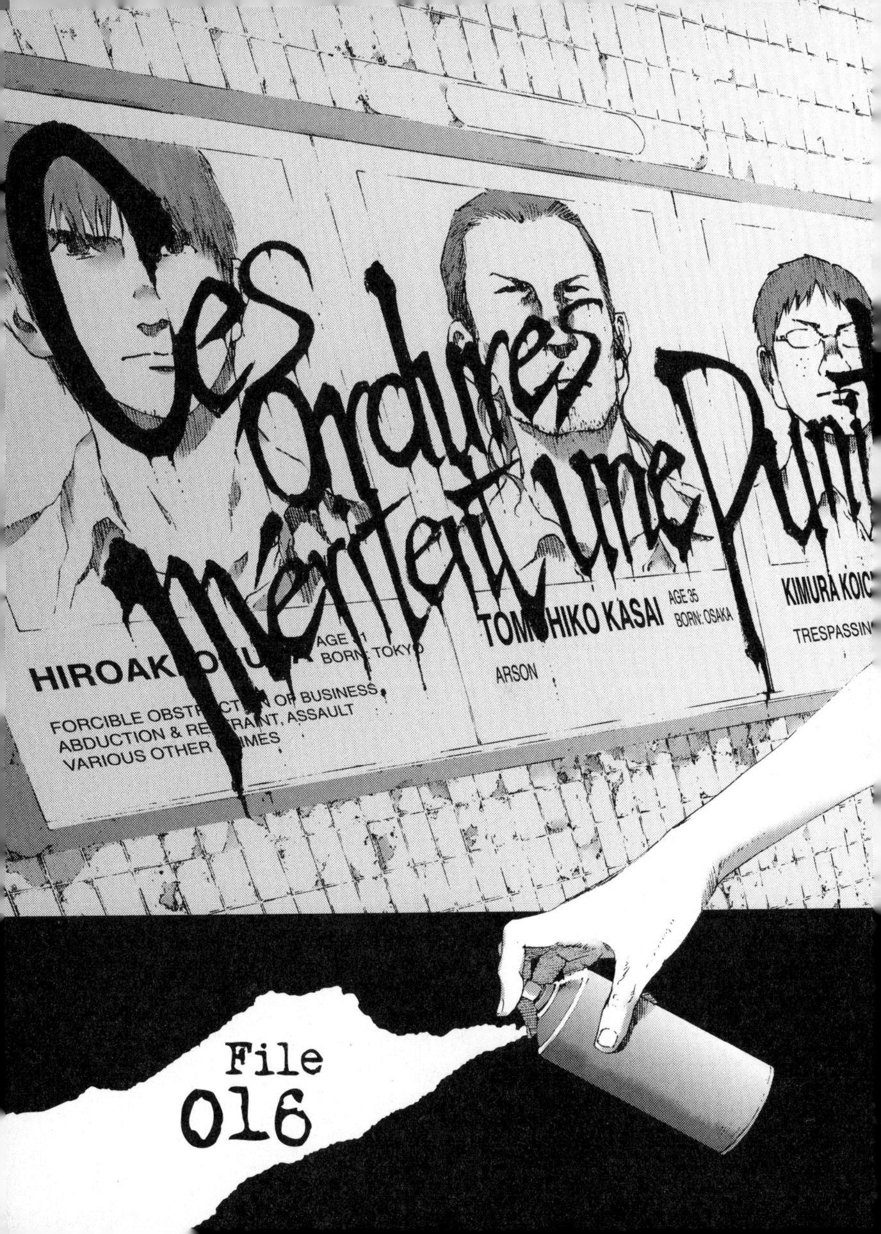

HIROAK
BORN: TOKYO
FORCIBLE OBSTR
OF BUSINESS,
ABDUCTION & RE
AINT, ASSAULT
VARIOUS OTHER
IMES
TOM HIKO KASAI
AGE 35
BORN: OSAKA
ARSON
KIMURA KOIC
TRESPASSIN
File
016

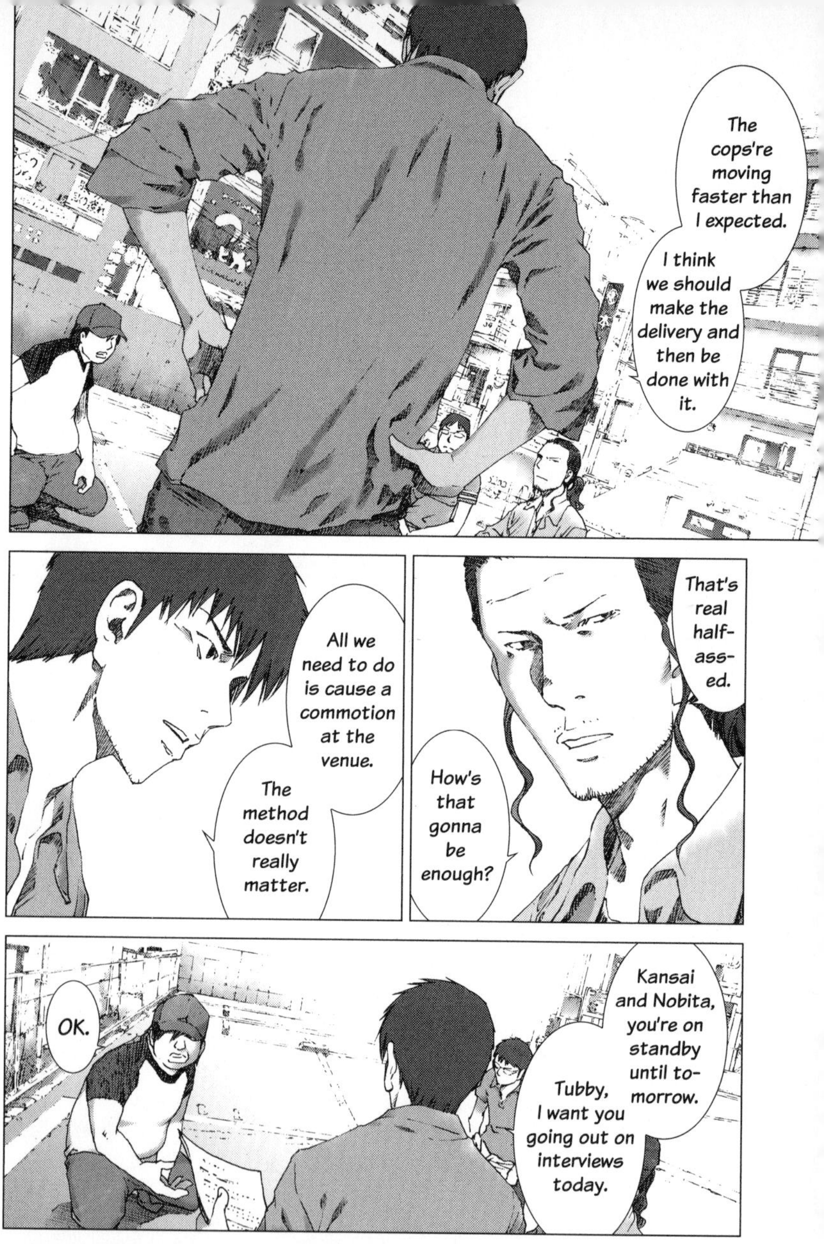
The cops're moving faster than I expected.
I think we should make the delivery and then be done with it.
That's real half-assed.
How's that gonna be enough?
All we need to do is cause a commotion at the venue.
The method doesn't really matter.
Kansai and Nobita, you're on standby until to-morrow.
Tubby, I want you going out on interviews today.
OK.

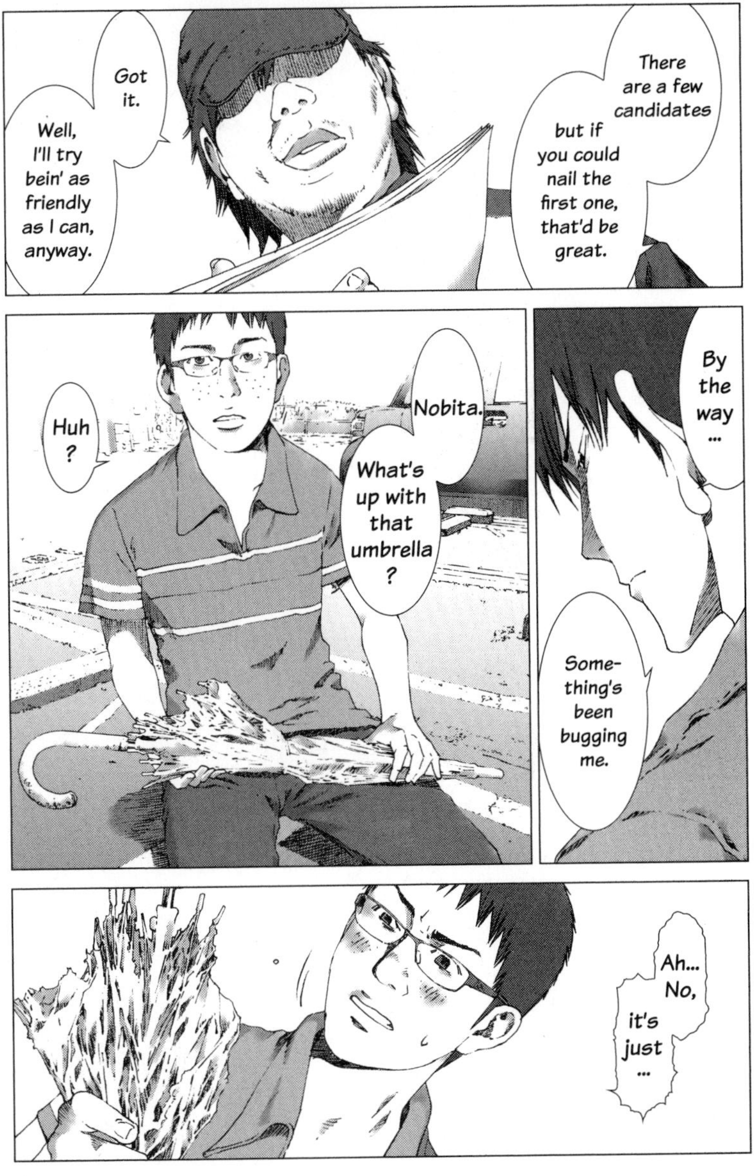
There are a few candidates
but if you could nail the first one, that'd be great.
Got it.
Well, I'll try bein' as friendly as I can, anyway.
By the way ...
Something's been bugging me.
Nobita.
What's up with that umbrella?
Huh?
Ah... No, it's just ...

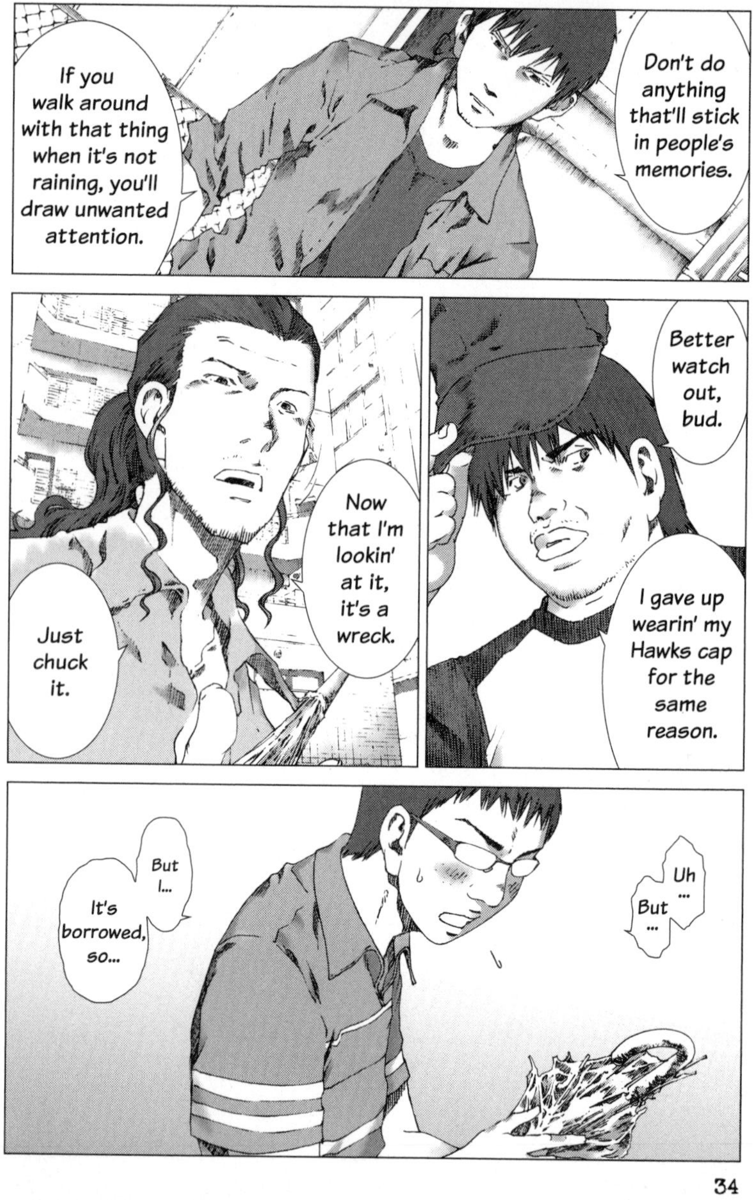
Don't do anything that'll stick in people's memories.
If you walk around with that thing when it's not raining, you'll draw unwanted attention.
Better watch out, bud.
I gave up wearin' my Hawks cap for the same reason.
Now that I'm lookin' at it, it's a wreck.
Just chuck it.
Uh... But...
But I...
It's borrowed, so...

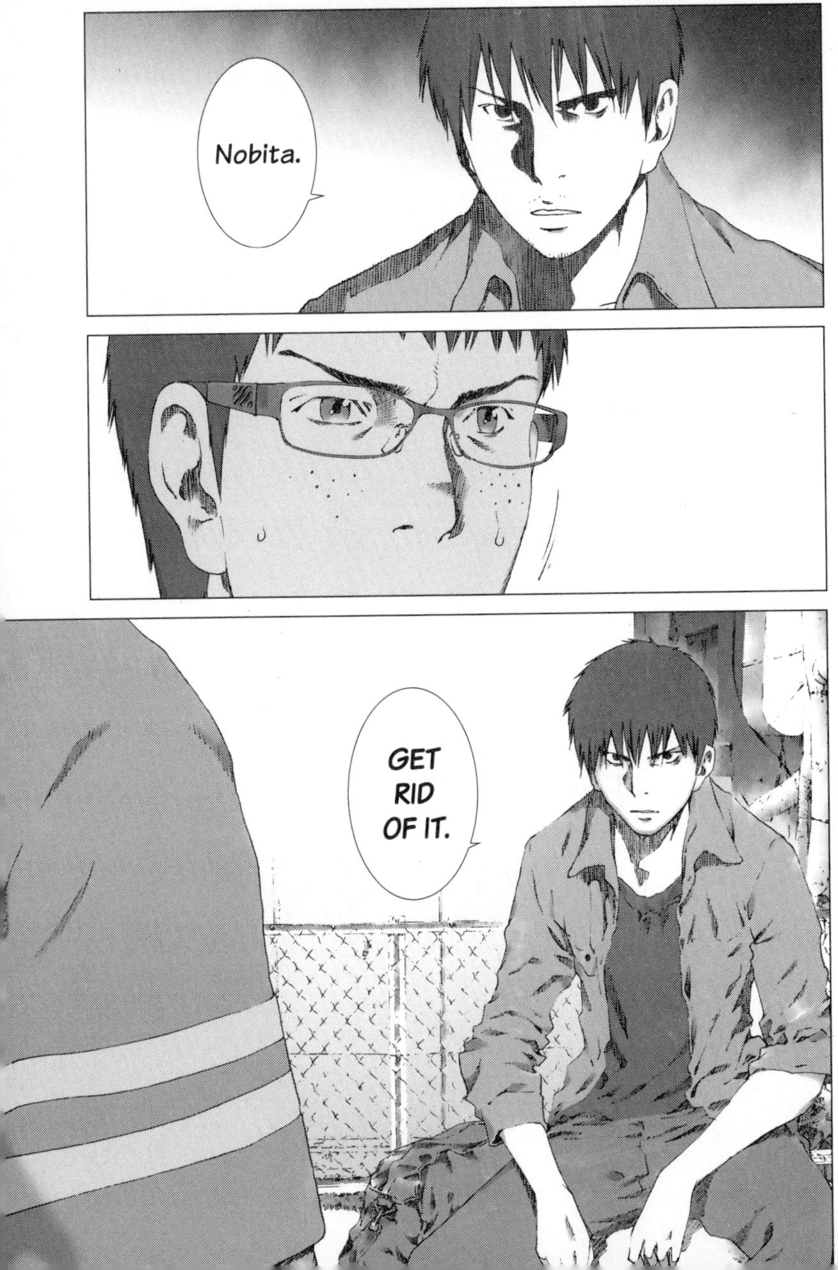
Nobita.
GET RID OF IT.

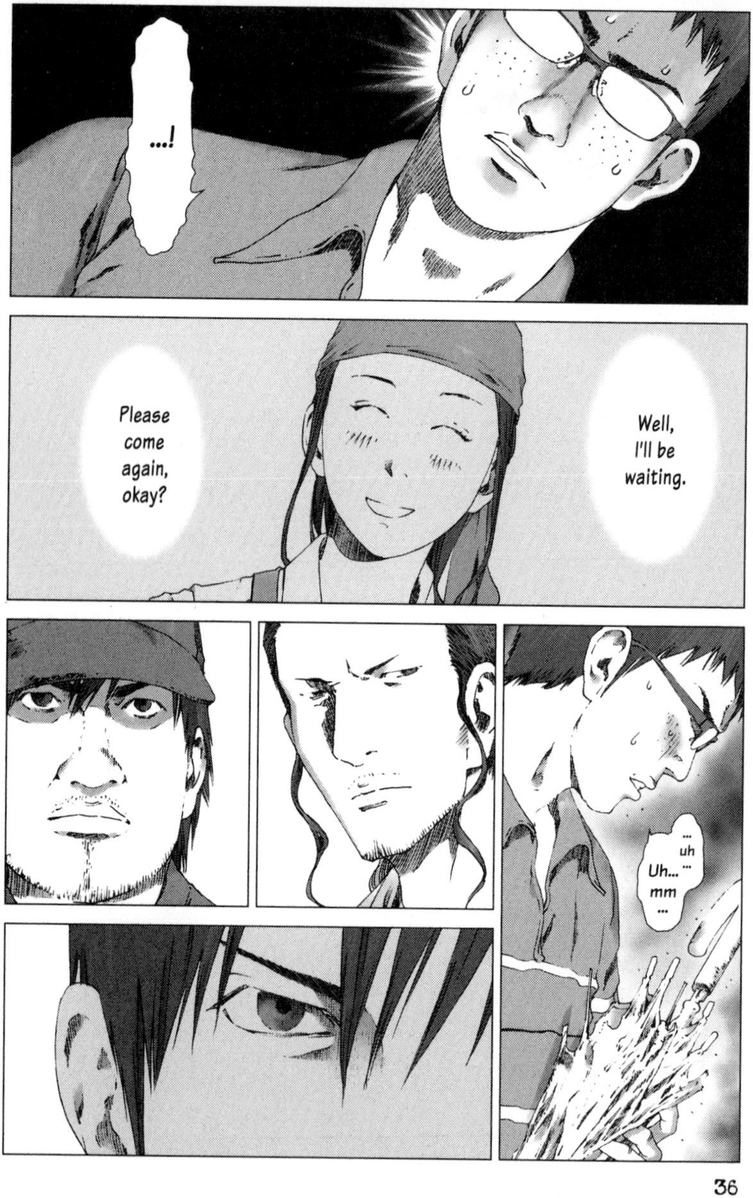
...!
Well, I'll be waiting.
Please come again, okay?
... uh ... Uh... mm ...

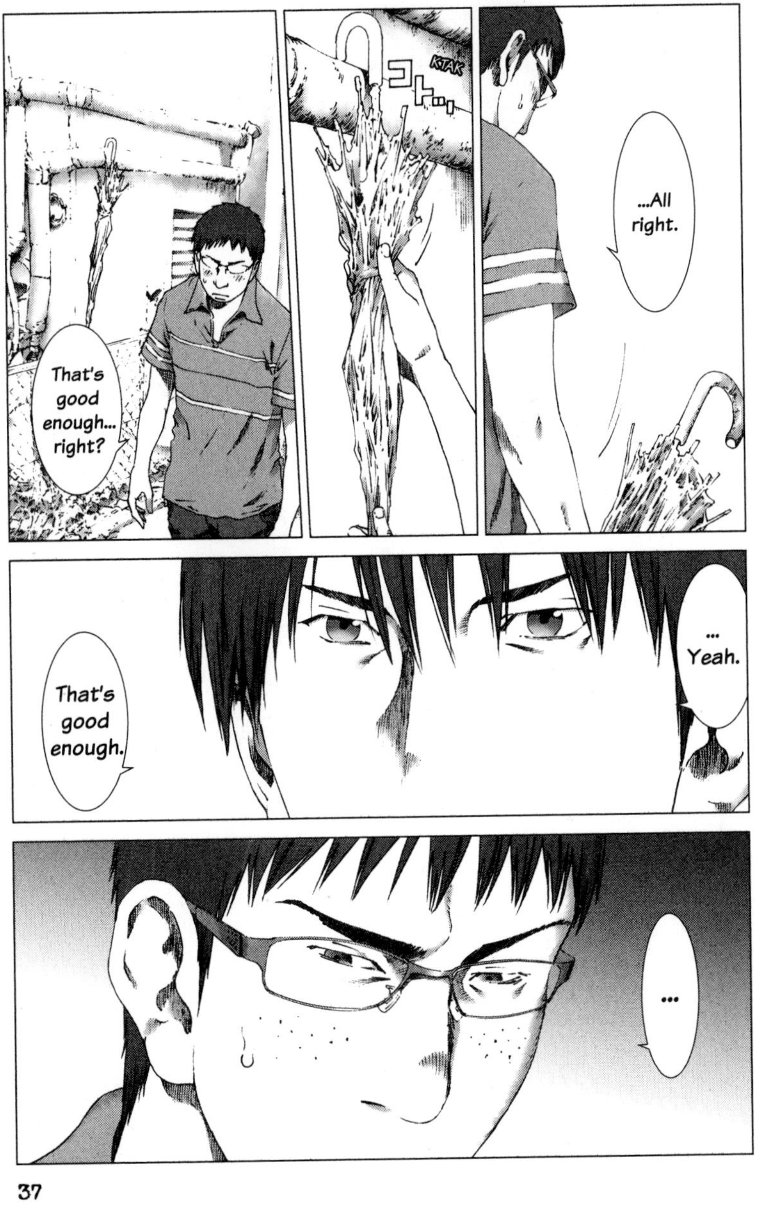
...All right.
KTAK
コトッ
That's good enough... right?
... Yeah.
That's good enough.
...

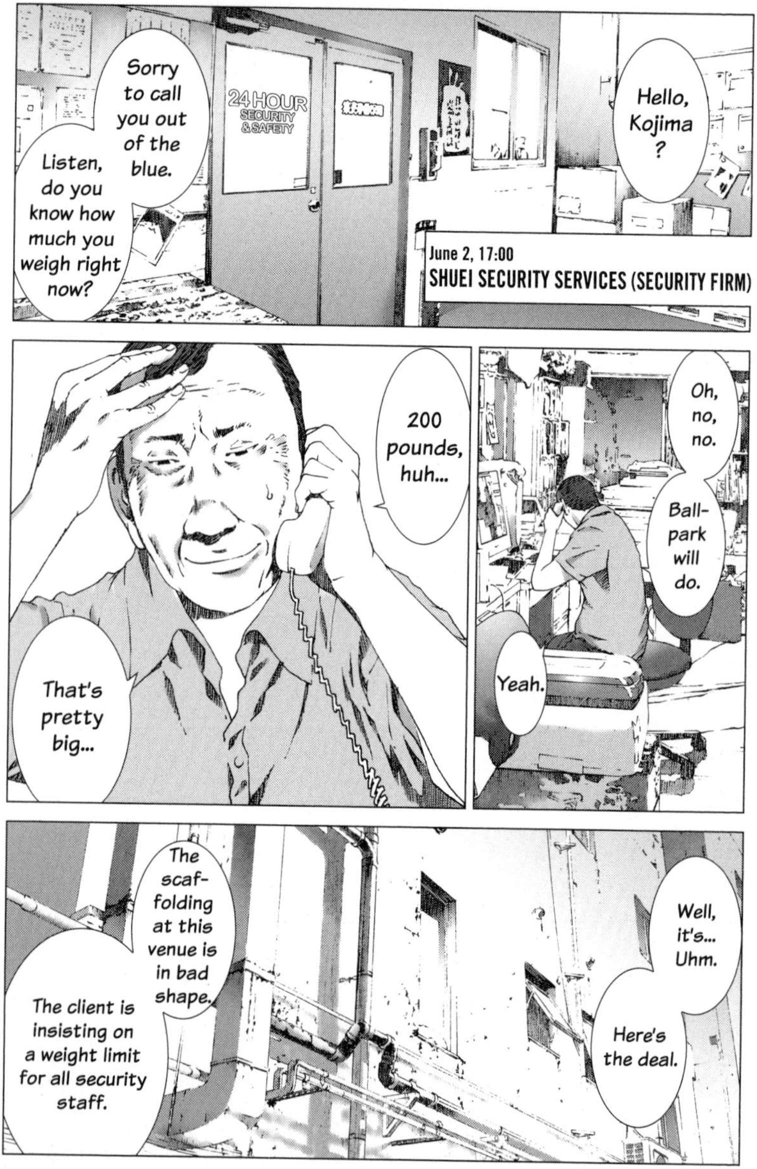
Hello, Kojima?
June 2, 17:00
SHUEI SECURITY SERVICES (SECURITY FIRM)
24 HOUR SECURITY & SAFETY
Sorry to call you out of the blue.
Listen, do you know how much you weigh right now?
Oh, no, no.
Ball-park will do.
Yeah.
200 pounds, huh...
That's pretty big...
Well, it's... Uhm.
Here's the deal.
The scaf-folding at this venue is in bad shape.
The client is insisting on a weight limit for all security staff.

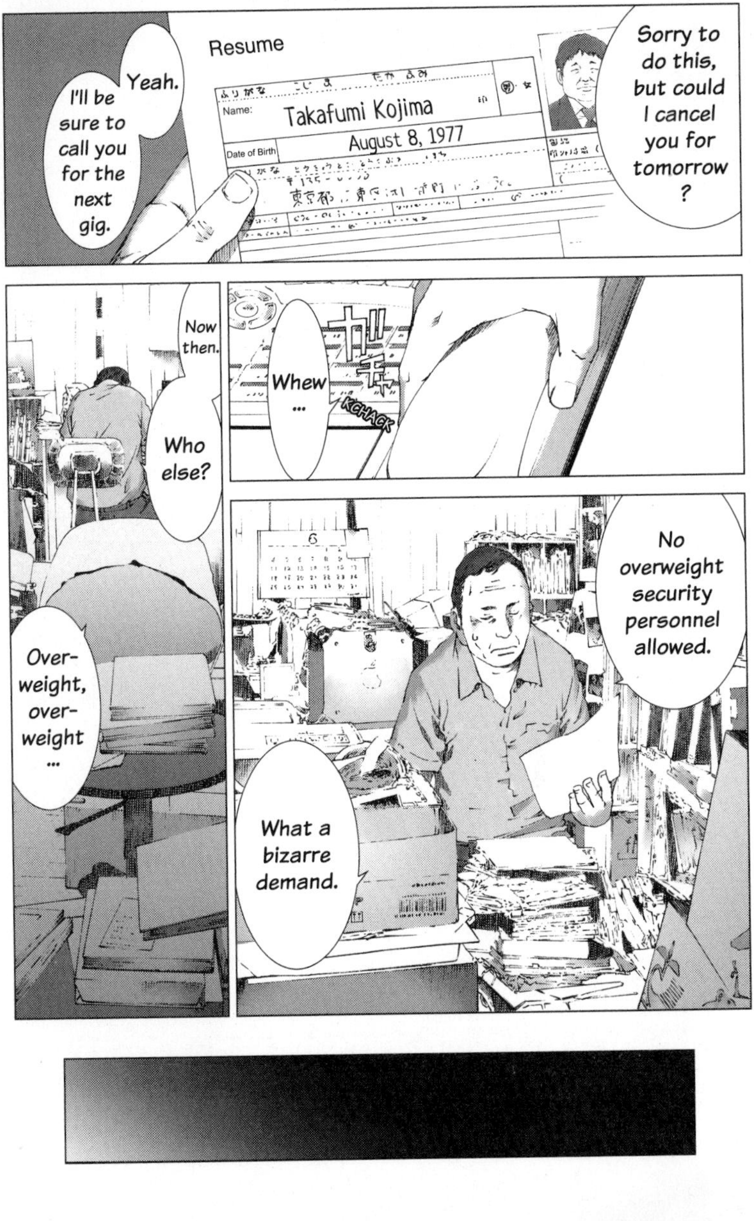
Sorry to do this, but could I cancel you for tomorrow?
Resume
Name:
Takafumi Kojima
Date of Birth
August 8, 1977
Yeah.
I'll be sure to call you for the next gig.
Whew...
KCHACK
No overweight security personnel allowed.
What a bizarre demand.
Now then.
Who else?
Over-weight, over-weight...

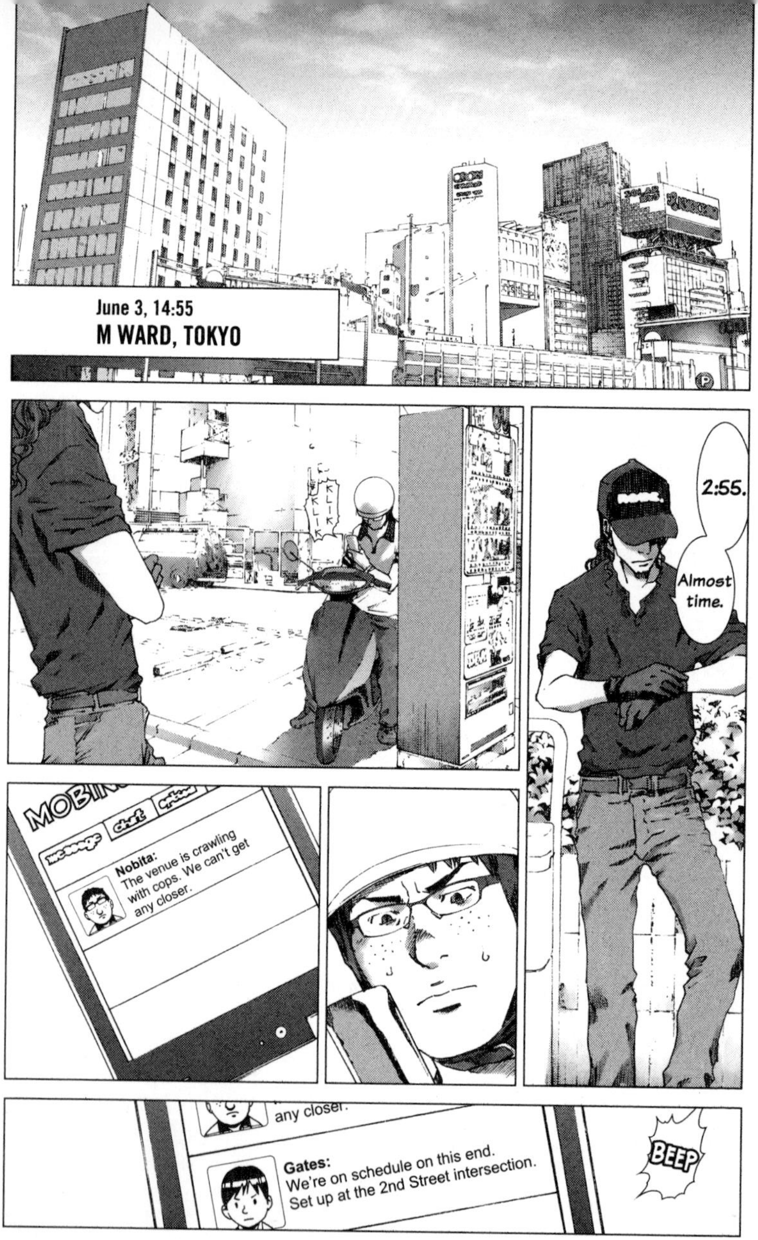
June 3, 14:55
M WARD, TOKYO
2:55.
Almost time.
KLIK KLIK
Nobita: The venue is crawling with cops. We can't get any closer.
BEEP
any closer.
Gates: We're on schedule on this end. Set up at the 2nd Street intersection.

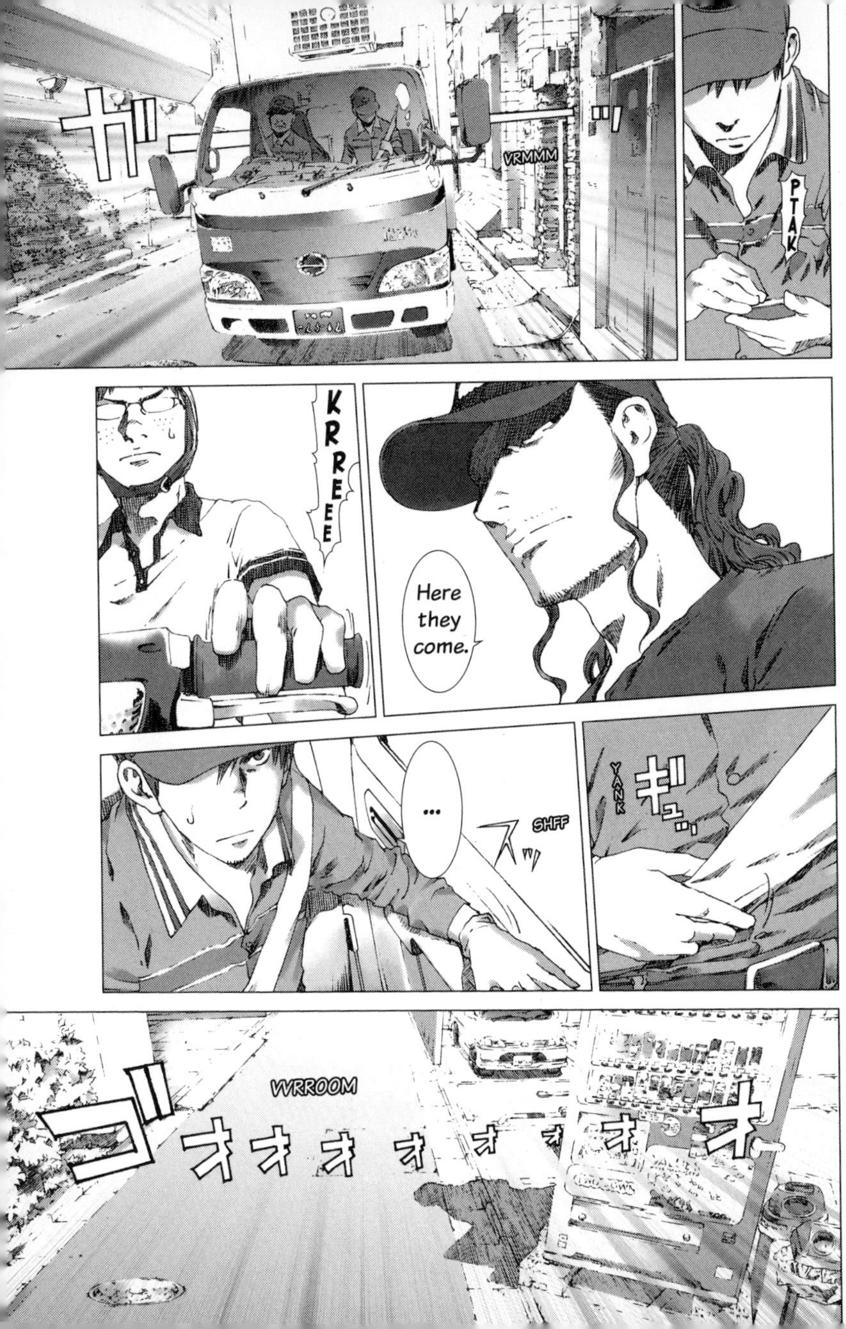
PTAK
VRMMM
Here they come.
KRREEE
YANK
...
SHFF
VVRROOM

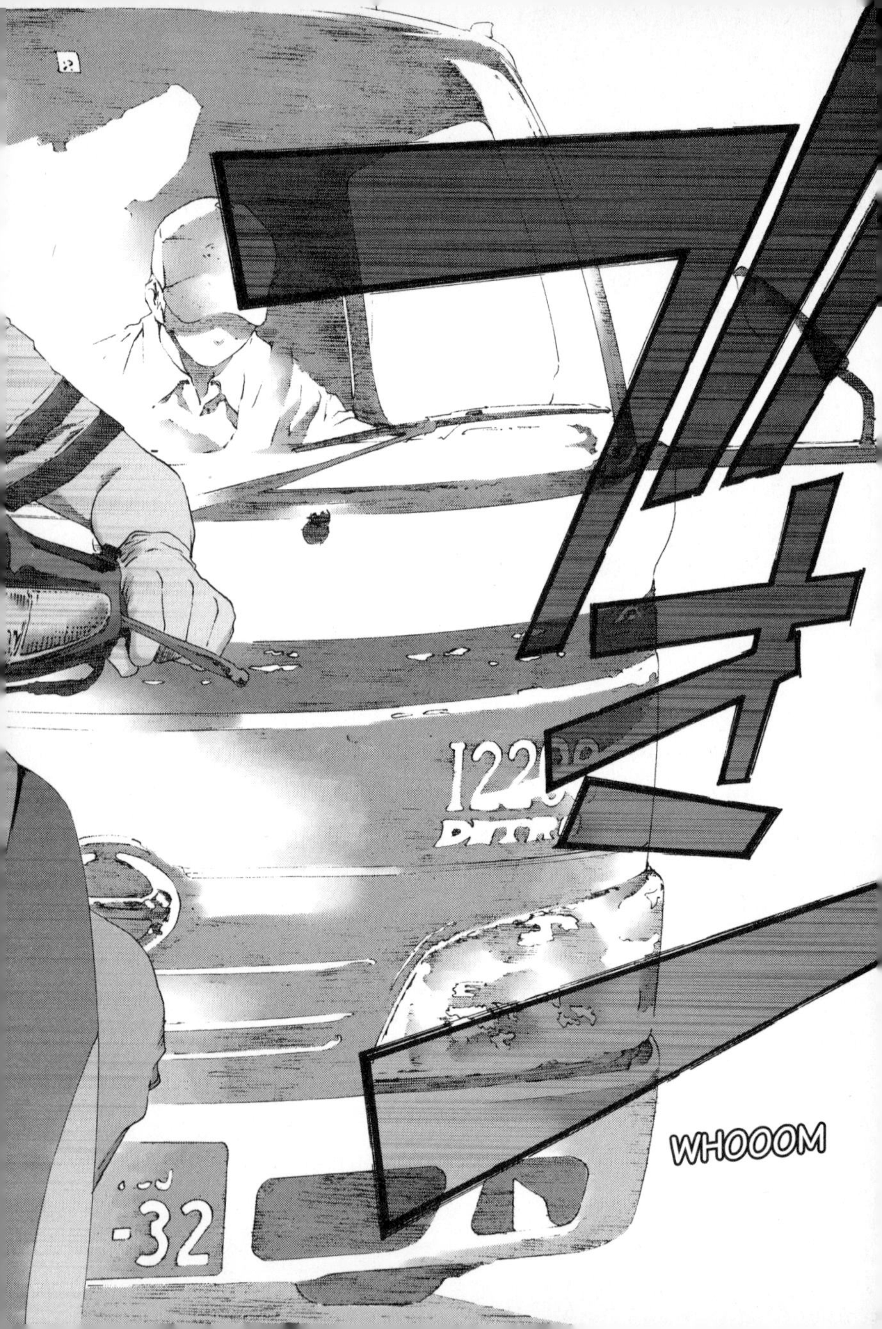
WHOOOM

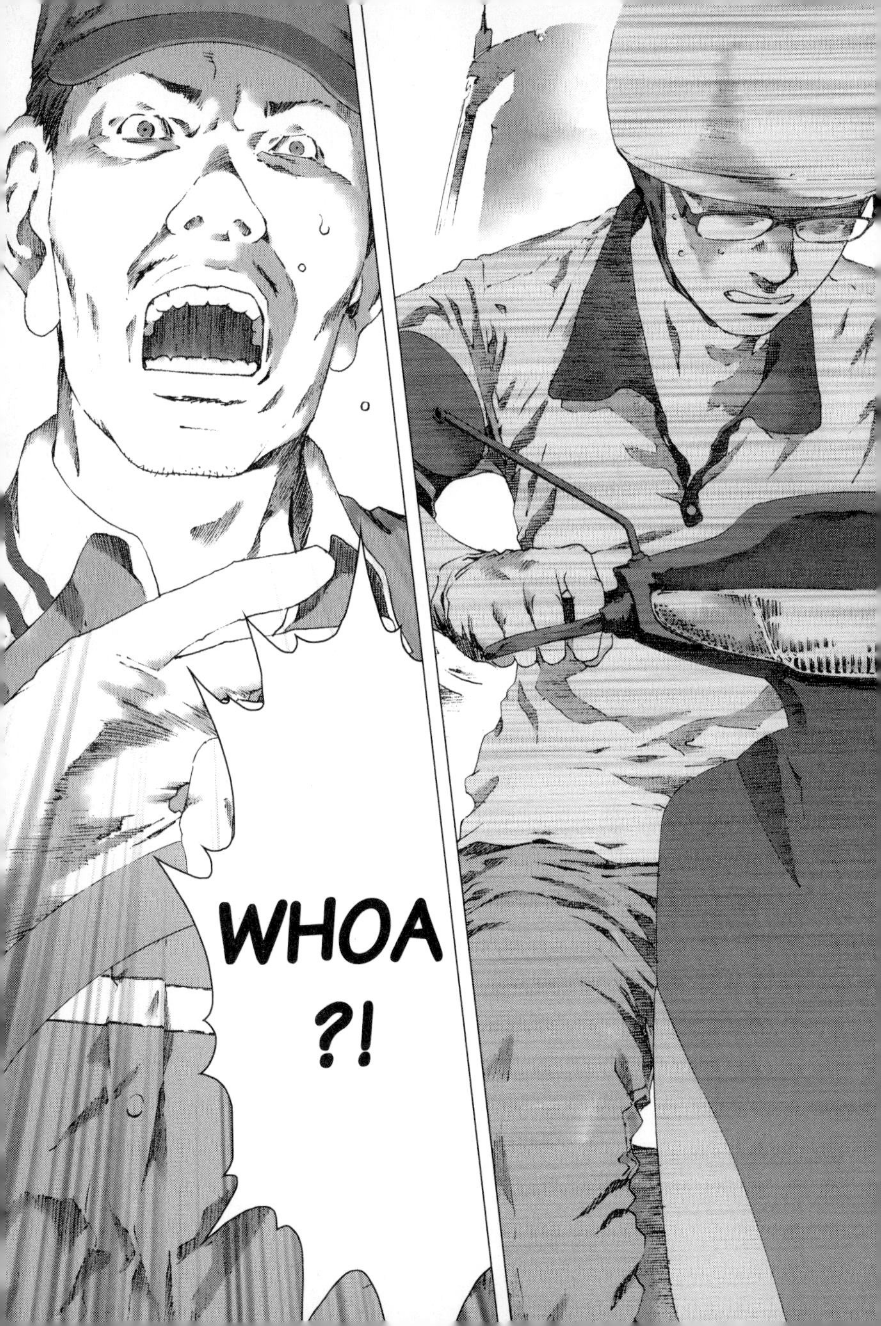
WHOA ?!

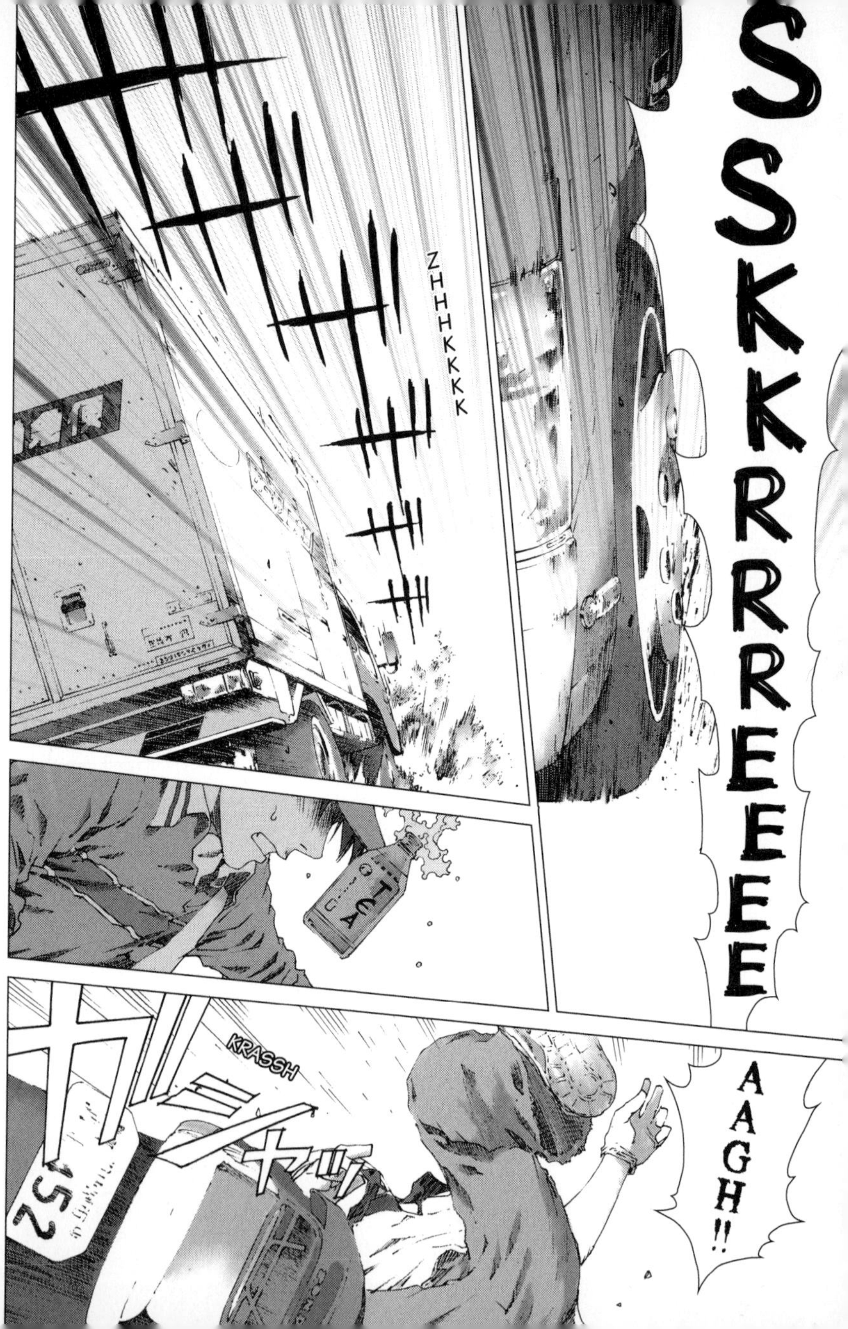
SSKKRRREEEE
ZHHHKKKK
TEA
AAGH!!
KRASSH
152

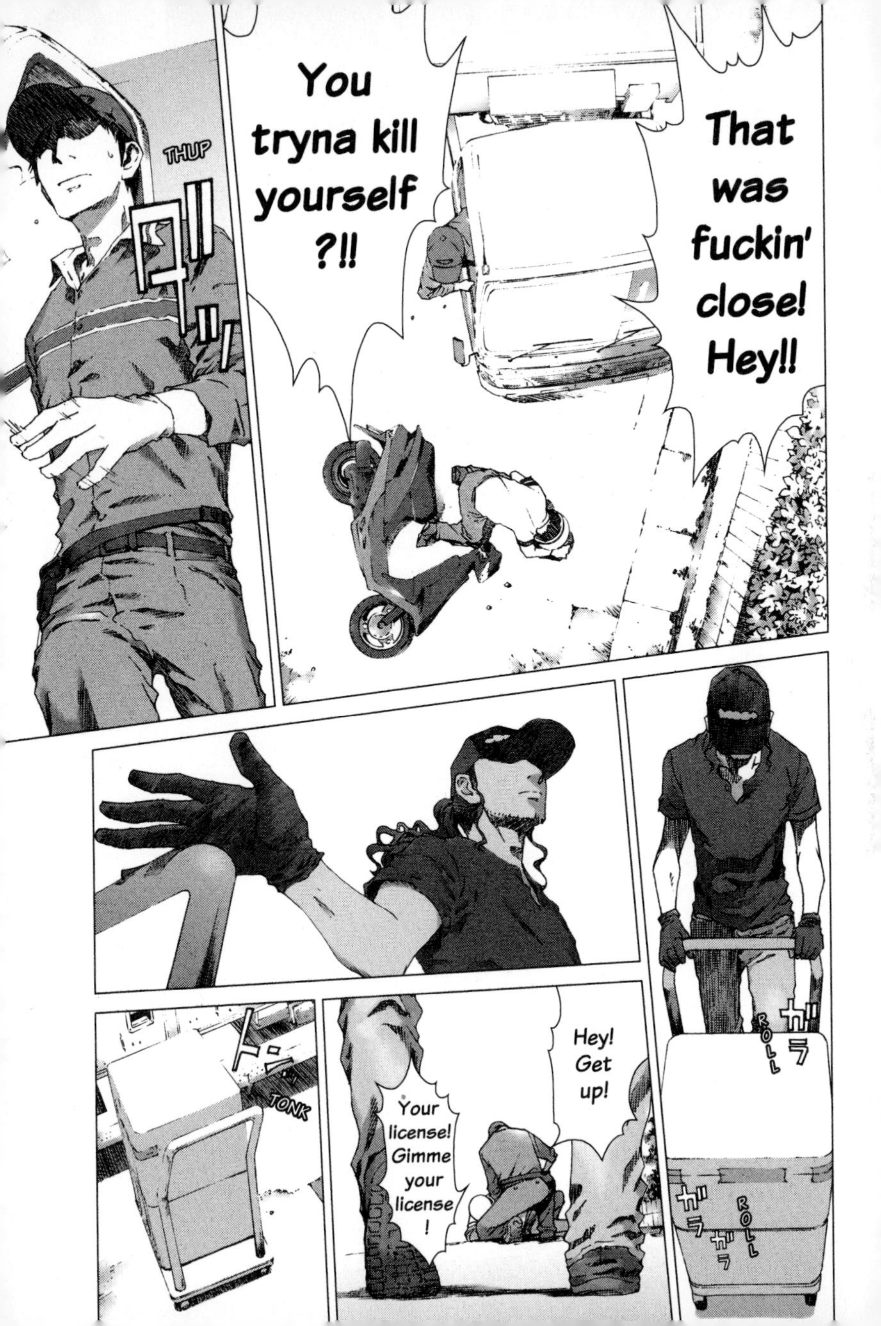
That was fuckin' close! Hey!!
You tryna kill yourself?!!
THUP
ROLL
ROLL
Hey! Get up!
Your license! Gimme your license!
TONK

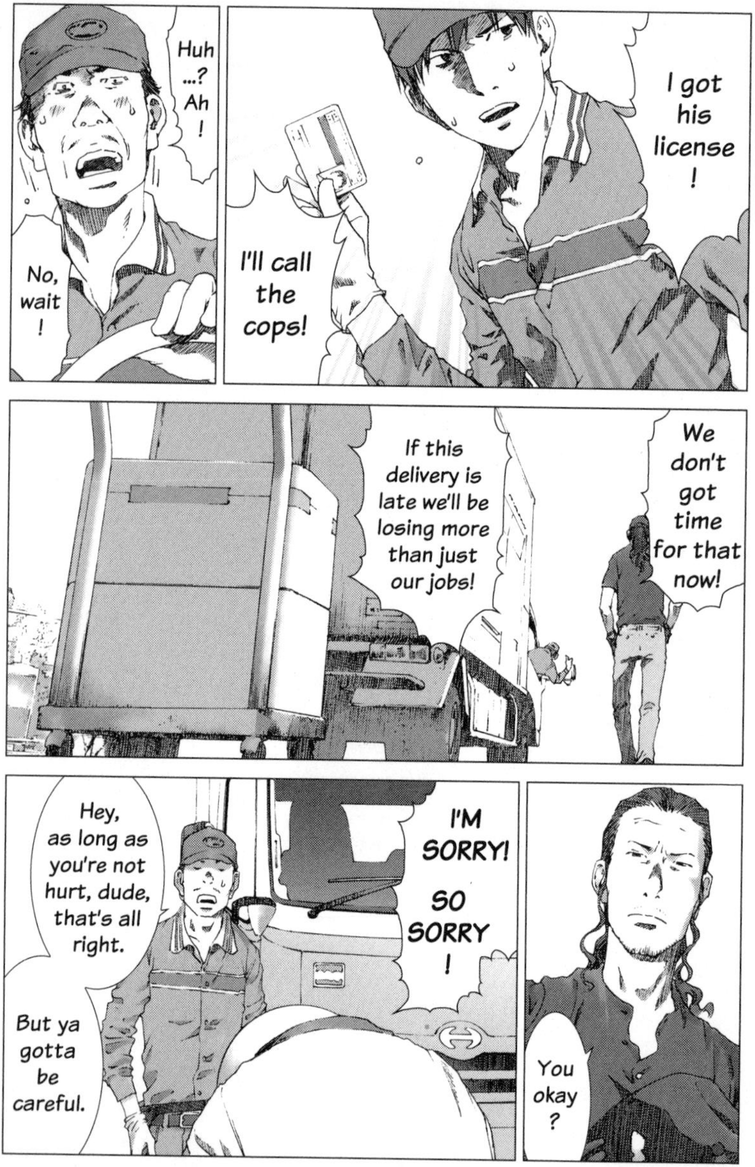
I got his license!
I'll call the cops!
Huh...? Ah!
No, wait!
We don't got time for that now!
If this delivery is late we'll be losing more than just our jobs!
You okay?
I'M SORRY!
SO SORRY!
Hey, as long as you're not hurt, dude, that's all right.
But ya gotta be careful.

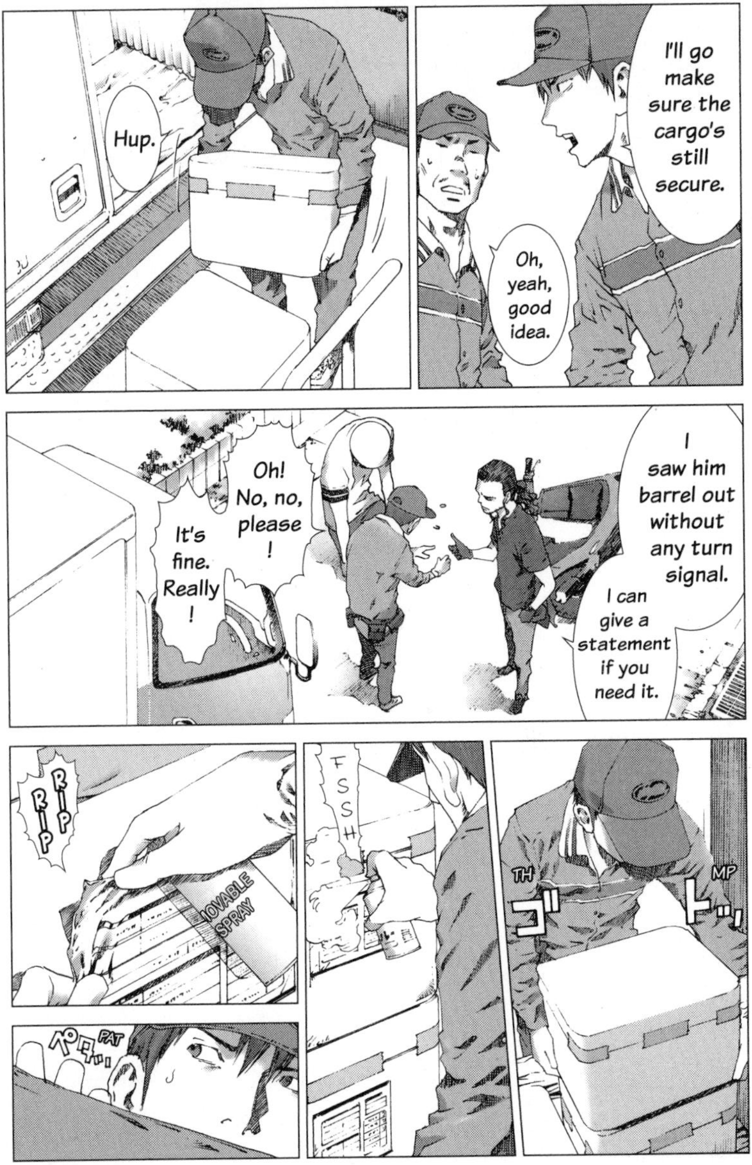
I'll go make sure the cargo's still secure.
Oh, yeah, good idea.
Hup.
I saw him barrel out without any turn signal.
I can give a statement if you need it.
Oh! No, no, please!
It's fine. Really!
TH MP
ゴトッ
FSSH
RIP RIP
SPRAY
PAT
ペタッ

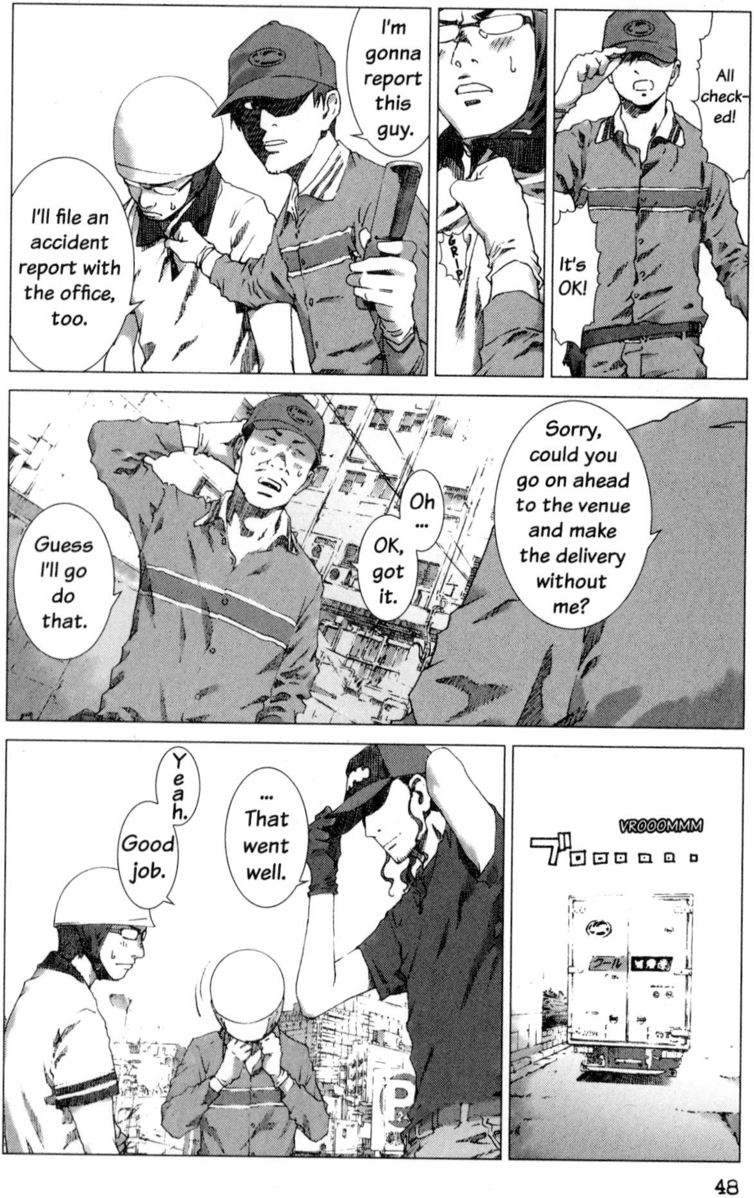
All check-ed!
It's OK!
GRIP
I'm gonna report this guy.
I'll file an accident report with the office, too.
Sorry, could you go on ahead to the venue and make the delivery without me?
Oh ... OK, got it.
Guess I'll go do that.
VROOOMMM
... That went well.
Yeah. Good job.

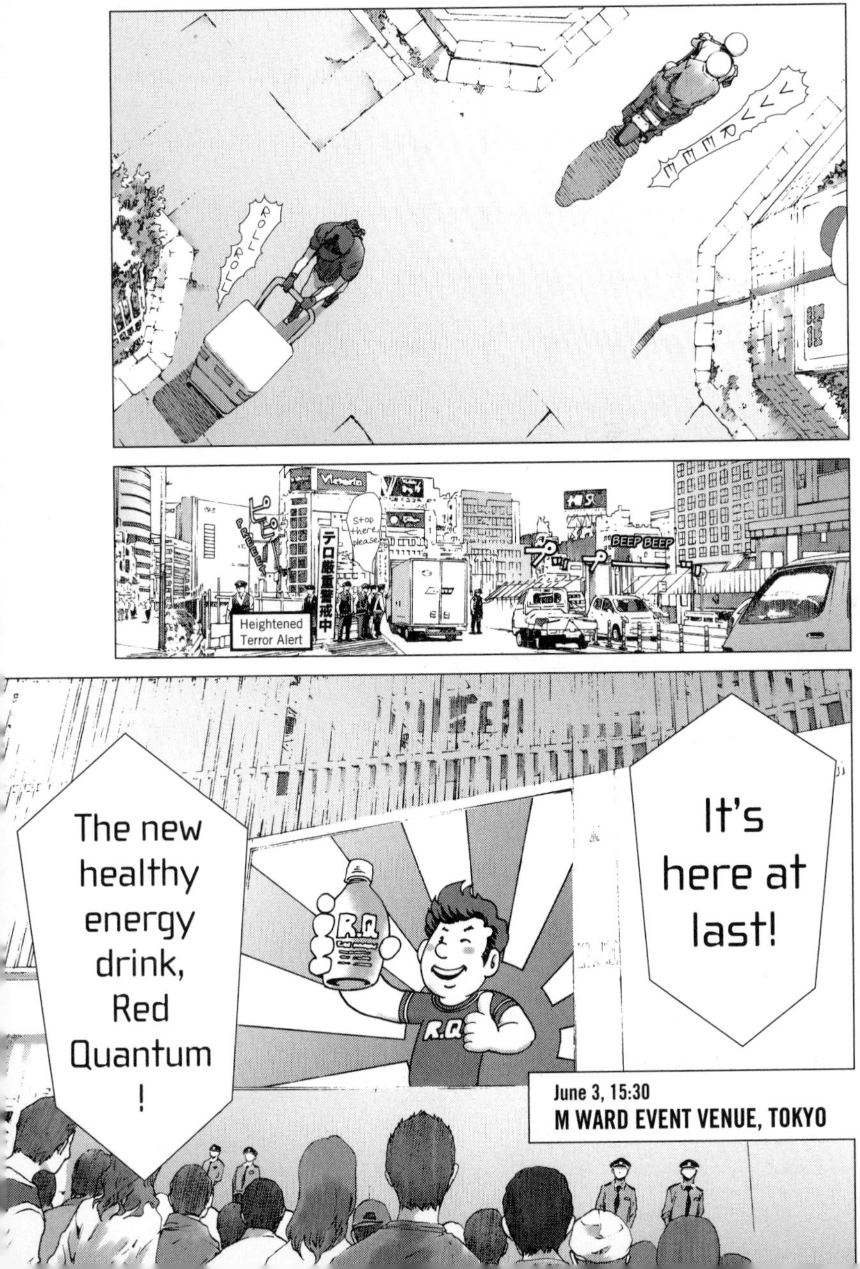
VVVREEE
ROLL ROLL
BEEP BEEP
Stop there, please.
テロ厳重警戒中
PREEET
Heightened Terror Alert
It's here at last!
The new healthy energy drink, Red Quantum!
June 3, 15:30
M WARD EVENT VENUE, TOKYO

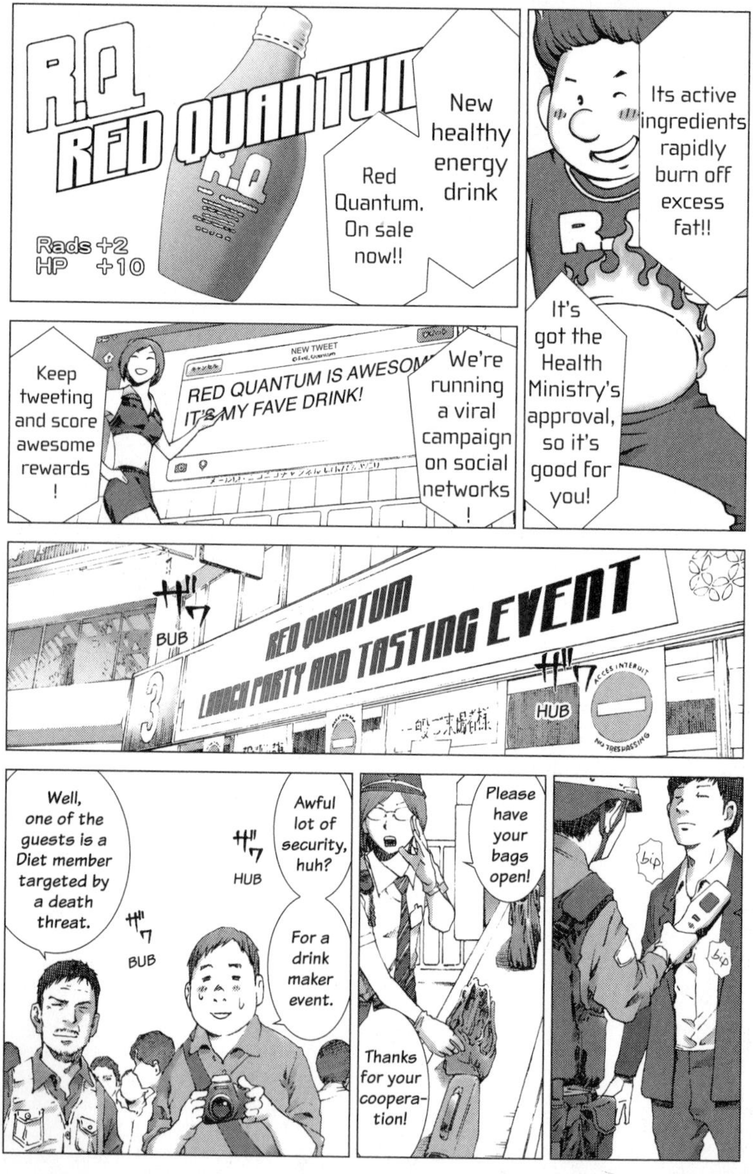

Its active ingredients rapidly burn off excess fat!!
R.Q
It's got the Health Ministry's approval, so it's good for you!
New healthy energy drink
Red Quantum. On sale now!!
R.Q
RED QUANTUM
R.Q
Rads +2
HP +10
We're running a viral campaign on social networks!
NEW TWEET
RED QUANTUM IS AWESOME
IT'S MY FAVE DRINK!
Keep tweeting and score awesome rewards!
HUB
ACCES INTERDIT
NO TRESPASSING
RED QUANTUM
LAUNCH PARTY AND TASTING EVENT
BUB
3
bip
bip
Please have your bags open!
Thanks for your cooperation!
Awful lot of security, huh?
For a drink maker event.
HUB
BUB
Well, one of the guests is a Diet member targeted by a death threat.

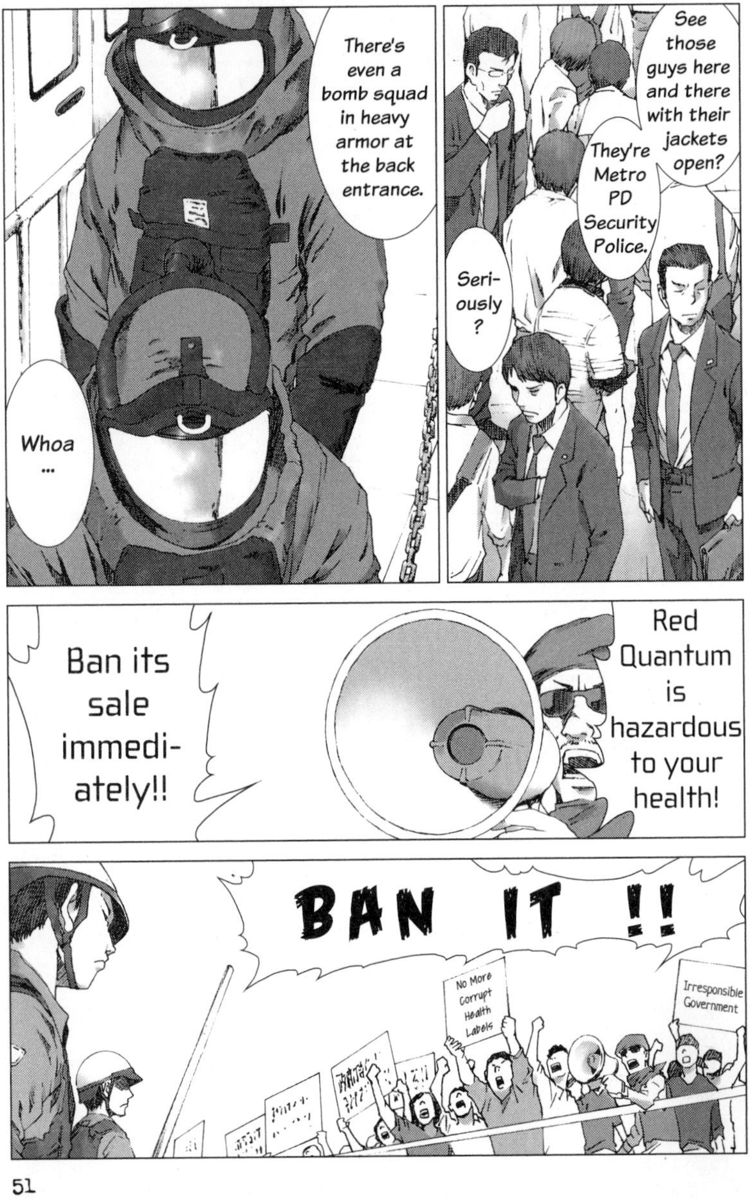
See those guys here and there with their jackets open?
They're Metro PD Security Police.
Seriously?
There's even a bomb squad in heavy armor at the back entrance.
Whoa ...
Red Quantum is hazardous to your health!
Ban its sale immediately!!
BAN IT !!
Irresponsible Government
No More Corrupt Health Labels

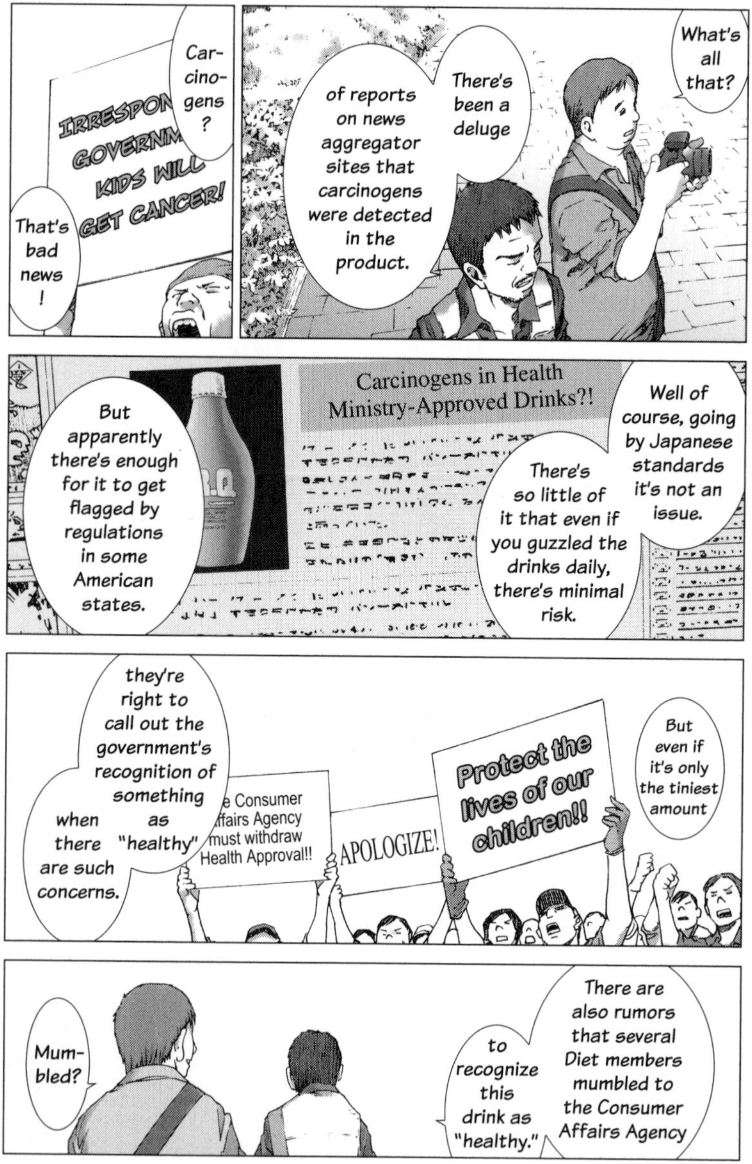
What's all that?
There's been a deluge
of reports on news aggregator sites that carcinogens were detected in the product.
IRRESPON GOVERNM KIDS WILL GET CANCER!
Car-cino-gens?
That's bad news!
Carcinogens in Health Ministry-Approved Drinks?!
Well of course, going by Japanese standards it's not an issue.
There's so little of it that even if you guzzled the drinks daily, there's minimal risk.
But apparently there's enough for it to get flagged by regulations in some American states.
But even if it's only the tiniest amount
Protect the lives of our children!!
APOLOGIZE!
e Consumer ffairs Agency must withdraw Health Approval!!
they're right to call out the government's recognition of something as "healthy"
when there are such concerns.
There are also rumors that several Diet members mumbled to the Consumer Affairs Agency
to recognize this drink as "healthy."
Mum-bled?

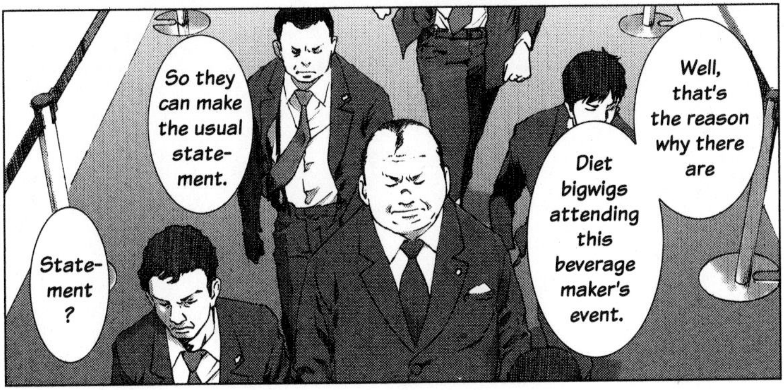
Well, that's the reason why there are
Diet bigwigs attending this beverage maker's event.
So they can make the usual statement.
Statement?

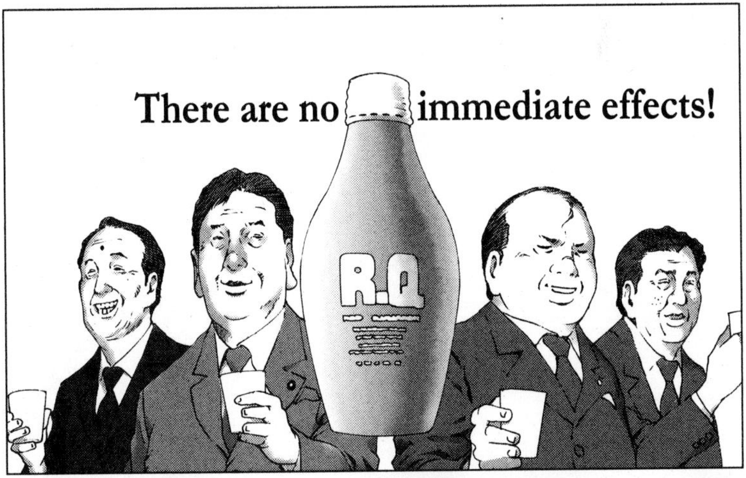
There are no immediate effects!
R.Q

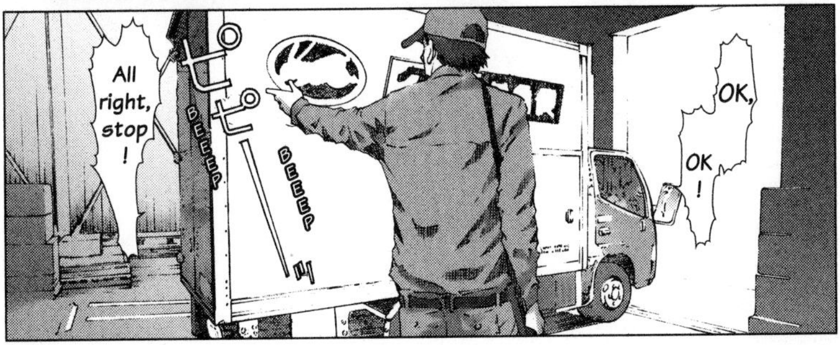
OK, OK!
BEEEP
BEEEP
All right, stop!

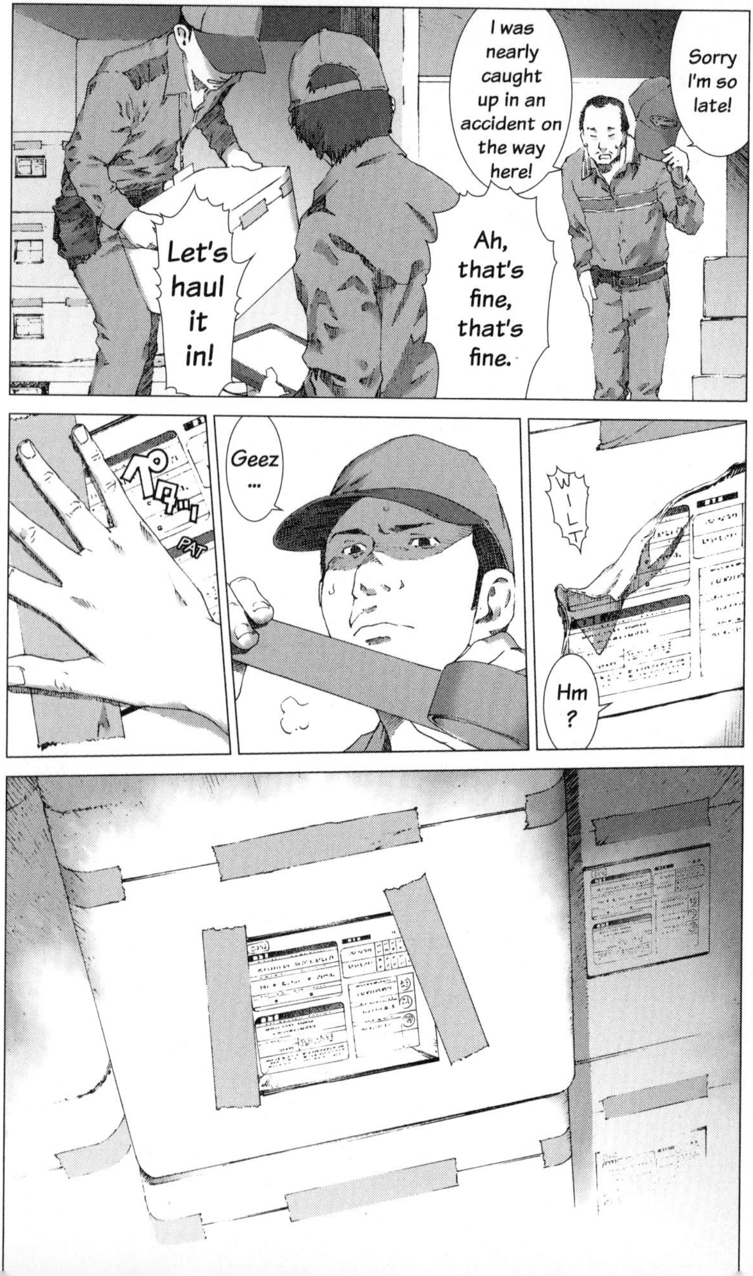
Sorry I'm so late!
I was nearly caught up in an accident on the way here!
Ah, that's fine, that's fine.
Let's haul it in!
WILT
Hm?
Geez...
PAT

File 017

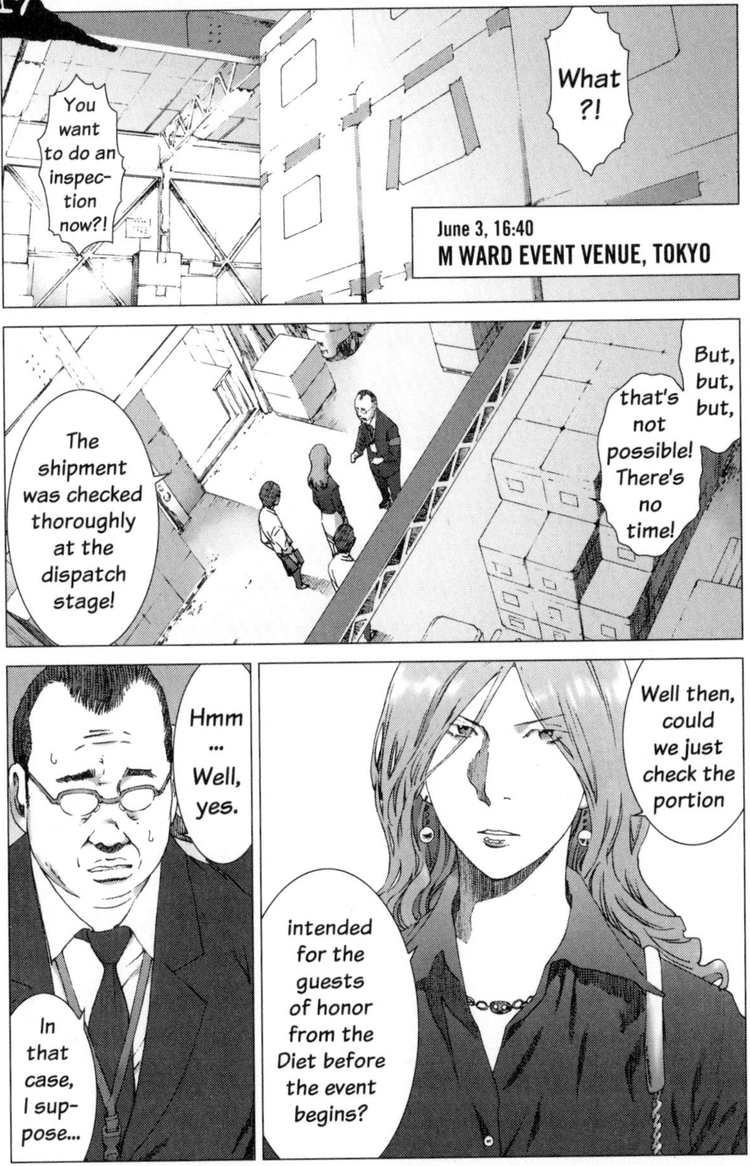
What?!
You want to do an inspection now?!
June 3, 16:40
M WARD EVENT VENUE, TOKYO
But, but, but,
that's not possible! There's no time!
The shipment was checked thoroughly at the dispatch stage!
Well then, could we just check the portion
intended for the guests of honor from the Diet before the event begins?
Hmm... Well, yes.
In that case, I suppose...

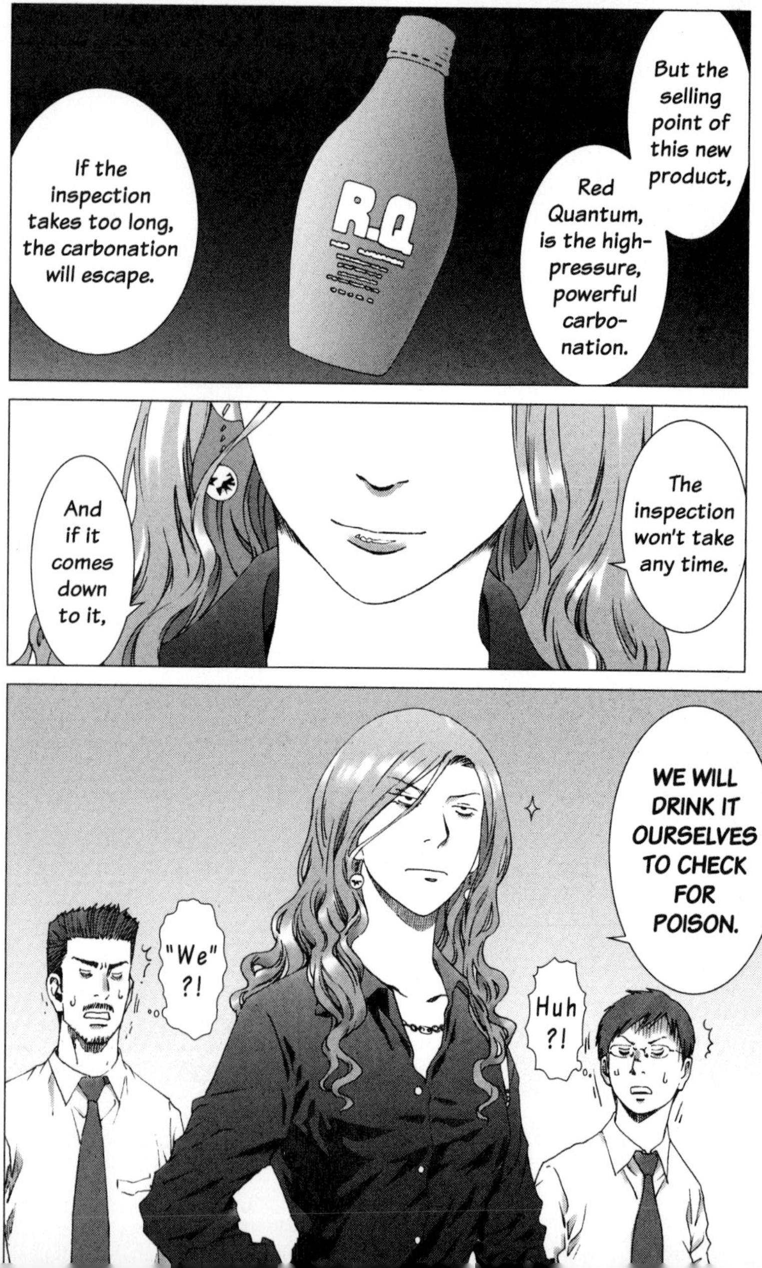
But the selling point of this new product,
Red Quantum, is the high-pressure, powerful carbonation.
R.Q
If the inspection takes too long, the carbonation will escape.
The inspection won't take any time.
And if it comes down to it,
WE WILL DRINK IT OURSELVES TO CHECK FOR POISON.
Huh?!
"We"?!

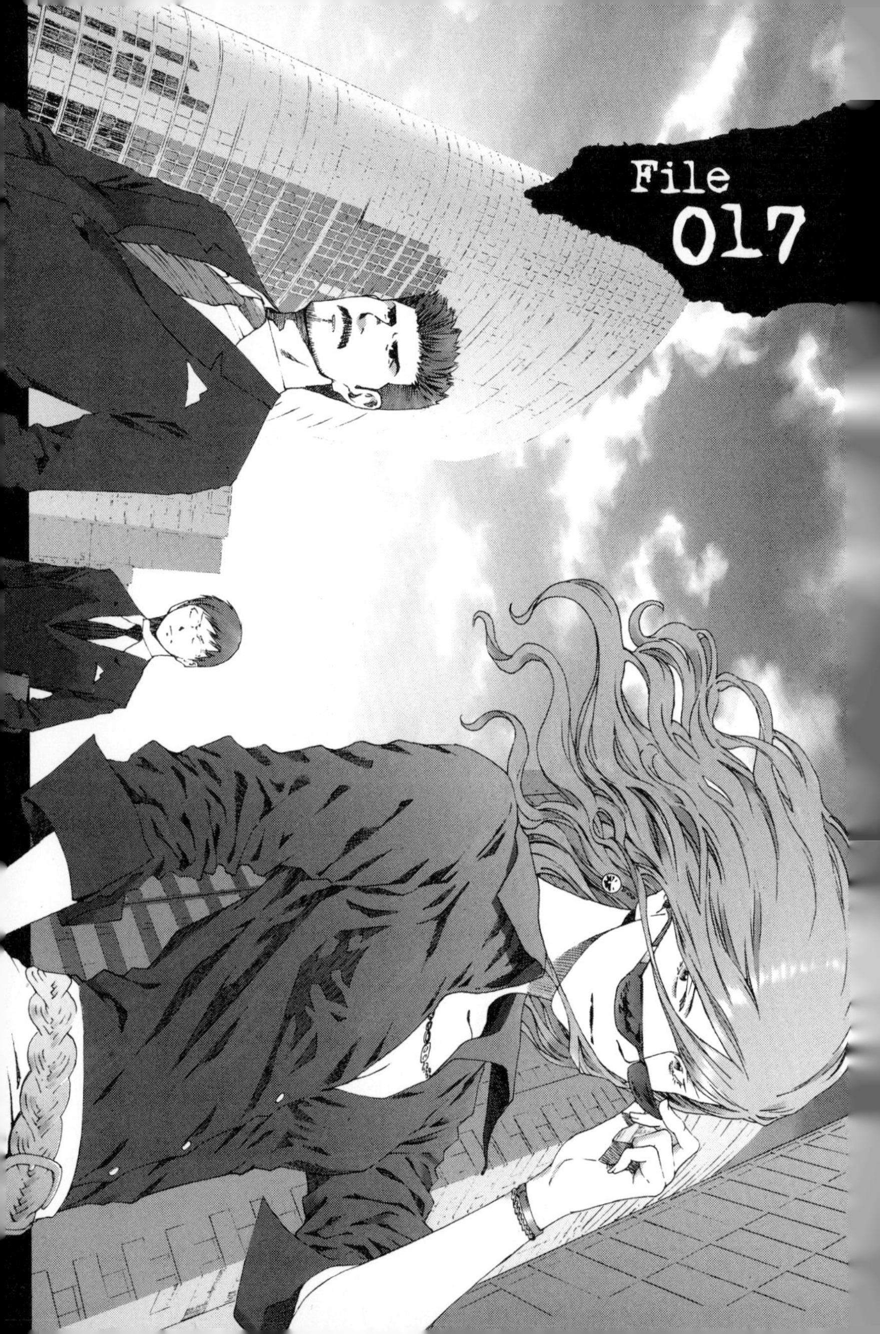
File
017

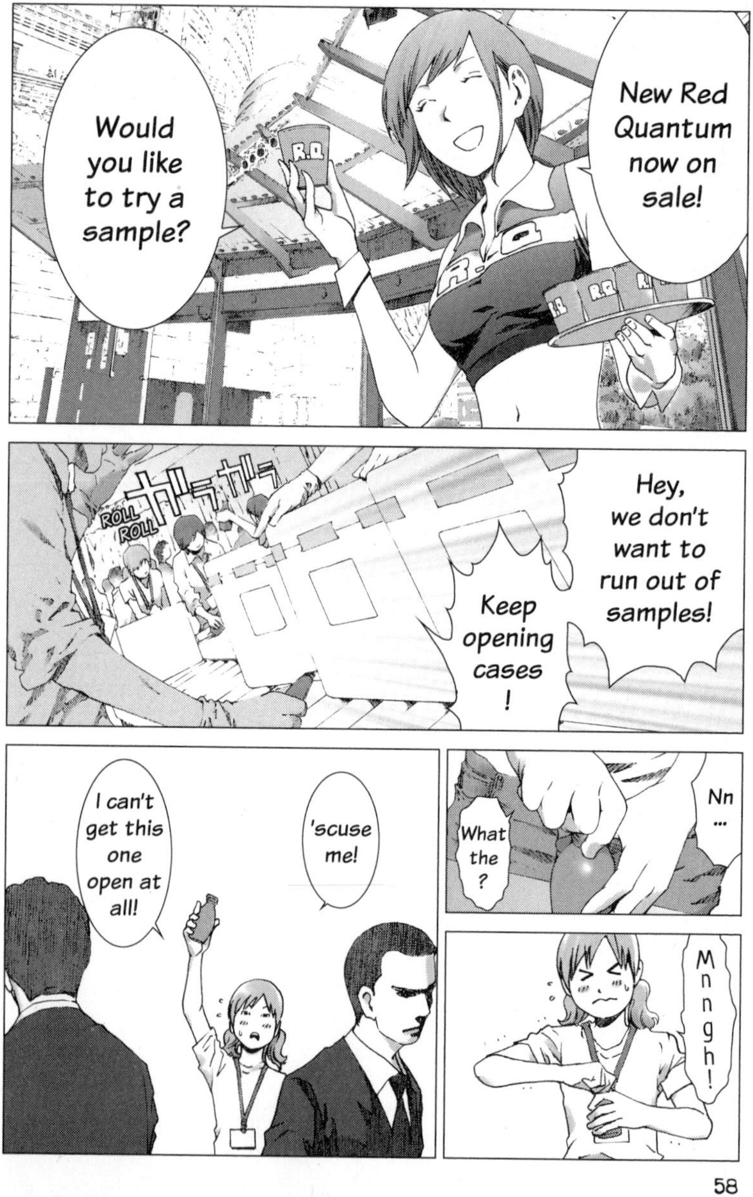
New Red Quantum now on sale!
Would you like to try a sample?
R.Q.
Hey, we don't want to run out of samples!
Keep opening cases!
ROLL ROLL
Nn...
What the?
Mnngh!
'scuse me!
I can't get this one open at all!

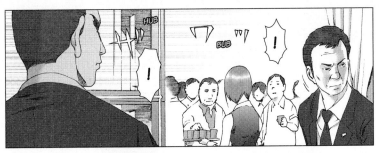

!
BUB
HUB
!
Put it on here.
Slowly please.
Huh? Uh.
OK...
BEEP
332 g
It's 27 grams over the standard weight.
It's been tam-pered with.
CHIK
The cap shows evidence of being opened.
The ring's been reattached with glue.

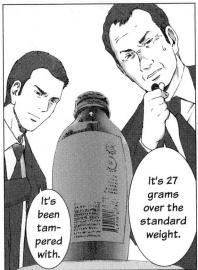

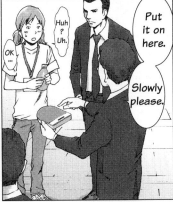

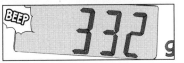

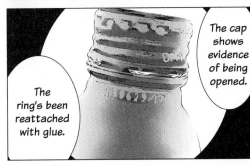

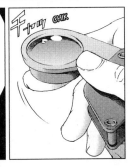

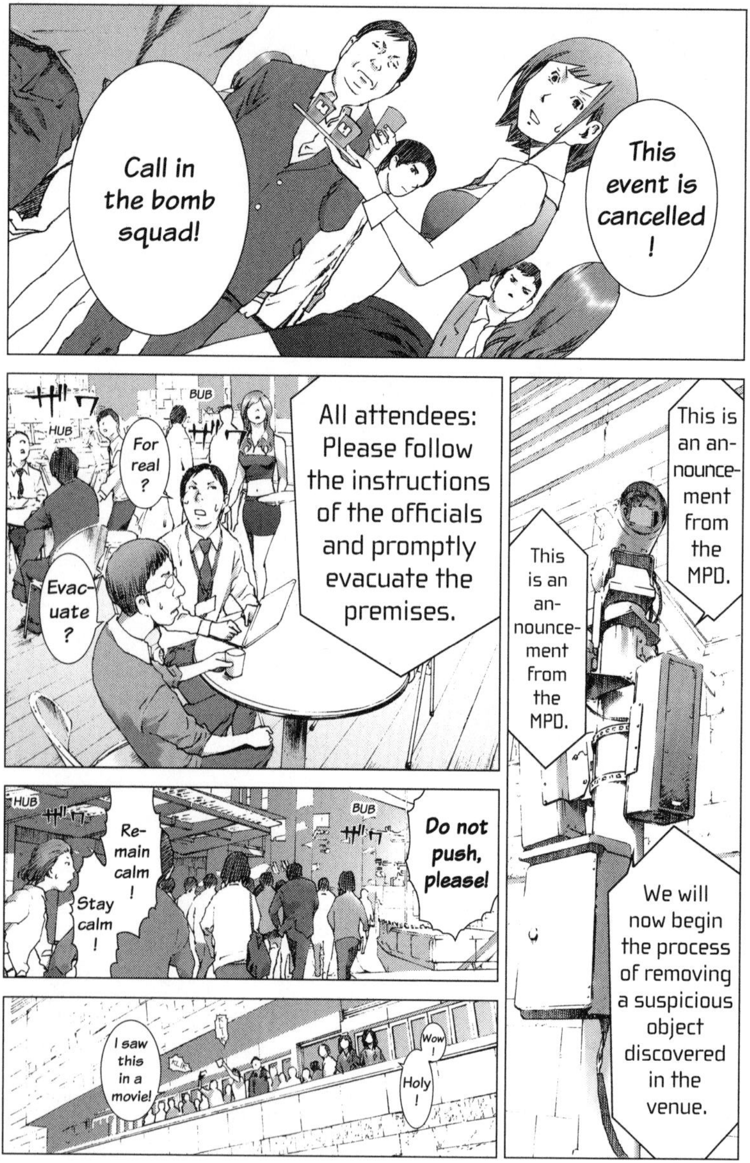
This event is cancelled!
Call in the bomb squad!
This is an announcement from the MPD.
This is an announcement from the MPD.
We will now begin the process of removing a suspicious object discovered in the venue.
All attendees: Please follow the instructions of the officials and promptly evacuate the premises.
BUB
For real?
HUB
Evacuate?
Do not push, please!
BUB
Re-main calm!
Stay calm!
HUB
Wow!
Holy!
KLIK
I saw this in a movie!
KLIK

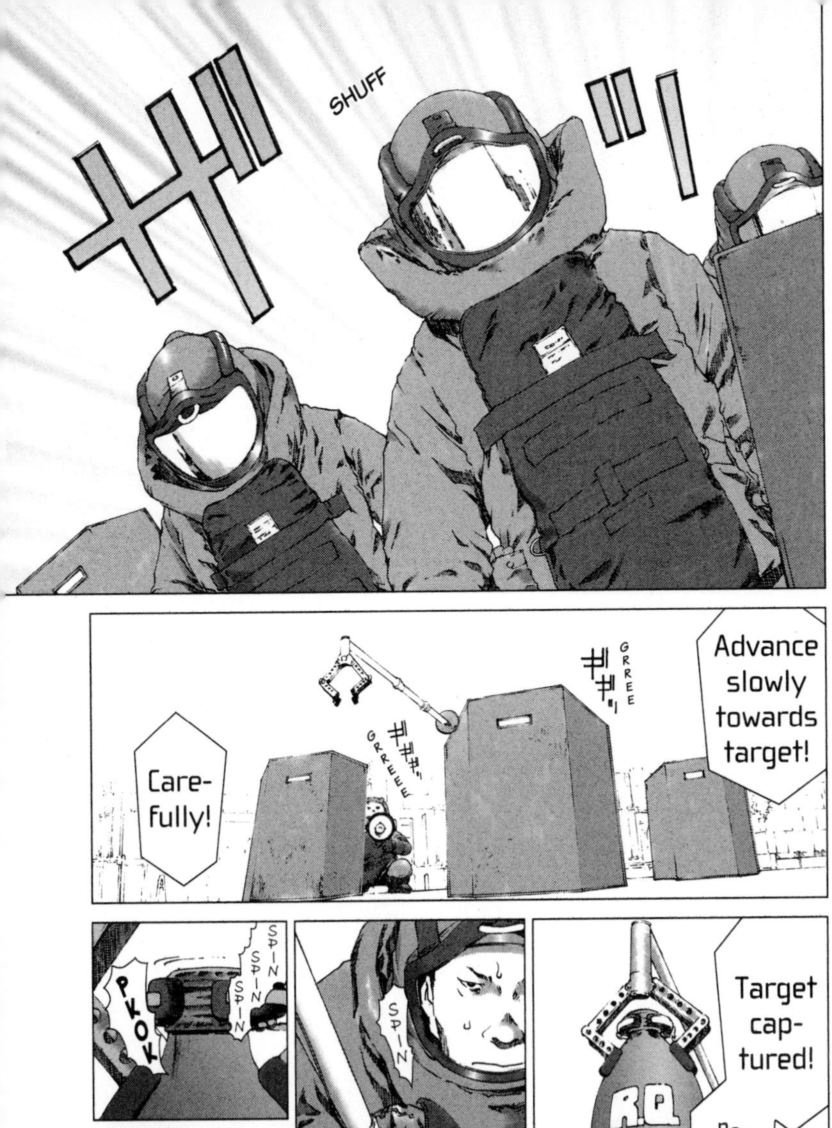
SHUFF
Advance slowly towards target!
GRREE
GRREEE
Care-fully!
Target cap-tured!
Re-moving cap!
SPIN
SPIN SPIN SPIN
PKOK
Hm?

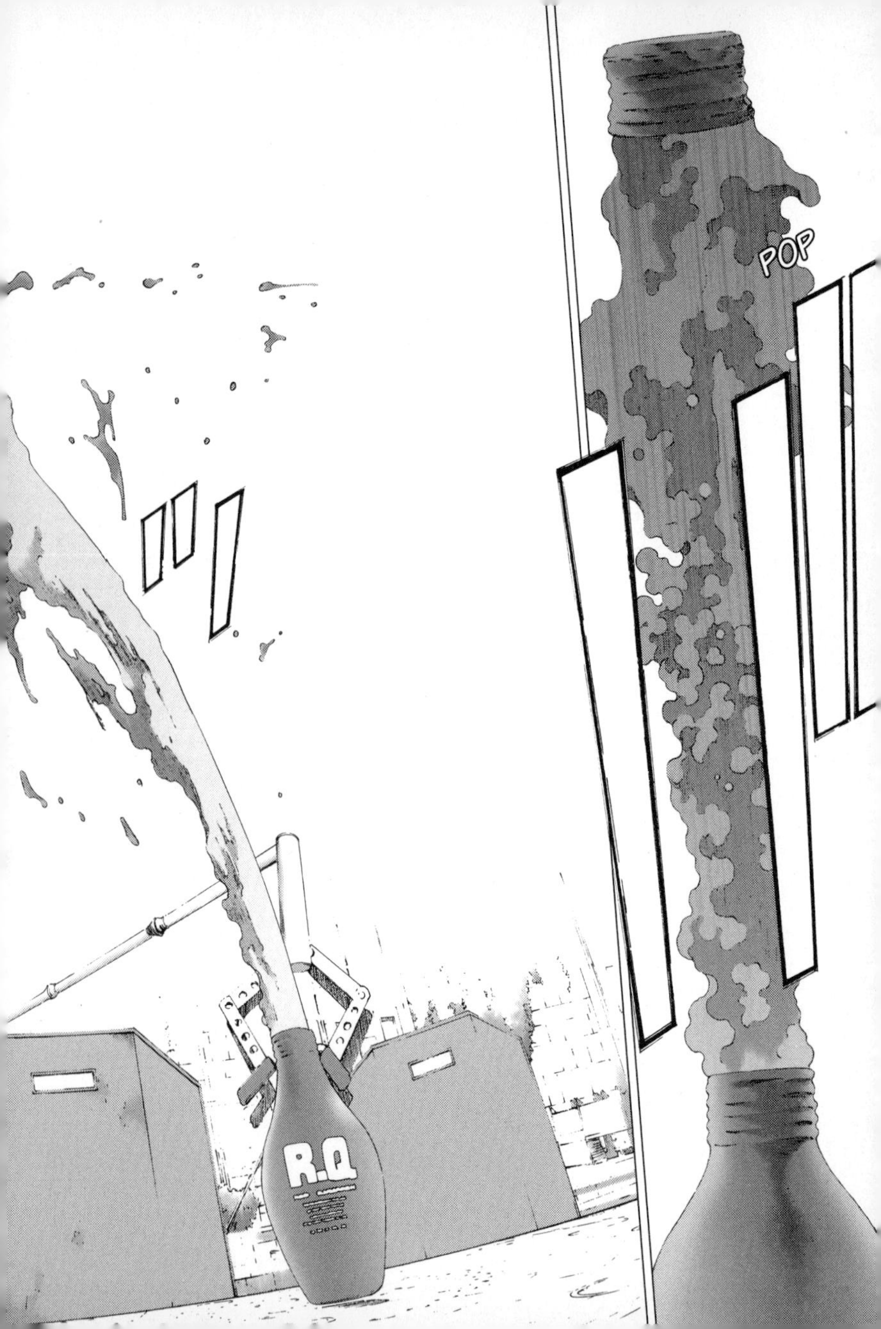
POP
R.Q

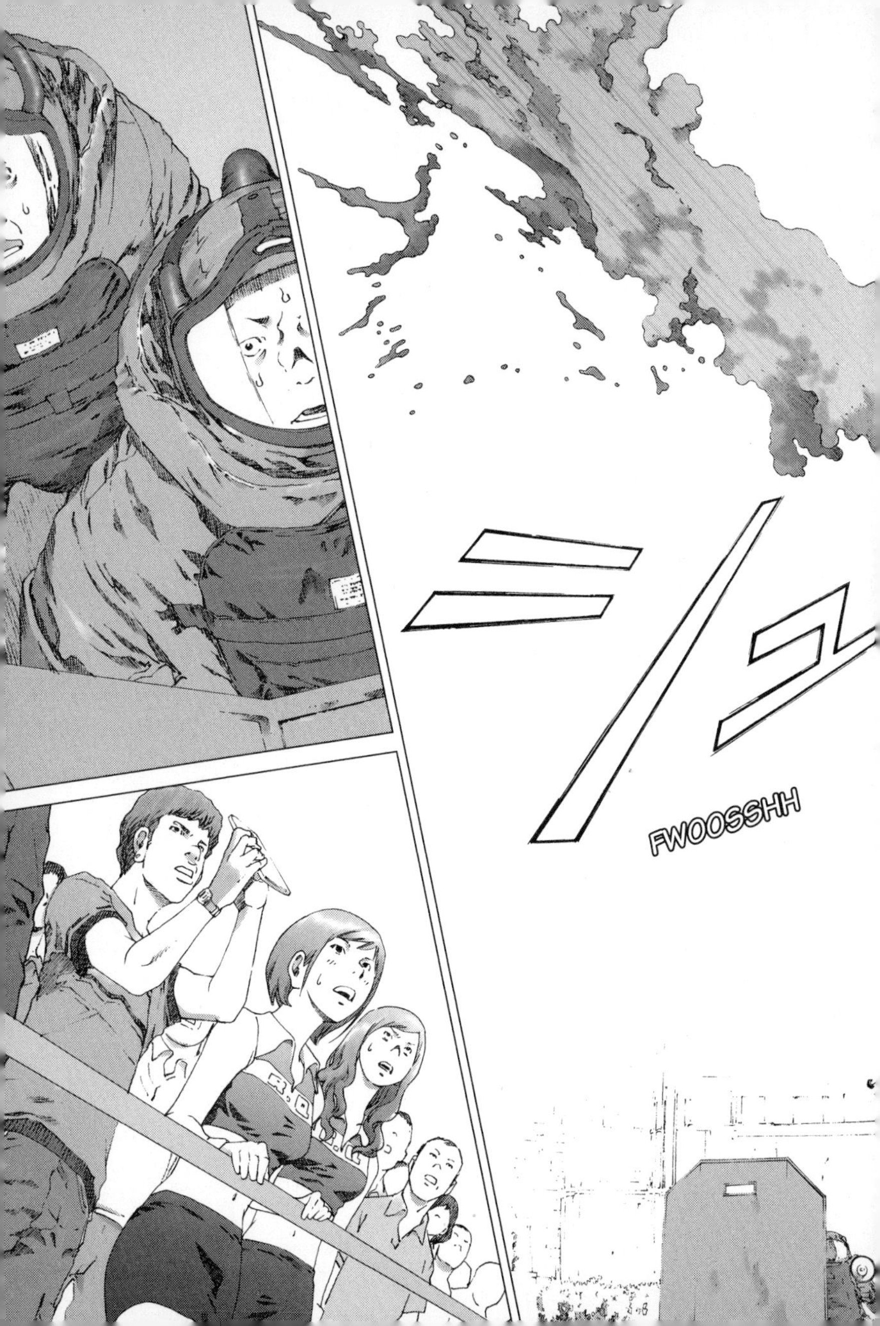
FWOOSSHH

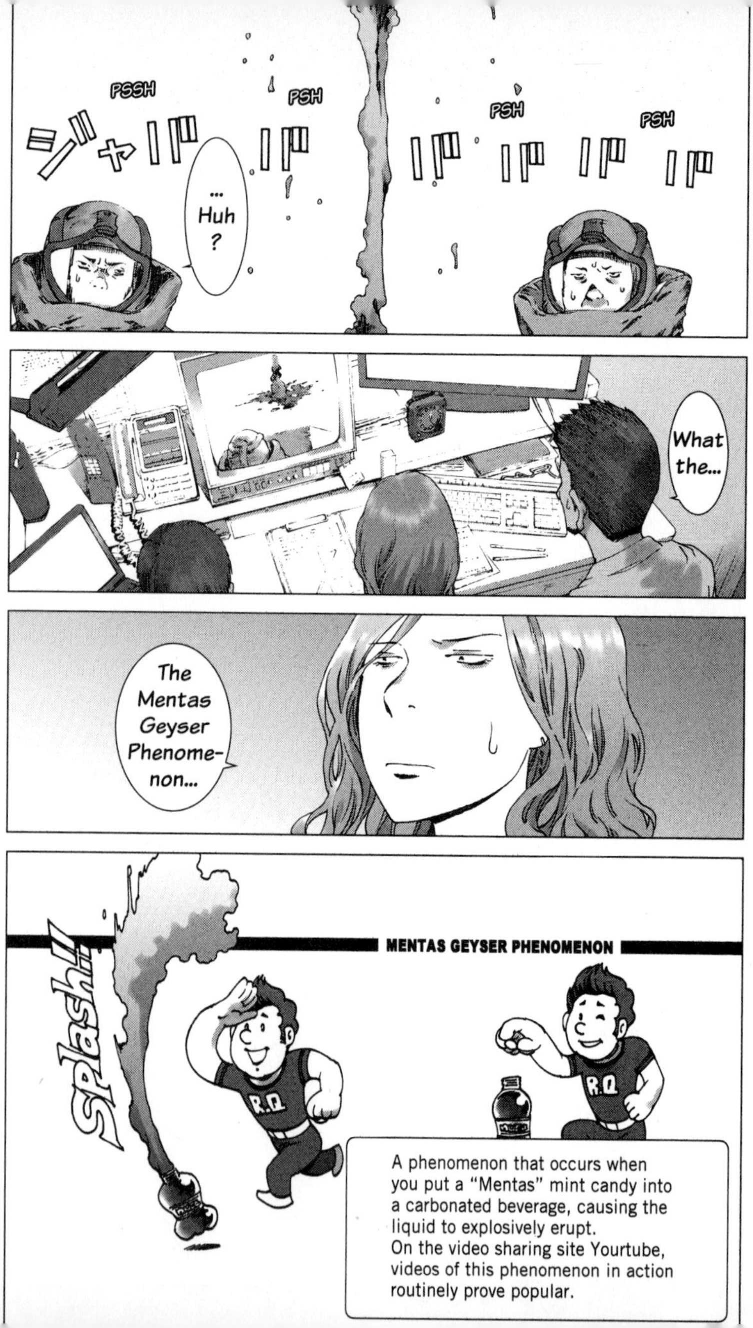

PSH
PSH
PSH
PSSH
... Huh?
What the...
The Mentas Geyser Phenomenon...
MENTAS GEYSER PHENOMENON
Splash!!
A phenomenon that occurs when you put a "Mentas" mint candy into a carbonated beverage, causing the liquid to explosively erupt.
On the video sharing site Yourtube, videos of this phenomenon in action routinely prove popular.

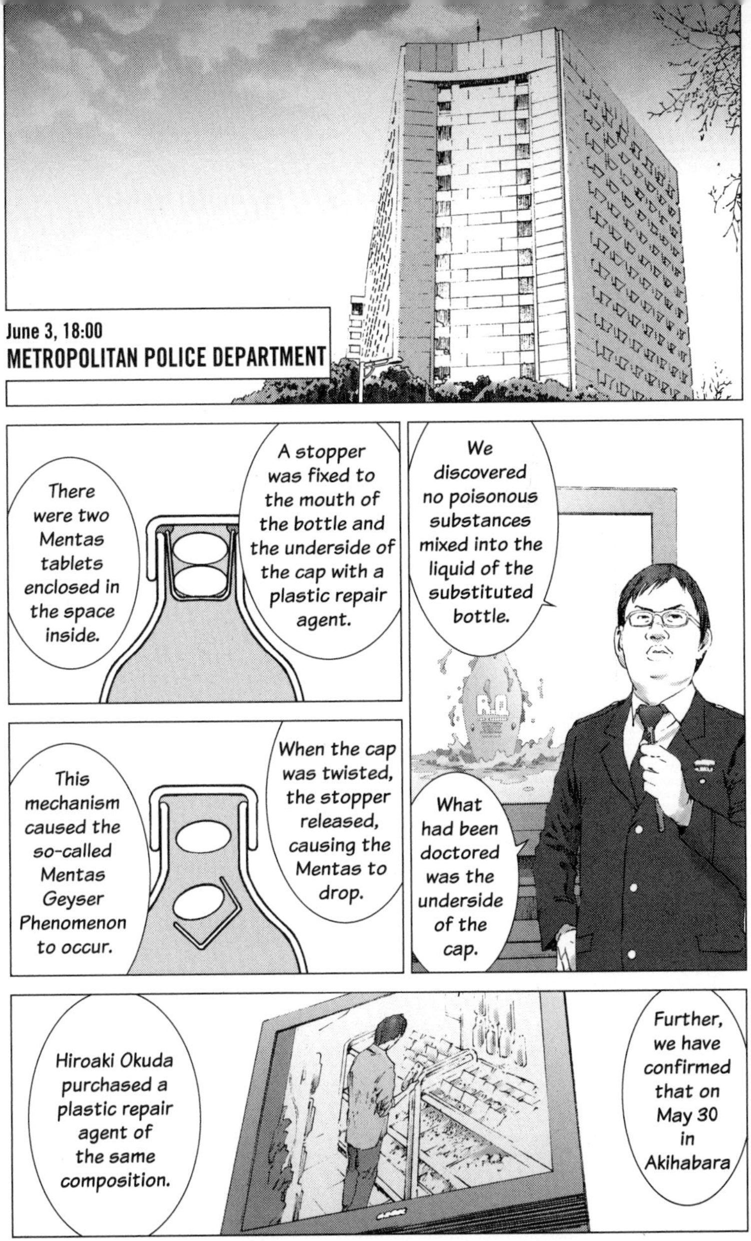
June 3, 18:00
METROPOLITAN POLICE DEPARTMENT
We discovered no poisonous substances mixed into the liquid of the substituted bottle.
What had been doctored was the underside of the cap.
A stopper was fixed to the mouth of the bottle and the underside of the cap with a plastic repair agent.
There were two Mentas tablets enclosed in the space inside.
When the cap was twisted, the stopper released, causing the Mentas to drop.
This mechanism caused the so-called Mentas Geyser Phenomenon to occur.
Further, we have confirmed that on May 30 in Akihabara
Hiroaki Okuda purchased a plastic repair agent of the same composition.

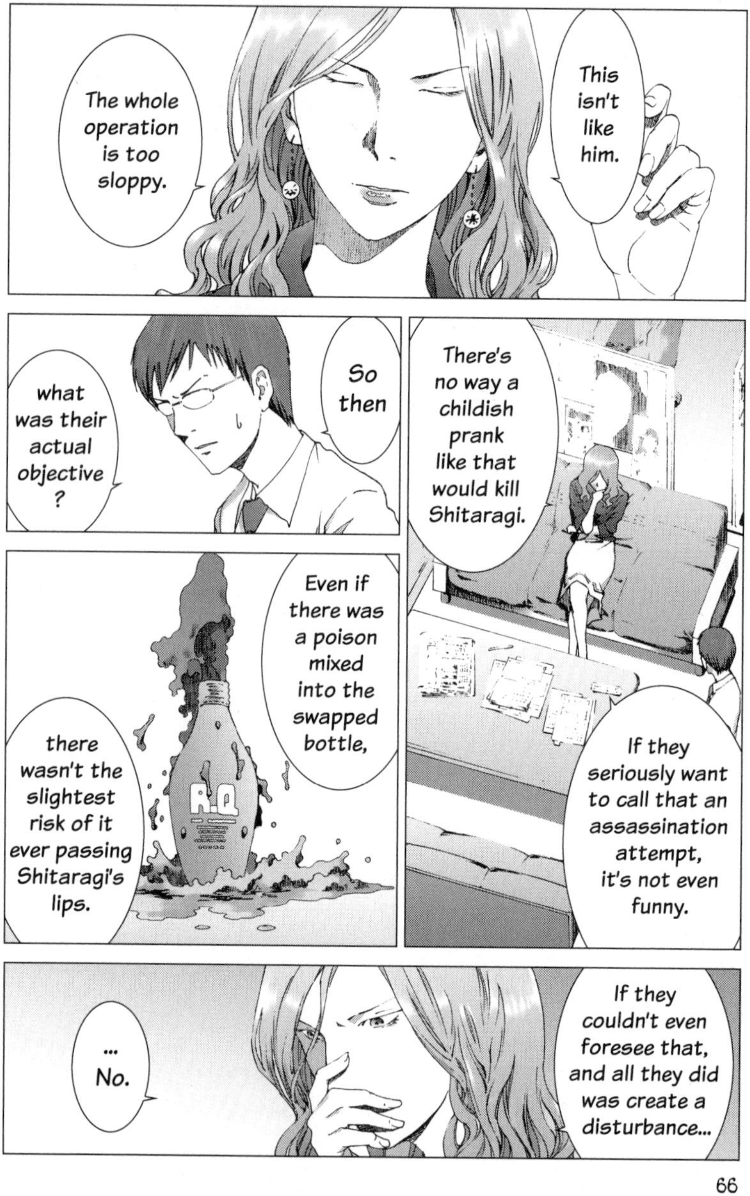
This isn't like him.
The whole operation is too sloppy.
There's no way a childish prank like that would kill Shitaragi.
If they seriously want to call that an assassination attempt, it's not even funny.
So then
what was their actual objective ?
Even if there was a poison mixed into the swapped bottle,
there wasn't the slightest risk of it ever passing Shitaragi's lips.
If they couldn't even foresee that, and all they did was create a disturbance...
... No.

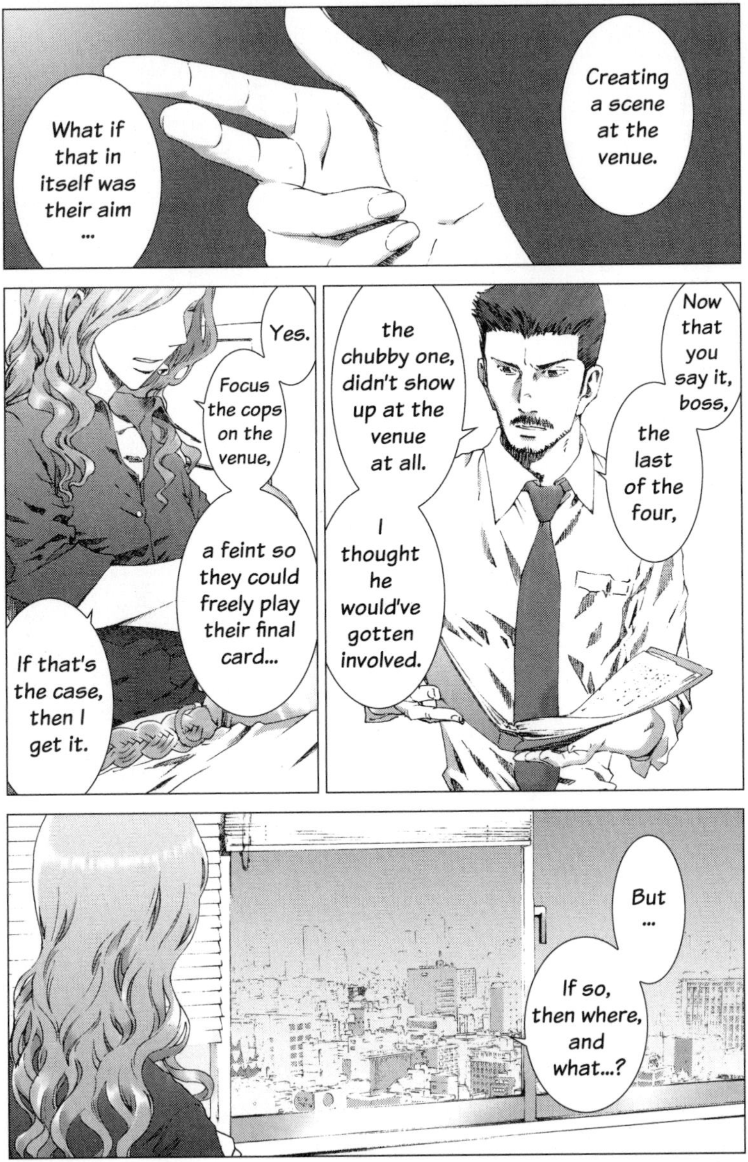

Creating a scene at the venue.
What if that in itself was their aim ...
Now that you say it, boss,
the last of the four,
the chubby one, didn't show up at the venue at all.
I thought he would've gotten involved.
Yes.
Focus the cops on the venue,
a feint so they could freely play their final card...
If that's the case, then I get it.
But ...
If so, then where, and what...?

June 3, 18:30
G BRANCH MANGA CAFÉ, Y CITY,
KANAGAWA PREFECTURE

CALL 911 IF YOU SEE THESE MEN!!

セ!!

!! ! !

RRIP

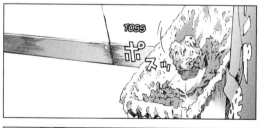

TOSS

ポ ス ッ

krsh

krsh

WHIRR

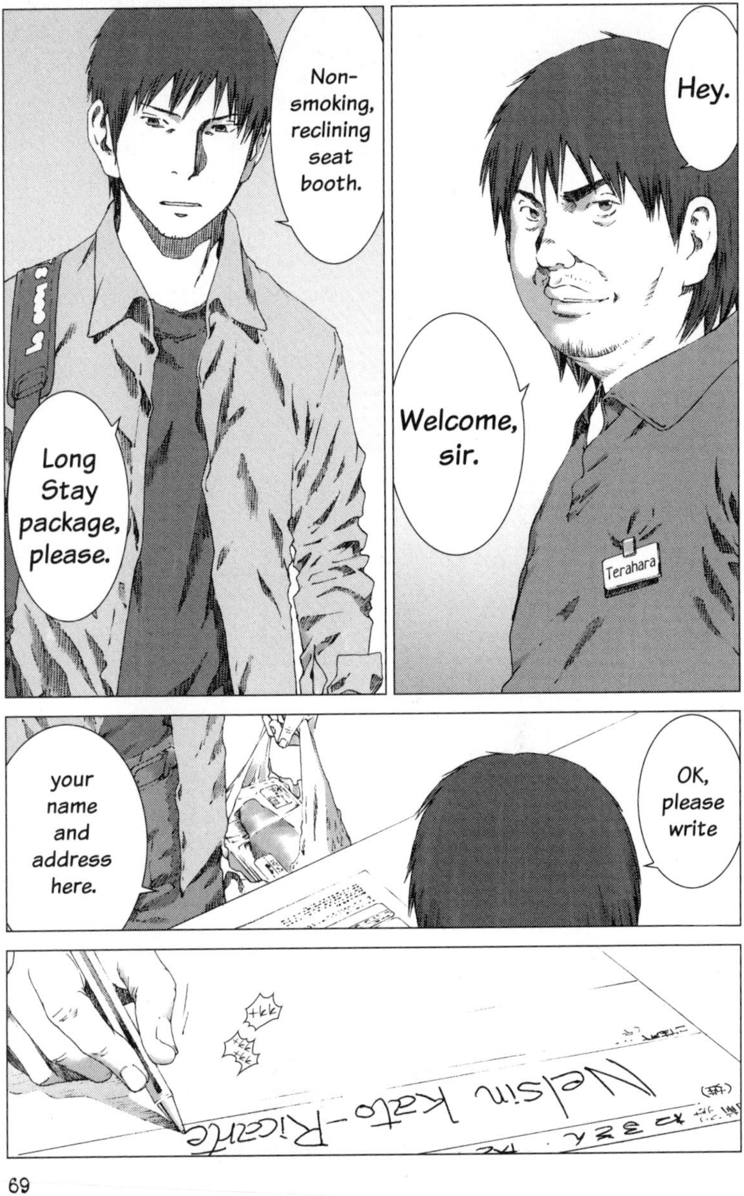
Hey.
Welcome, sir.
Terahara
Non-smoking, reclining seat booth.
Long Stay package, please.
OK, please write
your name and address here.

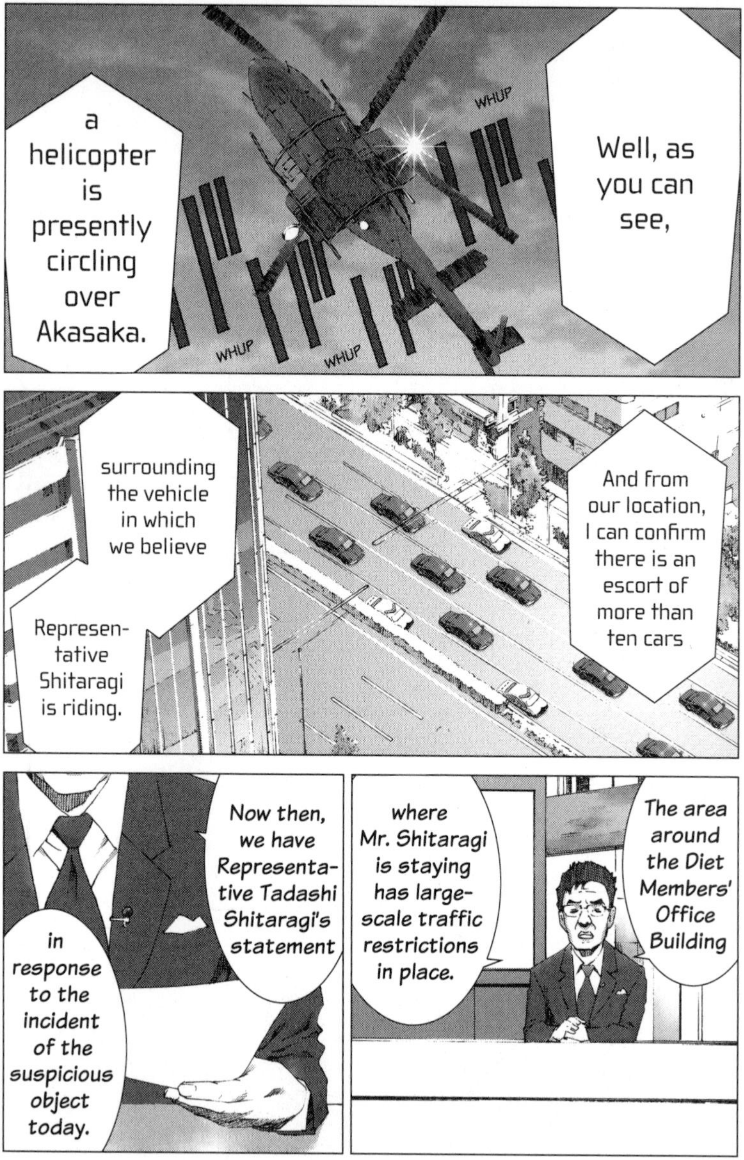
Well, as you can see,
WHUP
a helicopter is presently circling over Akasaka.
WHUP
WHUP
And from our location, I can confirm there is an escort of more than ten cars
surrounding the vehicle in which we believe
Representative Shitaragi is riding.
The area around the Diet Members' Office Building
where Mr. Shitaragi is staying has large-scale traffic restrictions in place.
Now then, we have Representative Tadashi Shitaragi's statement
in response to the incident of the suspicious object today.

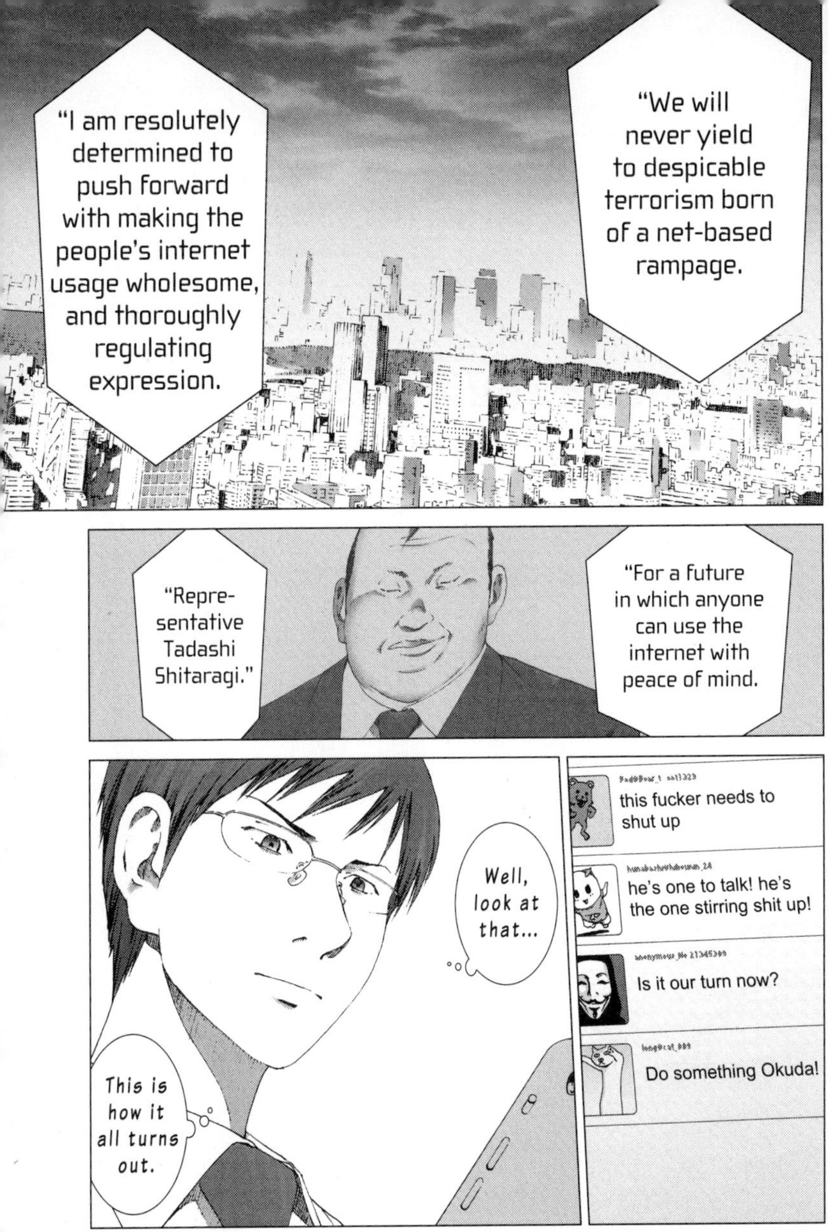
"We will never yield to despicable terrorism born of a net-based rampage.
"I am resolutely determined to push forward with making the people's internet usage wholesome, and thoroughly regulating expression.
"For a future in which anyone can use the internet with peace of mind.
"Representative Tadashi Shitaragi."
this fucker needs to shut up
he's one to talk! he's the one stirring shit up!
Is it our turn now?
Do something Okuda!
Well, look at that...
This is how it all turns out.

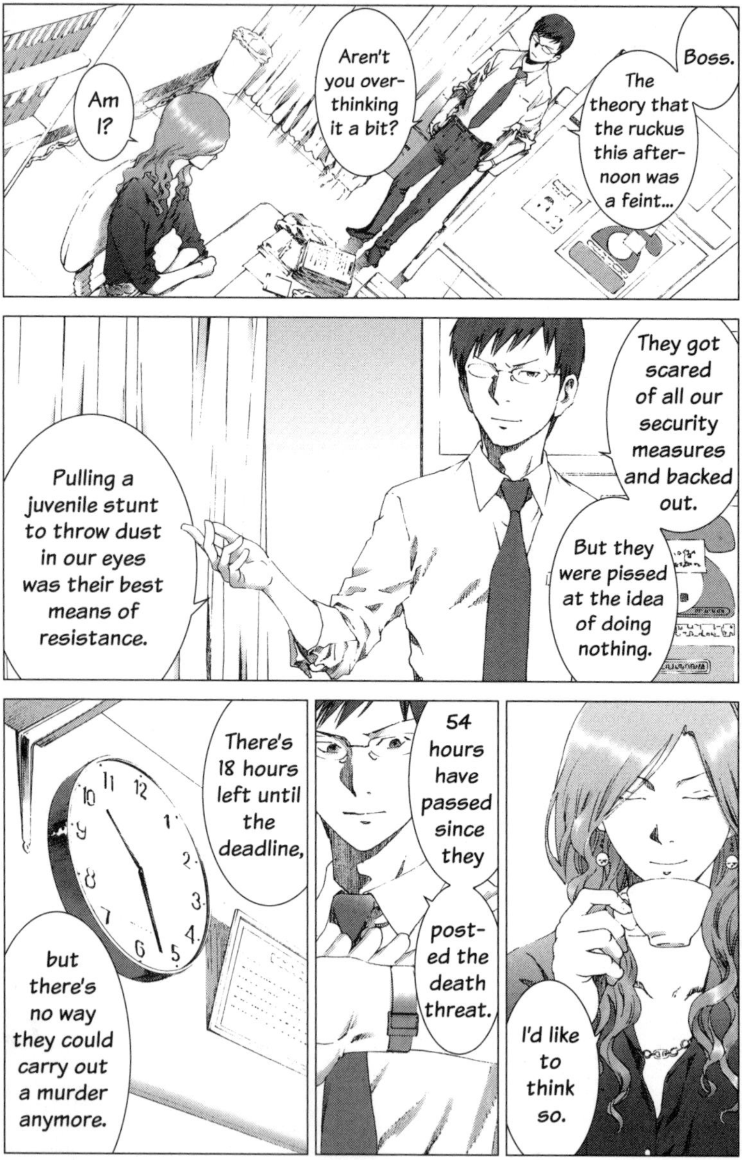
Boss.
The theory that the ruckus this afternoon was a feint...
Aren't you over-thinking it a bit?
Am I?
They got scared of all our security measures and backed out.
But they were pissed at the idea of doing nothing.
Pulling a juvenile stunt to throw dust in our eyes was their best means of resistance.
I'd like to think so.
54 hours have passed since they
post-ed the death threat.
There's 18 hours left until the deadline,
but there's no way they could carry out a murder anymore.

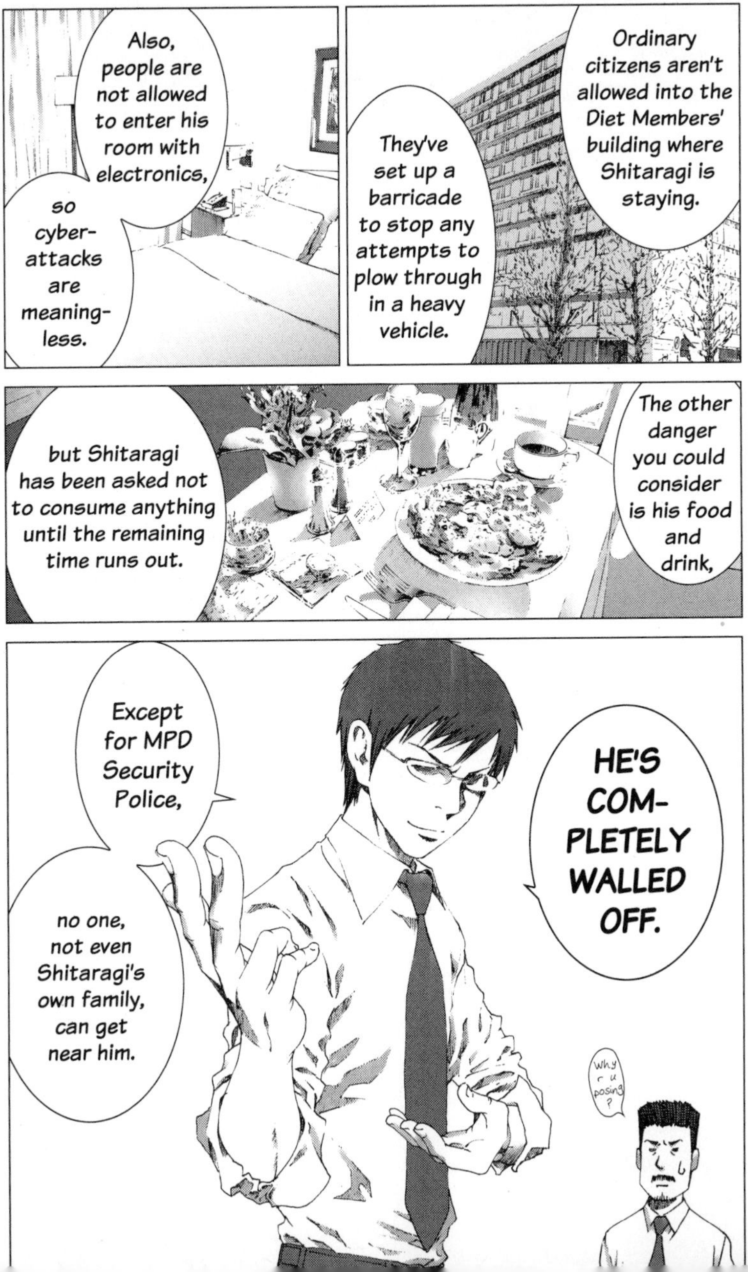
Ordinary citizens aren't allowed into the Diet Members' building where Shitaragi is staying.
They've set up a barricade to stop any attempts to plow through in a heavy vehicle.
Also, people are not allowed to enter his room with electronics,
so cyber-attacks are meaning-less.
The other danger you could consider is his food and drink,
but Shitaragi has been asked not to consume anything until the remaining time runs out.
Except for MPD Security Police,
no one, not even Shitaragi's own family, can get near him.
HE'S COM-PLETELY WALLED OFF.
Why r u posing?

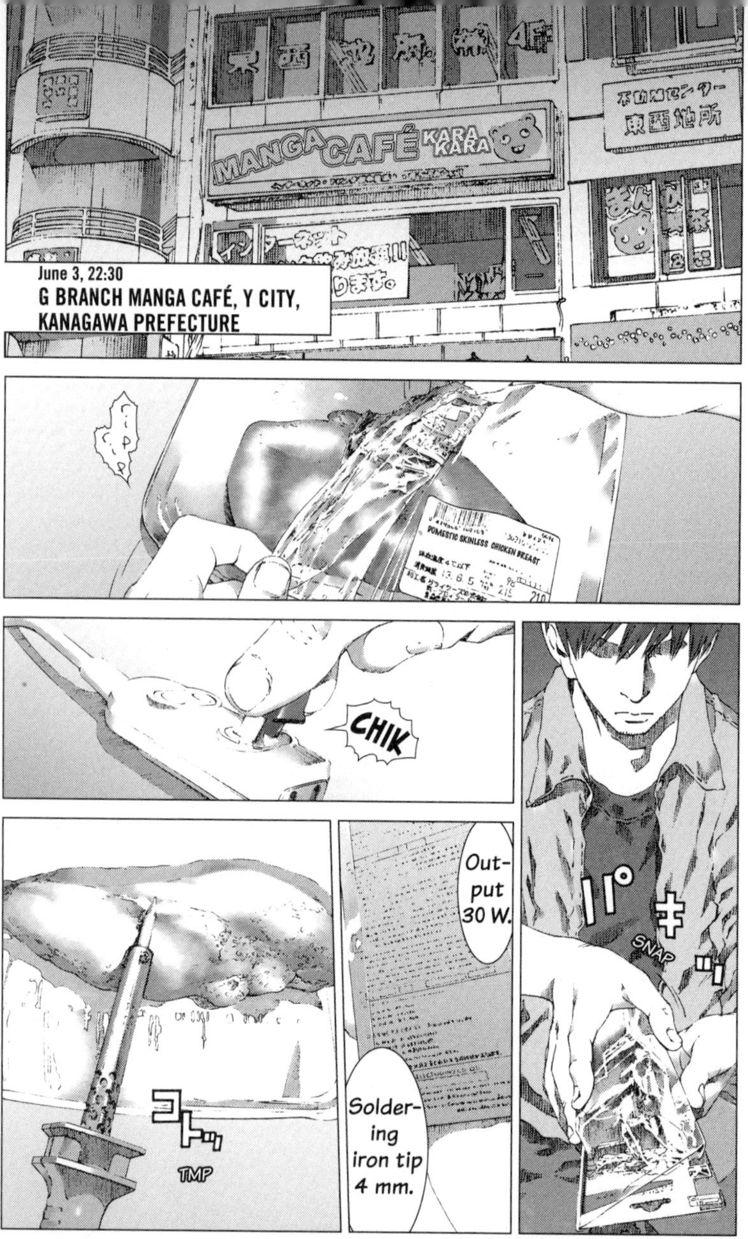
MANGA CAFÉ KARA KARA
June 3, 22:30
G BRANCH MANGA CAFÉ, Y CITY, KANAGAWA PREFECTURE
RIP RIP
DOMESTIC SKINLESS CHICKEN BREAST
パキッ
SNAP
CHIK
Output 30 W.
Soldering iron tip 4 mm.
コトッ
TMP

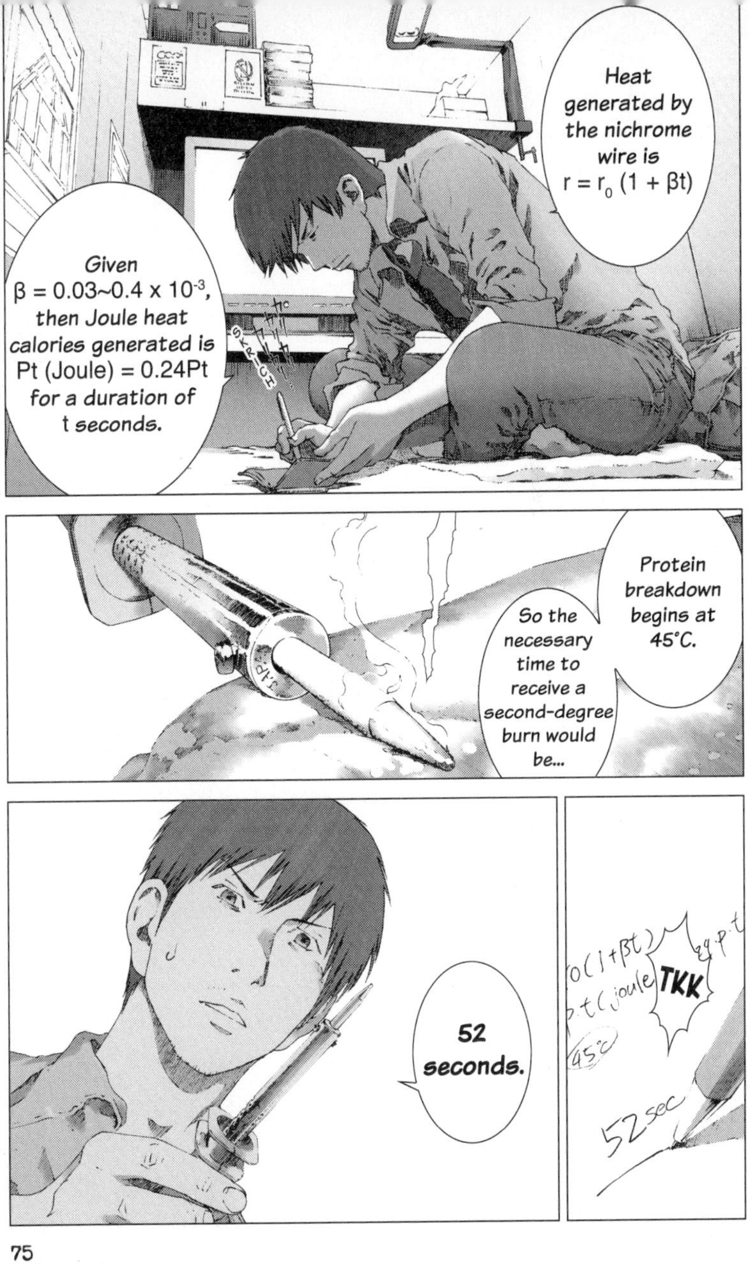
Heat generated by the nichrome wire is $r = r_0 (1 + \beta t)$
Given $\beta = 0.03\sim0.4 \times 10^{-3}$, then Joule heat calories generated is Pt (Joule) = 0.24Pt for a duration of t seconds.
SKRICH
Protein breakdown begins at 45°C.
So the necessary time to receive a second-degree burn would be...
TKK
52sec
52 seconds.

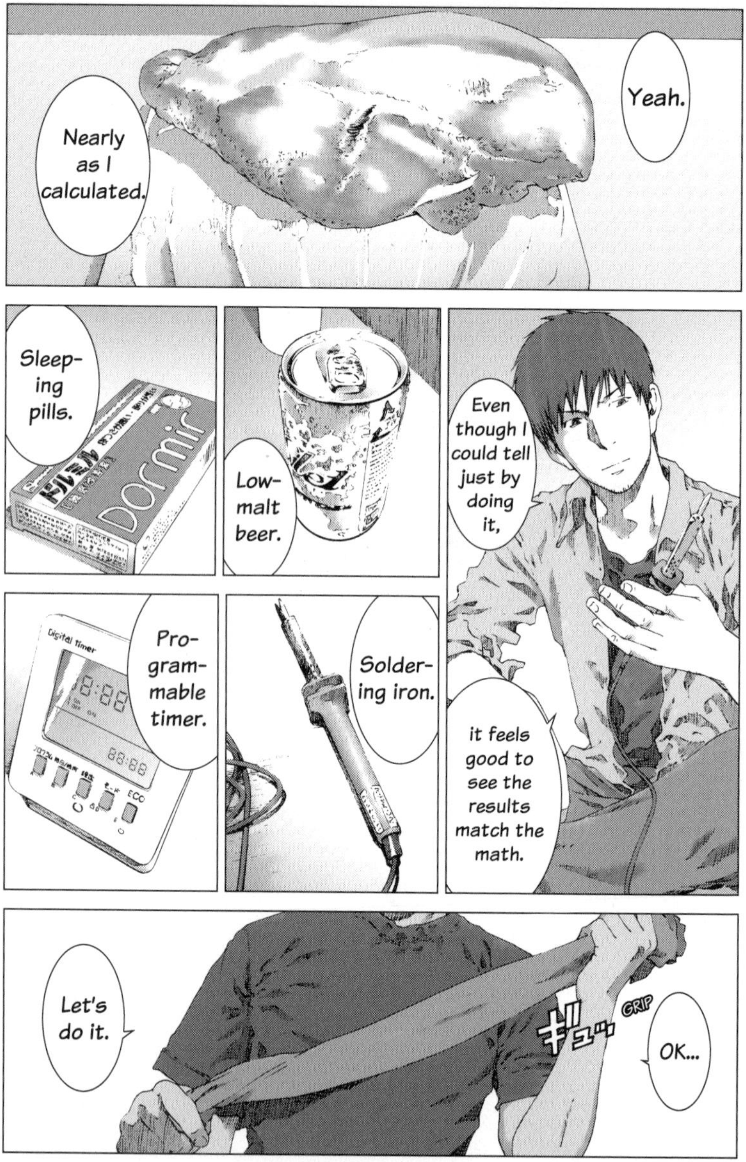
Yeah.
Nearly as I calculated.
Even though I could tell just by doing it,
it feels good to see the results match the math.
Low-malt beer.
Sleeping pills.
Dormir
Soldering iron.
Programable timer.
Digital timer
ECO
ギュッ GRIP
OK...
Let's do it.

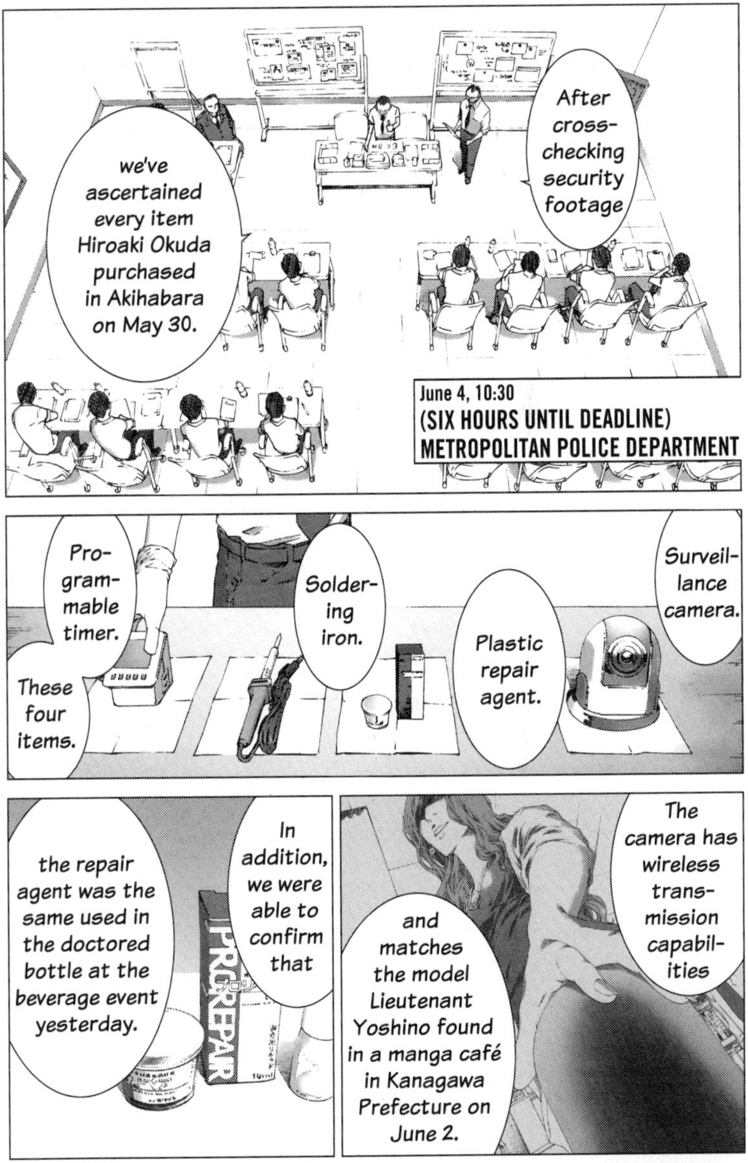
After cross-checking security footage
we've ascertained every item Hiroaki Okuda purchased in Akihabara on May 30.
June 4, 10:30
(SIX HOURS UNTIL DEADLINE)
METROPOLITAN POLICE DEPARTMENT
Surveil-lance camera.
Plastic repair agent.
Solder-ing iron.
Pro-gram-mable timer.
These four items.
The camera has wireless trans-mission capabil-ities
and matches the model Lieutenant Yoshino found in a manga café in Kanagawa Prefecture on June 2.
In addition, we were able to confirm that
the repair agent was the same used in the doctored bottle at the beverage event yesterday.
PRC REPAIR

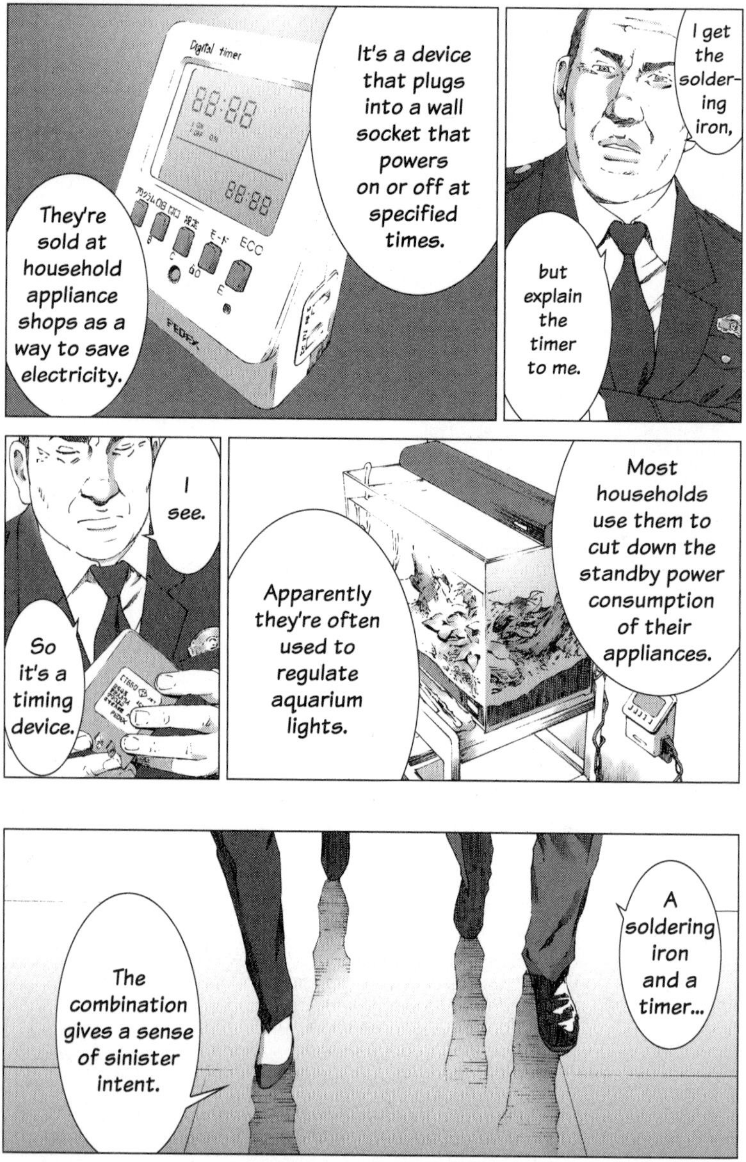
I get the soldering iron,
but explain the timer to me.
It's a device that plugs into a wall socket that powers on or off at specified times.
They're sold at household appliance shops as a way to save electricity.
Most households use them to cut down the standby power consumption of their appliances.
Apparently they're often used to regulate aquarium lights.
I see.
So it's a timing device.
A soldering iron and a timer...
The combination gives a sense of sinister intent.

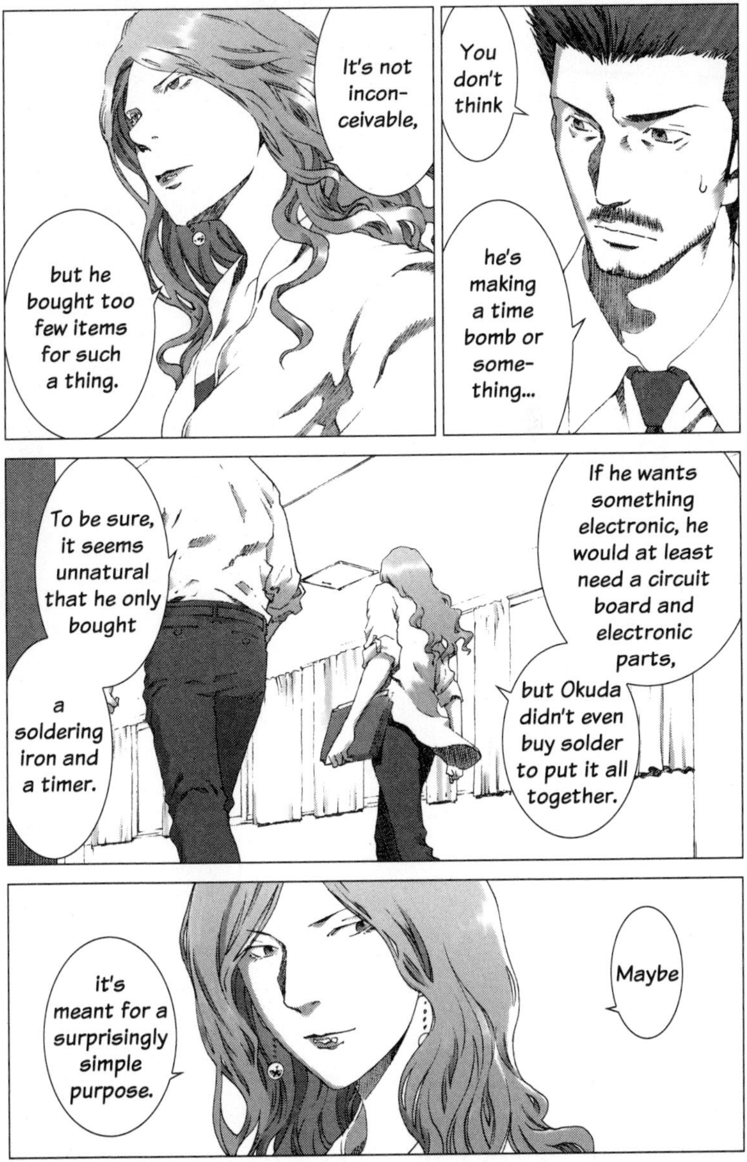
You don't think
he's making a time bomb or some-thing...
It's not incon-ceivable,
but he bought too few items for such a thing.
If he wants something electronic, he would at least need a circuit board and electronic parts,
but Okuda didn't even buy solder to put it all together.
To be sure, it seems unnatural that he only bought
a soldering iron and a timer.
Maybe
it's meant for a surprisingly simple purpose.

June 4, 12:30
(FOUR HOURS UNTIL DEADLINE)
G BRANCH MANGA CAFÉ

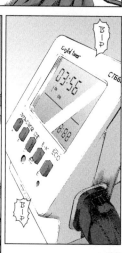

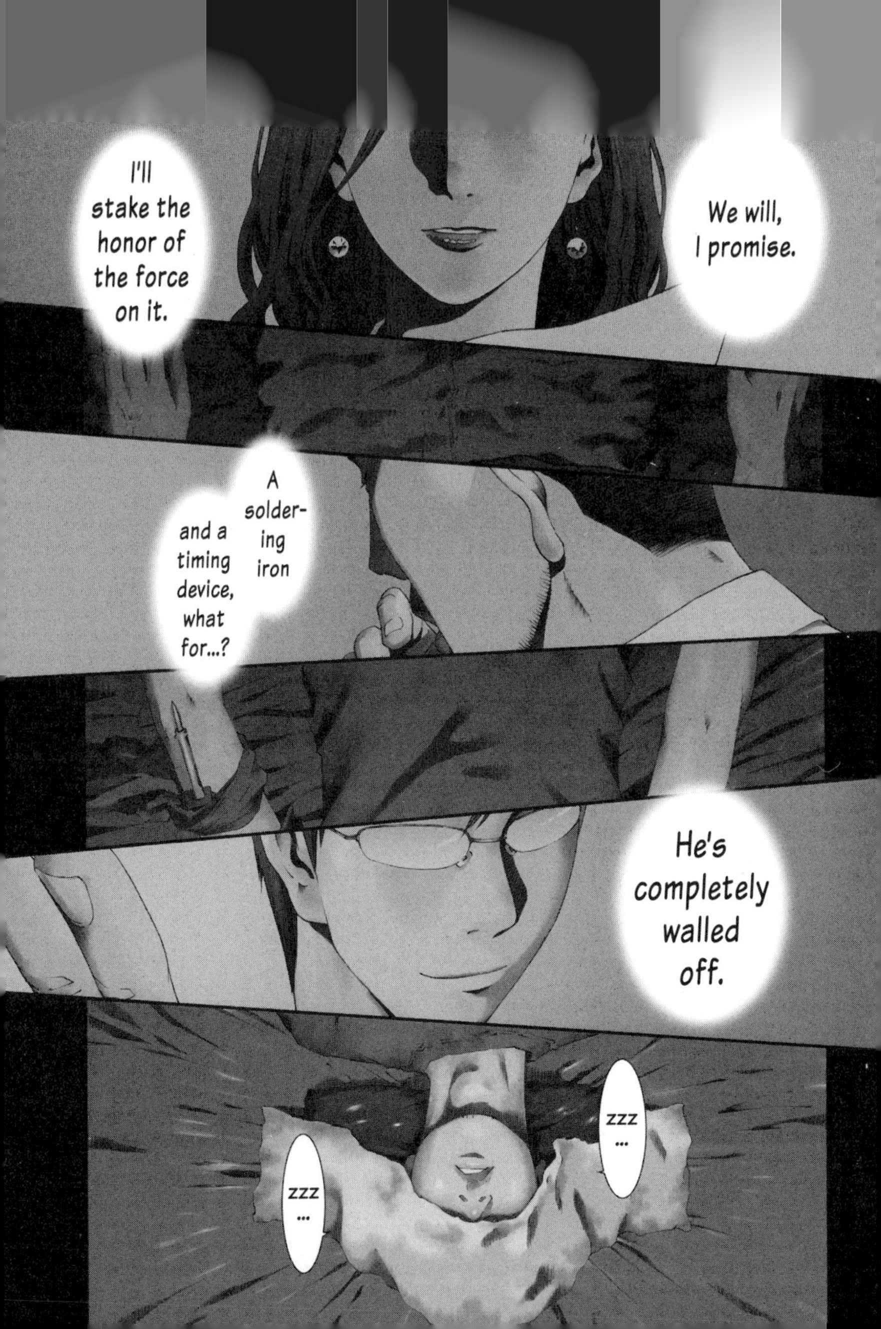
We will, I promise.
I'll stake the honor of the force on it.
A solder-ing iron
and a timing device, what for...?
He's completely walled off.
zzz...
zzz...

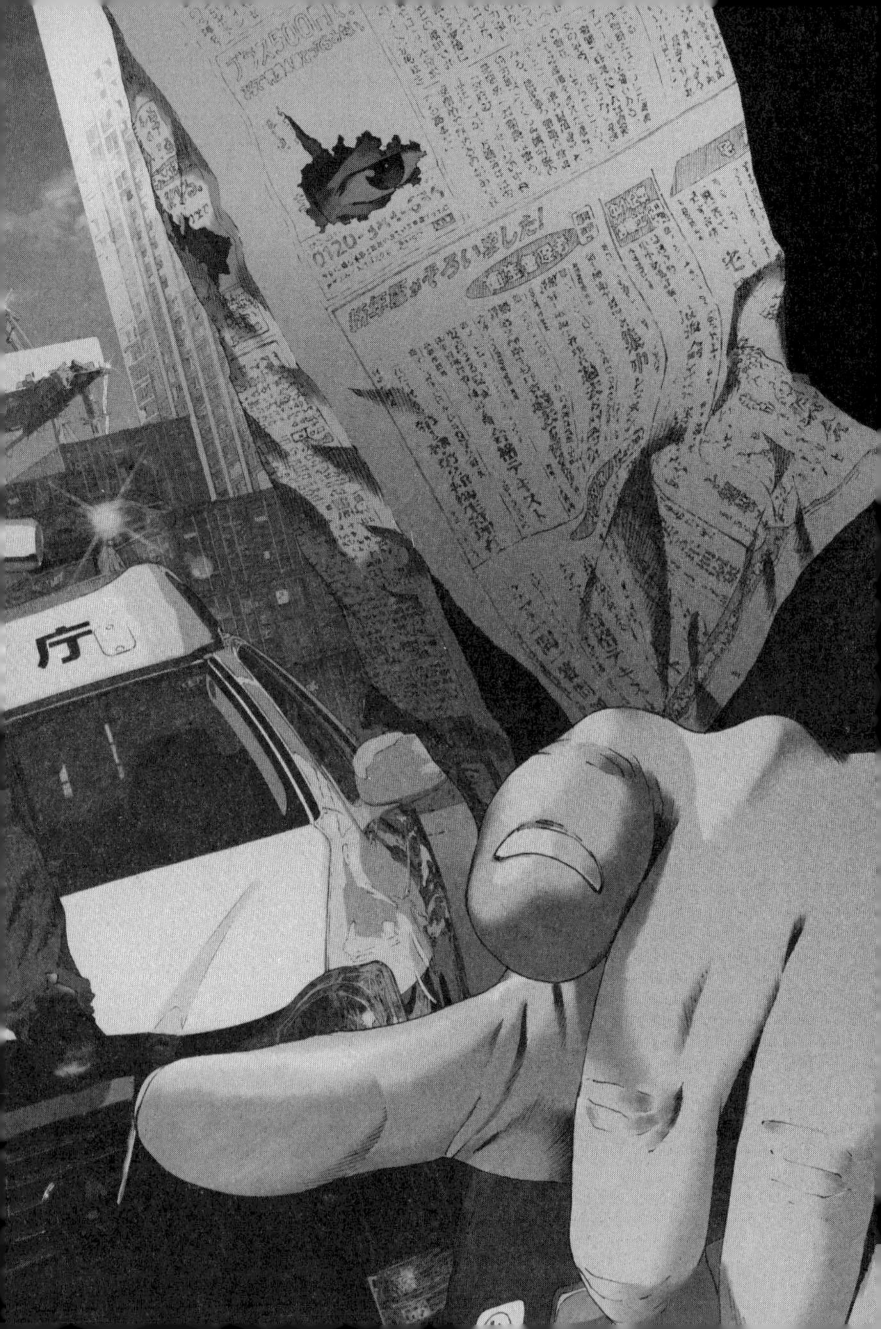
庁

File 018

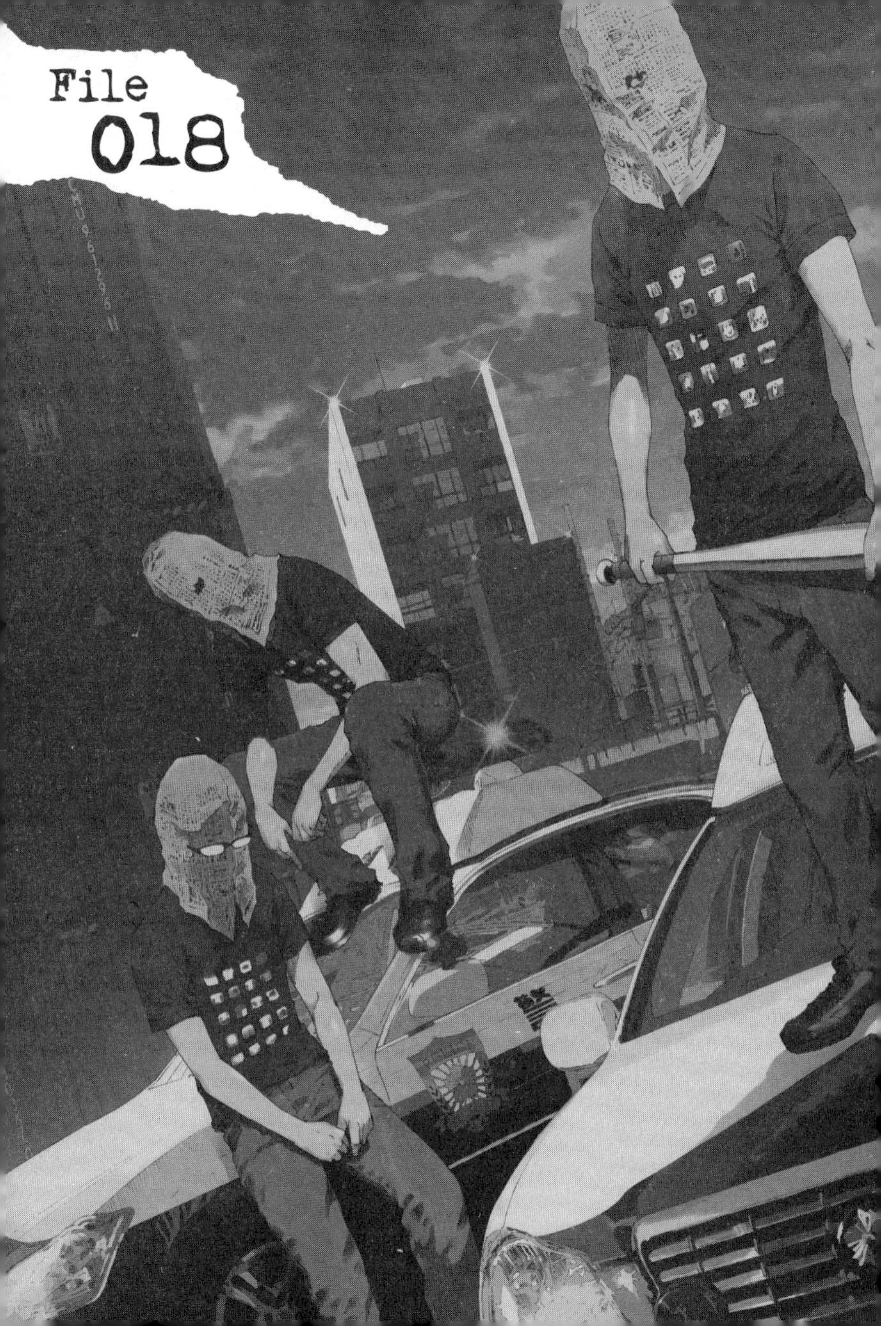

PROPHECY

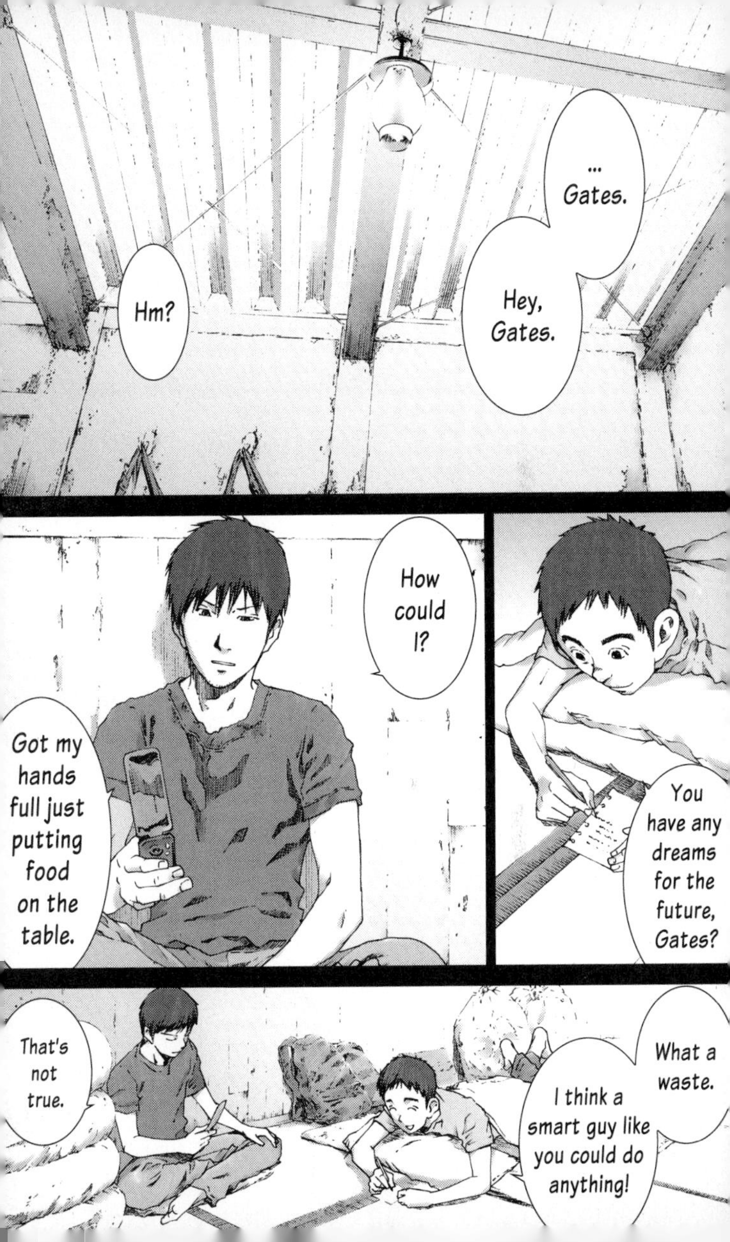
...
Gates.
Hey, Gates.
Hm?
You have any dreams for the future, Gates?
How could I?
Got my hands full just putting food on the table.
What a waste.
I think a smart guy like you could do anything!
That's not true.

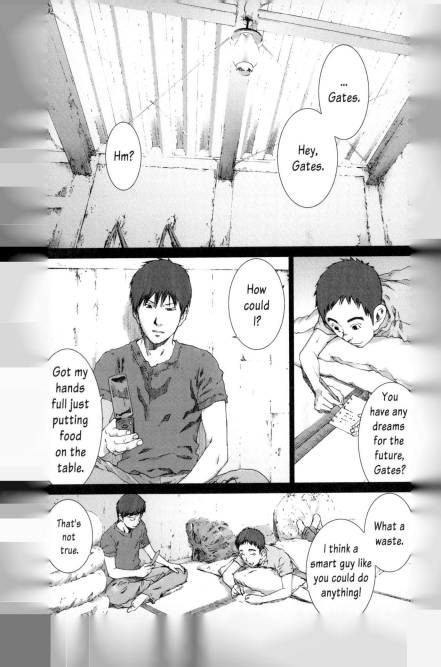

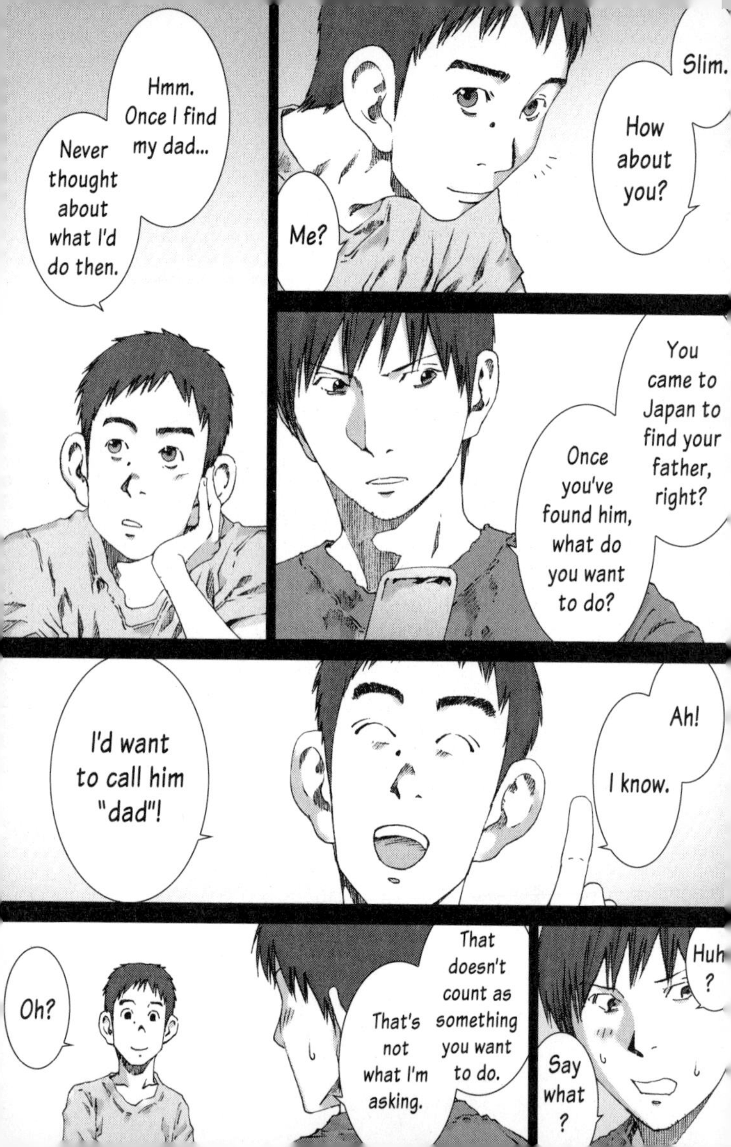
Slim.
How about you?
Me?
Hmm. Once I find my dad...
Never thought about what I'd do then.
You came to Japan to find your father, right?
Once you've found him, what do you want to do?
Ah! I know.
I'd want to call him "dad"!
Huh?
Say what?
That doesn't count as something you want to do.
That's not what I'm asking.
Oh?

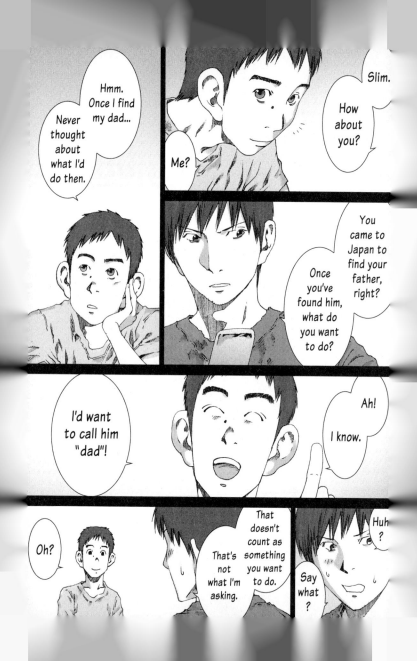

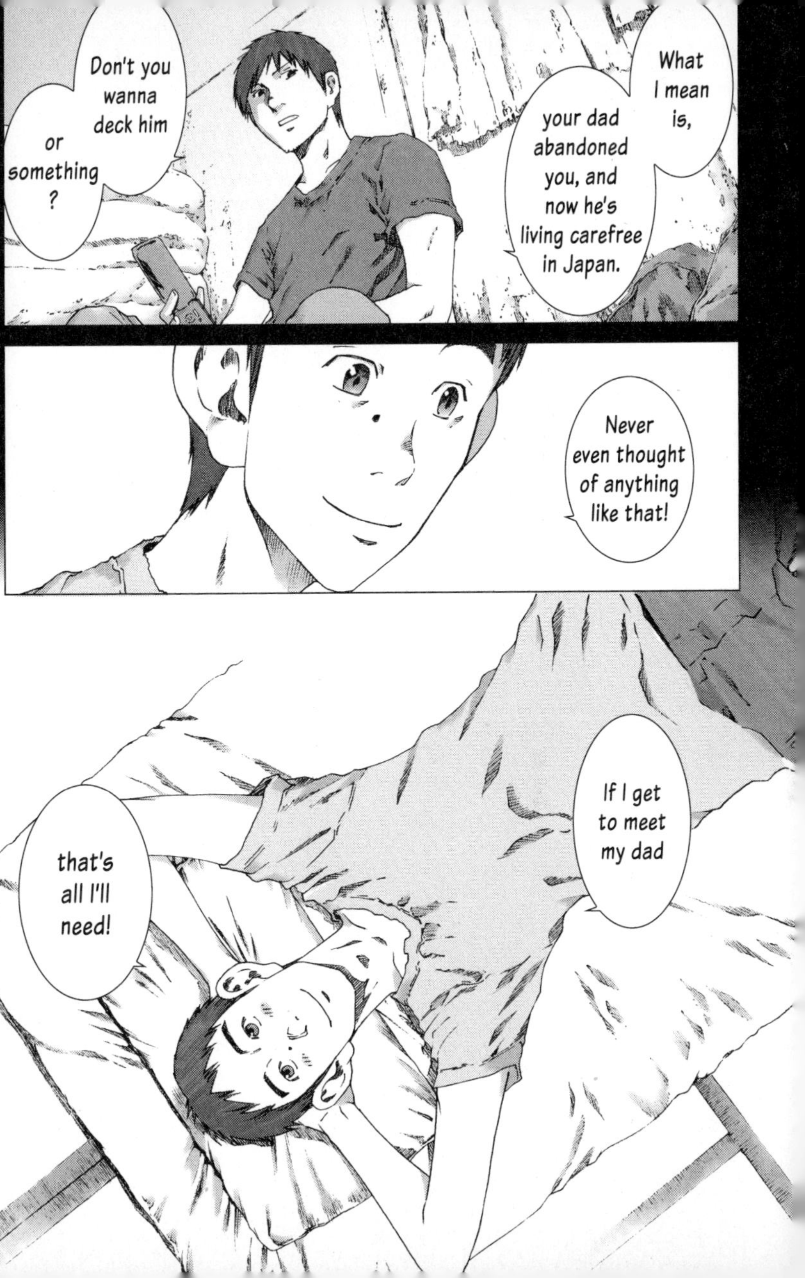
What I mean is, your dad abandoned you, and now he's living carefree in Japan.
Don't you wanna deck him or something?
Never even thought of anything like that!
If I get to meet my dad
that's all I'll need!

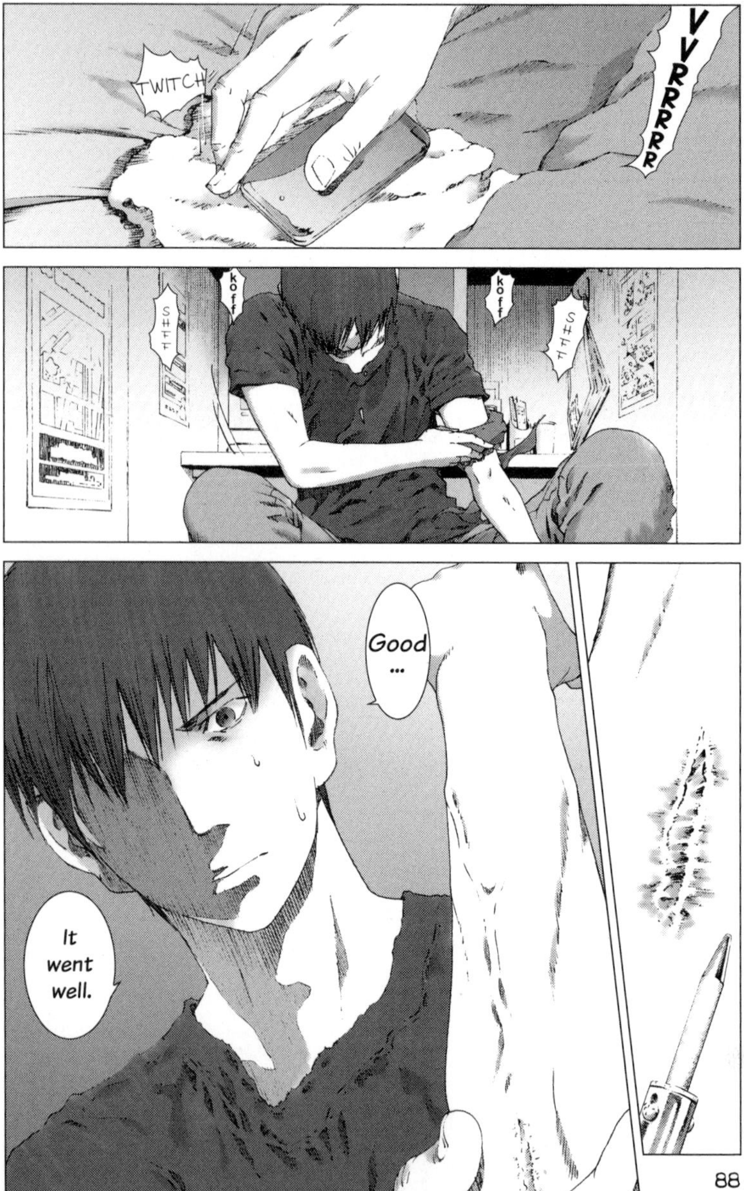
VVRRRRR
TWITCH
SHFF
koff
koff
SHFF
Good ...
It went well.

June 4, 15:30 (One hour remaining until deadline)
NEW HOUSE OF REPRESENTATIVES OFFICE BUILDING, C WARD, TOKYO

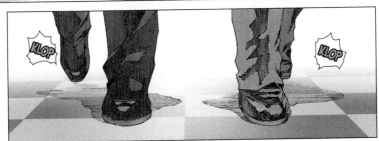

KLOP

KLOP

We have urgent business with Mr. Shitaragi.

Please let us through.

!

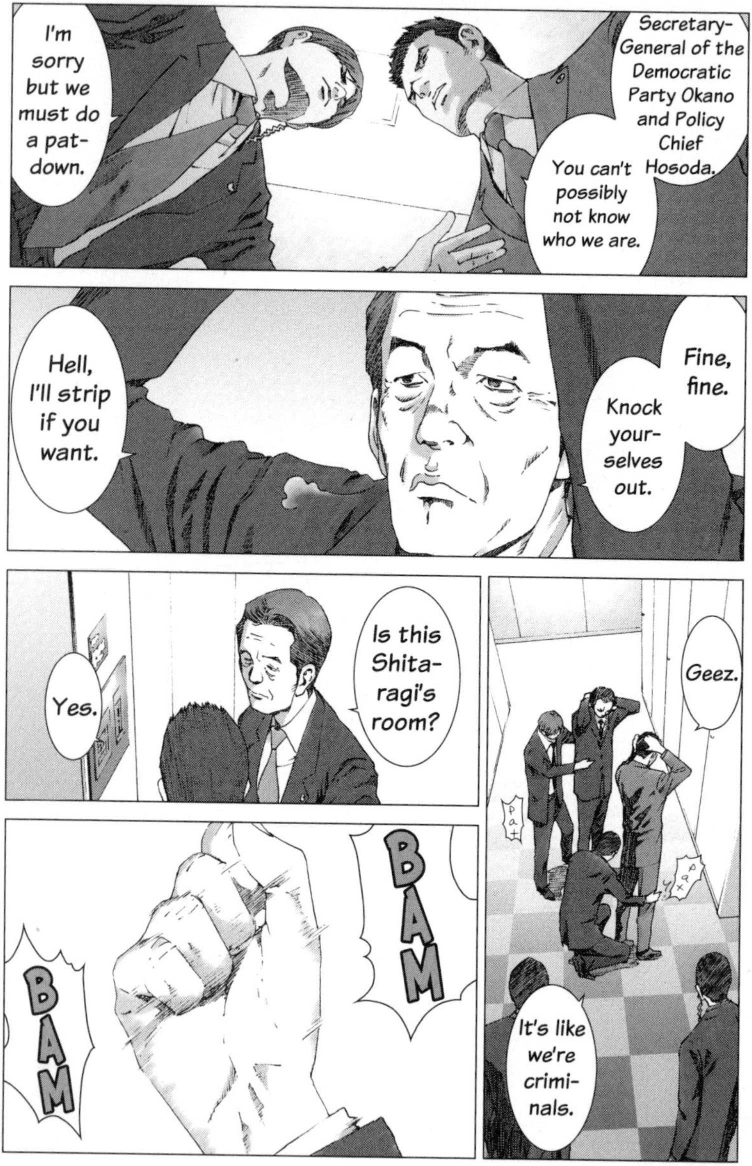
Secretary-General of the Democratic Party Okano and Policy Chief Hosoda.
You can't possibly not know who we are.
I'm sorry but we must do a pat-down.
Fine, fine.
Knock yourselves out.
Hell, I'll strip if you want.
Geez.
pat
pat
It's like we're criminals.
Is this Shitaragi's room?
Yes.
BAM
BAM

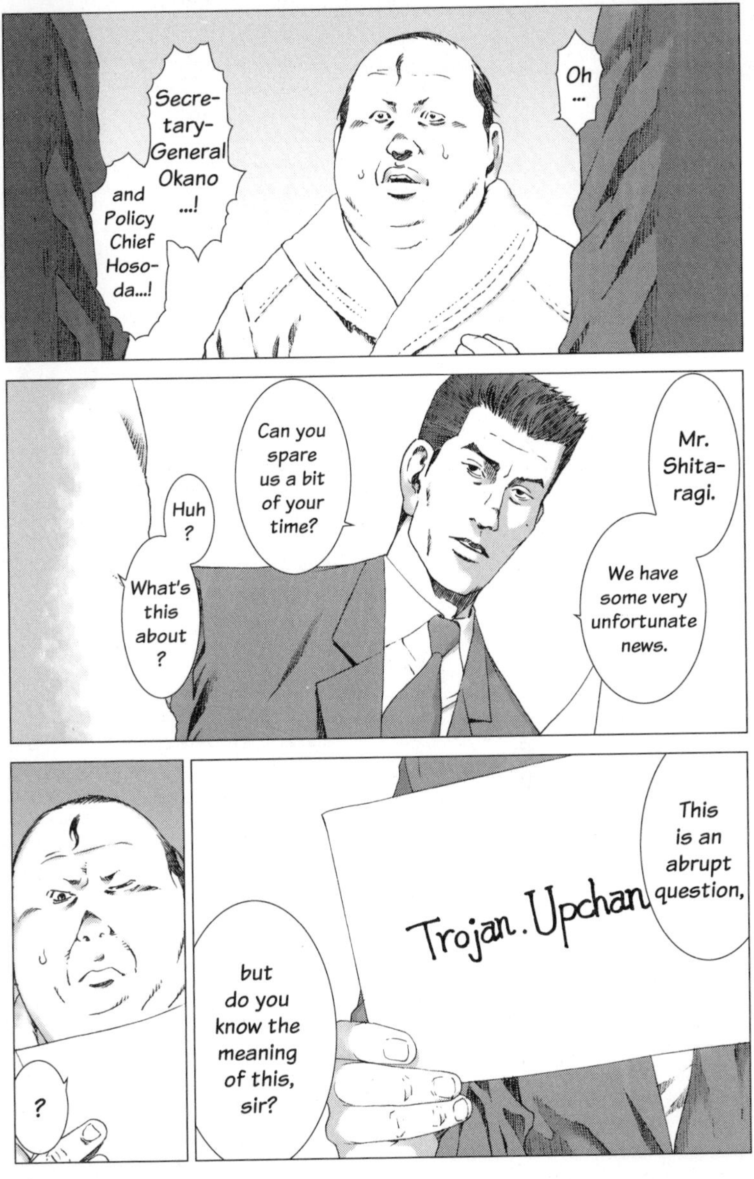
Oh ...
Secretary-General Okano ...!
and Policy Chief Hosoda...!
Mr. Shitaragi.
We have some very unfortunate news.
Can you spare us a bit of your time?
Huh?
What's this about?
This is an abrupt question,
Trojan.Upchan
but do you know the meaning of this, sir?
?

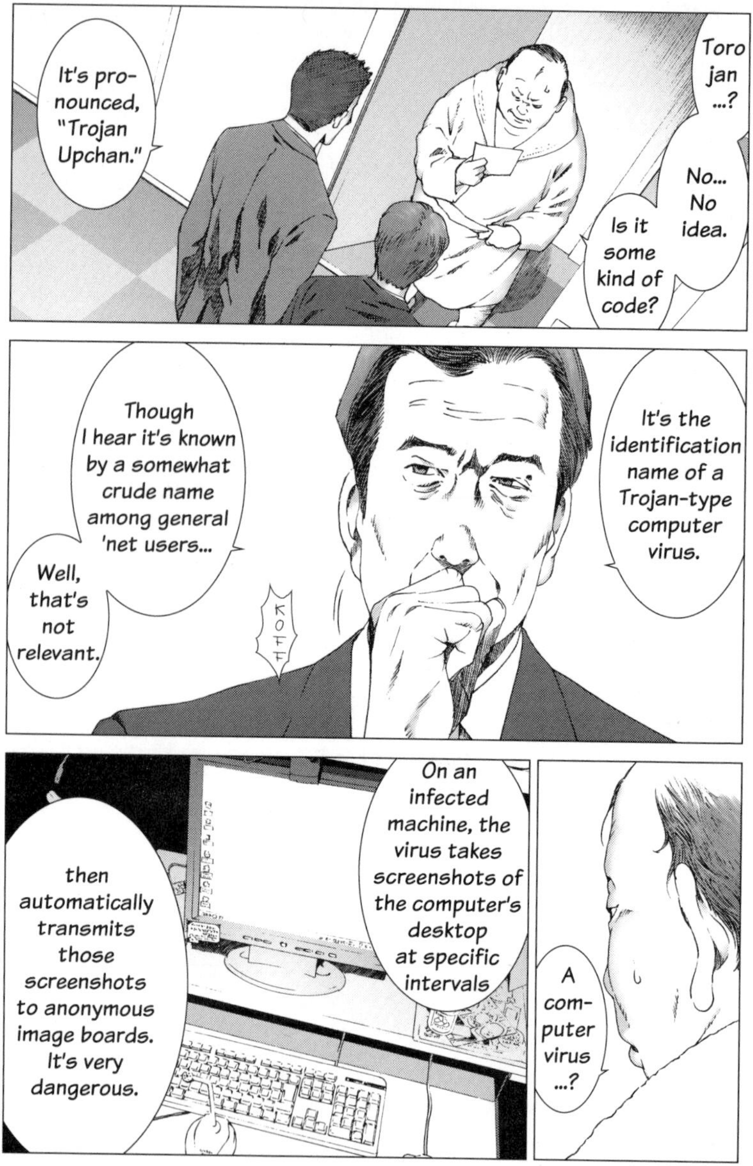
Toro jan ...?
No... No idea.
Is it some kind of code?
It's pro-nounced, "Trojan Upchan."
It's the identification name of a Trojan-type computer virus.
KOFF
Though I hear it's known by a somewhat crude name among general 'net users...
Well, that's not relevant.
A com-puter virus ...?
On an infected machine, the virus takes screenshots of the computer's desktop at specific intervals
then automatically transmits those screenshots to anonymous image boards. It's very dangerous.

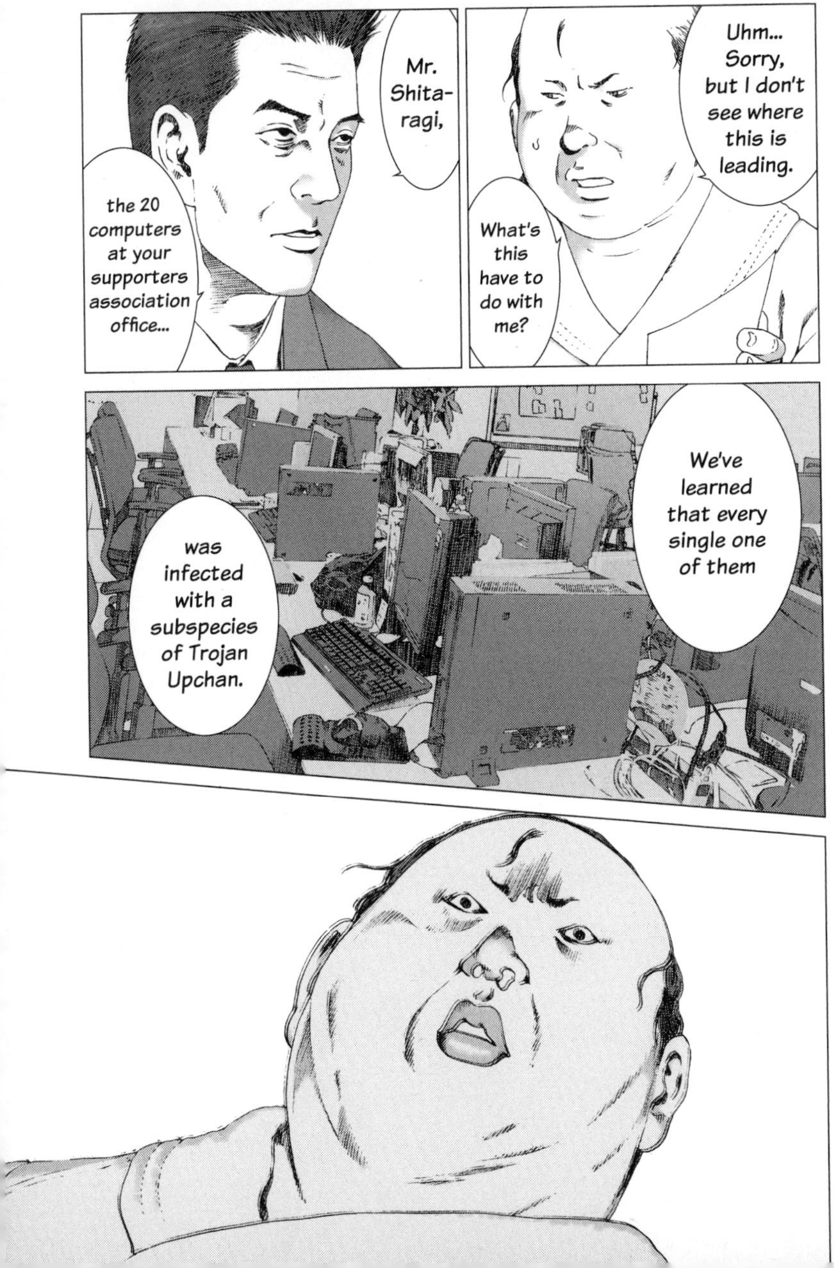
Uhm... Sorry, but I don't see where this is leading.
What's this have to do with me?
Mr. Shitaragi,
the 20 computers at your supporters association office...
We've learned that every single one of them
was infected with a subspecies of Trojan Upchan.

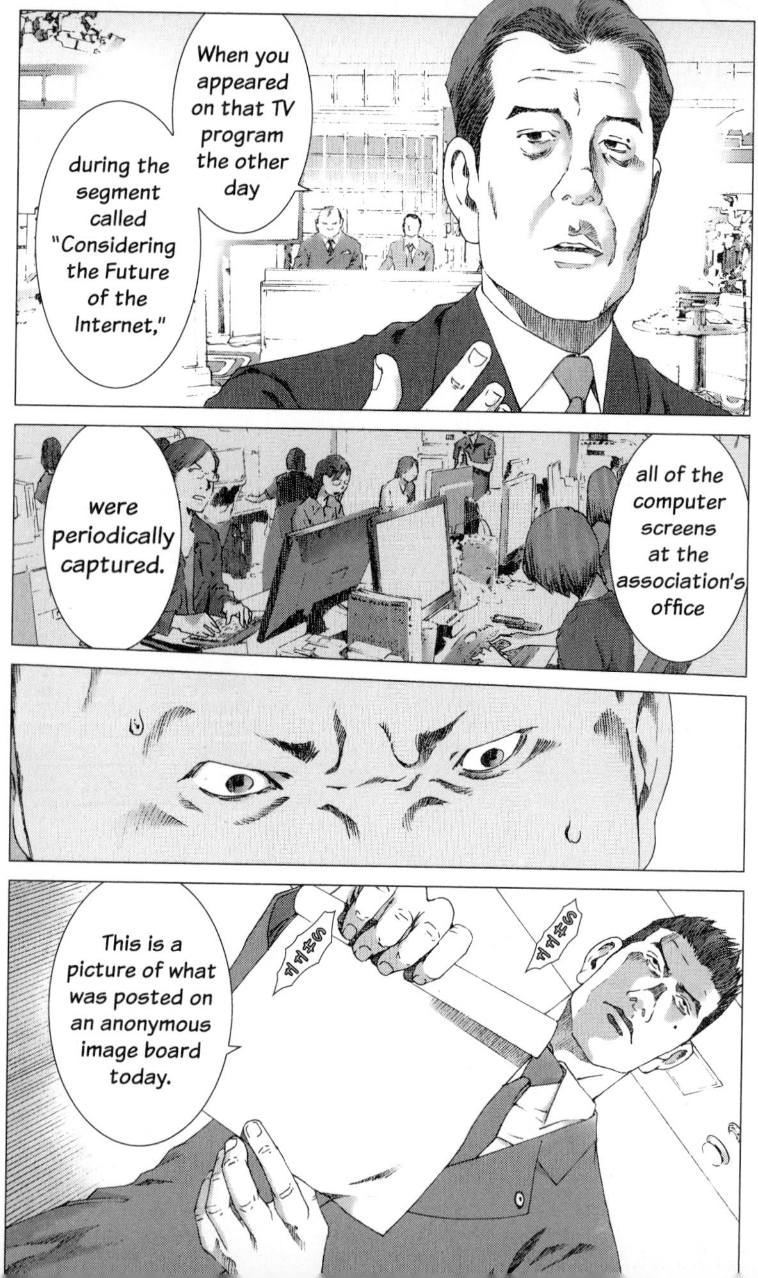
When you appeared on that TV program the other day
during the segment called "Considering the Future of the Internet,"
all of the computer screens at the association's office
were periodically captured.
This is a picture of what was posted on an anonymous image board today.

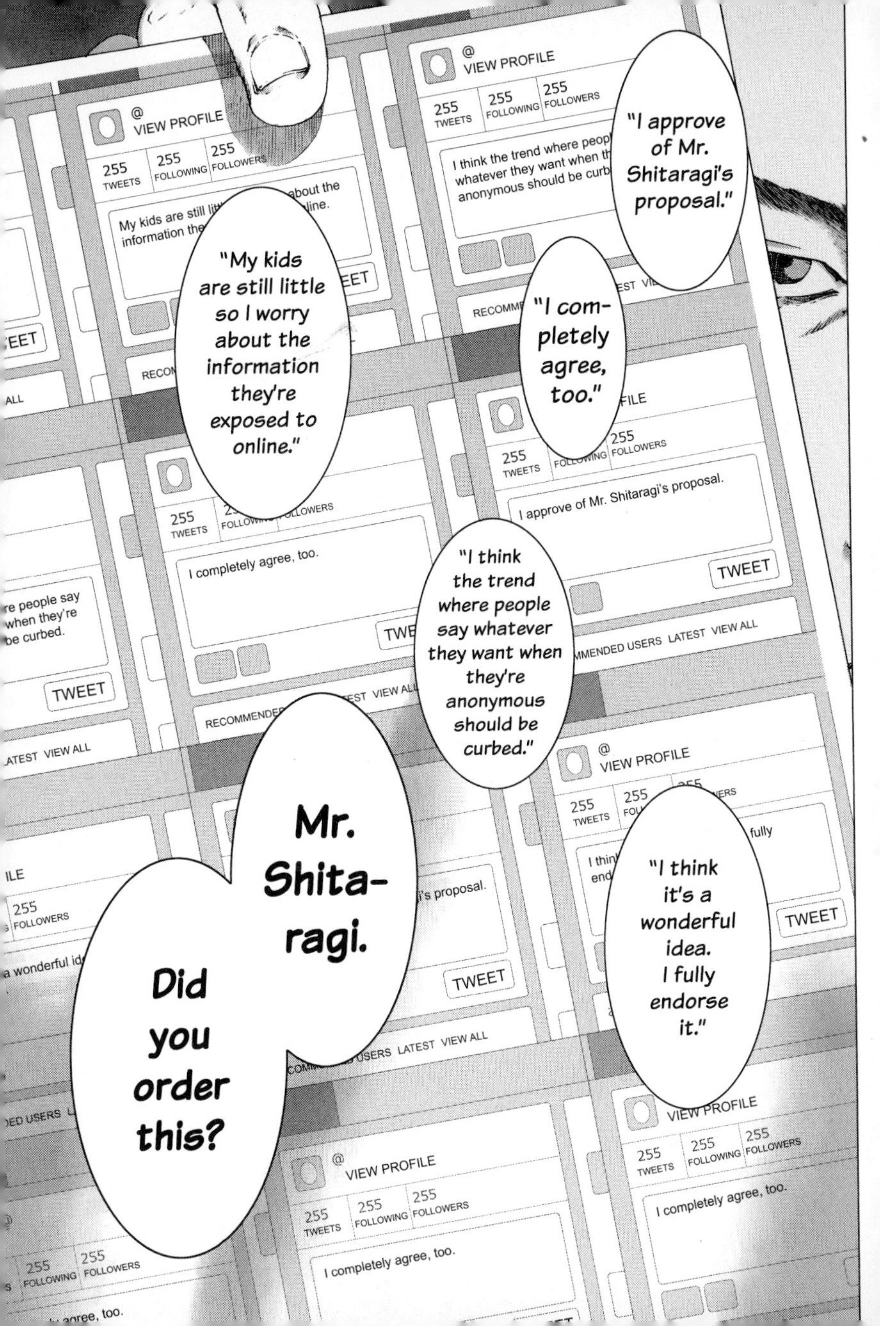
"I approve of Mr. Shitaragi's proposal."
"I com-pletely agree, too."
"My kids are still little so I worry about the information they're exposed to online."
"I think the trend where people say whatever they want when they're anonymous should be curbed."
"I think it's a wonderful idea. I fully endorse it."
Mr. Shita-ragi.
Did you order this?

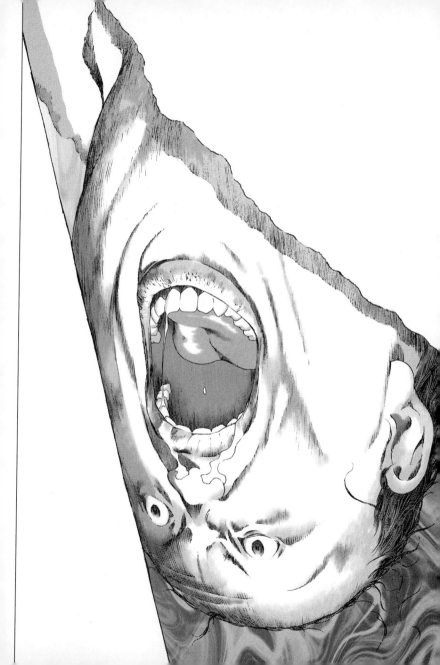

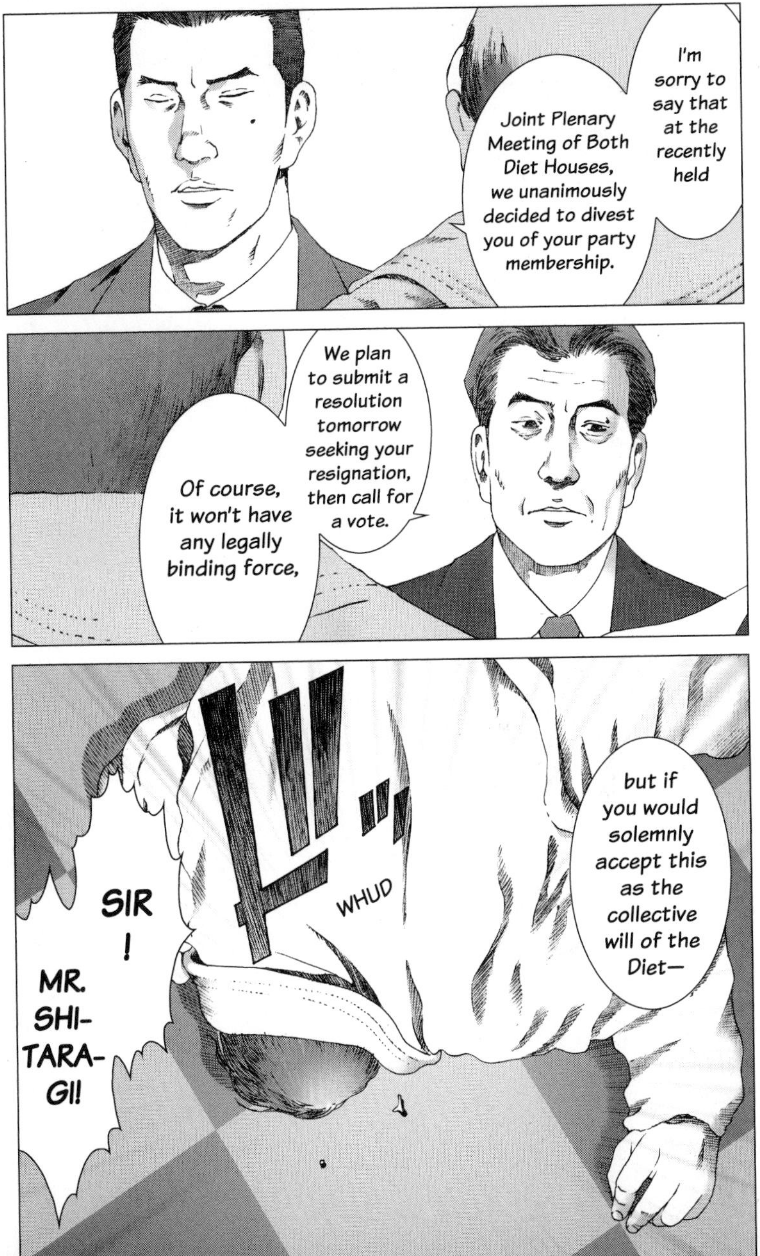
I'm sorry to say that at the recently held
Joint Plenary Meeting of Both Diet Houses, we unanimously decided to divest you of your party membership.
We plan to submit a resolution tomorrow seeking your resignation, then call for a vote.
Of course, it won't have any legally binding force,
but if you would solemnly accept this as the collective will of the Diet—
WHUD
SIR!
MR. SHI-TARA-GI!

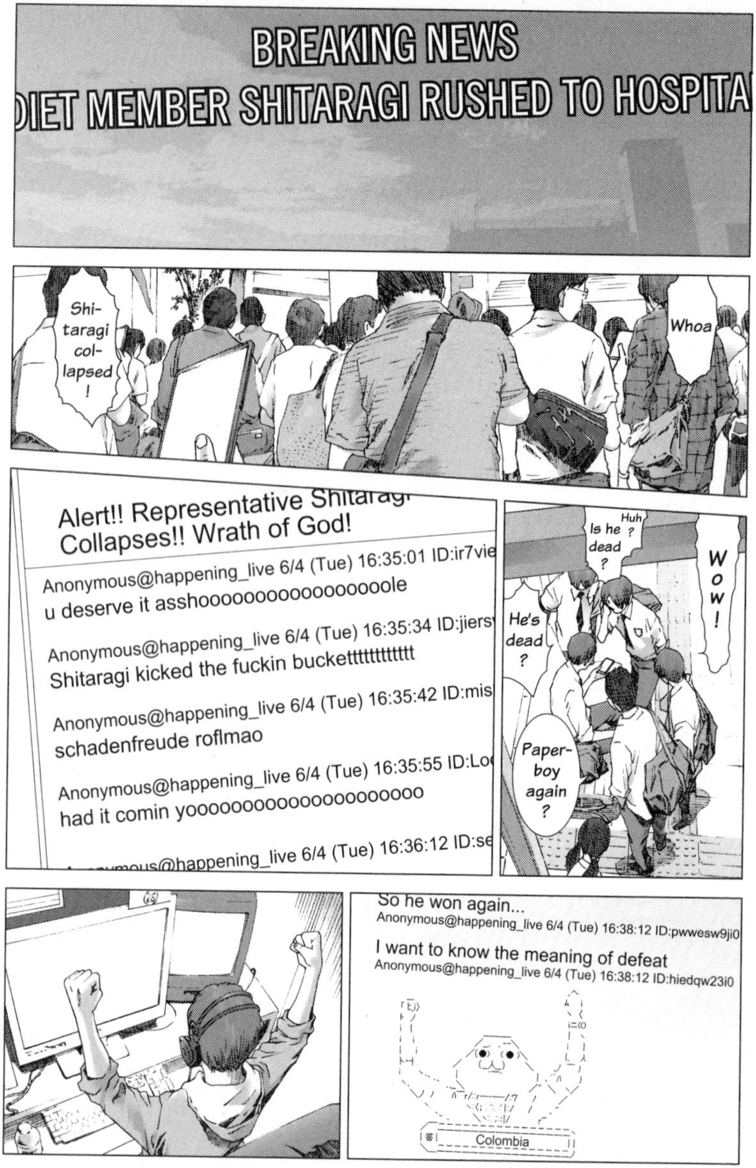
BREAKING NEWS
DIET MEMBER SHITARAGI RUSHED TO HOSPITAL
Whoa
Shi-taragi col-lapsed!
Wow!
Huh?
Is he dead?
He's dead?
Paper-boy again?
Alert!! Representative Shitaragi Collapses!! Wrath of God!
Anonymous@happening_live 6/4 (Tue) 16:35:01 ID:ir7vie
u deserve it asshoooooooooooooooooole
Anonymous@happening_live 6/4 (Tue) 16:35:34 ID:jiers
Shitaragi kicked the fuckin buckettttttttttttt
Anonymous@happening_live 6/4 (Tue) 16:35:42 ID:mis
schadenfreude roflmao
Anonymous@happening_live 6/4 (Tue) 16:35:55 ID:Lo
had it comin yooooooooooooooooooooo
Anonymous@happening_live 6/4 (Tue) 16:36:12 ID:se
So he won again...
Anonymous@happening_live 6/4 (Tue) 16:38:12 ID:pwwesw9ji0
I want to know the meaning of defeat
Anonymous@happening_live 6/4 (Tue) 16:38:12 ID:hiedqw23i0
Colombia

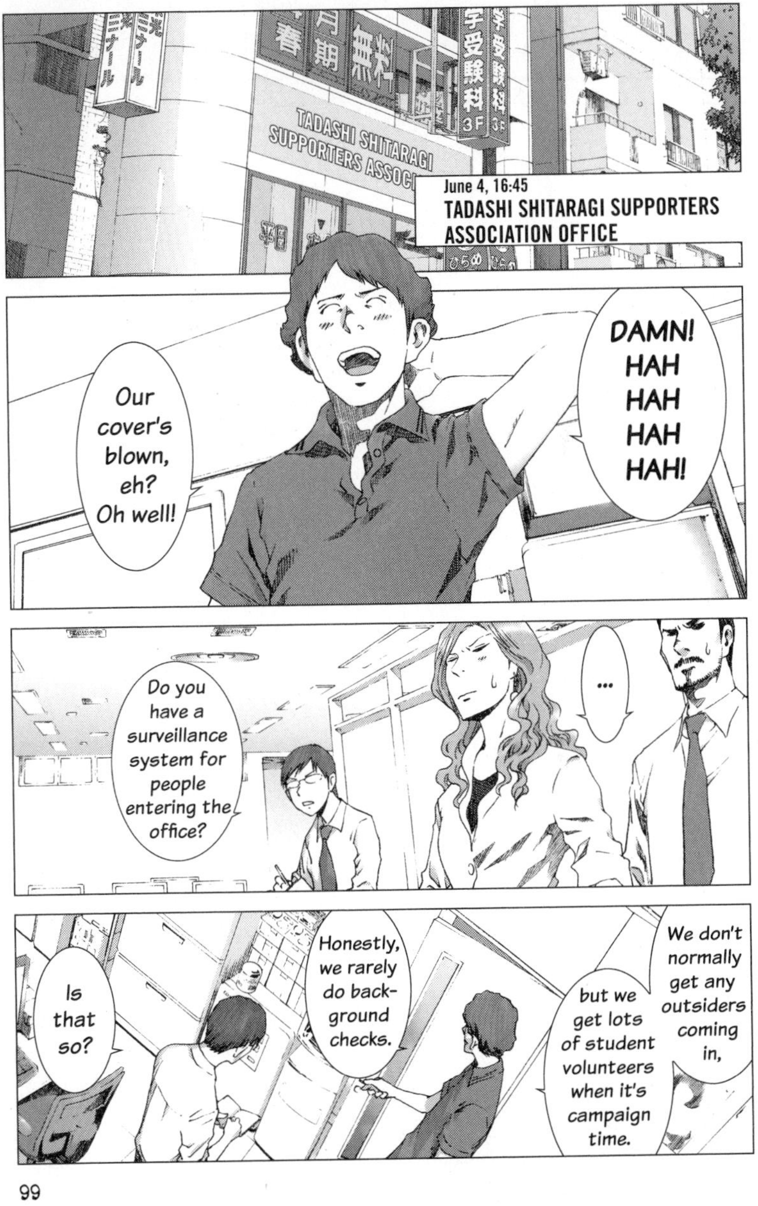
June 4, 16:45
TADASHI SHITARAGI SUPPORTERS ASSOCIATION OFFICE
DAMN! HAH HAH HAH HAH!
Our cover's blown, eh? Oh well!
...
Do you have a surveillance system for people entering the office?
We don't normally get any outsiders coming in,
but we get lots of student volunteers when it's campaign time.
Honestly, we rarely do back-ground checks.
Is that so?

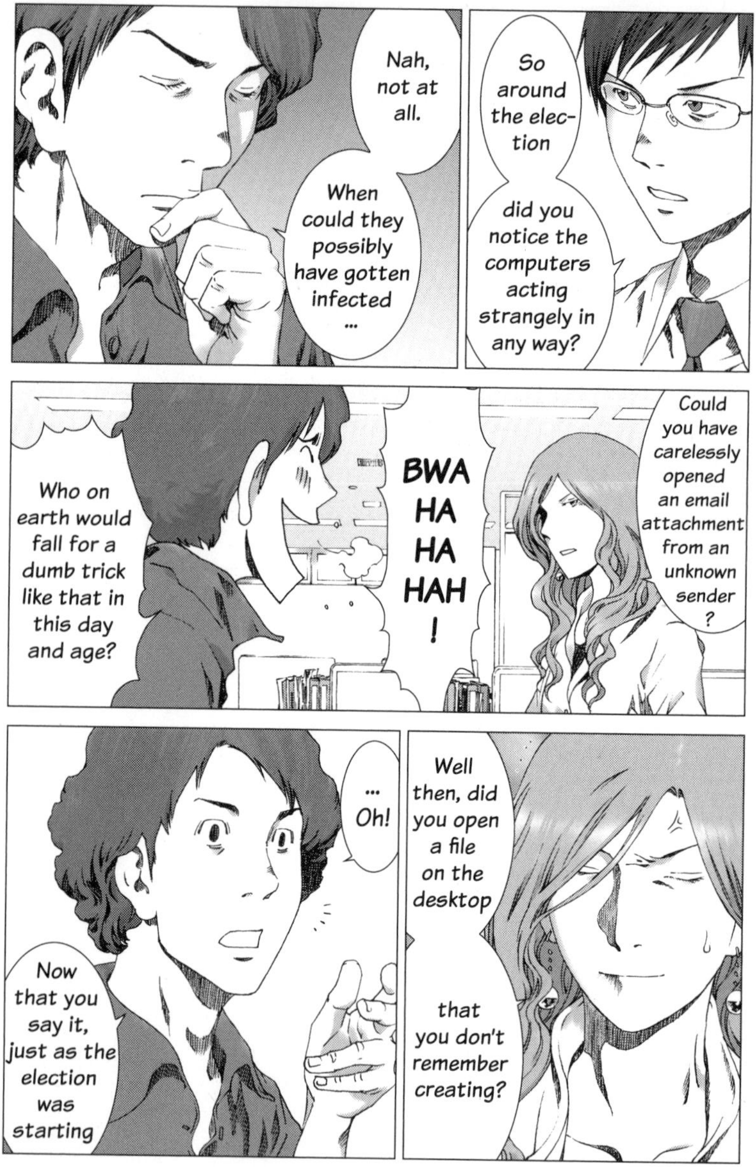
So around the election
did you notice the computers acting strangely in any way?
Nah, not at all.
When could they possibly have gotten infected ...
Could you have carelessly opened an email attachment from an unknown sender ?
BWA HA HA HAH !
Who on earth would fall for a dumb trick like that in this day and age?
Well then, did you open a file on the desktop
that you don't remember creating?
... Oh!
Now that you say it, just as the election was starting

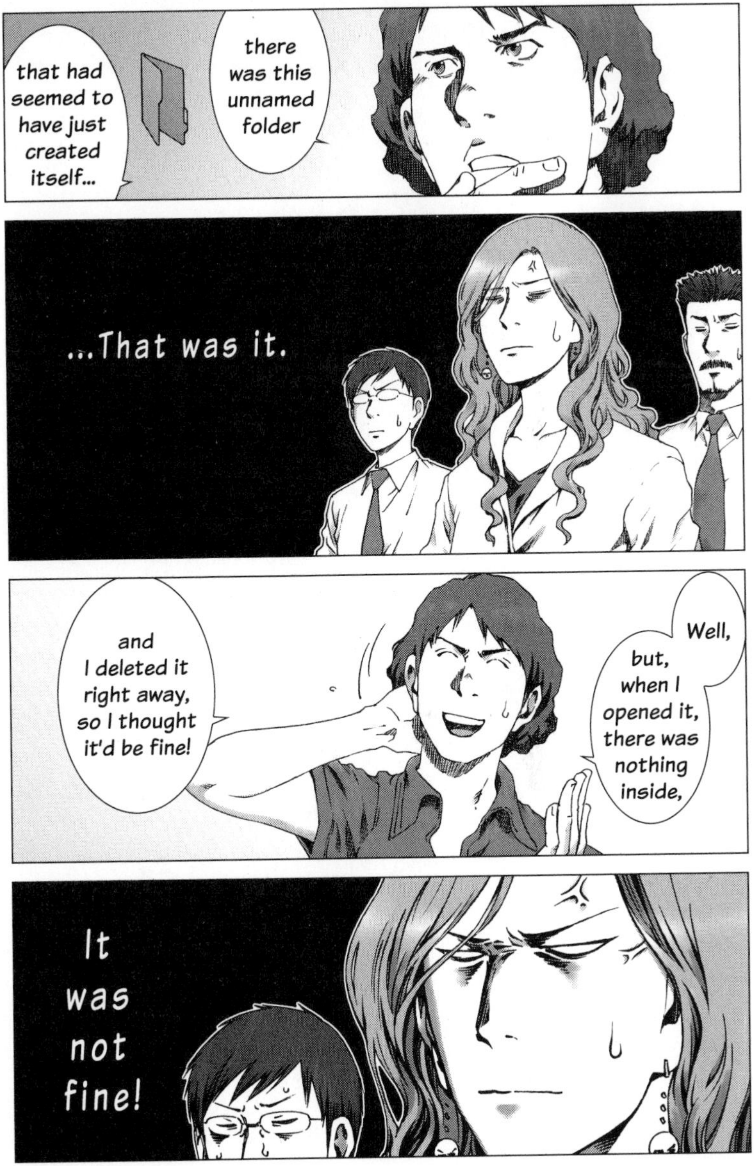
there was this unnamed folder
that had seemed to have just created itself...
...That was it.
Well, but, when I opened it, there was nothing inside,
and I deleted it right away, so I thought it'd be fine!
It was not fine!

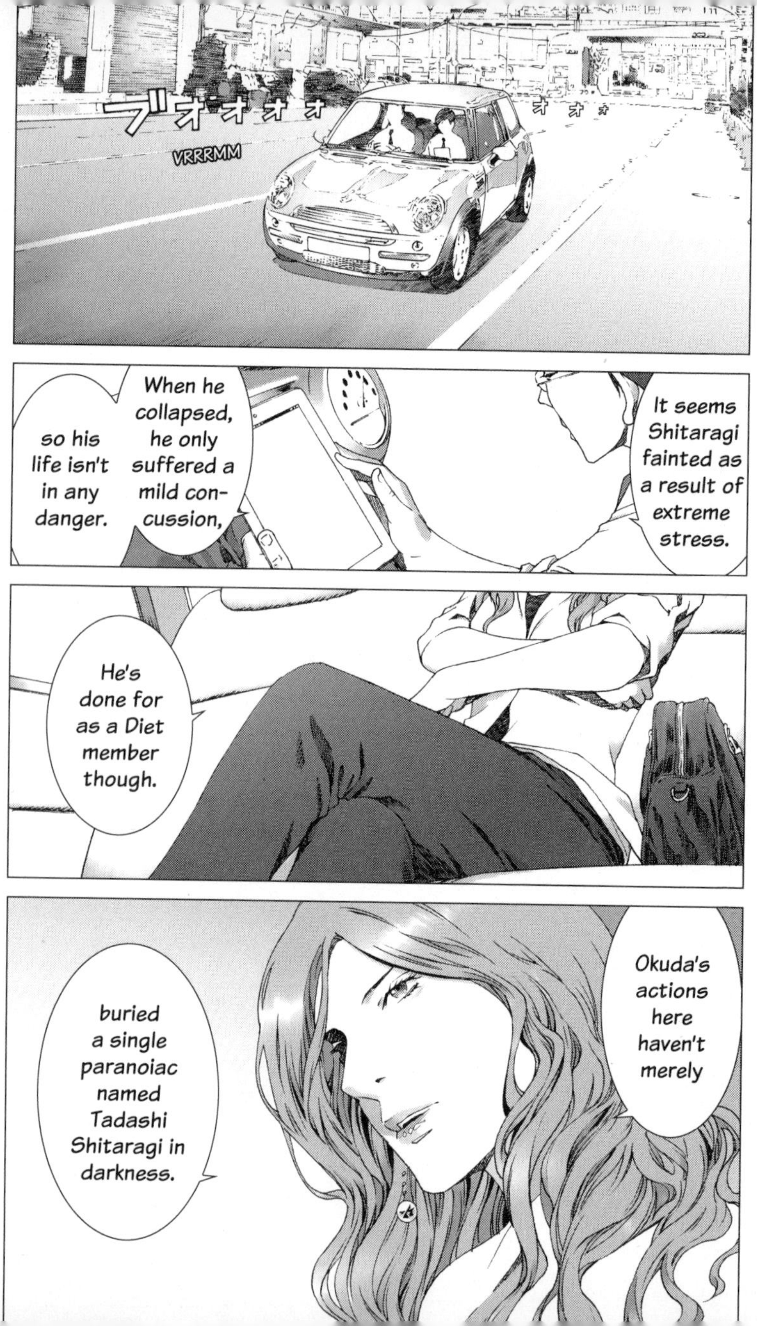
ブオオオオ
オオォ
VRRRMM
It seems Shitaragi fainted as a result of extreme stress.
When he collapsed, he only suffered a mild concussion,
so his life isn't in any danger.
He's done for as a Diet member though.
Okuda's actions here haven't merely
buried a single paranoiac named Tadashi Shitaragi in darkness.

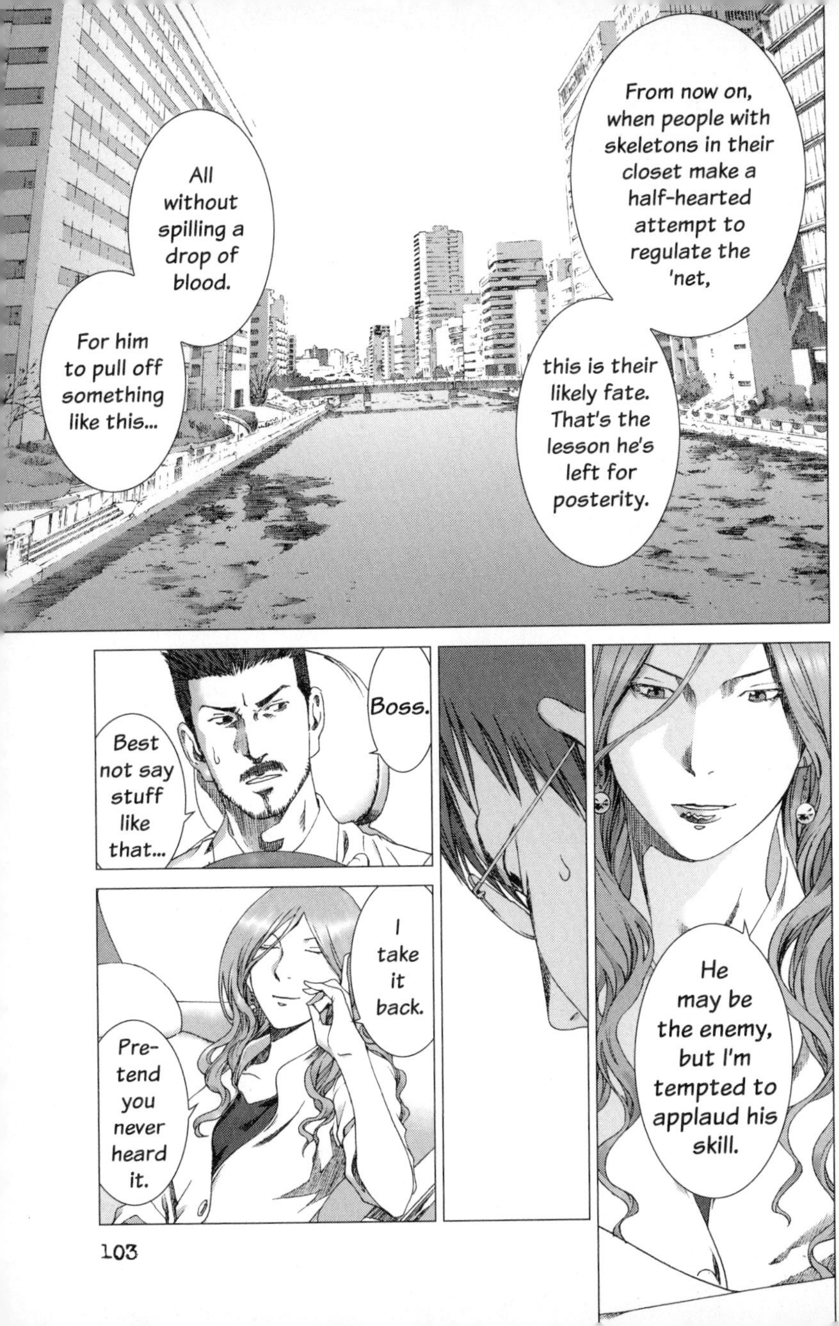
From now on, when people with skeletons in their closet make a half-hearted attempt to regulate the 'net,
this is their likely fate. That's the lesson he's left for posterity.
All without spilling a drop of blood.
For him to pull off something like this...
He may be the enemy, but I'm tempted to applaud his skill.
Boss.
Best not say stuff like that...
I take it back.
Pretend you never heard it.

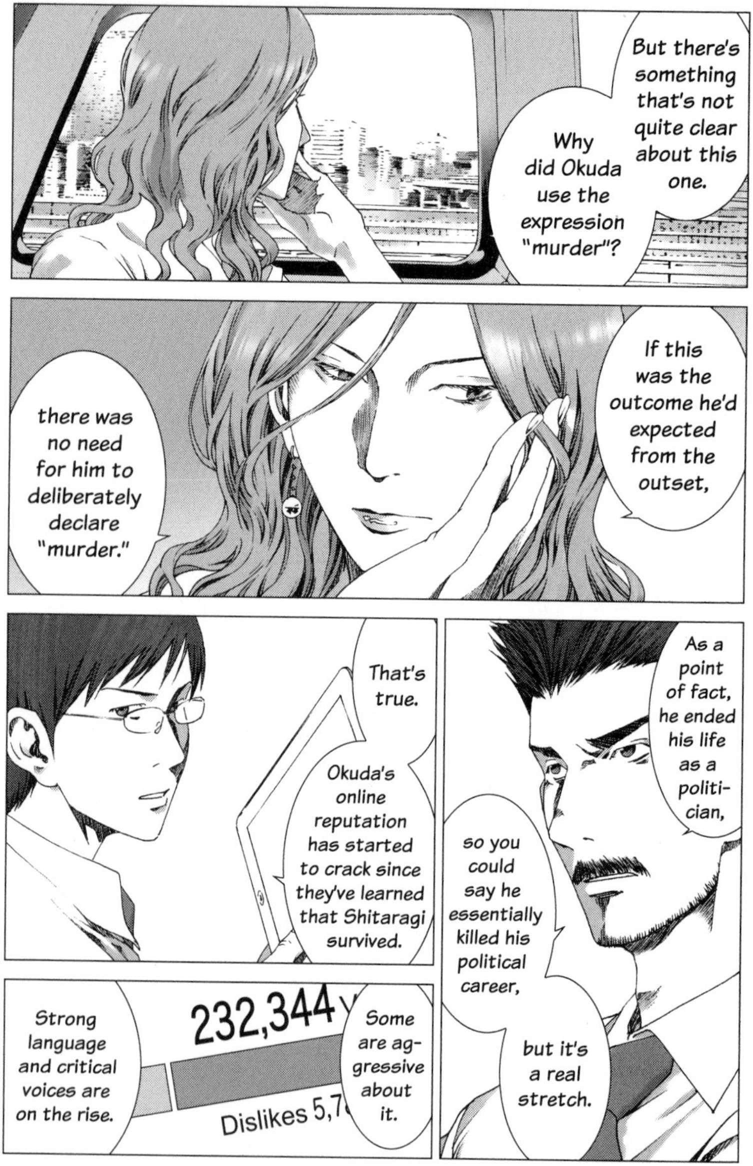

But there's something that's not quite clear about this one.
Why did Okuda use the expression "murder"?
If this was the outcome he'd expected from the outset,
there was no need for him to deliberately declare "murder."
As a point of fact, he ended his life as a politician,
so you could say he essentially killed his political career,
but it's a real stretch.
That's true.
Okuda's online reputation has started to crack since they've learned that Shitaragi survived.
232,344
Dislikes
Some are aggressive about it.
Strong language and critical voices are on the rise.

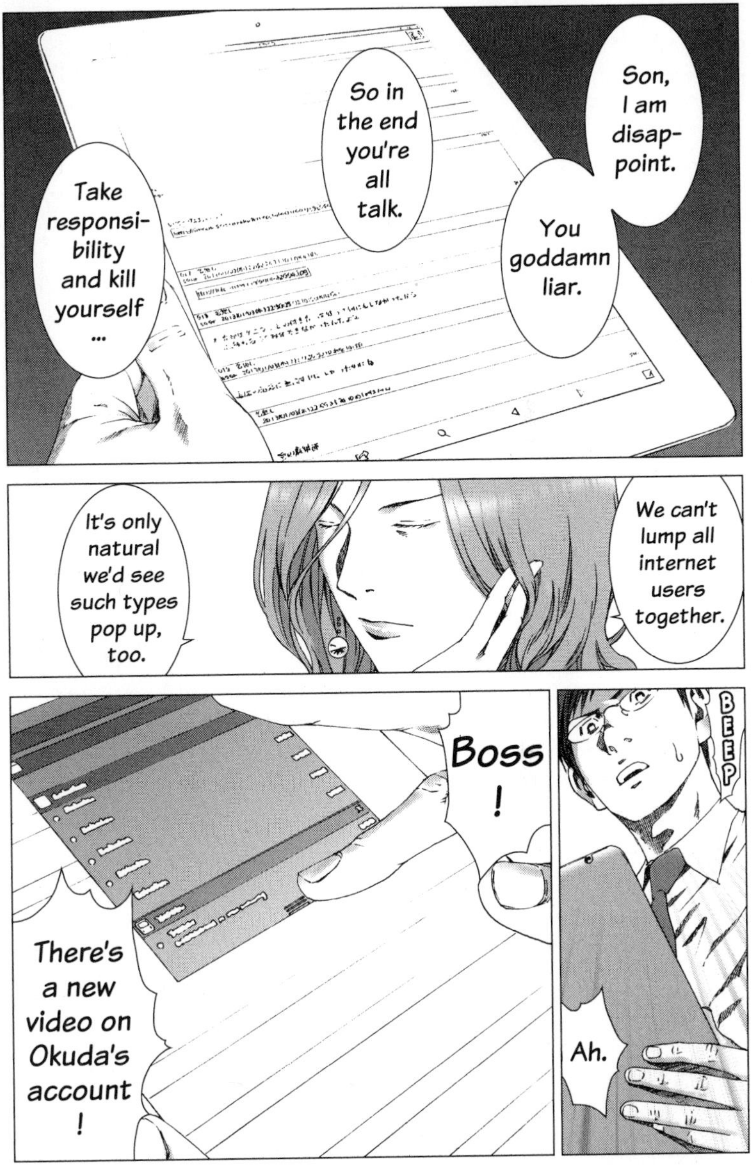
Son, I am disap-point.
You goddamn liar.
So in the end you're all talk.
Take responsi-bility and kill yourself ...
We can't lump all internet users together.
It's only natural we'd see such types pop up, too.
BEEP
Ah.
Boss!
There's a new video on Okuda's account!

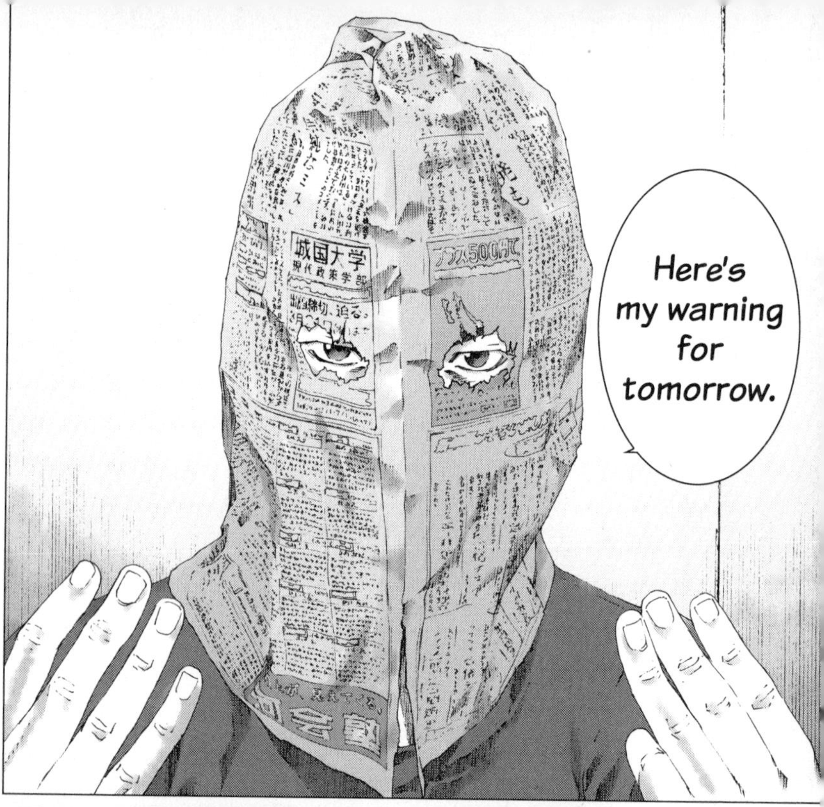
Here's my warning for tomorrow.

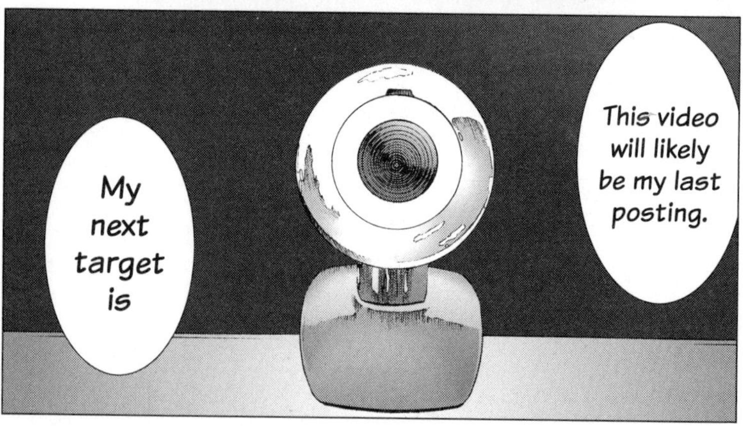
This video will likely be my last posting.
My next target is

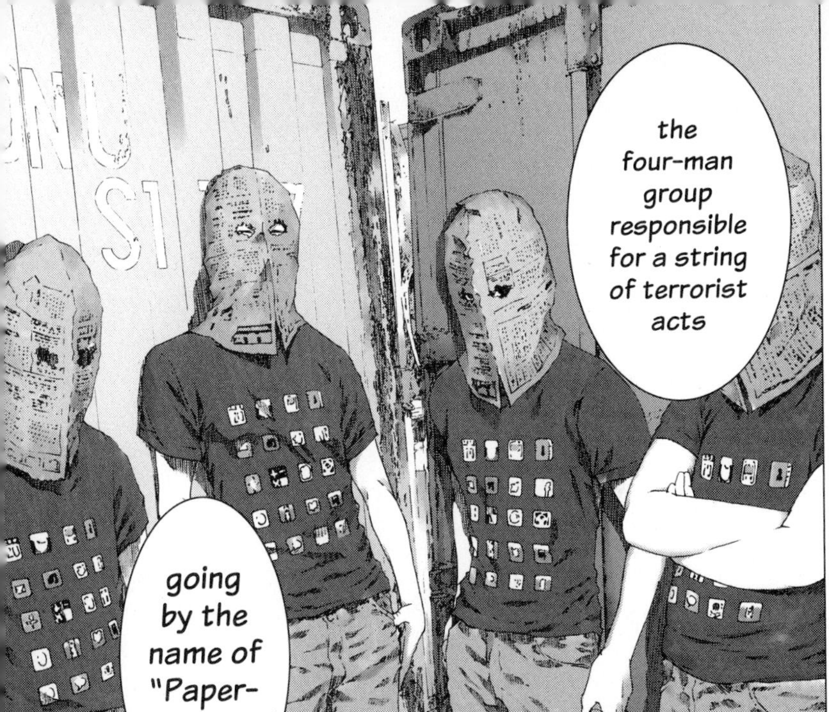
the four-man group responsible for a string of terrorist acts
going by the name of "Paper-boy."

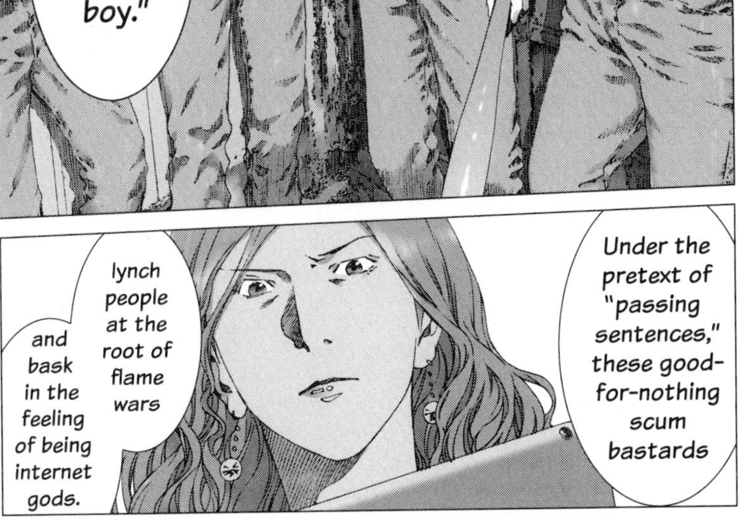
Under the pretext of "passing sentences," these good-for-nothing scum bastards
lynch people at the root of flame wars
and bask in the feeling of being internet gods.

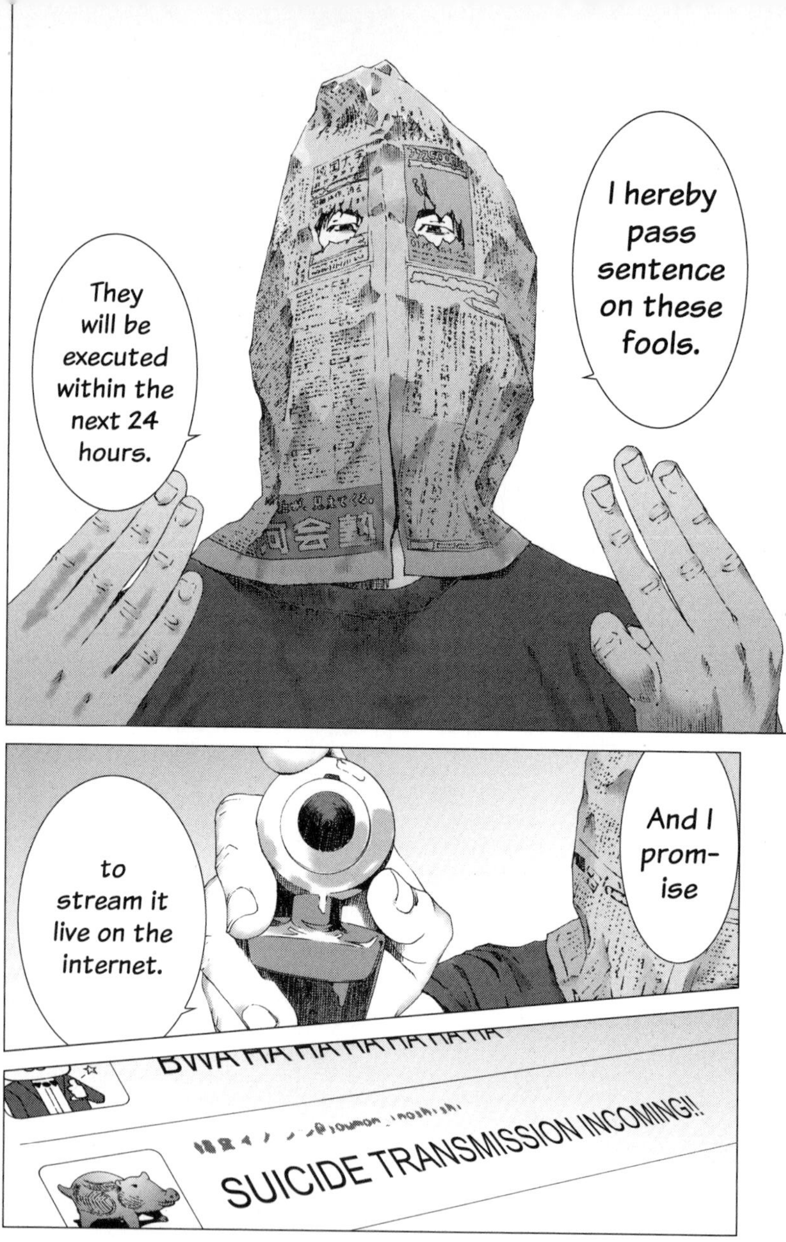
I hereby pass sentence on these fools.
They will be executed within the next 24 hours.
And I promise
to stream it live on the internet.
BWA HA HA HA HA HA HA
SUICIDE TRANSMISSION INCOMING!!

File 019

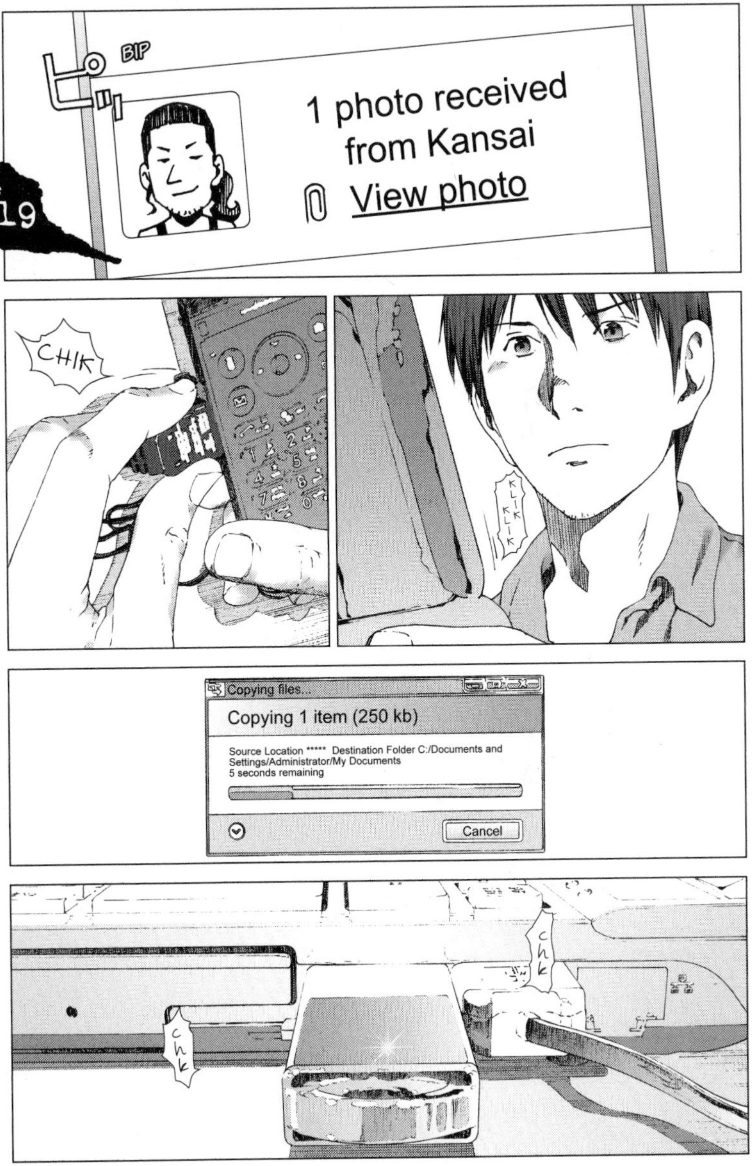

ピピッ
BIP
1 photo received from Kansai
View photo
KLIK KLIK
CHIK
Copying files...
Copying 1 item (250 kb)
Source Location ***** Destination Folder C:/Documents and Settings/Administrator/My Documents
5 seconds remaining
Cancel
chk
chk

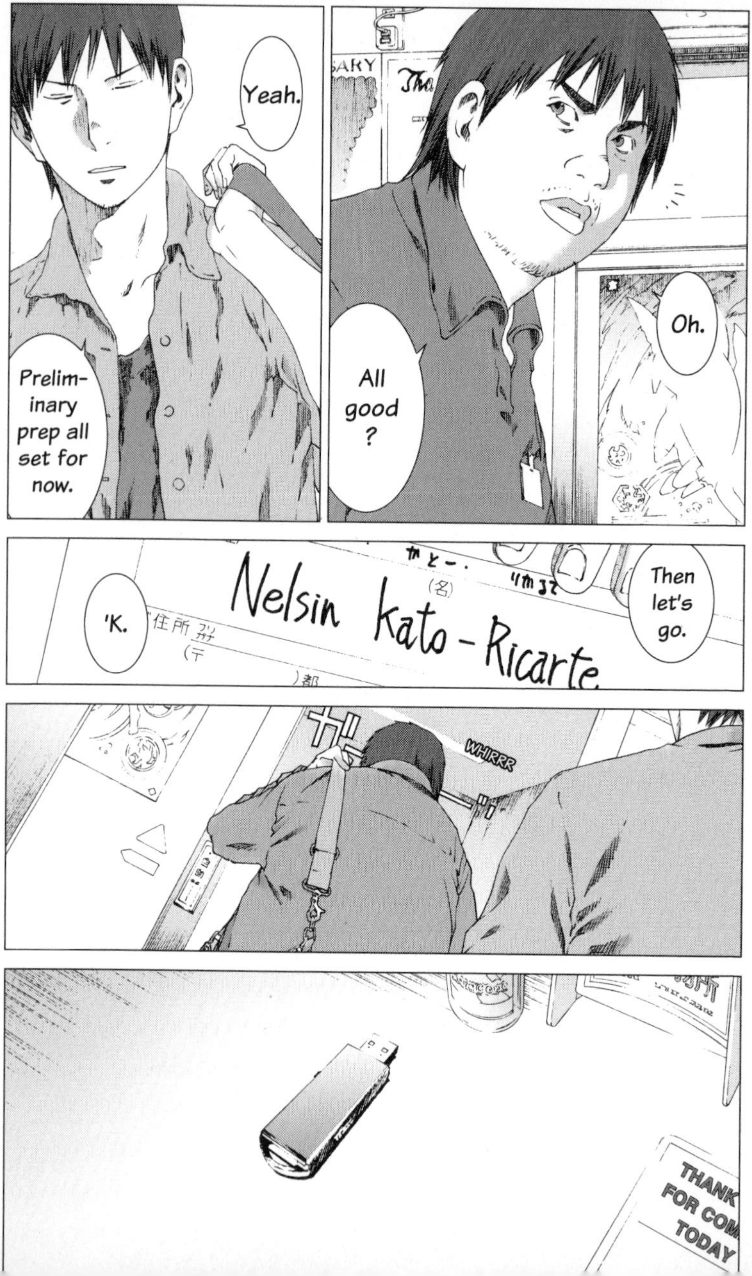
Oh.
All good?
Yeah.
Prelim-inary prep all set for now.
Then let's go.
Nelsin Kato-Ricarte
'K.
WHIRRR
THANK
FOR COM
TODAY

File 019

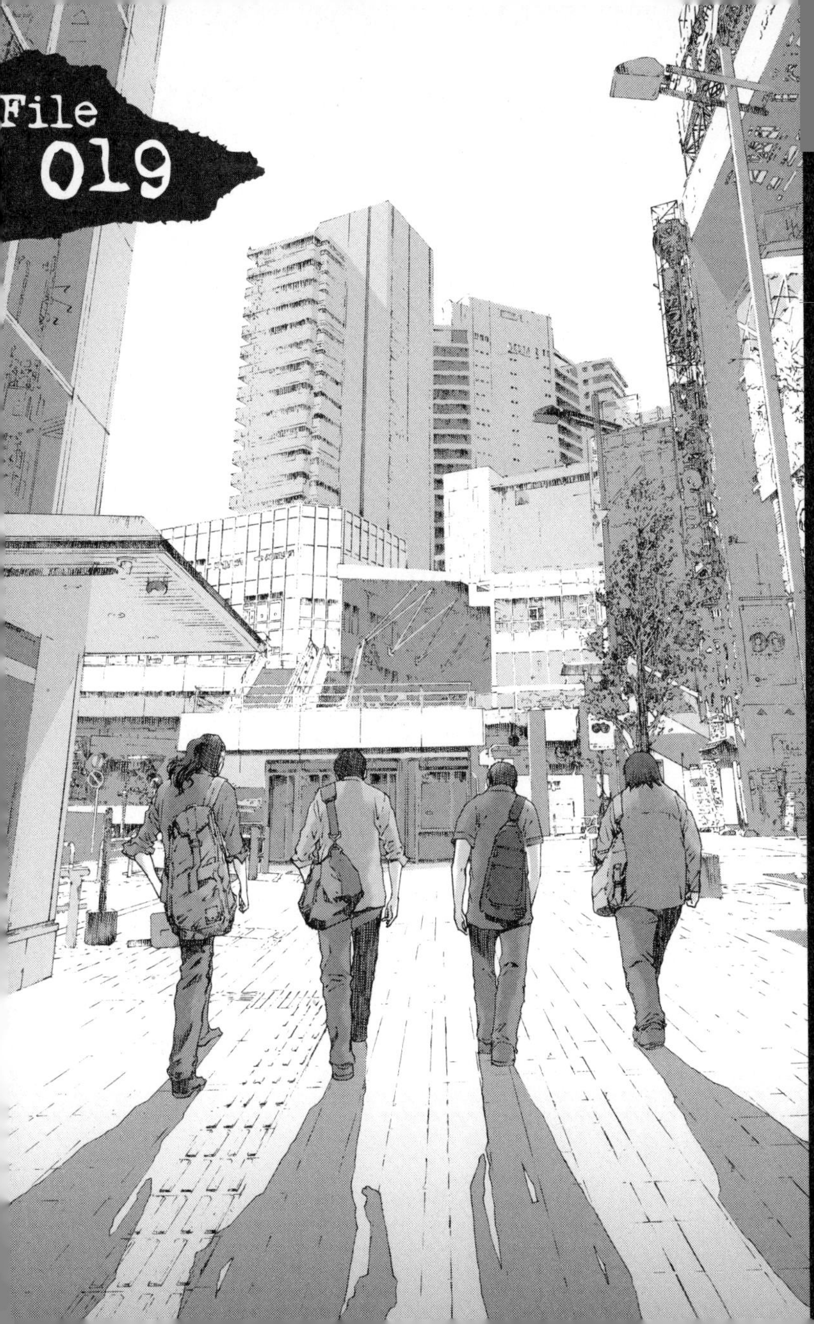

SKREE

June 4, 18:20
G BRANCH MANGA CAFÉ, Y CITY, KANAGAWA PREFECTURE

Got it!

According to the analysis by the Cyber Force, the video was posted from booth 8 at G Branch.

The log shows him being here up until 20 minutes ago.

CHAK

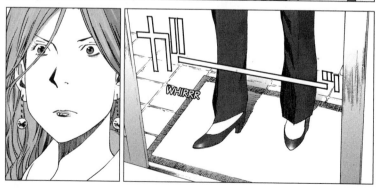

WHIRRR

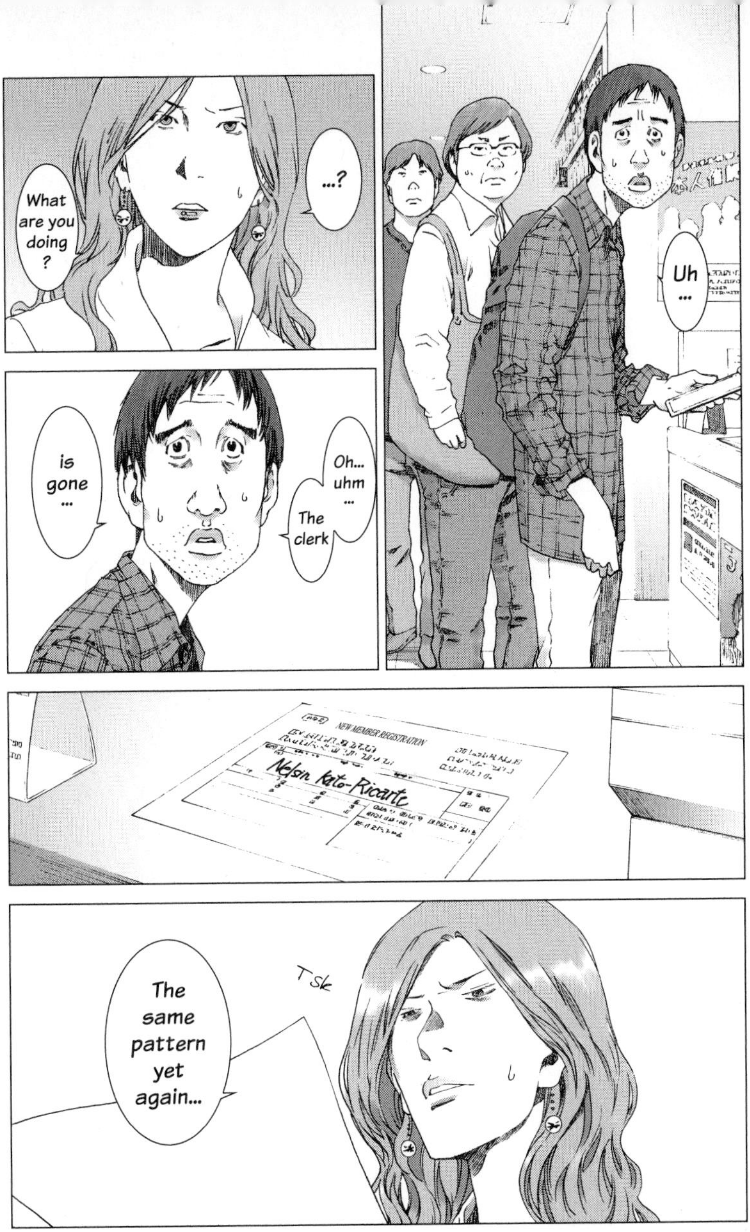
Uh ...
...?
What are you doing ?
Oh... uhm ...
The clerk
is gone ...
NEW MEMBER REGISTRATION
Nelson Kato-Ricarte
Tsk
The same pattern yet again...

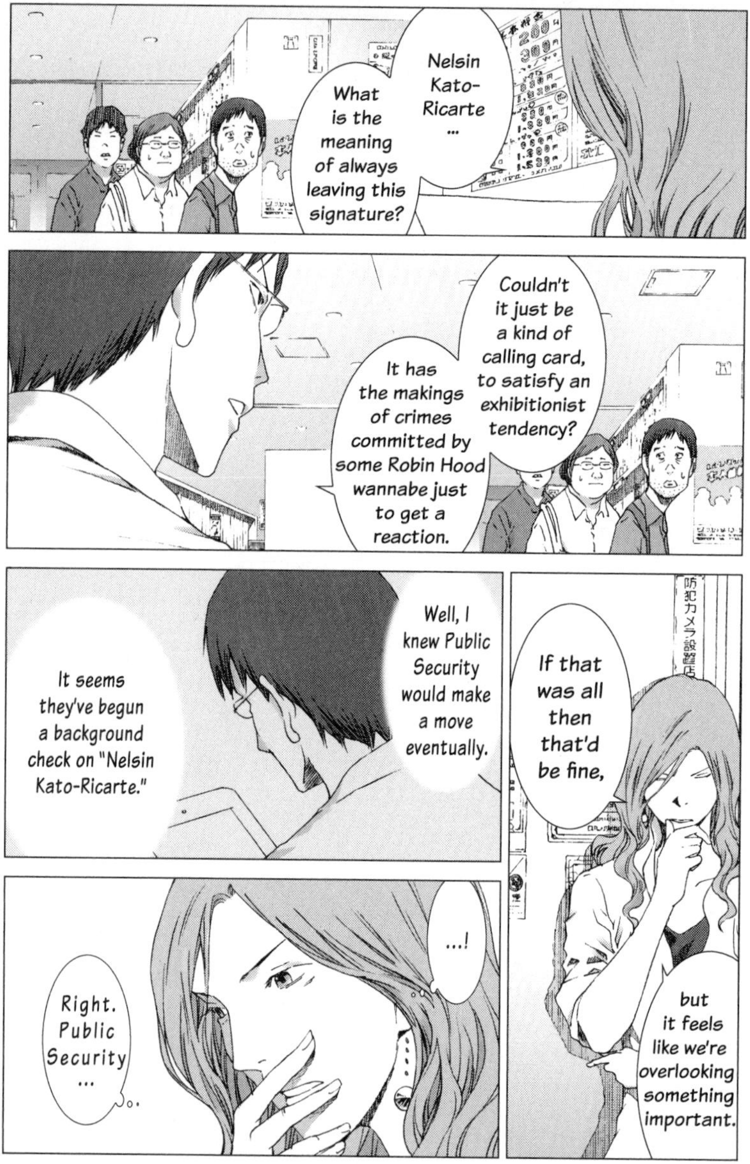
Nelsin Kato-Ricarte ...
What is the meaning of always leaving this signature?
Couldn't it just be a kind of calling card, to satisfy an exhibitionist tendency?
It has the makings of crimes committed by some Robin Hood wannabe just to get a reaction.
防犯カメラ設置店
If that was all then that'd be fine,
but it feels like we're overlooking something important.
Well, I knew Public Security would make a move eventually.
It seems they've begun a background check on "Nelsin Kato-Ricarte."
...!
Right. Public Security ...

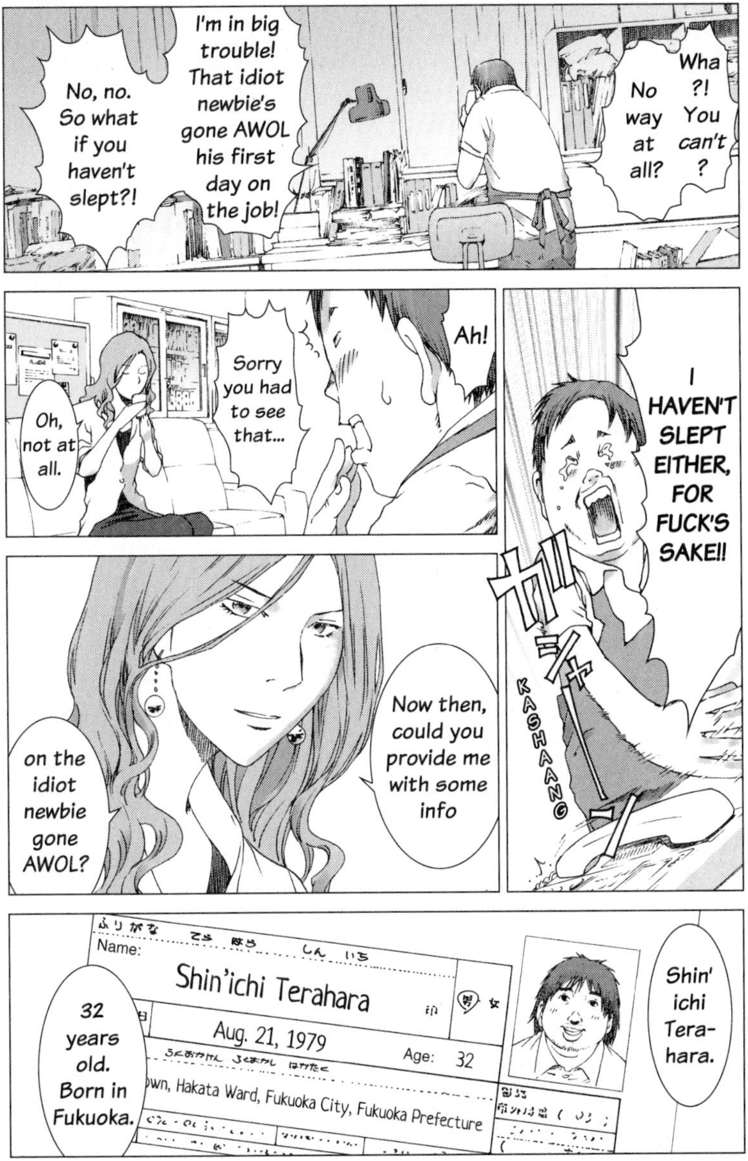
Wha?! You can't?
No way at all?
I'm in big trouble! That idiot newbie's gone AWOL his first day on the job!
No, no. So what if you haven't slept?!
I HAVEN'T SLEPT EITHER, FOR FUCK'S SAKE!!
KASHAANG
Ah!
Sorry you had to see that...
Oh, not at all.
Now then, could you provide me with some info
on the idiot newbie gone AWOL?
Shin'ichi Terahara.
ふりがな
Name:
Shin'ichi Terahara
Aug. 21, 1979
Age: 32
own, Hakata Ward, Fukuoka City, Fukuoka Prefecture
32 years old. Born in Fukuoka.

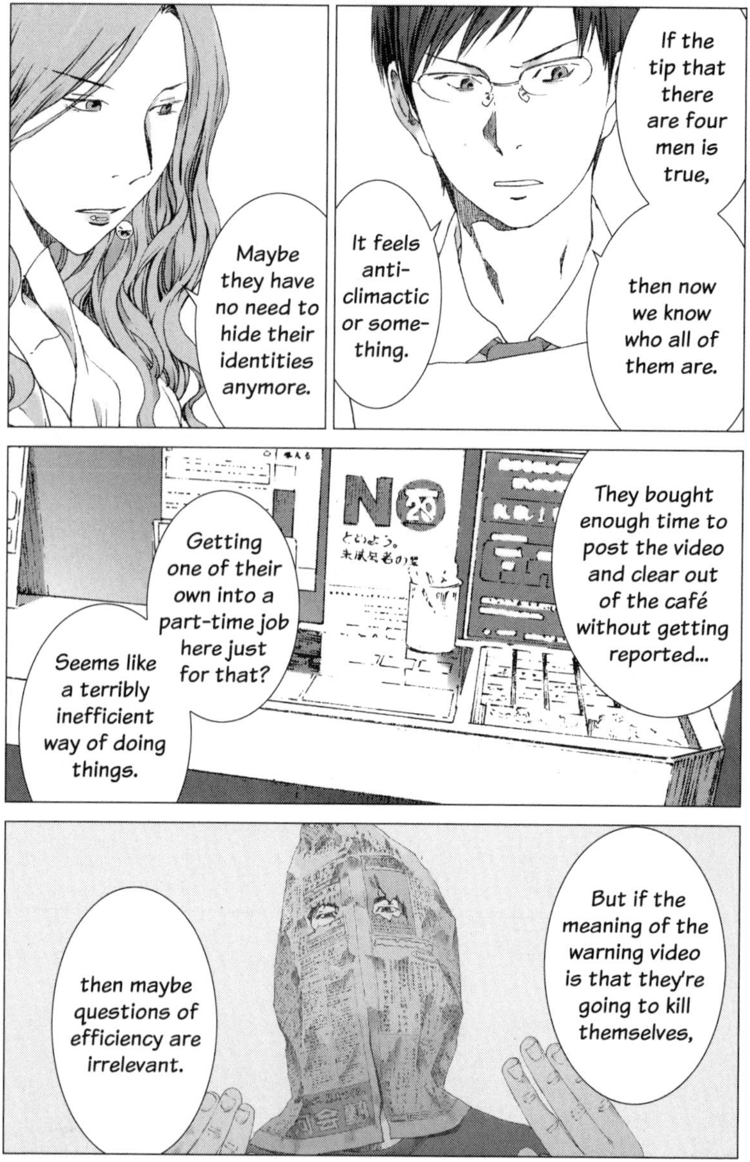
If the tip that there are four men is true,
then now we know who all of them are.
It feels anti-climactic or some-thing.
Maybe they have no need to hide their identities anymore.
They bought enough time to post the video and clear out of the café without getting reported...
Getting one of their own into a part-time job here just for that?
Seems like a terribly inefficient way of doing things.
But if the meaning of the warning video is that they're going to kill themselves,
then maybe questions of efficiency are irrelevant.

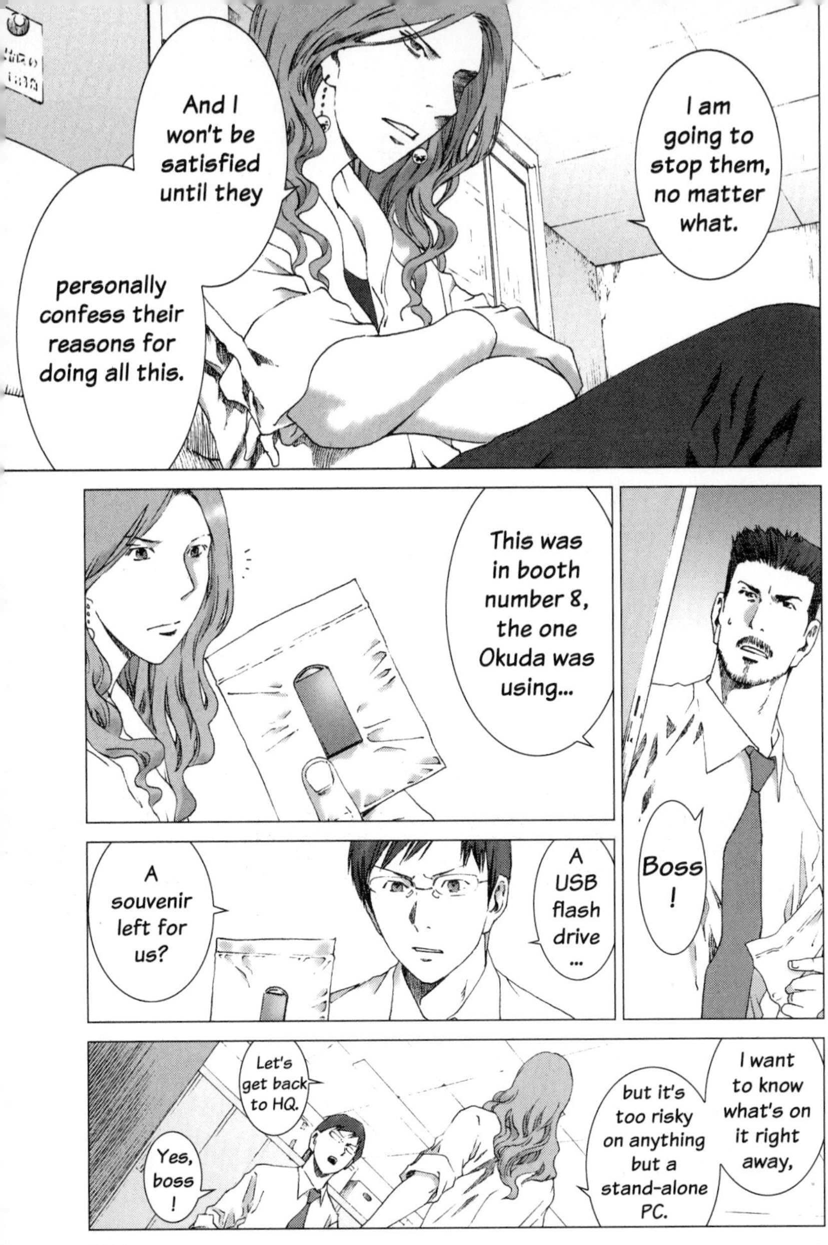
I am going to stop them, no matter what.
And I won't be satisfied until they
personally confess their reasons for doing all this.
Boss!
This was in booth number 8, the one Okuda was using...
A USB flash drive...
A souvenir left for us?
I want to know what's on it right away,
but it's too risky on anything but a stand-alone PC.
Let's get back to HQ.
Yes, boss!

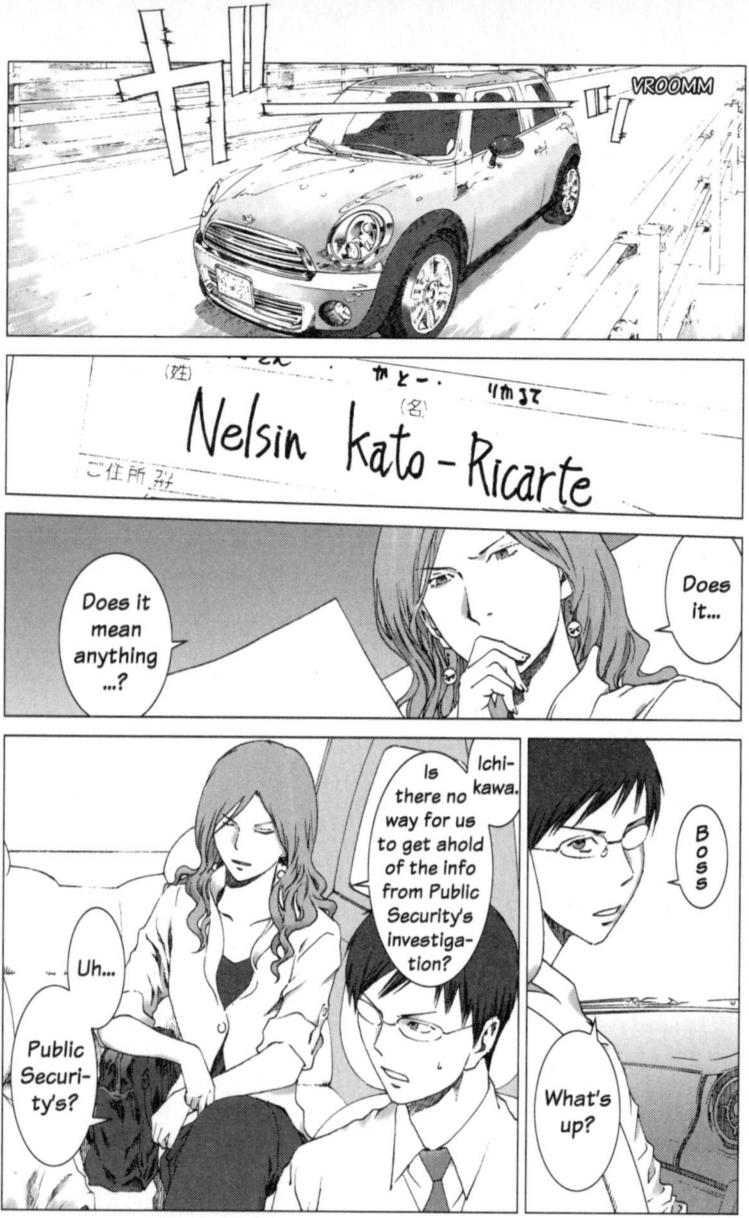
VROOMM
(姓)
(名)
Nelsin kato-Ricarte
ご住所
Does it...
Does it mean anything...?
Boss
What's up?
Ichi-kawa.
Is there no way for us to get ahold of the info from Public Security's investigation?
Uh...
Public Securi-ty's?

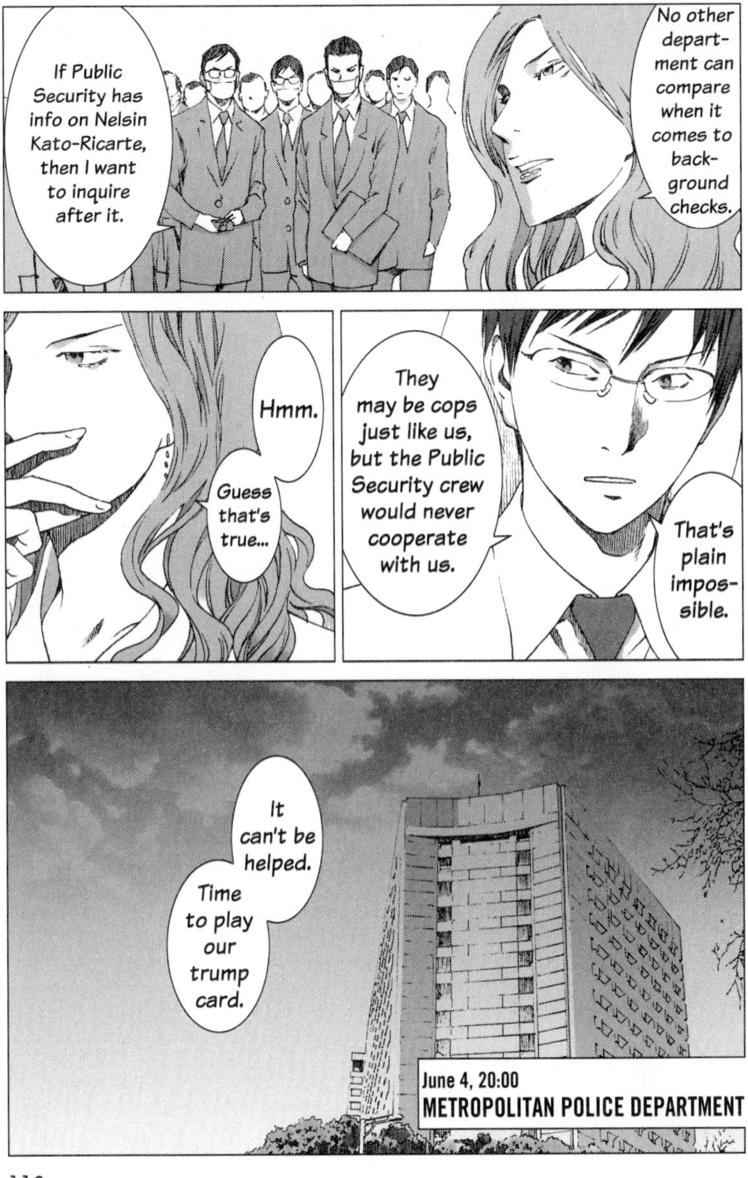
No other department can compare when it comes to background checks.
If Public Security has info on Nelsin Kato-Ricarte, then I want to inquire after it.
They may be cops just like us, but the Public Security crew would never cooperate with us.
That's plain impossible.
Hmm.
Guess that's true...
It can't be helped.
Time to play our trump card.
June 4, 20:00
METROPOLITAN POLICE DEPARTMENT

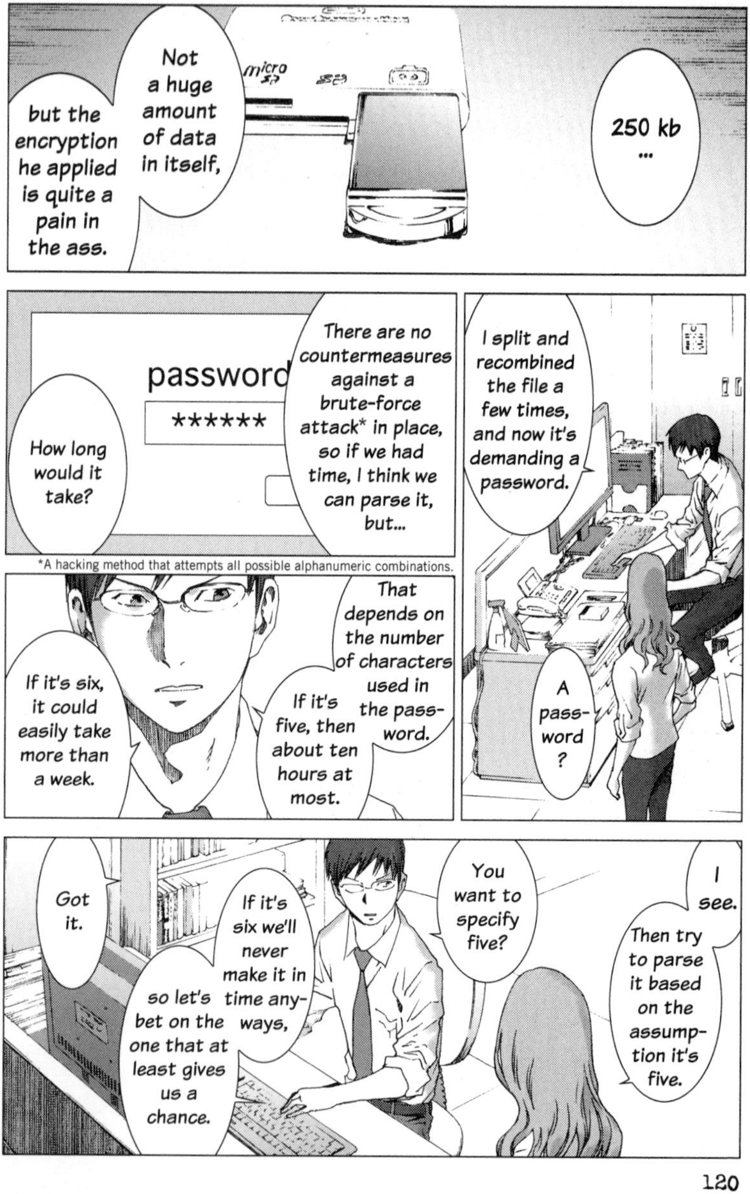
250 kb ...
Not a huge amount of data in itself,
but the encryption he applied is quite a pain in the ass.
I split and recombined the file a few times, and now it's demanding a password.
A pass-word ?
password
******
There are no countermeasures against a brute-force attack* in place, so if we had time, I think we can parse it, but...
How long would it take?
That depends on the number of characters used in the pass-word.
If it's five, then about ten hours at most.
If it's six, it could easily take more than a week.
I see.
Then try to parse it based on the assump-tion it's five.
You want to specify five?
If it's six we'll never make it in time any-ways,
so let's bet on the one that at least gives us a chance.
Got it.
*A hacking method that attempts all possible alphanumeric combinations.

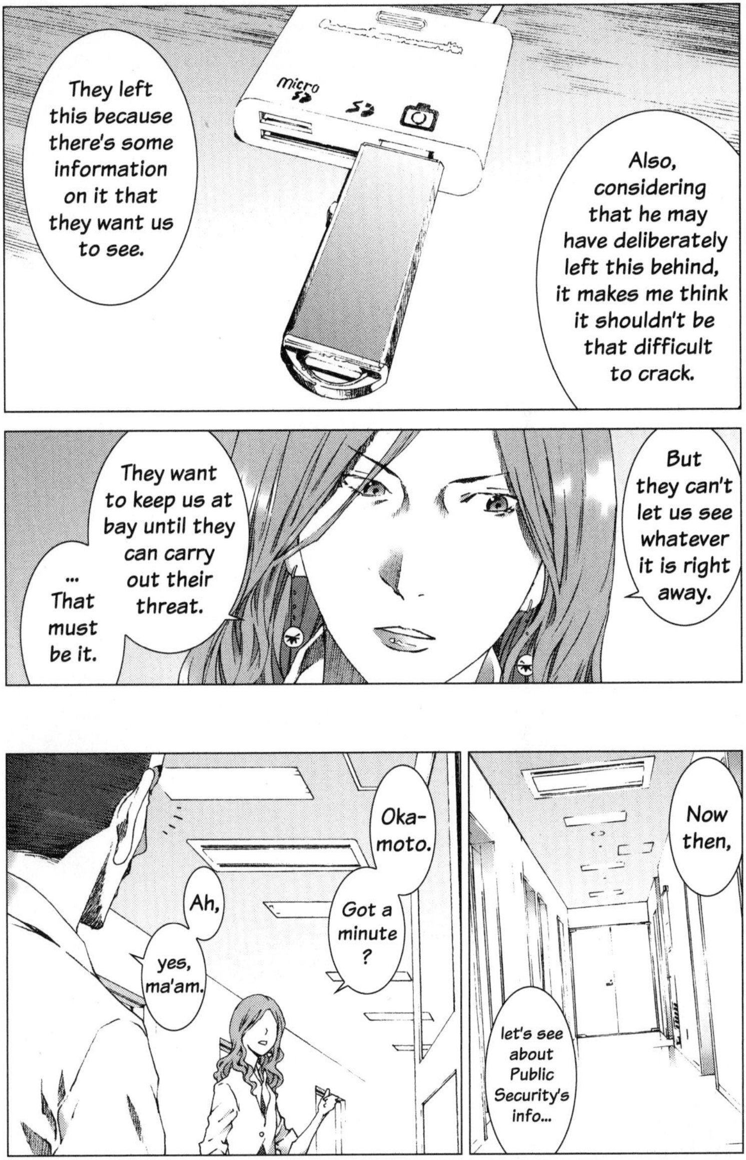

They left this because there's some information on it that they want us to see.
Also, considering that he may have deliberately left this behind, it makes me think it shouldn't be that difficult to crack.
But they can't let us see whatever it is right away.
They want to keep us at bay until they can carry out their threat.
... That must be it.
Now then,
let's see about Public Security's info...
Oka-moto.
Got a minute?
Ah,
yes, ma'am.

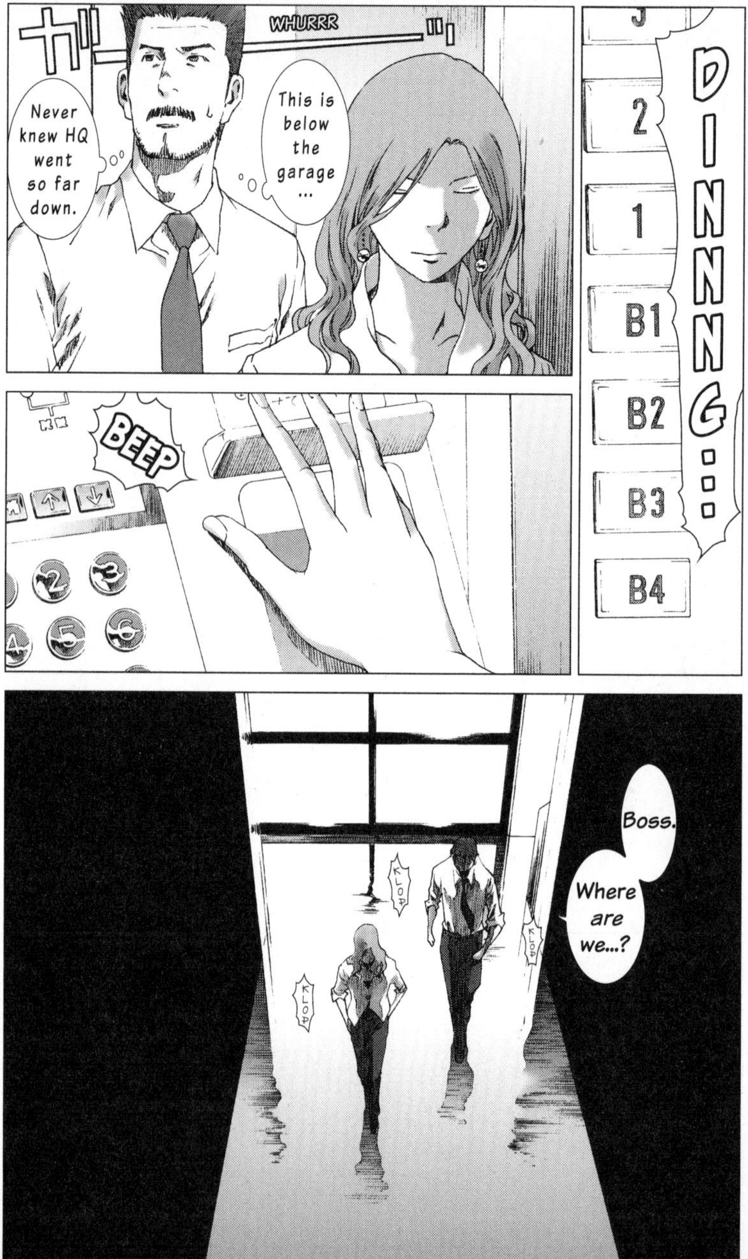
DINNNG...
2
1
B1
B2
B3
B4
WHURRR
This is below the garage...
Never knew HQ went so far down.
BEEP
Boss.
Where are we...?
KLOP
KLOP
KLOP

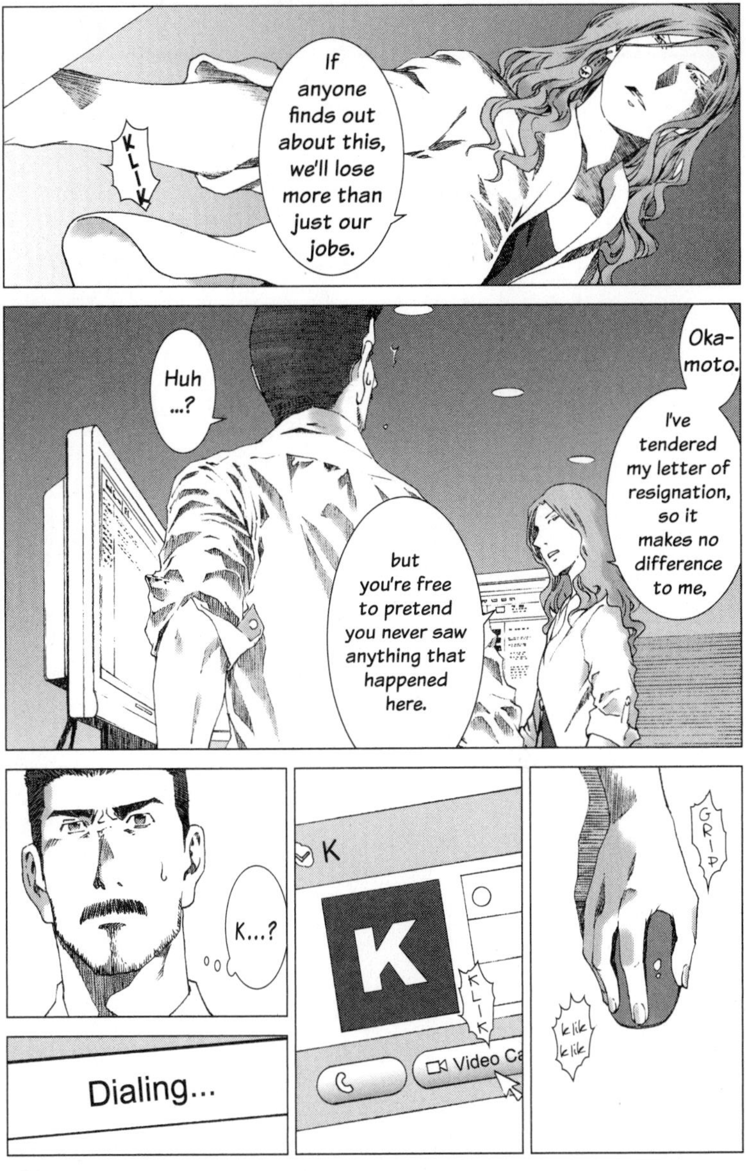
If anyone finds out about this, we'll lose more than just our jobs.
KLIK
Oka-moto.
I've tendered my letter of resignation, so it makes no difference to me,
but you're free to pretend you never saw anything that happened here.
Huh ...?
GRIP
klik klik
K
K
KLIK
Video Ca
K...?
Dialing...

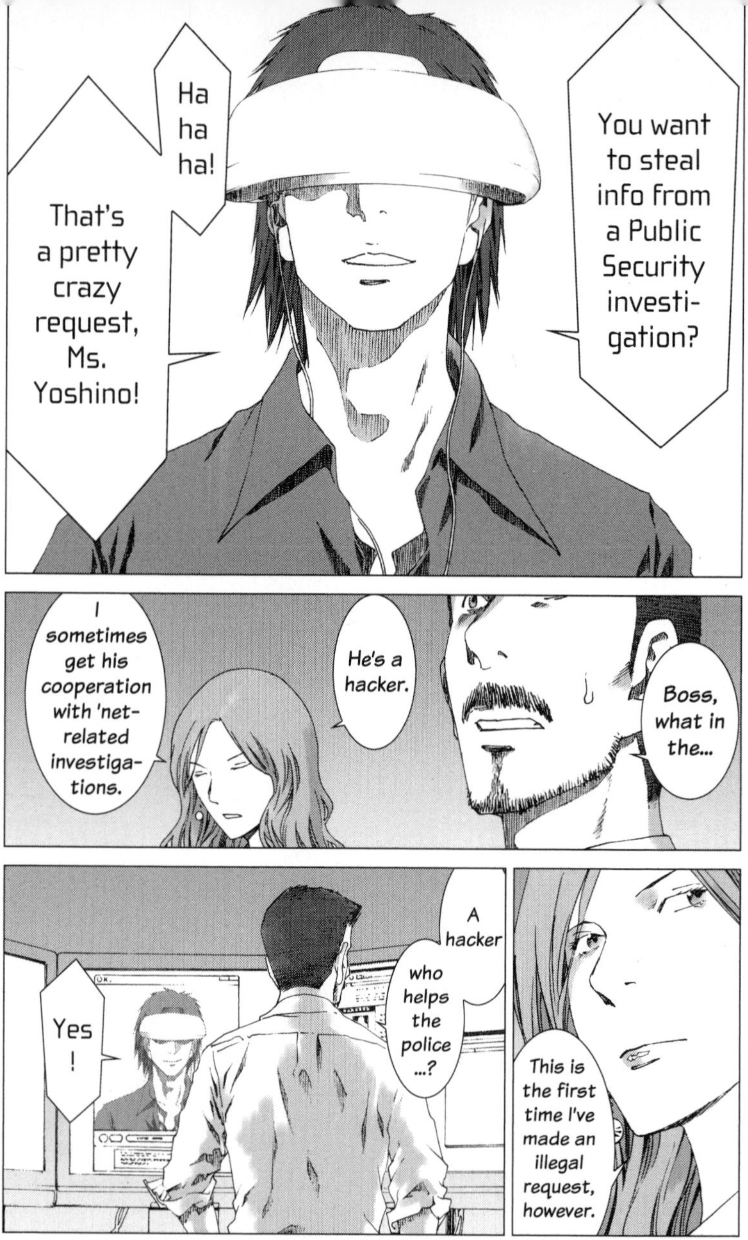
You want to steal info from a Public Security investigation?
Ha ha ha!
That's a pretty crazy request, Ms. Yoshino!
Boss, what in the...
He's a hacker.
I sometimes get his cooperation with 'net-related investigations.
This is the first time I've made an illegal request, however.
A hacker who helps the police ...?
Yes!

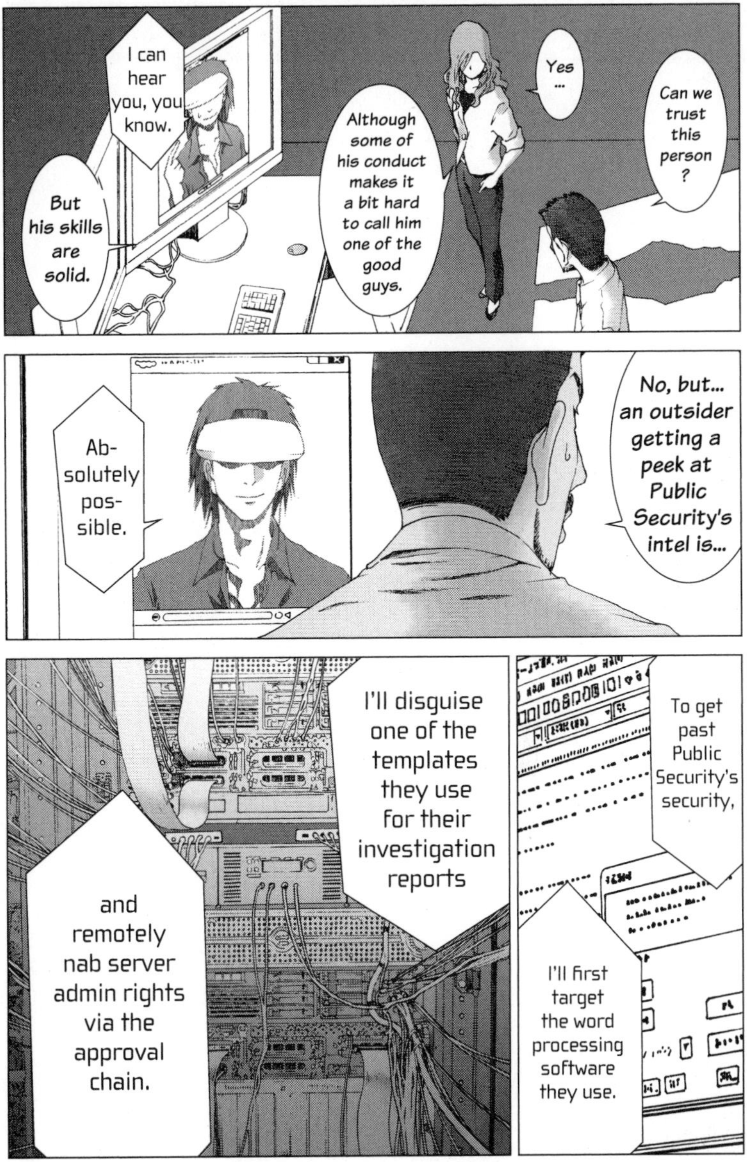
Can we trust this person?
Yes...
Although some of his conduct makes it a bit hard to call him one of the good guys.
But his skills are solid.
I can hear you, you know.
No, but... an outsider getting a peek at Public Security's intel is...
Ab-solutely pos-sible.
To get past Public Security's security,
I'll first target the word processing software they use.
I'll disguise one of the templates they use for their investigation reports
and remotely nab server admin rights via the approval chain.

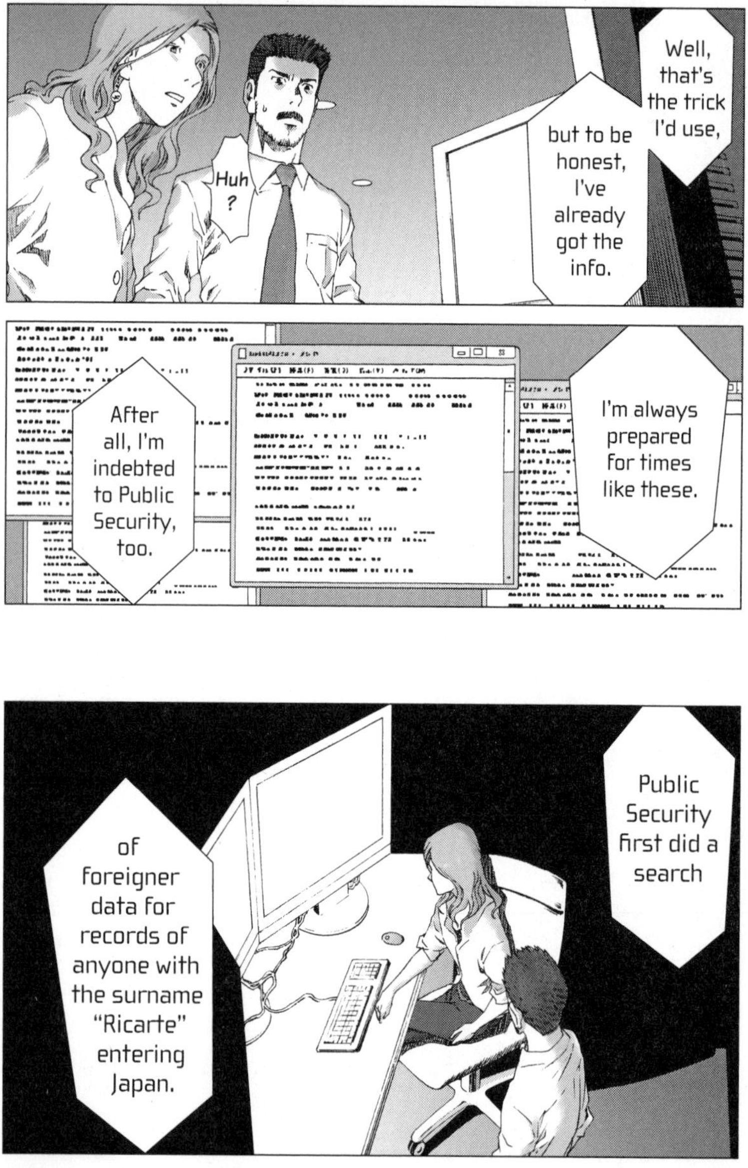
Well, that's the trick I'd use,
but to be honest, I've already got the info.
Huh?
I'm always prepared for times like these.
After all, I'm indebted to Public Security, too.
Public Security first did a search
of foreigner data for records of anyone with the surname "Ricarte" entering Japan.

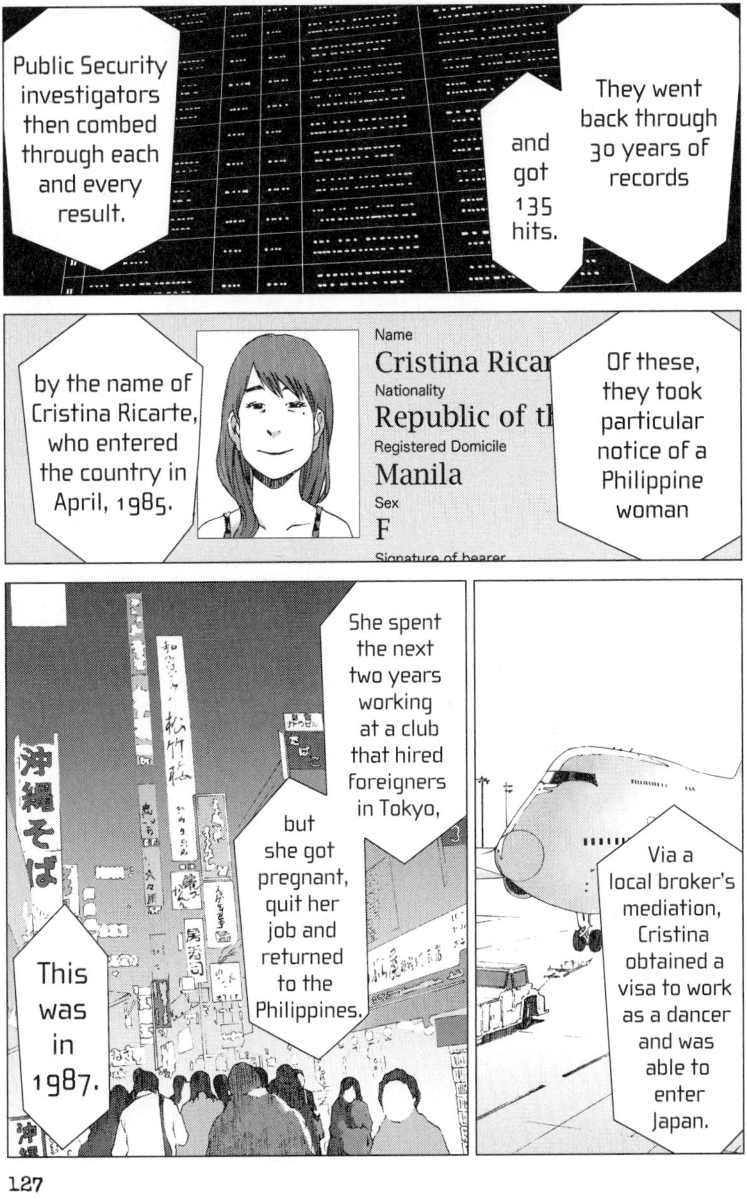
They went back through 30 years of records
and got 135 hits.
Public Security investigators then combed through each and every result.
Of these, they took particular notice of a Philippine woman
Name
Cristina Ricar
Nationality
Republic of th
Registered Domicile
Manila
Sex
F
by the name of Cristina Ricarte, who entered the country in April, 1985.
Via a local broker's mediation, Cristina obtained a visa to work as a dancer and was able to enter Japan.
She spent the next two years working at a club that hired foreigners in Tokyo,
but she got pregnant, quit her job and returned to the Philippines.
This was in 1987.
沖縄そば

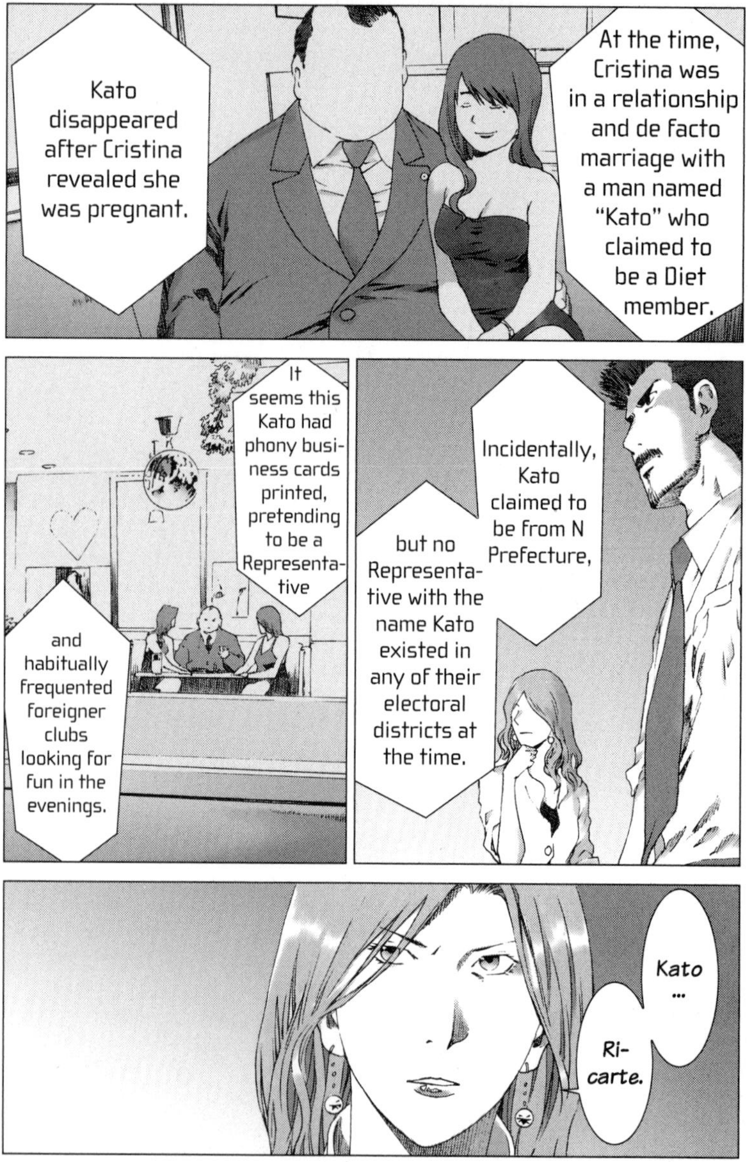
At the time, Cristina was in a relationship and de facto marriage with a man named "Kato" who claimed to be a Diet member.
Kato disappeared after Cristina revealed she was pregnant.
Incidentally, Kato claimed to be from N Prefecture,
but no Representa-tive with the name Kato existed in any of their electoral districts at the time.
It seems this Kato had phony busi-ness cards printed, pretending to be a Representa-tive
and habitually frequented foreigner clubs looking for fun in the evenings.
Kato ...
Ri-carte.

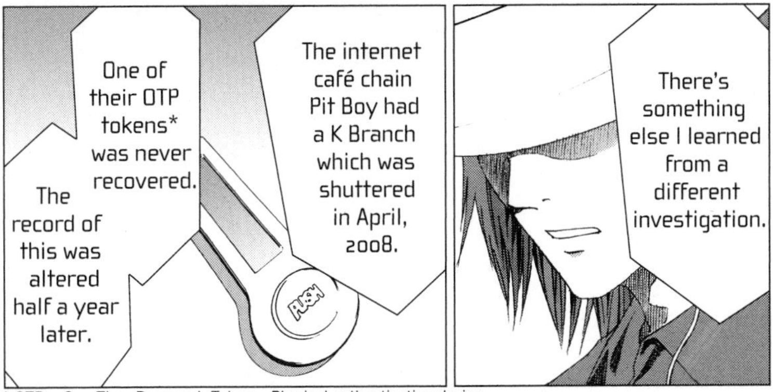
There's something else I learned from a different investigation.
The internet café chain Pit Boy had a K Branch which was shuttered in April, 2008.
One of their OTP tokens* was never recovered.
PUSH
The record of this was altered half a year later.

* OTP = One-Time Password. Token = Physical authentication device.

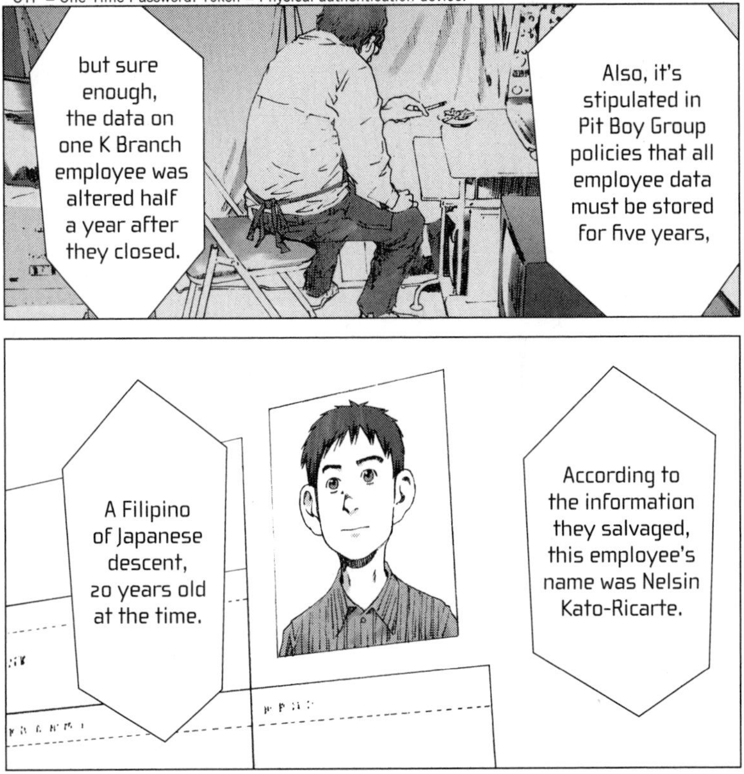
Also, it's stipulated in Pit Boy Group policies that all employee data must be stored for five years,
but sure enough, the data on one K Branch employee was altered half a year after they closed.
According to the information they salvaged, this employee's name was Nelsin Kato-Ricarte.
A Filipino of Japanese descent, 20 years old at the time.

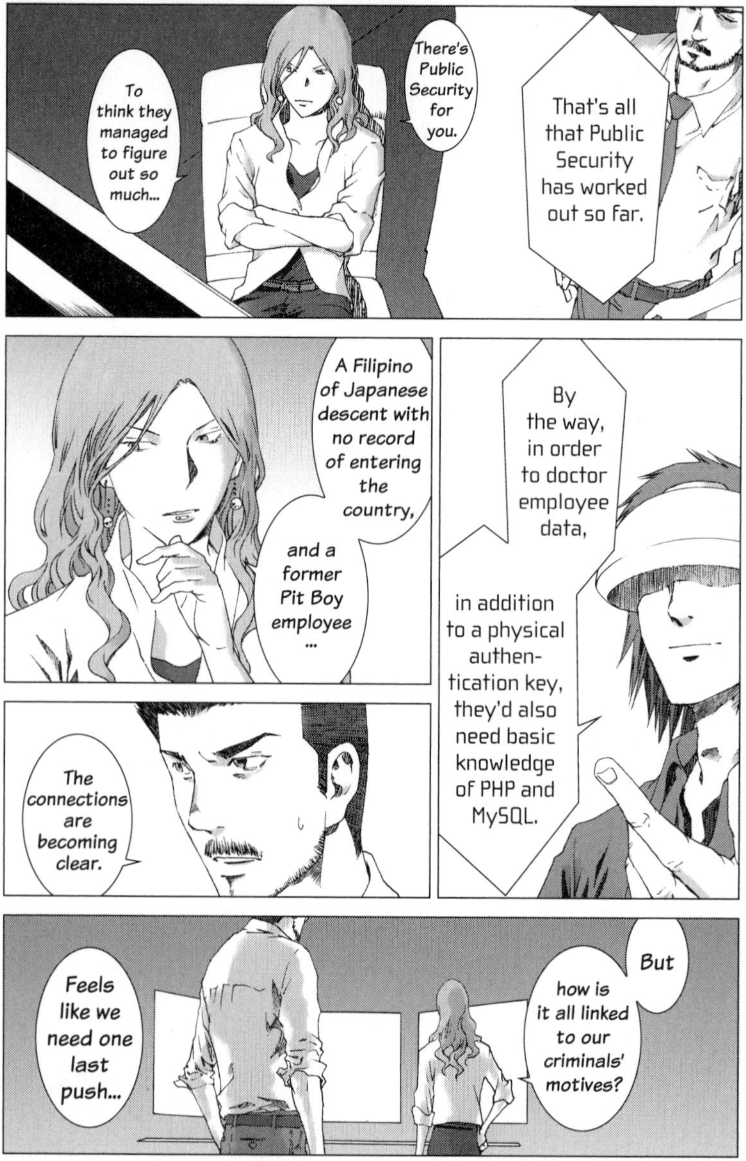
That's all that Public Security has worked out so far.
There's Public Security for you.
To think they managed to figure out so much...
By the way, in order to doctor employee data,
in addition to a physical authen-tication key, they'd also need basic knowledge of PHP and MySQL.
A Filipino of Japanese descent with no record of entering the country,
and a former Pit Boy employee ...
The connections are becoming clear.
But how is it all linked to our criminals' motives?
Feels like we need one last push...

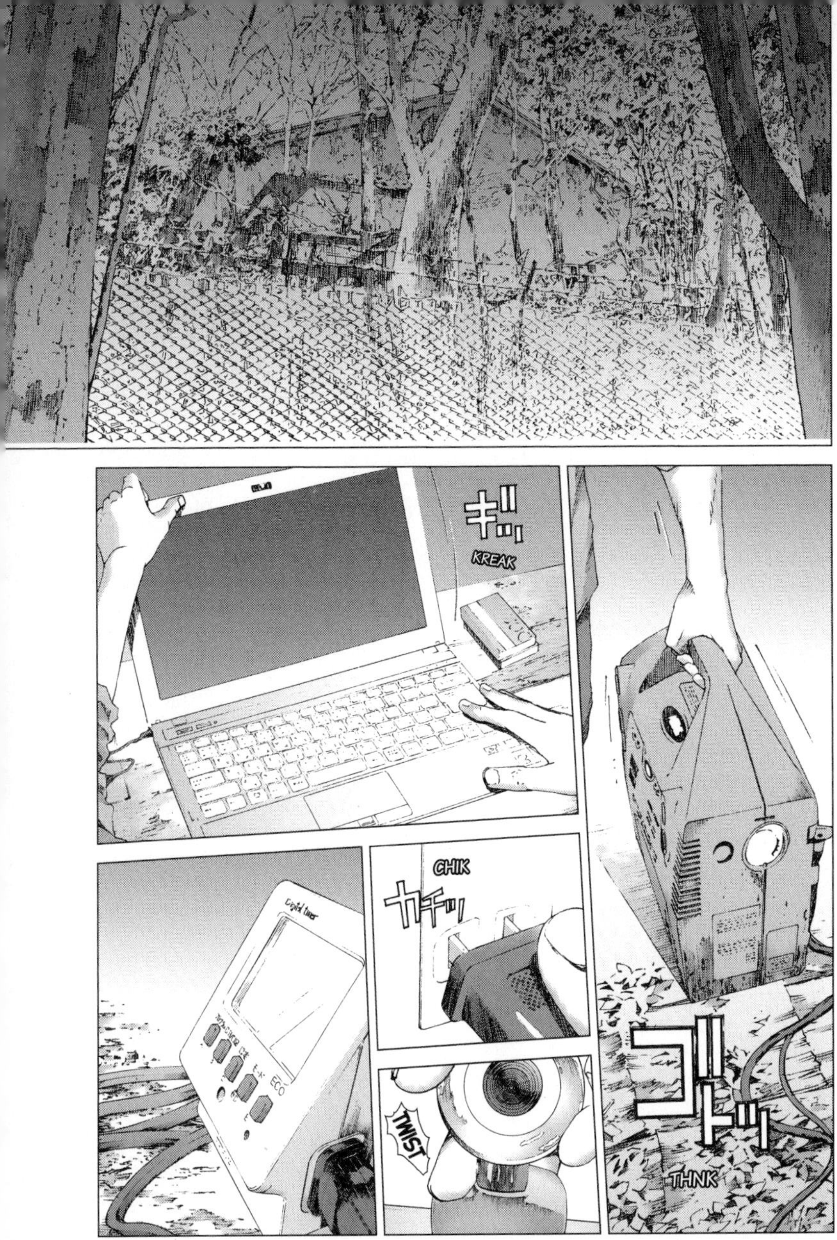
ゴトッ
THNK
ギッ
KREAK
CHIK
カチッ
TWIST
Digital timer
ECO

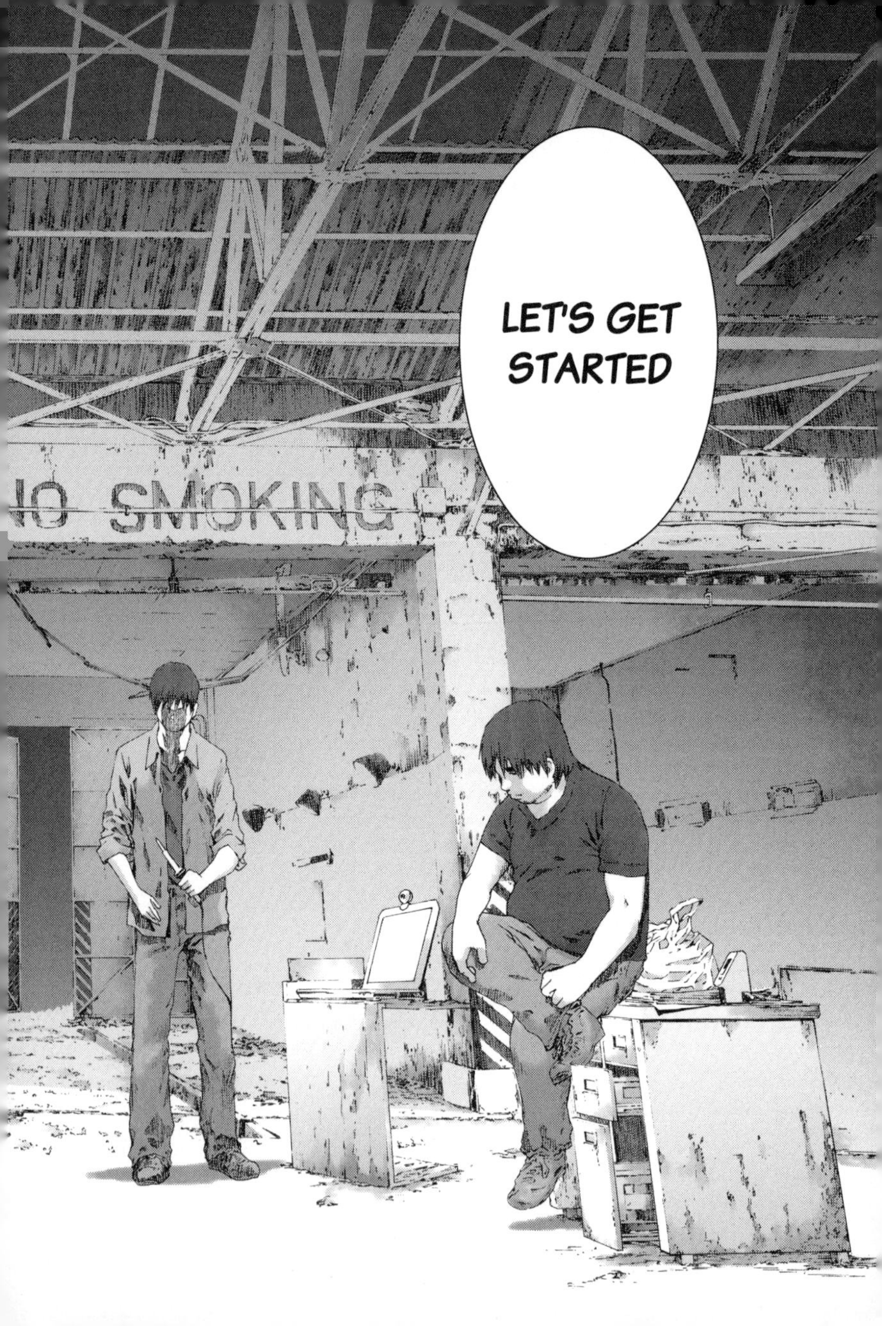
LET'S GET STARTED
NO SMOKING

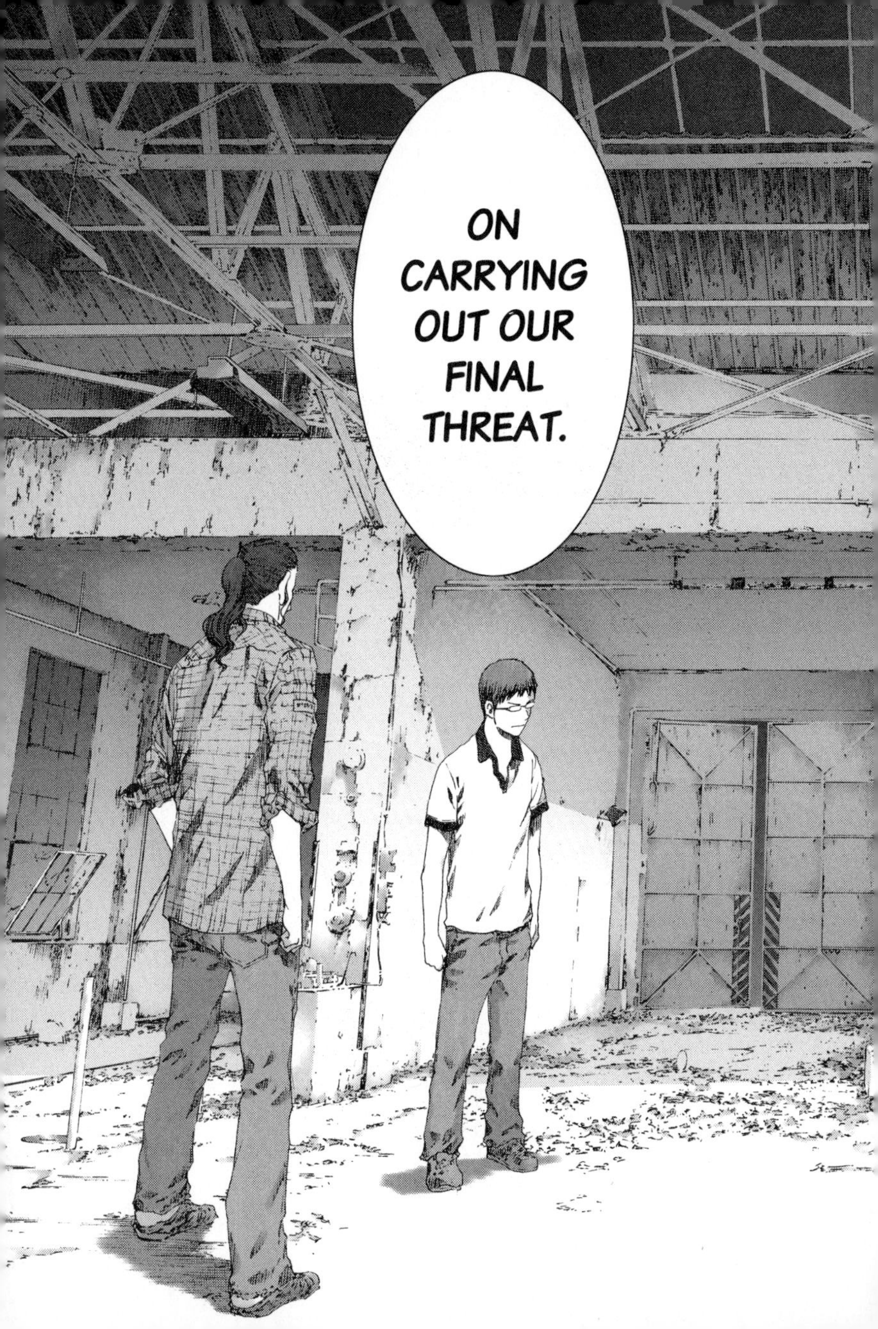
ON CARRYING OUT OUR FINAL THREAT.

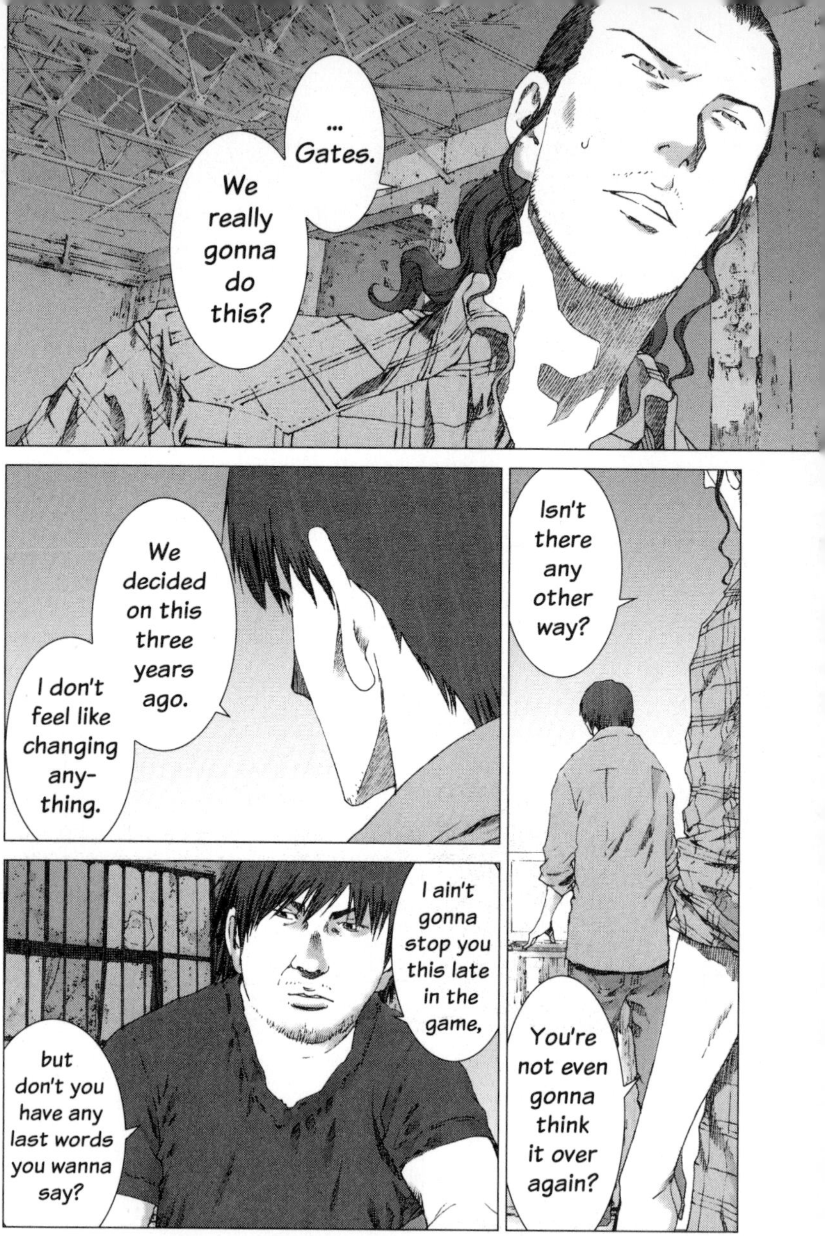
... Gates.
We really gonna do this?
Isn't there any other way?
You're not even gonna think it over again?
We decided on this three years ago.
I don't feel like changing any-thing.
I ain't gonna stop you this late in the game,
but don't you have any last words you wanna say?

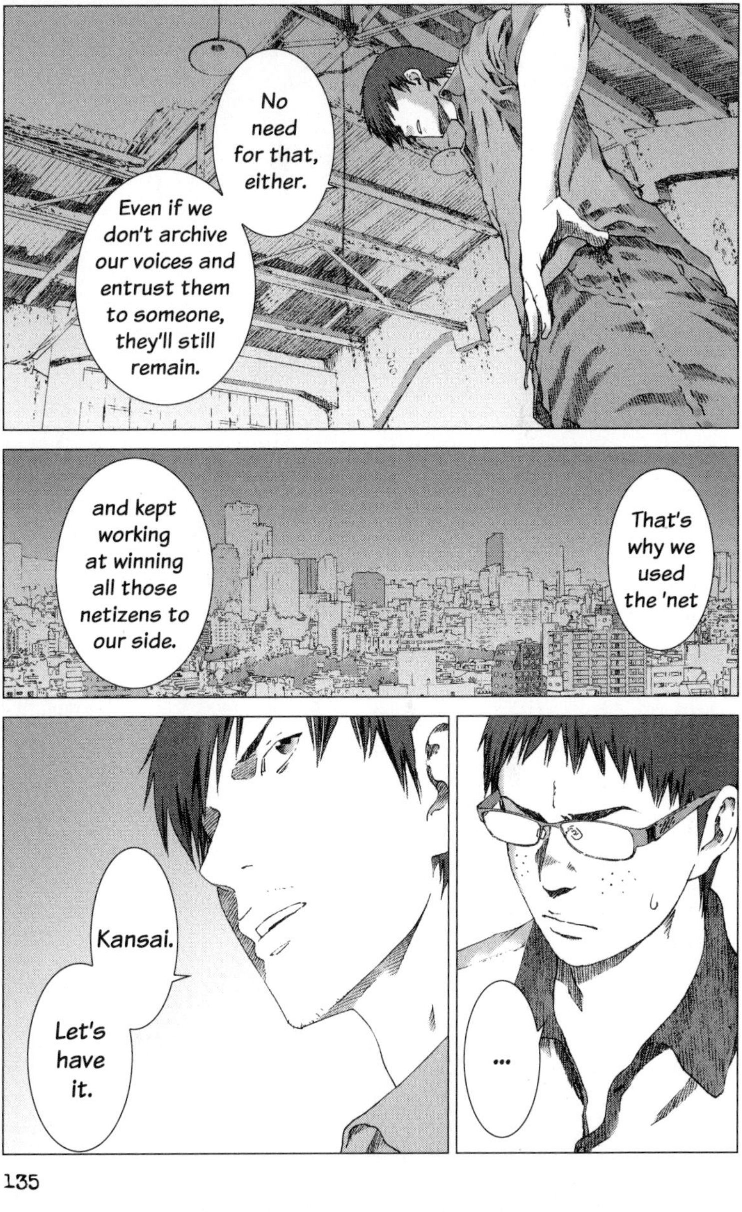
No need for that, either.
Even if we don't archive our voices and entrust them to someone, they'll still remain.
That's why we used the 'net
and kept working at winning all those netizens to our side.
...
Kansai.
Let's have it.

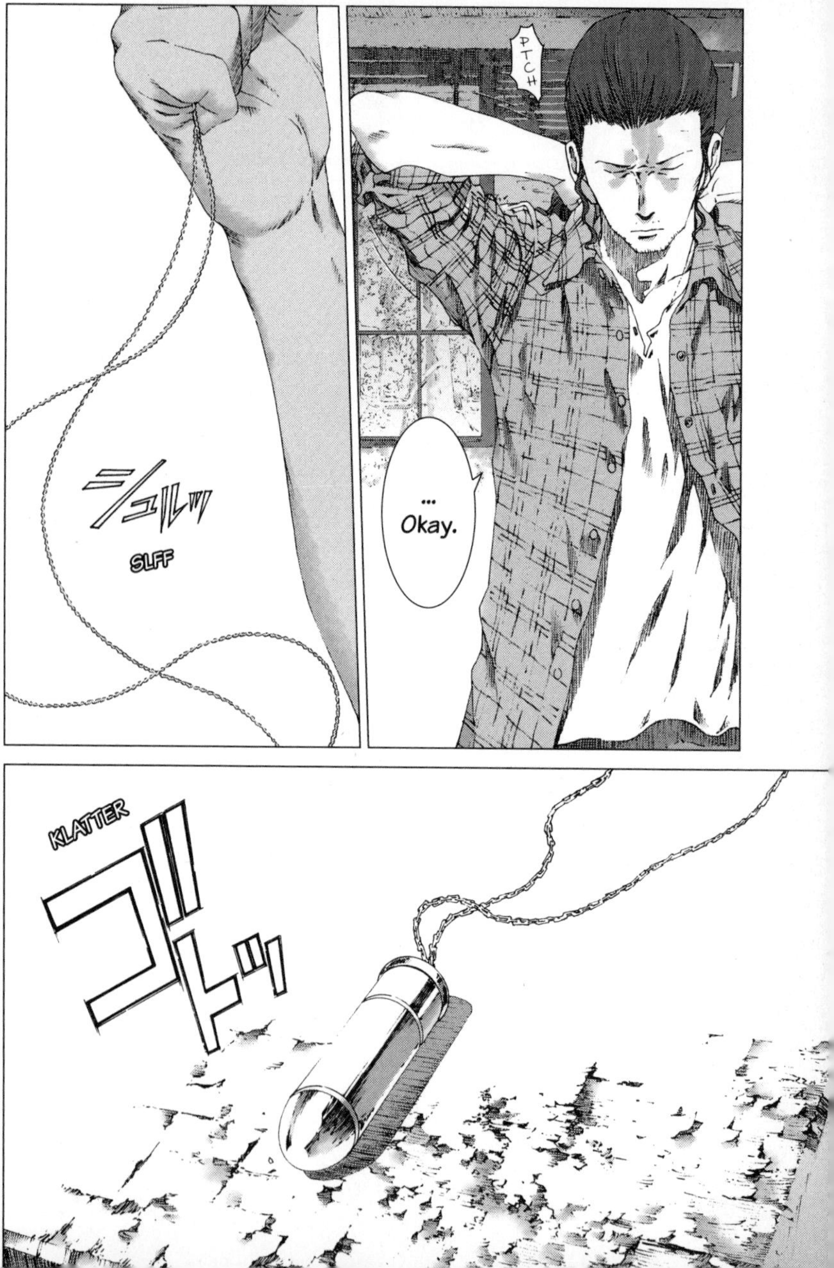
PTCH
... Okay.
シュルッ
SLFF
KLATTER
ゴトッ

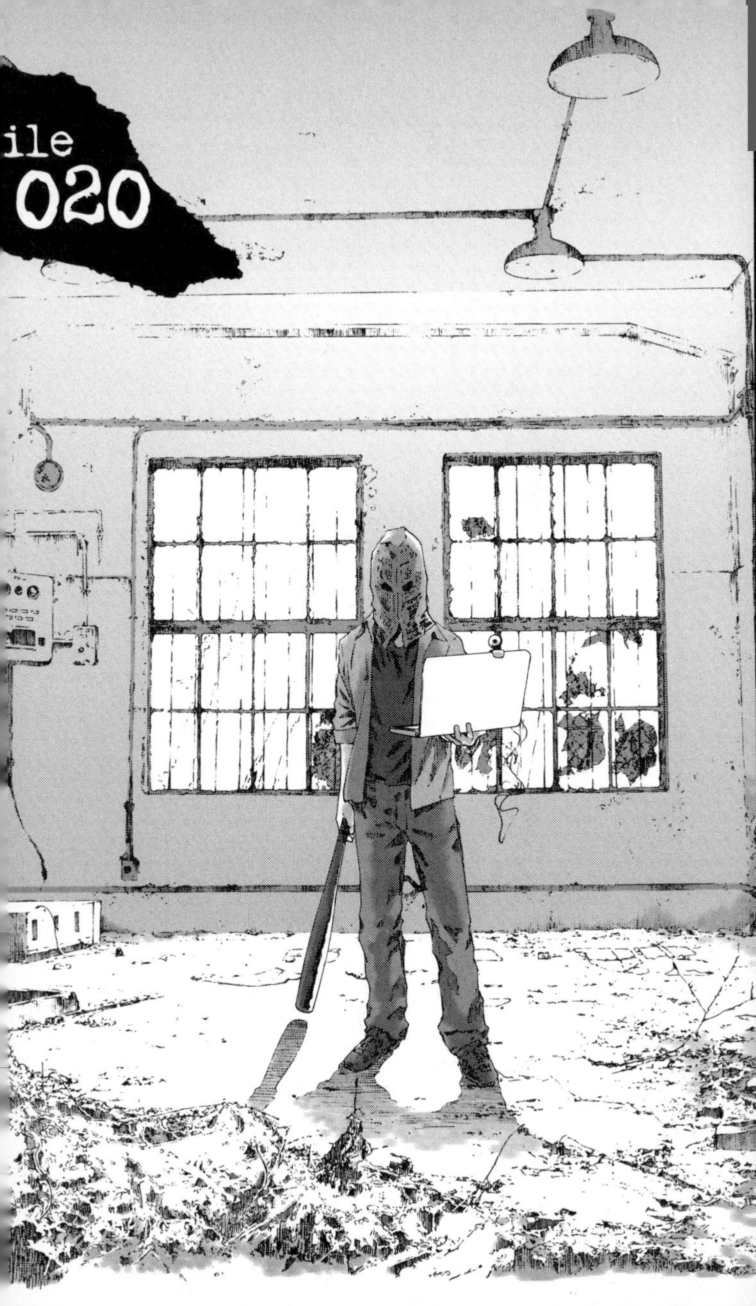
ile
020

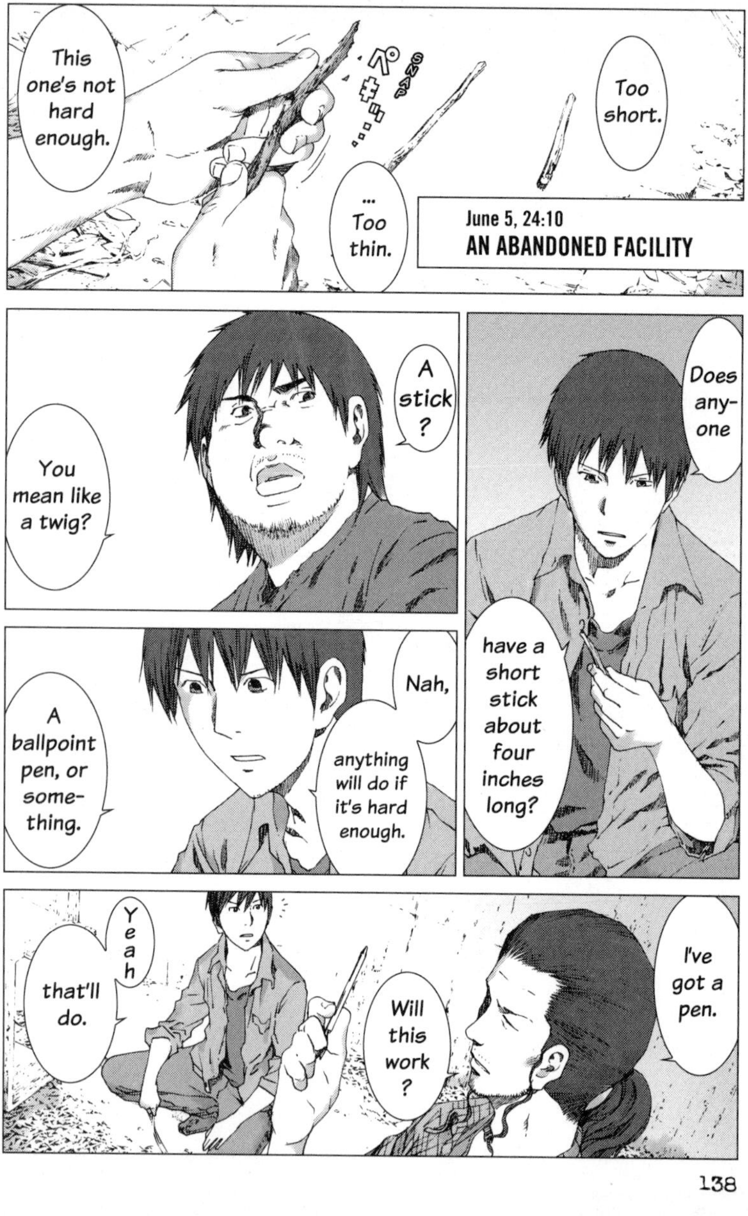
Too short.
SNAP
... Too thin.
This one's not hard enough.
June 5, 24:10
AN ABANDONED FACILITY
Does anyone
have a short stick about four inches long?
A stick?
You mean like a twig?
Nah,
anything will do if it's hard enough.
A ballpoint pen, or something.
I've got a pen.
Will this work?
Yeah
that'll do.

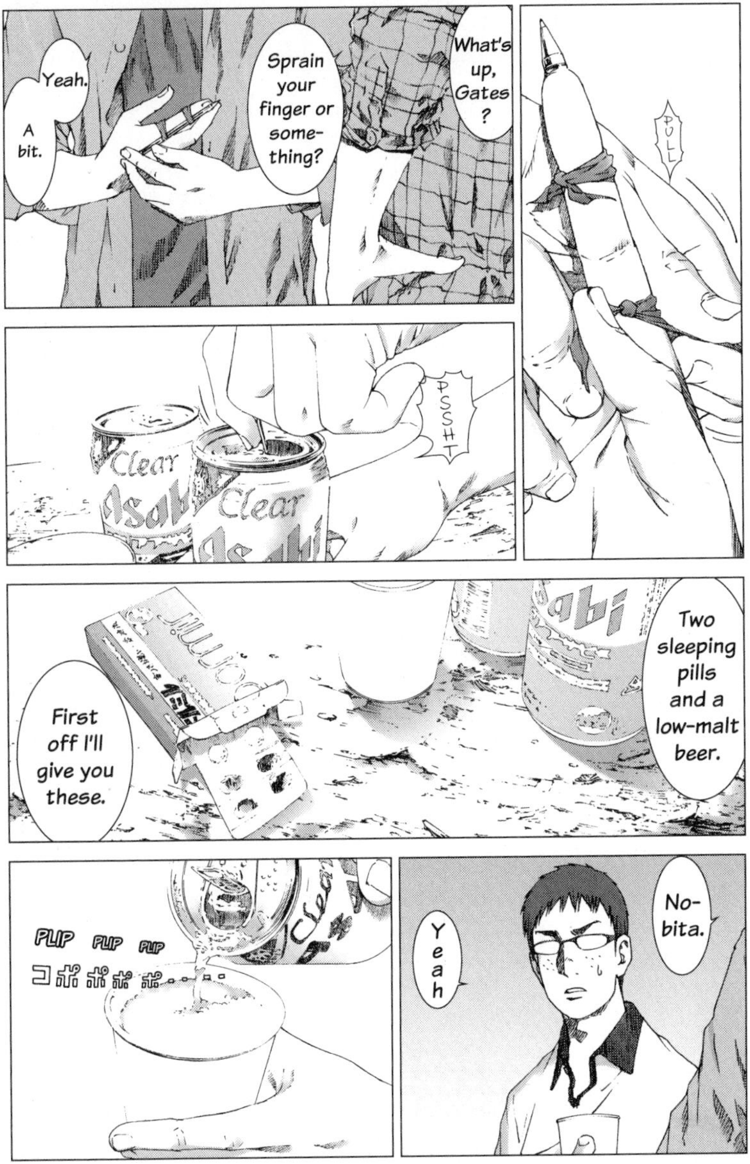
PULL
What's up, Gates?
Sprain your finger or some-thing?
Yeah.
A bit.
PSSHT
Two sleeping pills and a low-malt beer.
First off I'll give you these.
No-bita.
Yeah
PLIP PLIP PLIP
コポポポポ・・・・

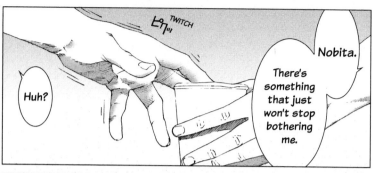

TWITCH

Nobita.

There's something that just won't stop bothering me.

Huh?

...?

Hiding ... something?

You're

hiding something from us, aren't you.

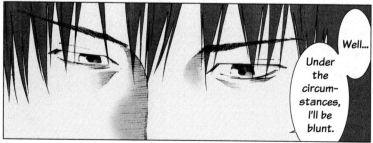

Well...

Under the circumstances, I'll be blunt.

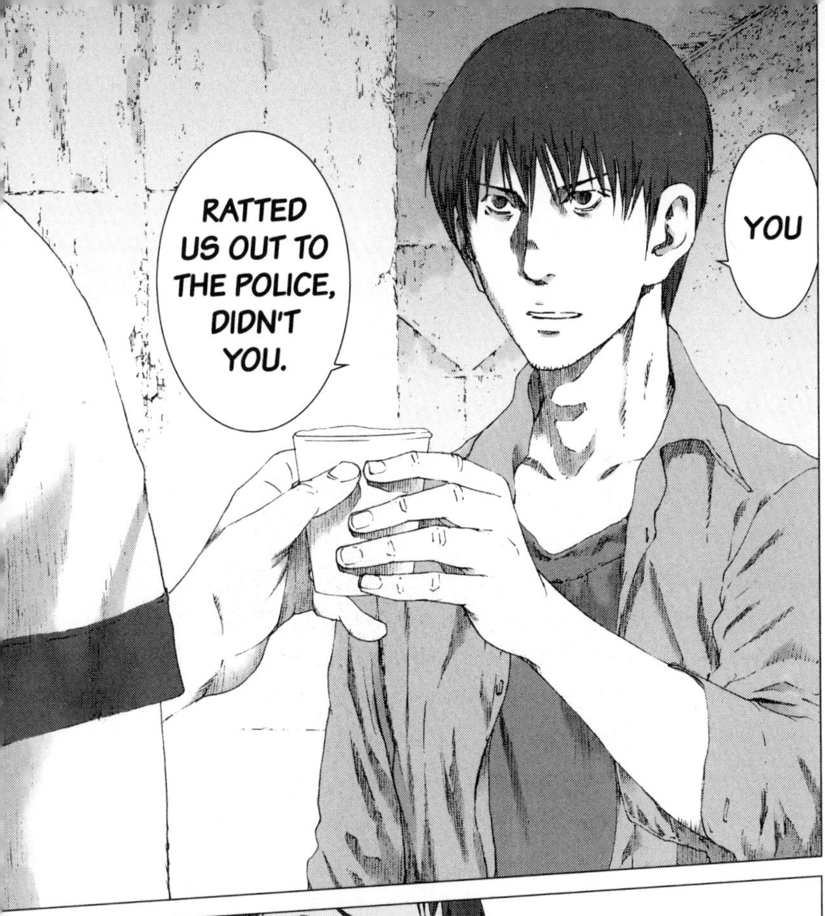
YOU
RATTED US OUT TO THE POLICE, DIDN'T YOU.

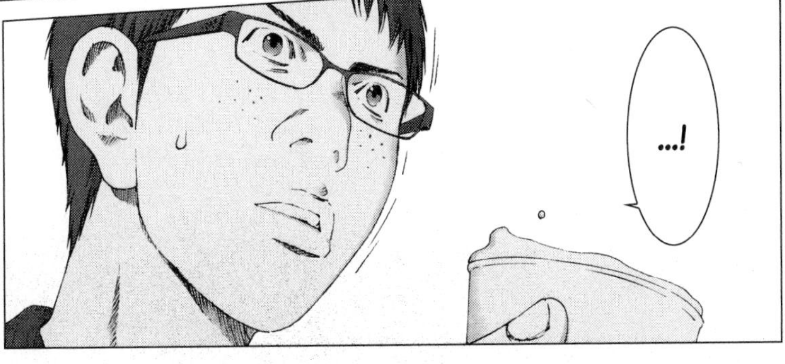
...!

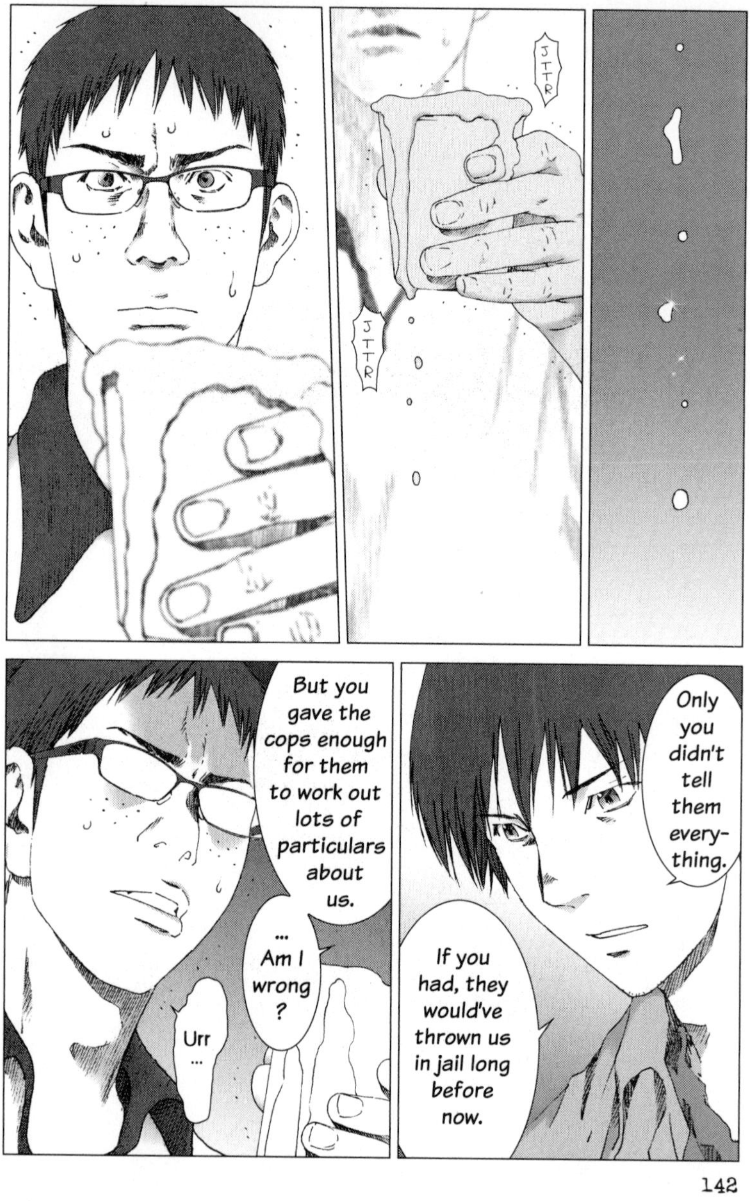
JTTR
JTTR
Only you didn't tell them every-thing.
If you had, they would've thrown us in jail long before now.
But you gave the cops enough for them to work out lots of particulars about us.
... Am I wrong?
Urr ...

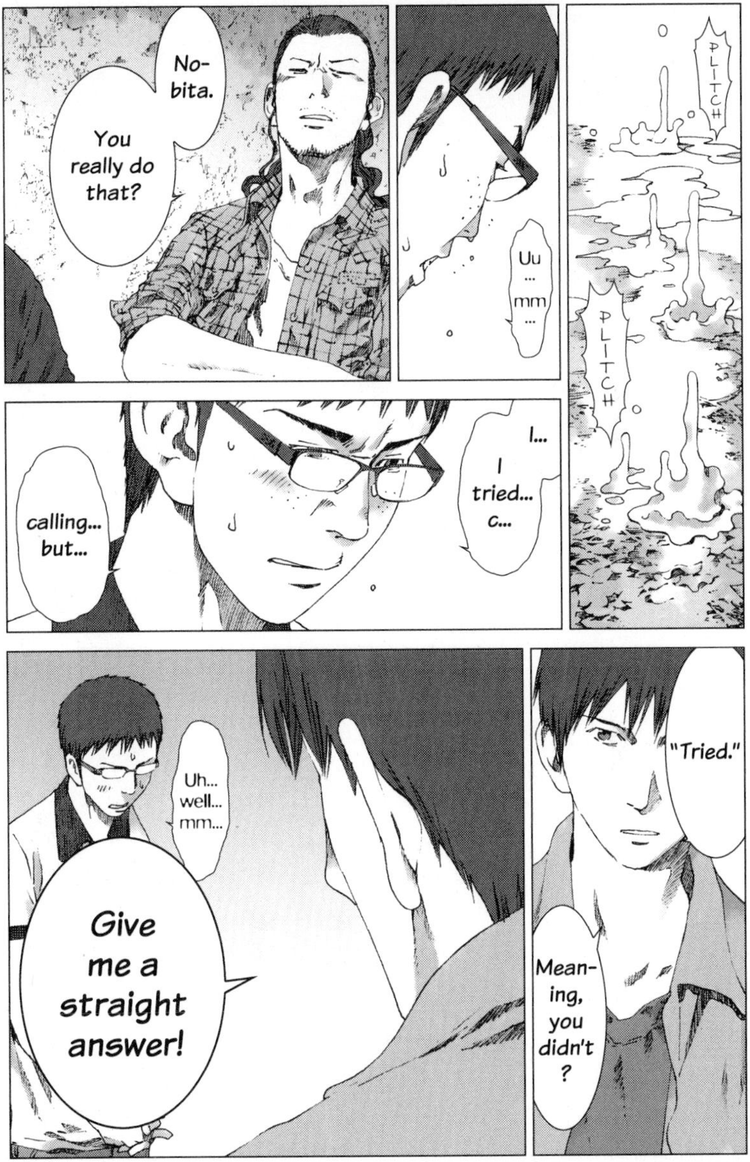

PLITCH
PLITCH
Uu ... mm ...
No-bita.
You really do that?
I...
I tried... c...
calling... but...
"Tried."
Meaning, you didn't ?
Uh... well... mm...
Give me a straight answer!

...and hung up in the middle...

No, I...

I got scared...

So you did call them.

You hung up in the middle.

No-bita. You...

I'm... I'm so sorry.

I... I was afraid.

Now what, Gates?

Tsk...

144

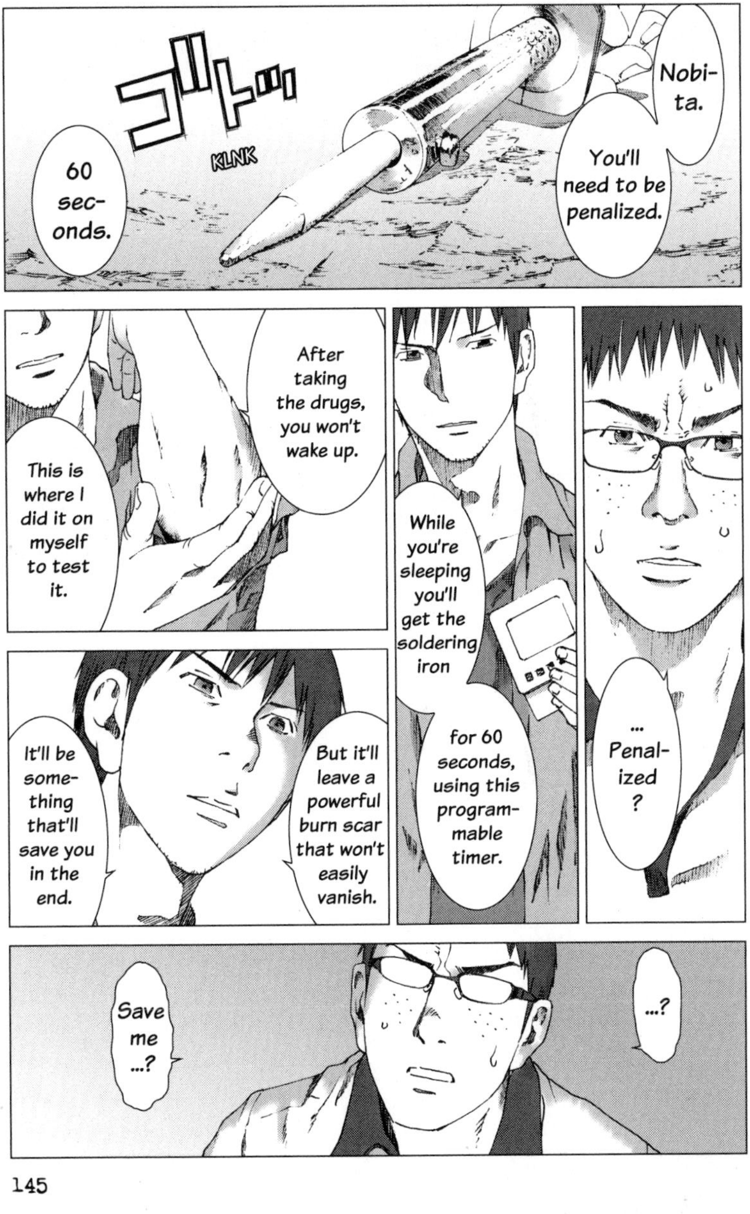
Nobita.
You'll need to be penalized.
ゴトッ
KLNK
60 seconds.
... Penalized?
While you're sleeping you'll get the soldering iron
for 60 seconds, using this programmable timer.
After taking the drugs, you won't wake up.
This is where I did it on myself to test it.
But it'll leave a powerful burn scar that won't easily vanish.
It'll be something that'll save you in the end.
...?
Save me ...?

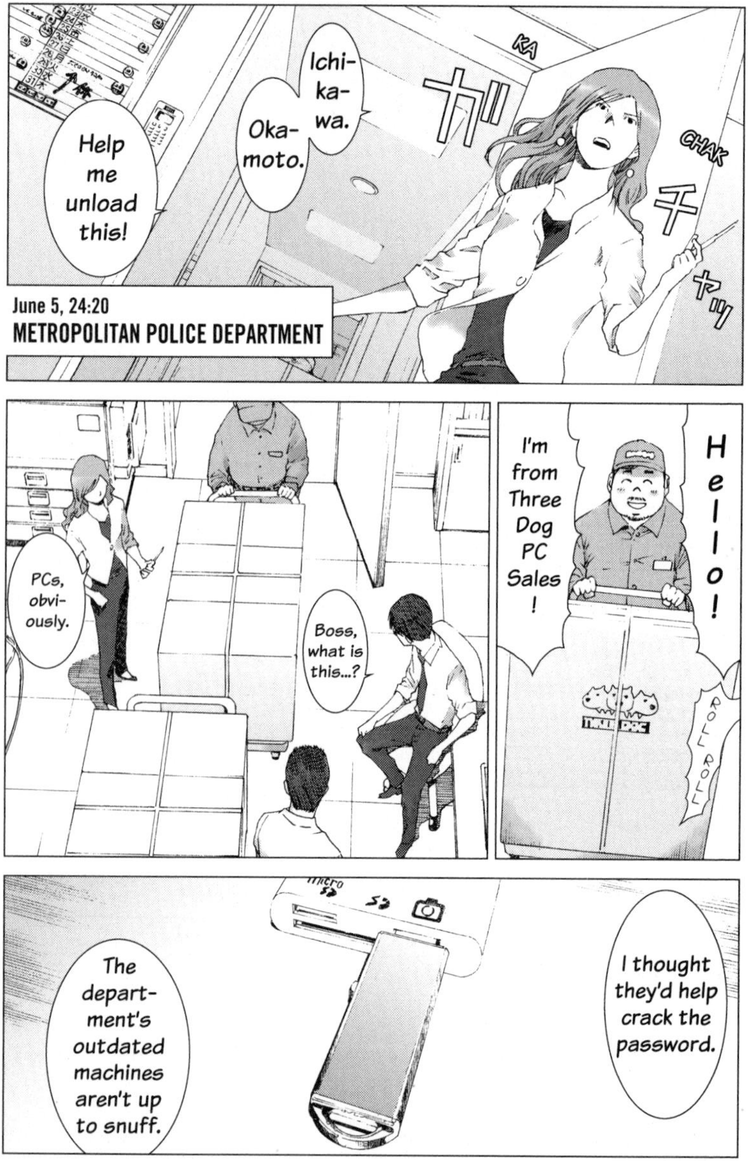
CHAK
チャッ
KA
ガ
Ichi-ka-wa.
Oka-moto.
Help me unload this!
June 5, 24:20
METROPOLITAN POLICE DEPARTMENT
Hello!
I'm from Three Dog PC Sales!
ROLL ROLL
Boss, what is this...?
PCs, obviously.
I thought they'd help crack the password.
The department's outdated machines aren't up to snuff.

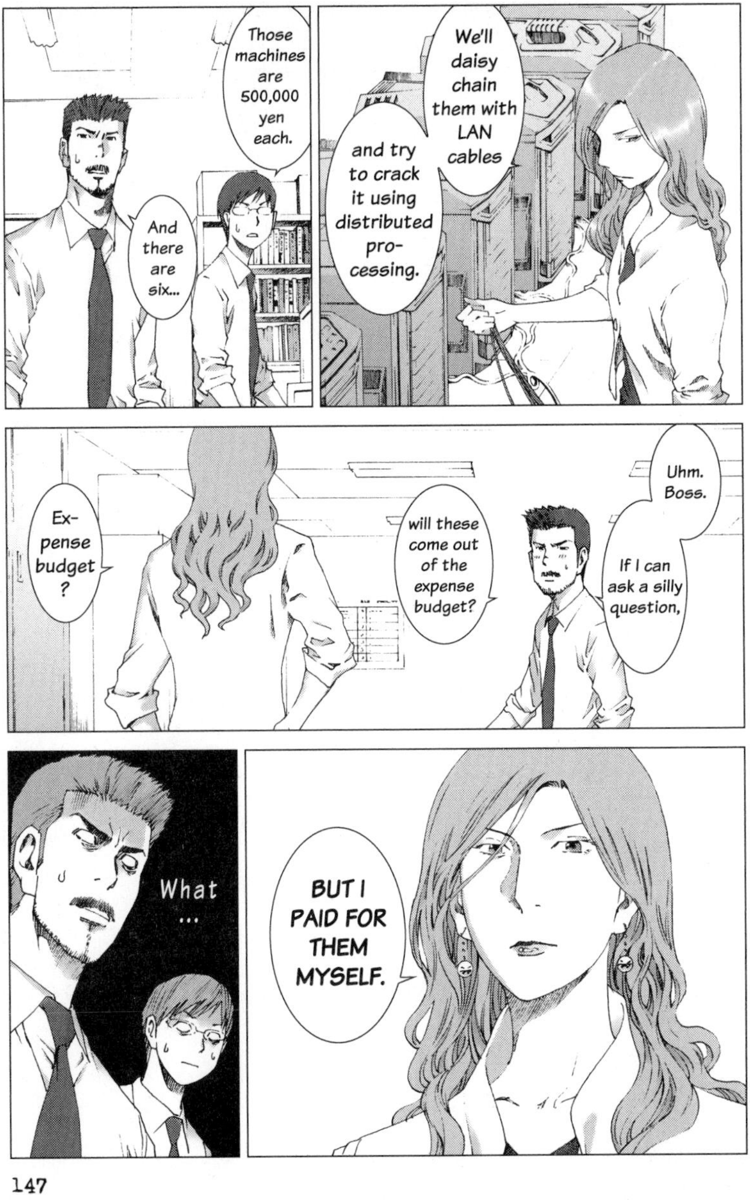
We'll daisy chain them with LAN cables
and try to crack it using distributed pro-cessing.
Those machines are 500,000 yen each.
And there are six...
Uhm. Boss.
If I can ask a silly question,
will these come out of the expense budget?
Ex-pense budget?
BUT I PAID FOR THEM MYSELF.
What ...

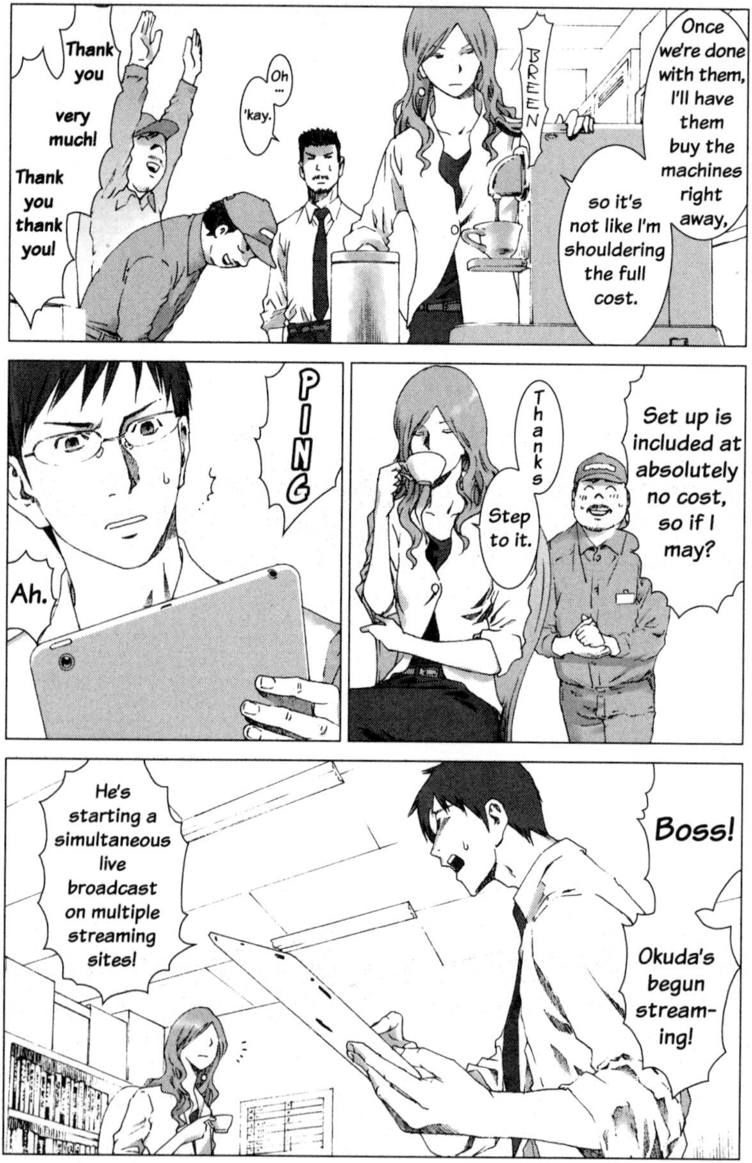
Once we're done with them, I'll have them buy the machines right away,
so it's not like I'm shouldering the full cost.
BREEN
Oh... 'kay.
Thank you very much!
Thank you thank you!
Set up is included at absolutely no cost, so if I may?
Thanks
Step to it.
PING
Ah.
Boss!
Okuda's begun stream-ing!
He's starting a simultaneous live broadcast on multiple streaming sites!

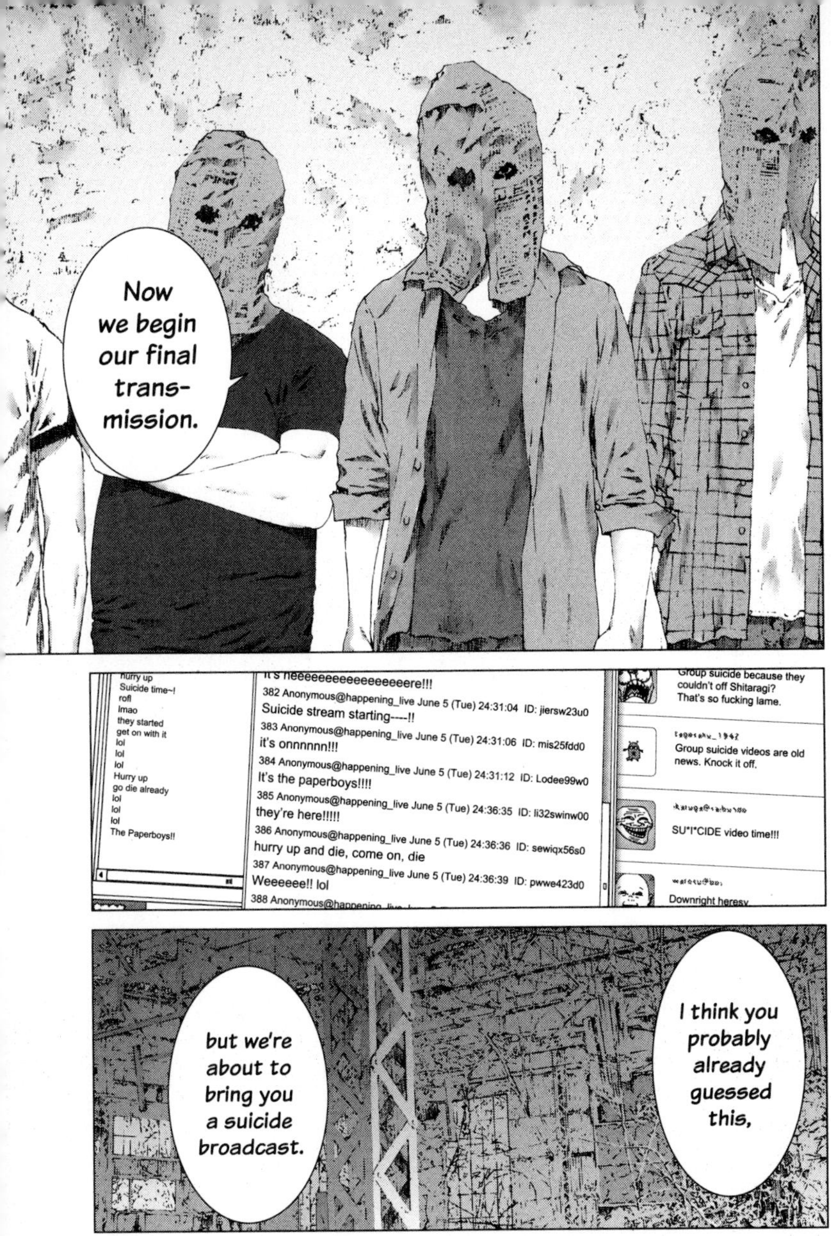
Now we begin our final trans-mission.
Group suicide because they couldn't off Shitaragi? That's so fucking lame.
Group suicide videos are old news. Knock it off.
SU*I*CIDE video time!!!
Downright heresy
382 Anonymous@happening_live June 5 (Tue) 24:31:04 ID: jiersw23u0
Suicide stream starting----!!
383 Anonymous@happening_live June 5 (Tue) 24:31:06 ID: mis25fdd0
it's onnnnnn!!!
384 Anonymous@happening_live June 5 (Tue) 24:31:12 ID: Lodee99w0
It's the paperboys!!!!
385 Anonymous@happening_live June 5 (Tue) 24:36:35 ID: li32swinw00
they're here!!!!!
386 Anonymous@happening_live June 5 (Tue) 24:36:36 ID: sewiqx56s0
hurry up and die, come on, die
387 Anonymous@happening_live June 5 (Tue) 24:36:39 ID: pwwe423d0
Weeeeee!! lol
hurry up
Suicide time~!
rofl
lmao
they started
get on with it
lol
lol
lol
Hurry up
go die already
lol
lol
lol
The Paperboys!!
I think you probably already guessed this,
but we're about to bring you a suicide broadcast.

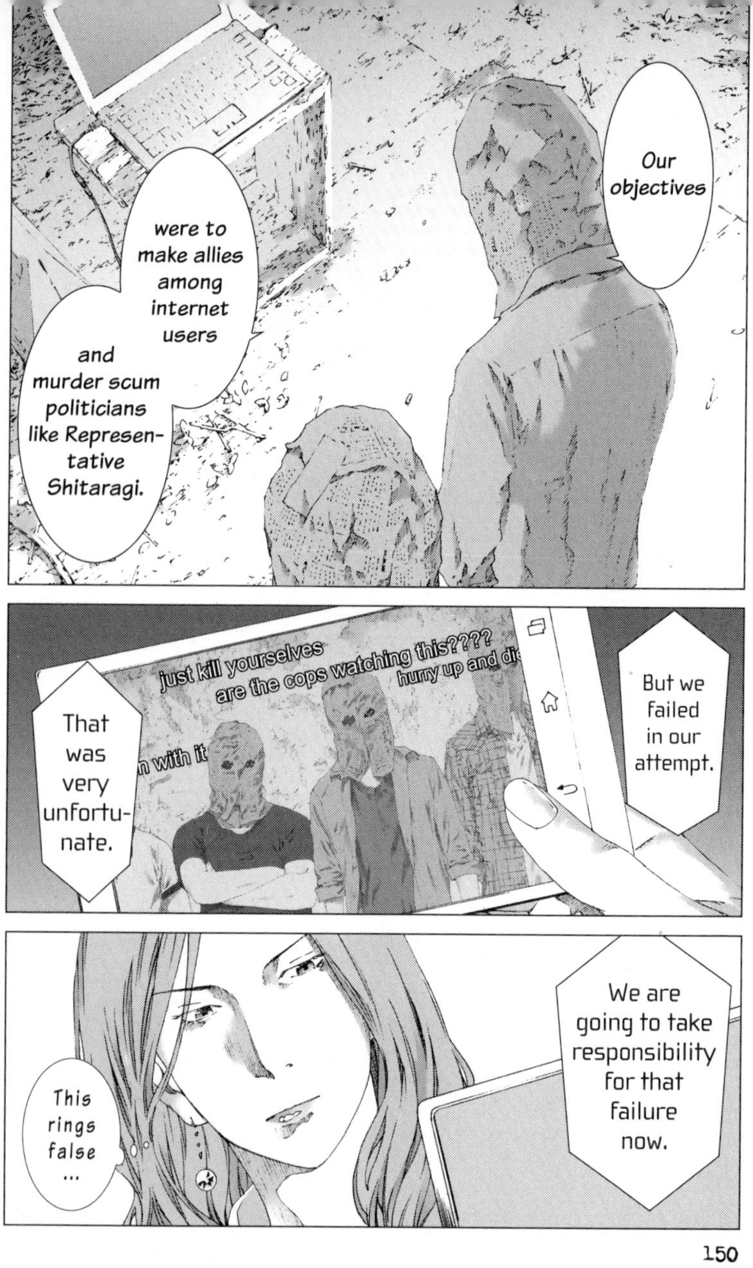
Our objectives
were to make allies among internet users
and murder scum politicians like Representative Shitaragi.
But we failed in our attempt.
just kill yourselves
are the cops watching this????
hurry up and di
n with it
That was very unfortunate.
We are going to take responsibility for that failure now.
This rings false ...

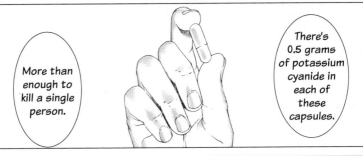

There's 0.5 grams of potassium cyanide in each of these capsules.
More than enough to kill a single person.
The pills will dissolve in our stomachs in about 30 minutes.
We will surely die in our sleep.
...
There's no reason for us to wear these masks any more.
SHRRRIP

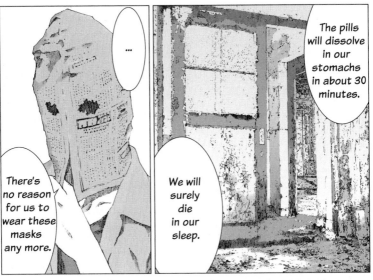

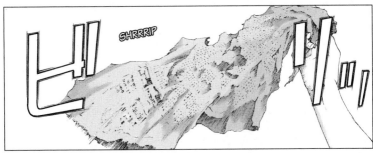

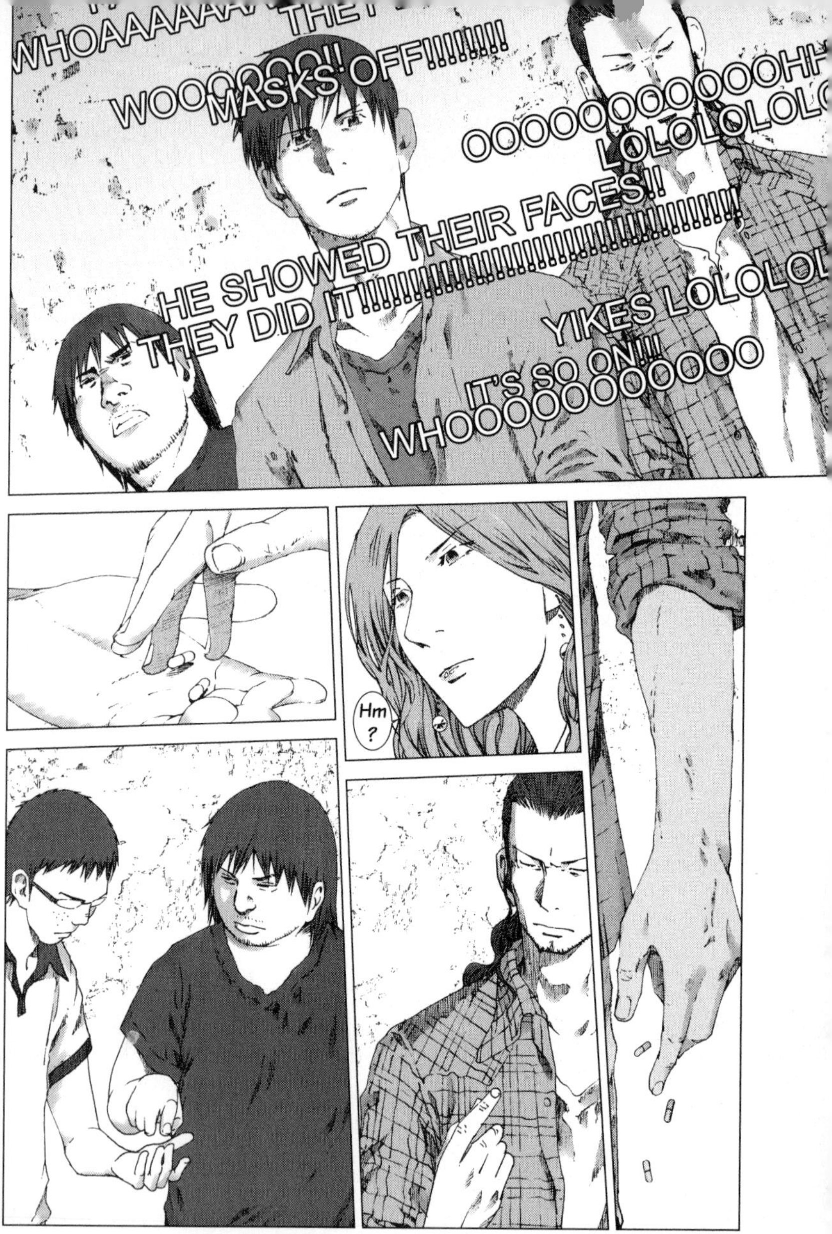
OOOOOOOOOOOOOHH
LOLOLOLOLO
WHOAAAAAAA
MASKS OFF!!!!!!!!
WOOOOOOO!!
HE SHOWED THEIR FACES!!
THEY DID IT!!!
YIKES LOLOLOL
IT'S SO ON!!!
WHOOOOOOOOOOOO
Hm?

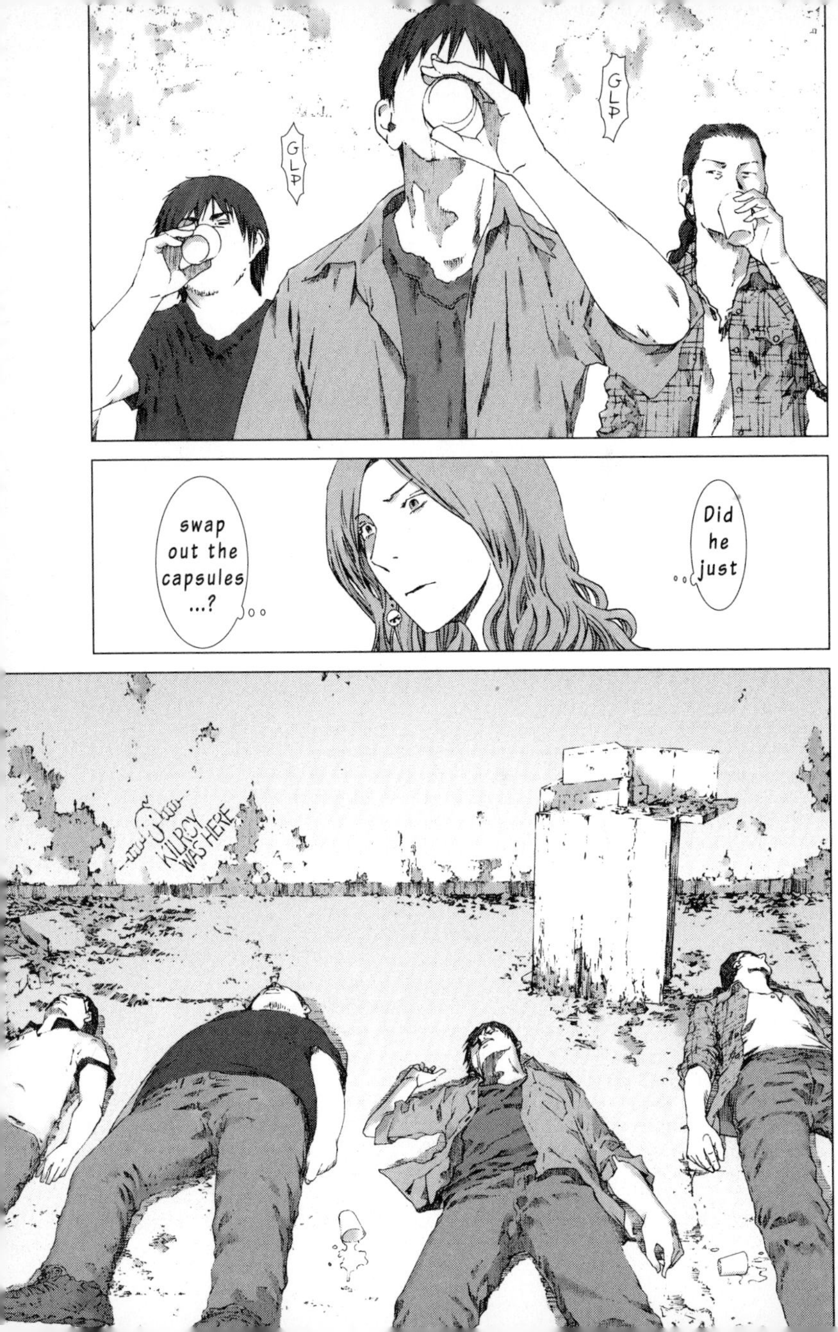
GLP
GLP
Did he just
swap out the capsules ...?
KILROY WAS HERE

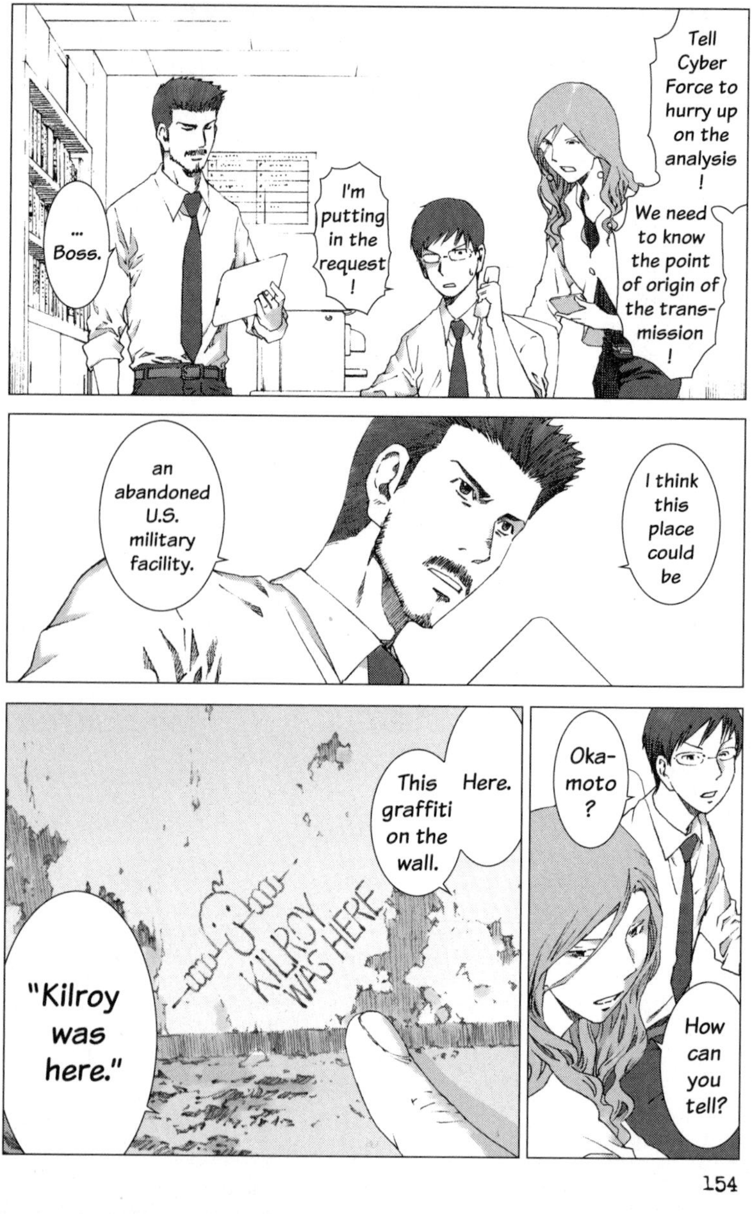
Tell Cyber Force to hurry up on the analysis!
We need to know the point of origin of the trans-mission!
I'm putting in the request!
... Boss.
I think this place could be
an abandoned U.S. military facility.
Oka-moto?
How can you tell?
Here.
This graffiti on the wall.
KILROY WAS HERE
"Kilroy was here."

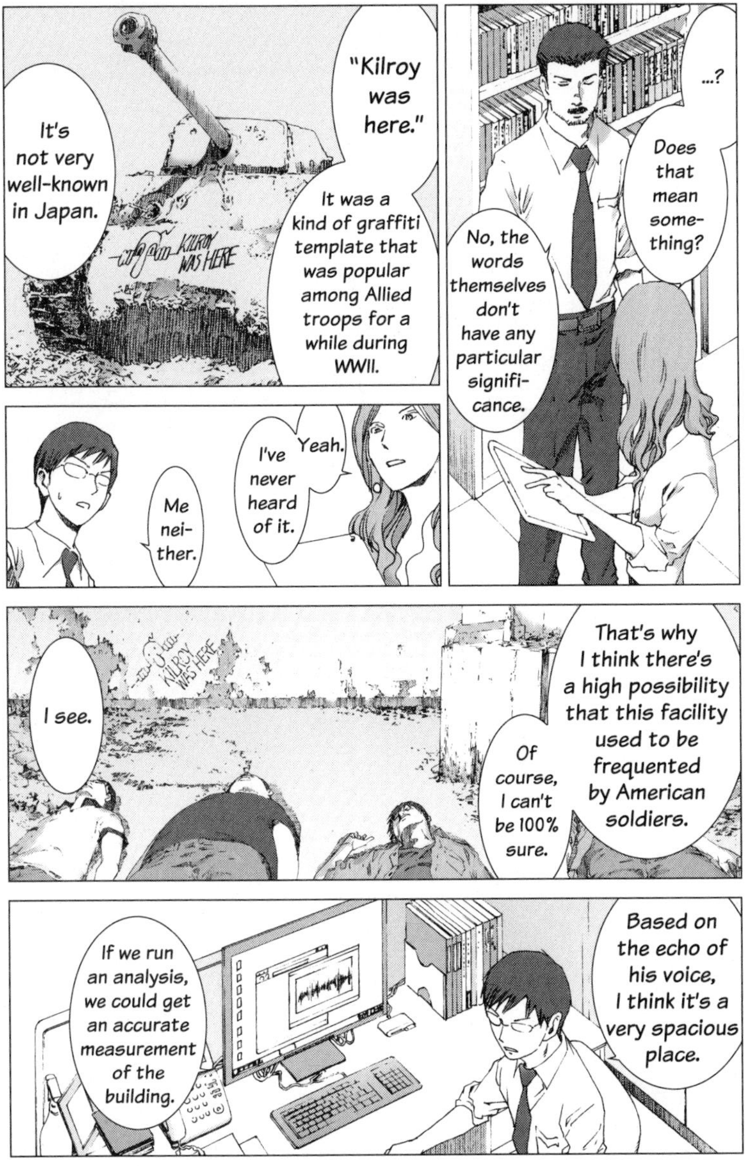
...?
Does that mean some-thing?
No, the words themselves don't have any particular signifi-cance.
"Kilroy was here."
It was a kind of graffiti template that was popular among Allied troops for a while during WWII.
KILROY WAS HERE
It's not very well-known in Japan.
Yeah.
I've never heard of it.
Me nei-ther.
That's why I think there's a high possibility that this facility used to be frequented by American soldiers.
Of course, I can't be 100% sure.
KILROY WAS HERE
I see.
Based on the echo of his voice, I think it's a very spacious place.
If we run an analysis, we could get an accurate measurement of the building.

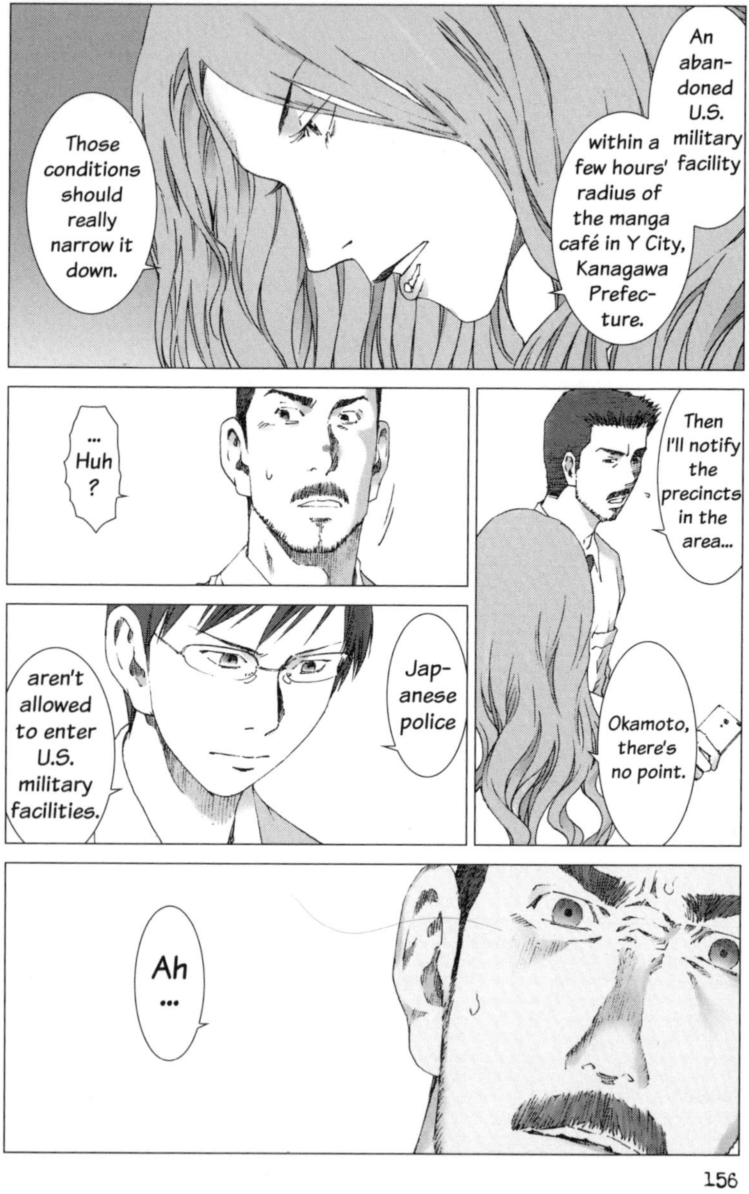
An abandoned U.S. military facility
within a few hours' radius of the manga café in Y City, Kanagawa Prefecture.
Those conditions should really narrow it down.
Then I'll notify the precincts in the area...
Okamoto, there's no point.
...Huh?
Japanese police
aren't allowed to enter U.S. military facilities.
Ah...

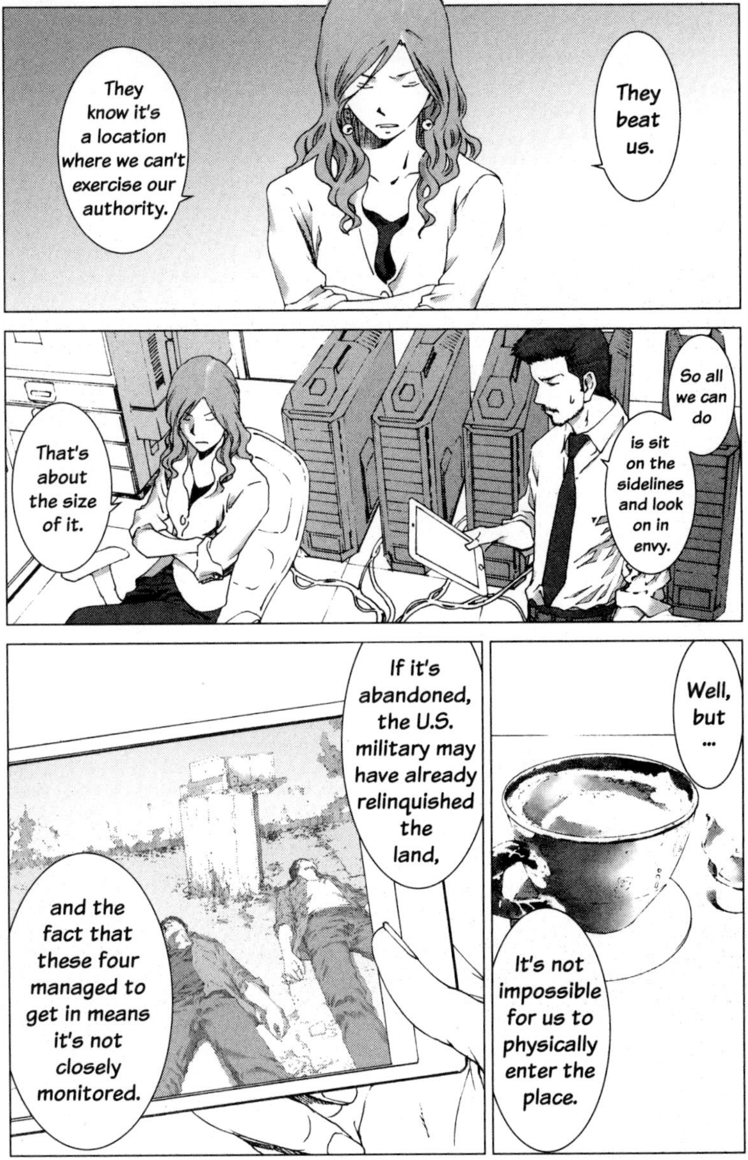
They beat us.
They know it's a location where we can't exercise our authority.
So all we can do
is sit on the sidelines and look on in envy.
That's about the size of it.
Well, but ...
It's not impossible for us to physically enter the place.
If it's abandoned, the U.S. military may have already relinquished the land,
and the fact that these four managed to get in means it's not closely monitored.

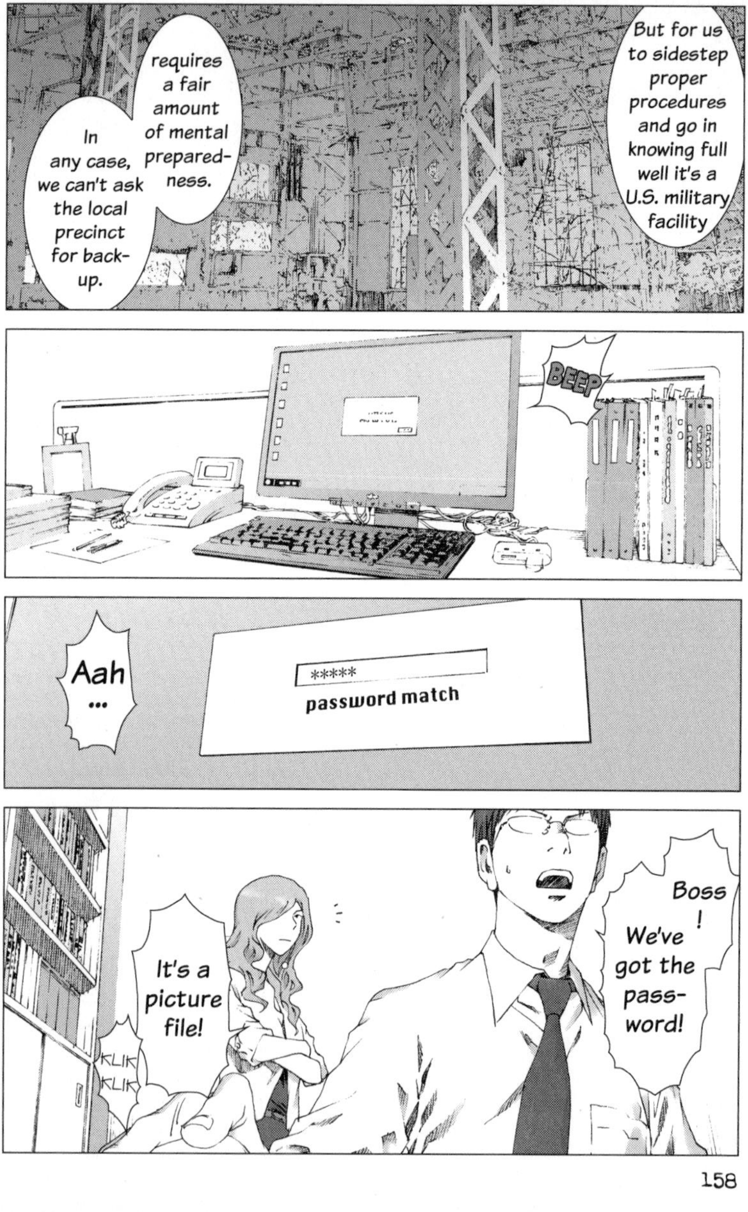
But for us to sidestep proper procedures and go in knowing full well it's a U.S. military facility
requires a fair amount of mental prepared-ness.
In any case, we can't ask the local precinct for back-up.
BEEP
*****
password match
Aah ...
Boss! We've got the pass-word!
It's a picture file!
KLIK KLIK

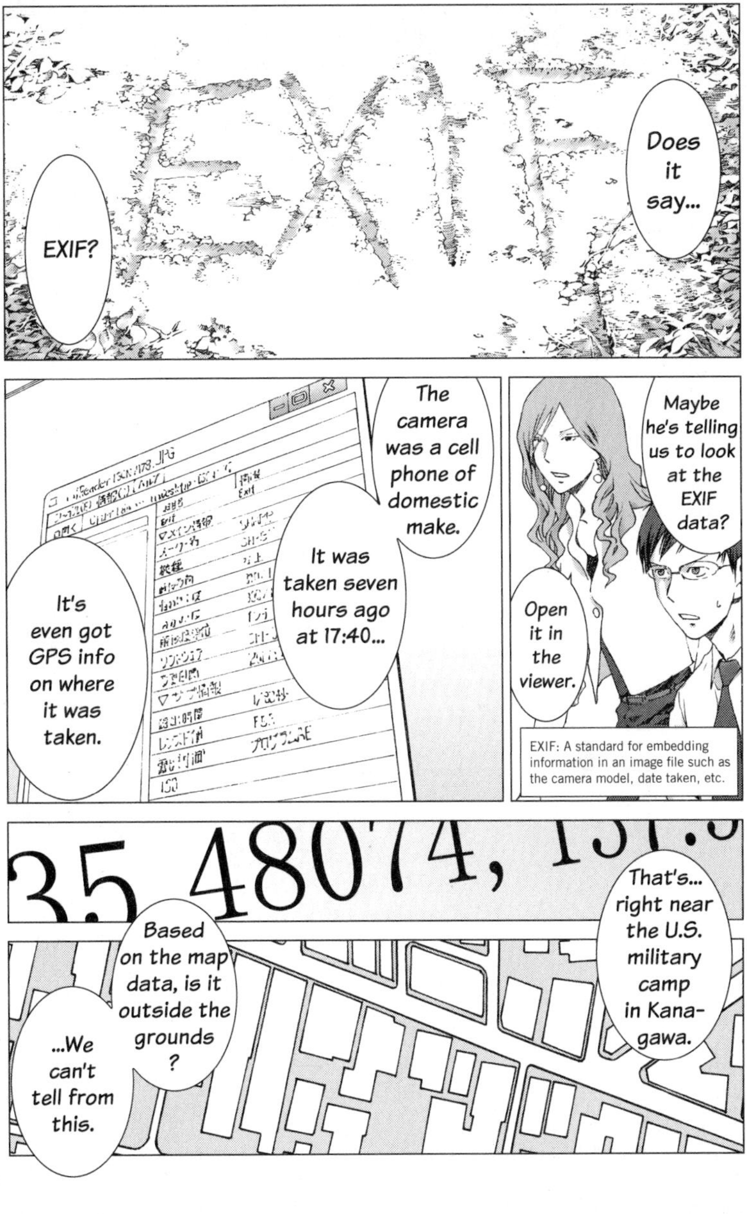
EXIF
Does it say...
EXIF?
Maybe he's telling us to look at the EXIF data?
Open it in the viewer.
EXIF: A standard for embedding information in an image file such as the camera model, date taken, etc.
The camera was a cell phone of domestic make.
It was taken seven hours ago at 17:40...
It's even got GPS info on where it was taken.
35 48074,
That's... right near the U.S. military camp in Kana-gawa.
Based on the map data, is it outside the grounds?
...We can't tell from this.

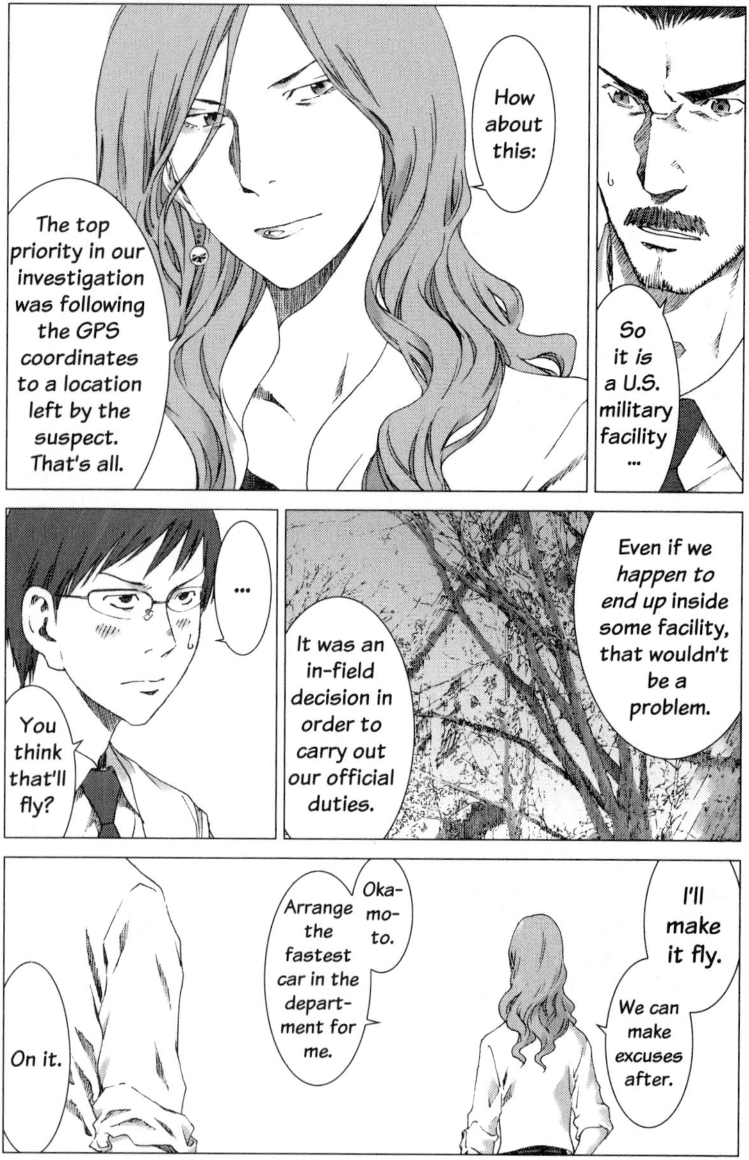
So it *is* a U.S. military facility...
How about this:
The top priority in our investigation was following the GPS coordinates to a location left by the suspect. That's all.
Even if we happen to end up inside some facility, that wouldn't be a problem.
It was an in-field decision in order to carry out our official duties.
...
You think that'll fly?
I'll make it fly.
We can make excuses after.
Okamoto.
Arrange the fastest car in the department for me.
On it.

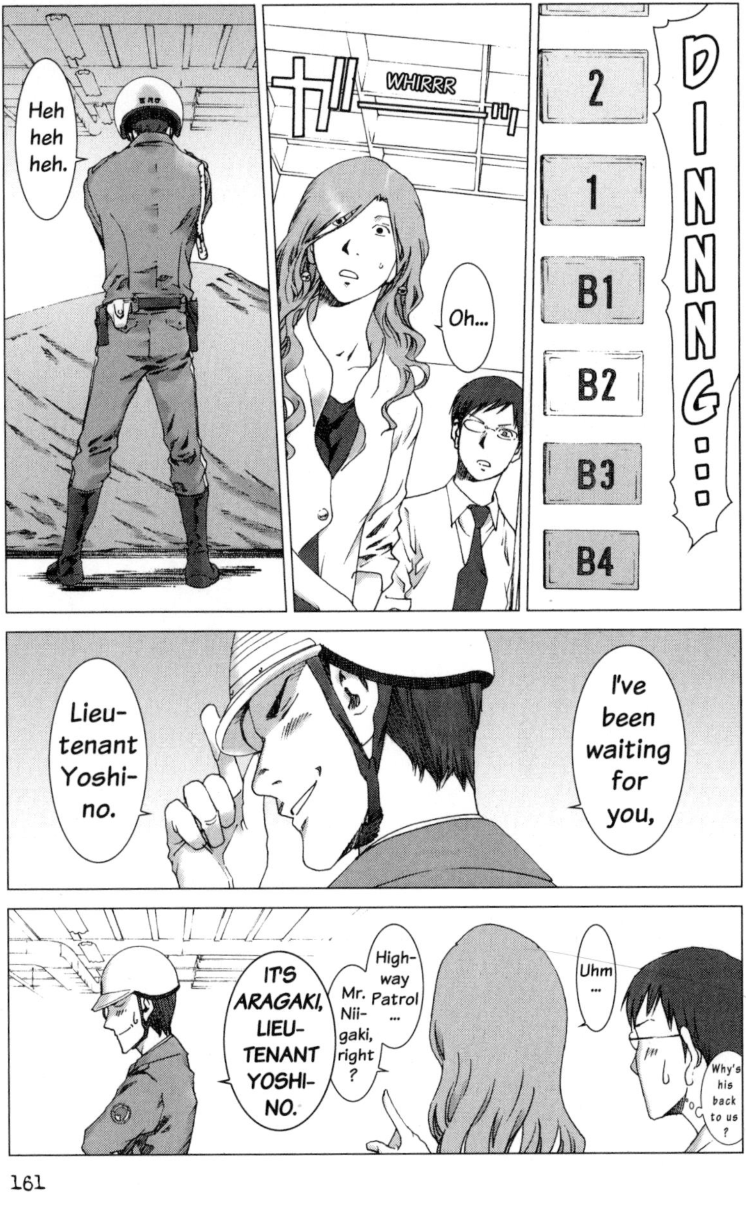
2
1
B1
B2
B3
B4
DINNNG...
WHIRRR
Oh...
Heh heh heh.
I've been waiting for you,
Lieutenant Yoshino.
Why's his back to us?
Uhm...
Highway Patrol...
Mr. Niigaki, right?
IT'S ARAGAKI, LIEUTENANT YOSHINO.

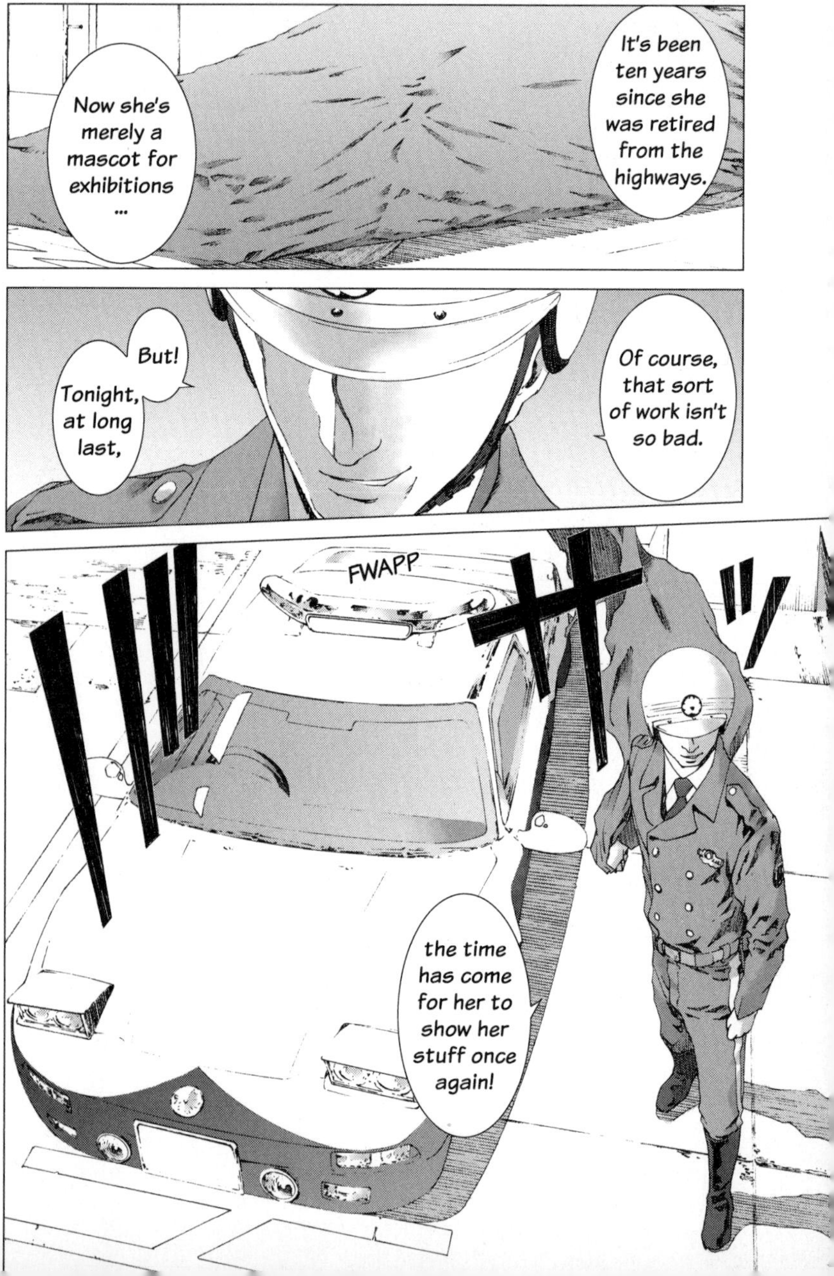
It's been ten years since she was retired from the highways.
Now she's merely a mascot for exhibitions ...
Of course, that sort of work isn't so bad.
But!
Tonight, at long last,
FWAPP
the time has come for her to show her stuff once again!

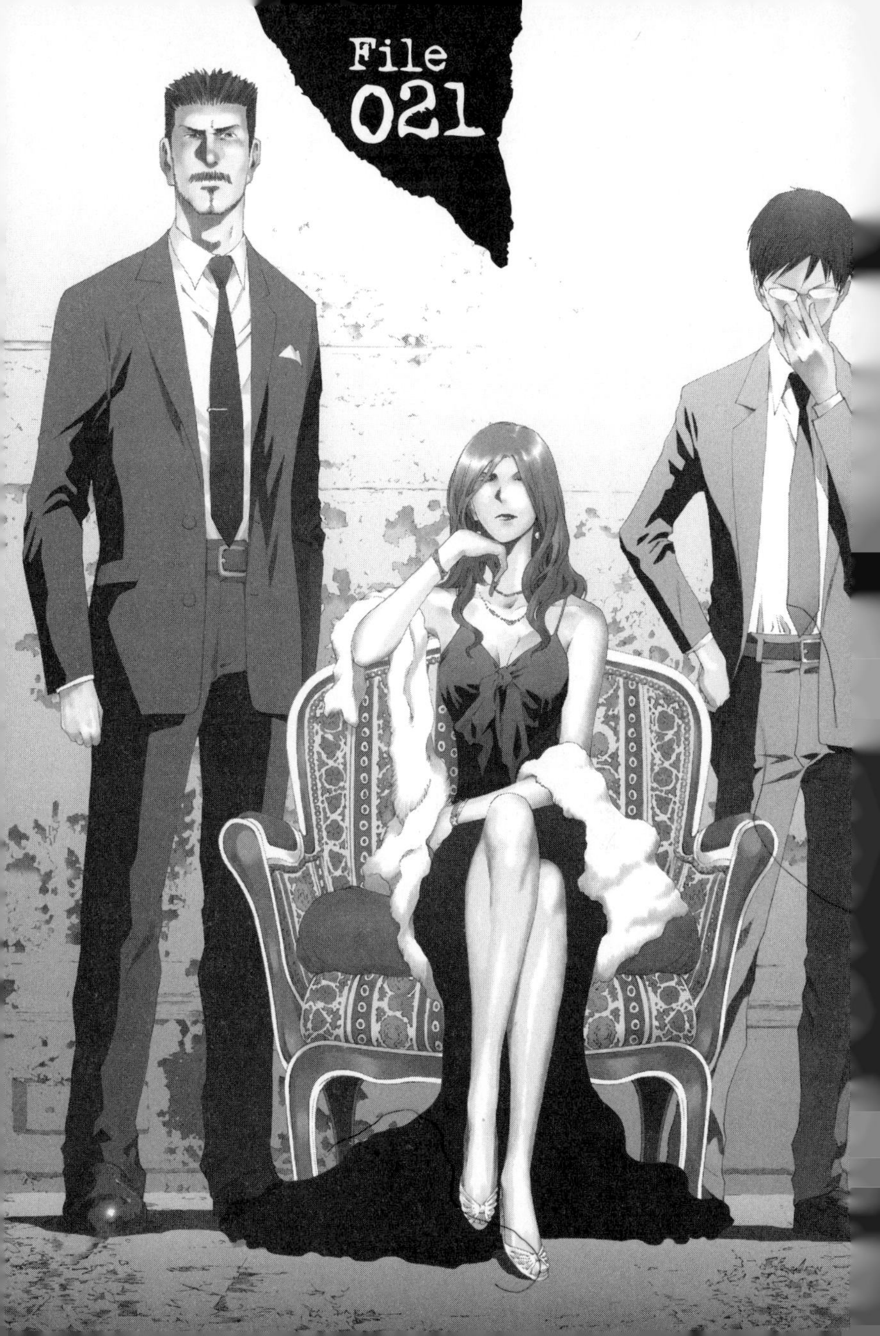
File
021

PROPHECY

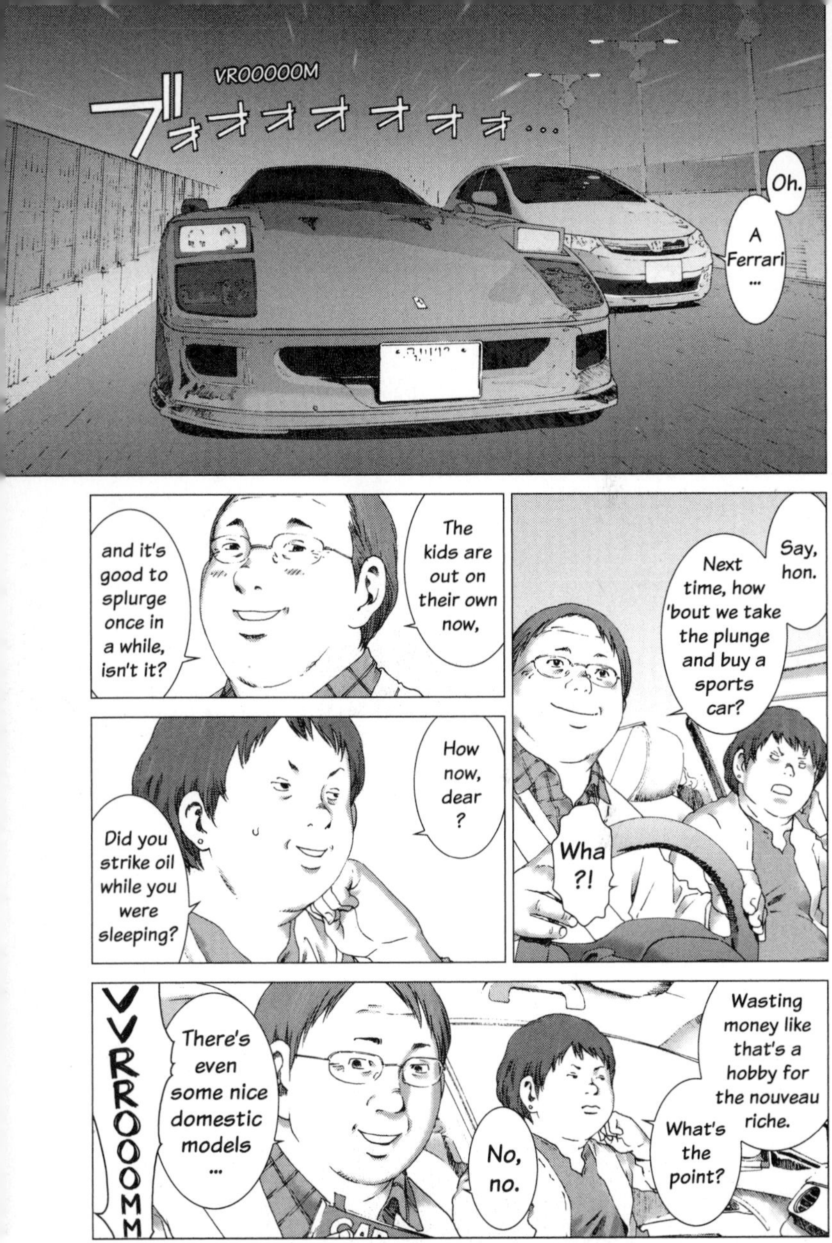
VROOOOOM
ブォォォォォォォ…
Oh.
A Ferrari …
Say, hon.
Next time, how 'bout we take the plunge and buy a sports car?
Wha ?!
The kids are out on their own now,
and it's good to splurge once in a while, isn't it?
How now, dear ?
Did you strike oil while you were sleeping?
Wasting money like that's a hobby for the nouveau riche.
What's the point?
No, no.
There's even some nice domestic models …
VVRROOOOMM

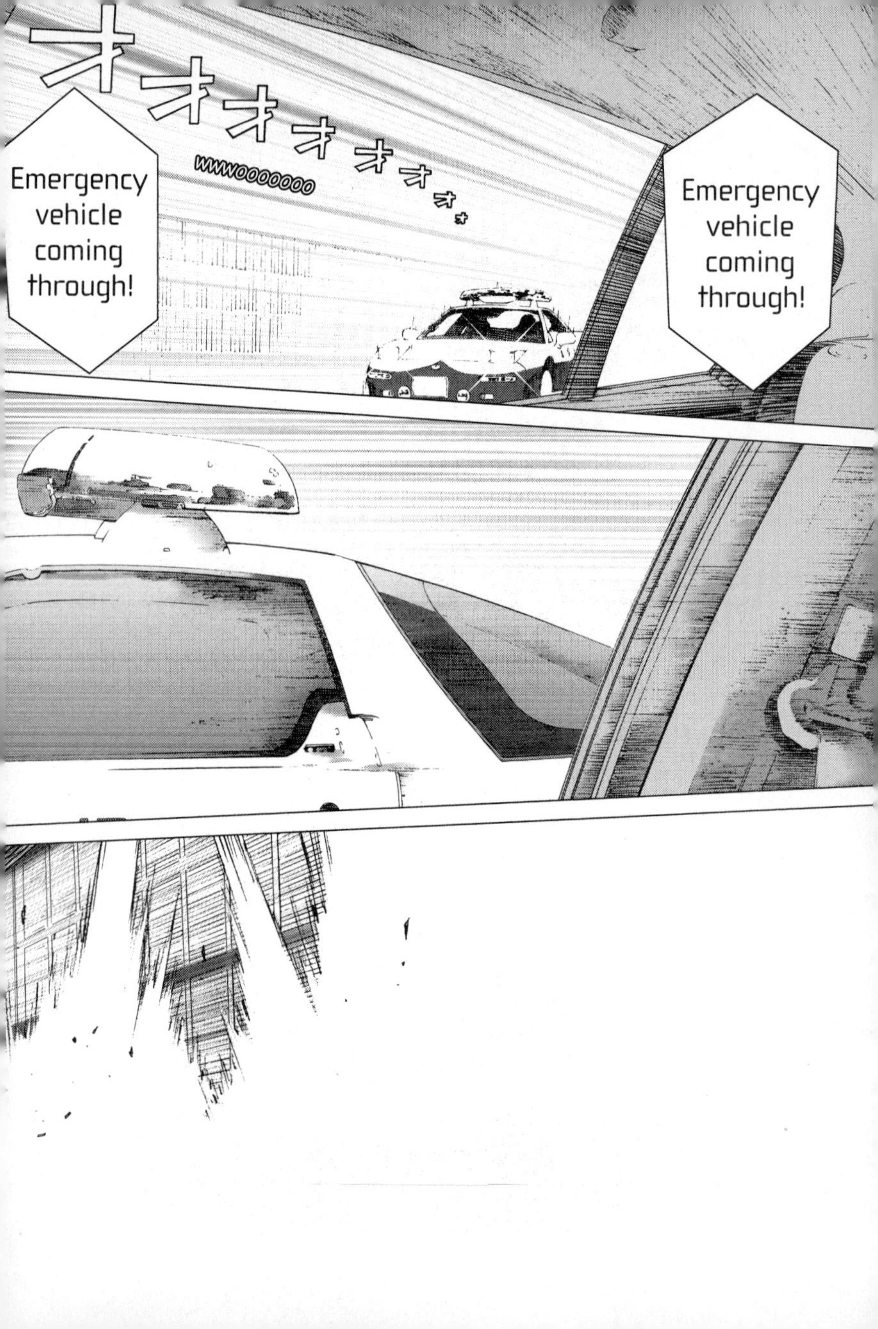
Emergency vehicle coming through!
Emergency vehicle coming through!
オオオオオオォォ
WWWOOOOOOO

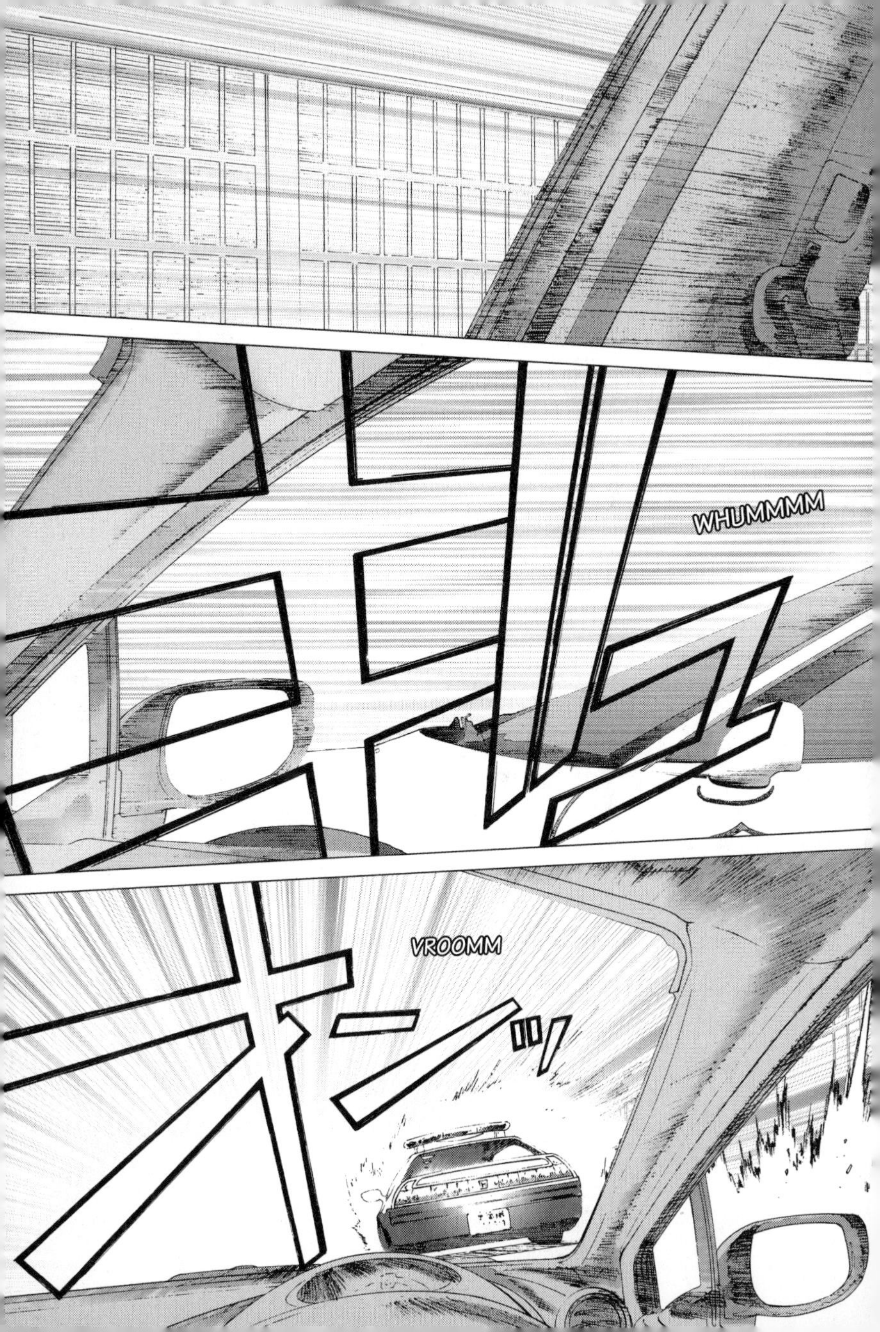
WHUMMMM
VROOMM

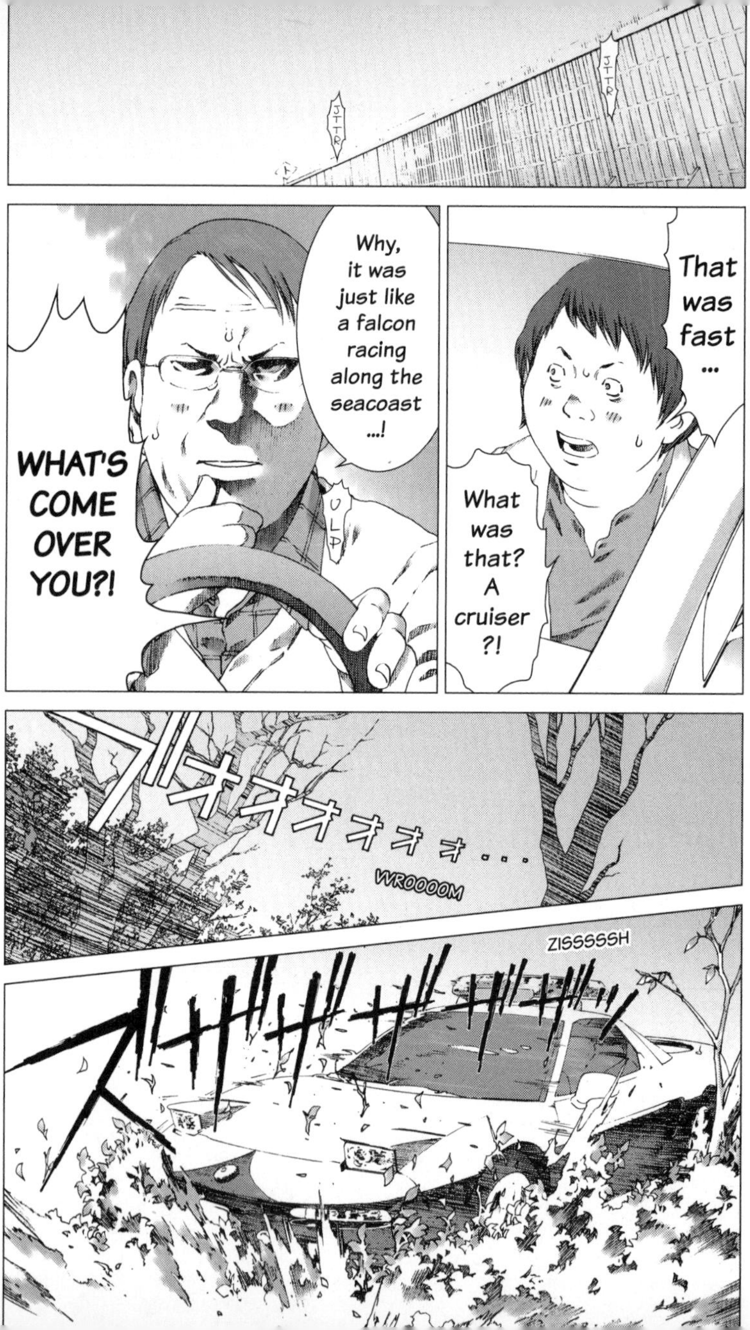
JTTR
JTTR
That was fast ...
What was that? A cruiser ?!
Why, it was just like a falcon racing along the seacoast ...!
WHAT'S COME OVER YOU?!
ULP
VVROOOOM
ZISSSSSH

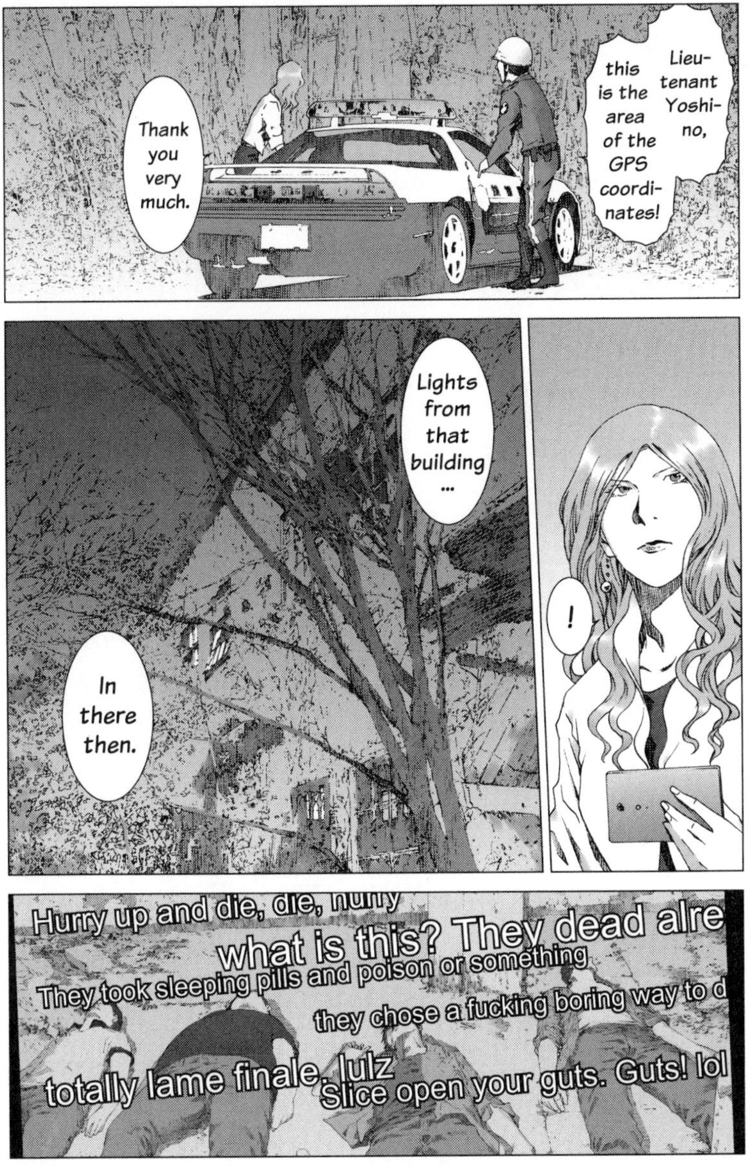

Lieutenant Yoshino, this is the area of the GPS coordinates!
Thank you very much.
!
Lights from that building ...
In there then.
Hurry up and die, die, hurry
what is this? They dead alre
They took sleeping pills and poison or something
they chose a fucking boring way to d
totally lame finale, lulz
Slice open your guts. Guts! lol

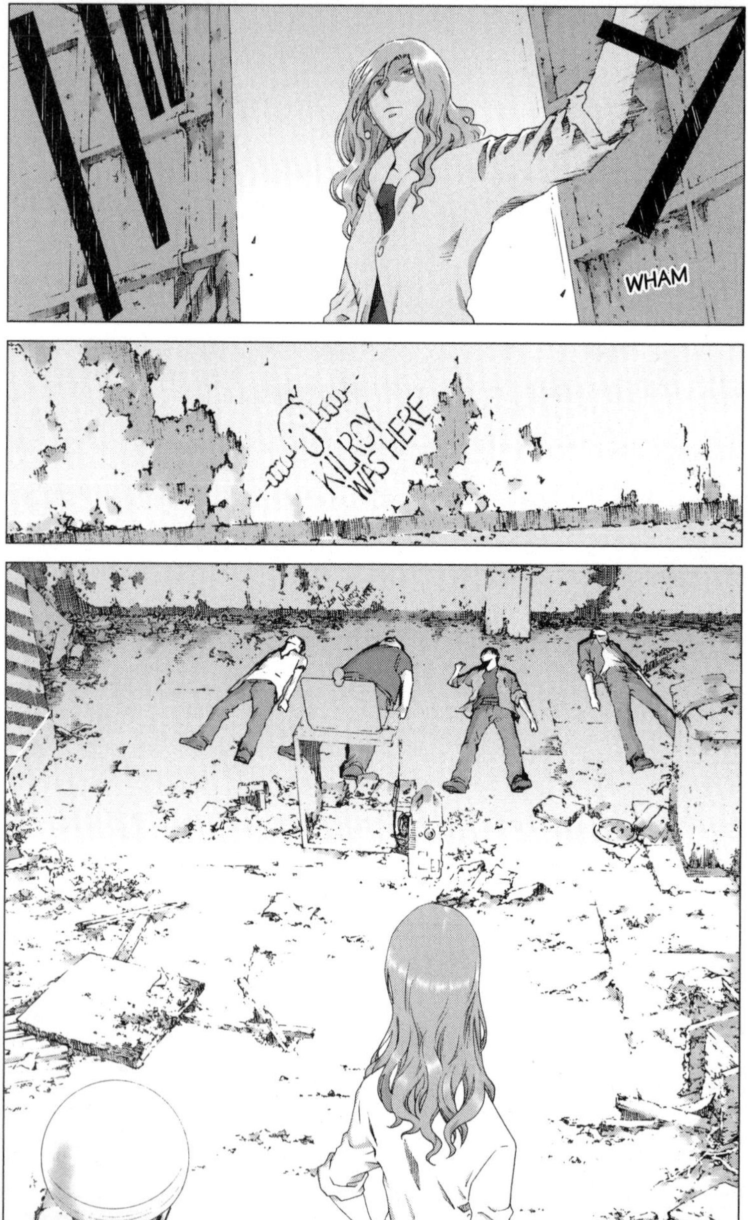
WHAM
KILROY WAS HERE

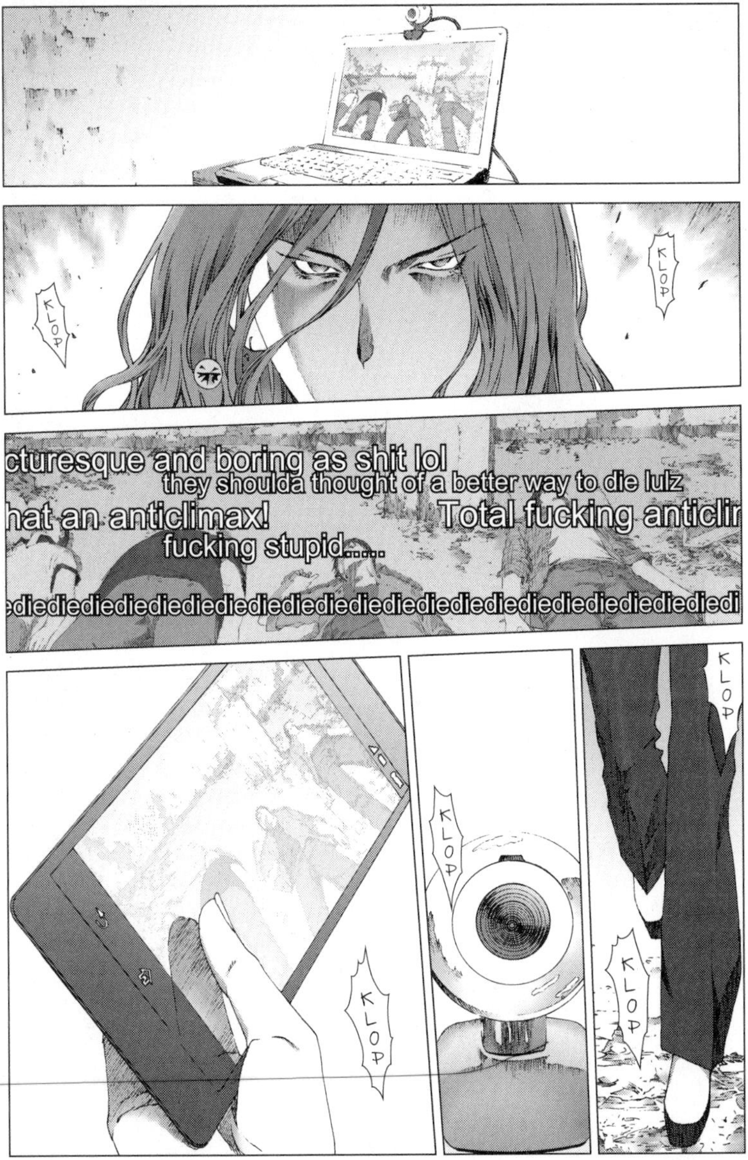
KLOP
KLOP
cturesque and boring as shit lol
they shoulda thought of a better way to die lulz
hat an anticlimax!
Total fucking anticli
fucking stupid.....
ediediediediediediediediediediediediediediediediediediediediedi
KLOP
KLOP
KLOP
KLOP

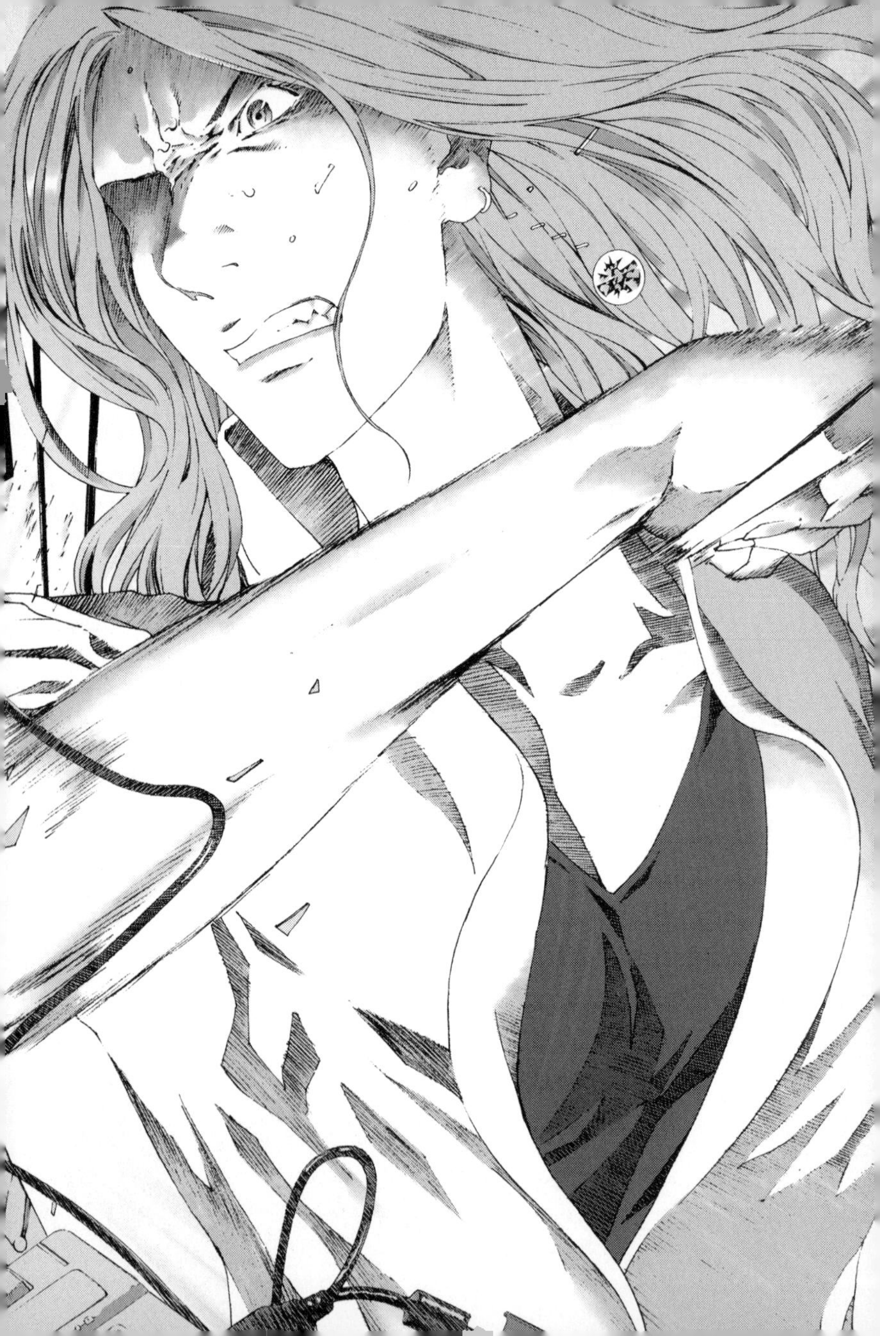

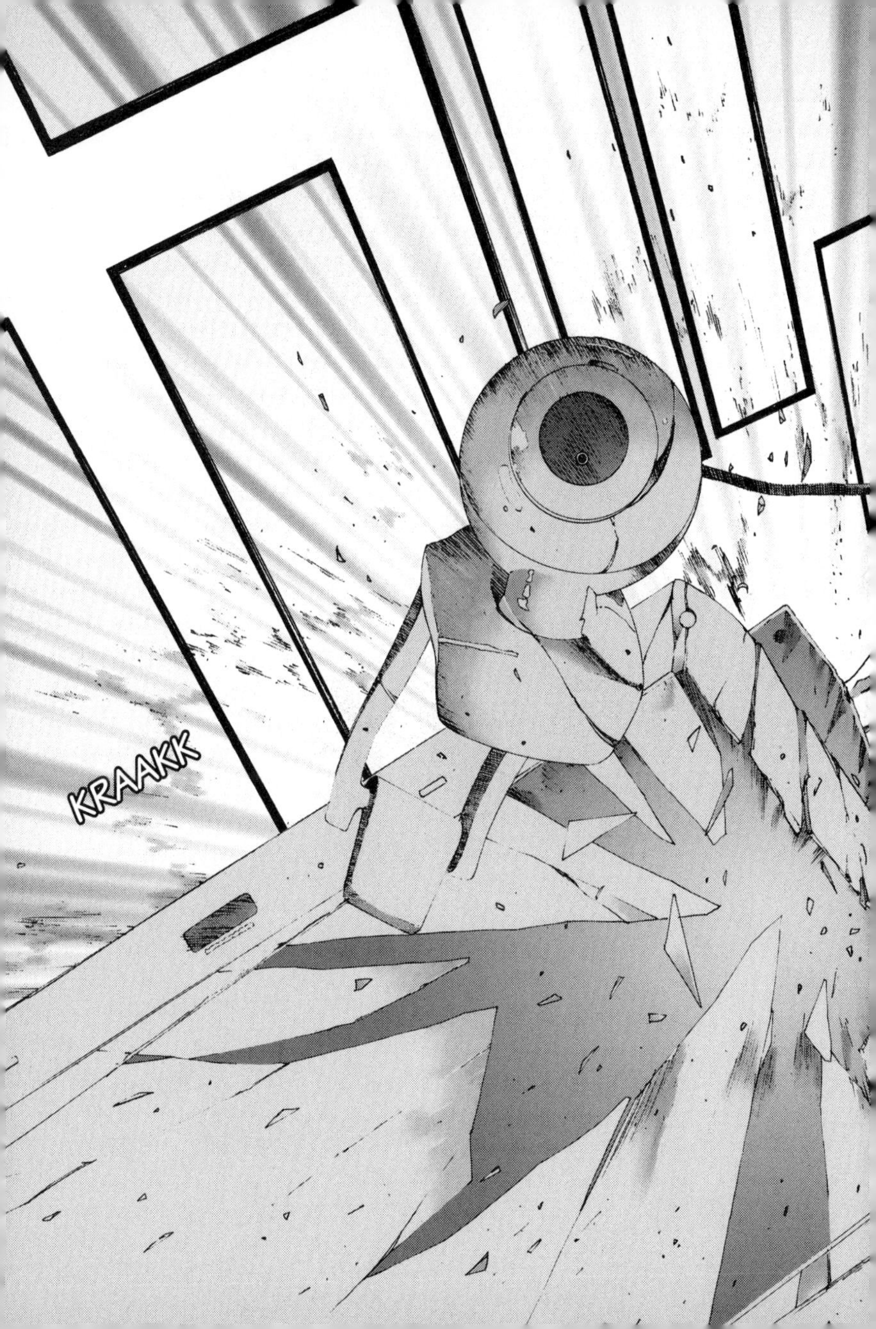
KRAAKK

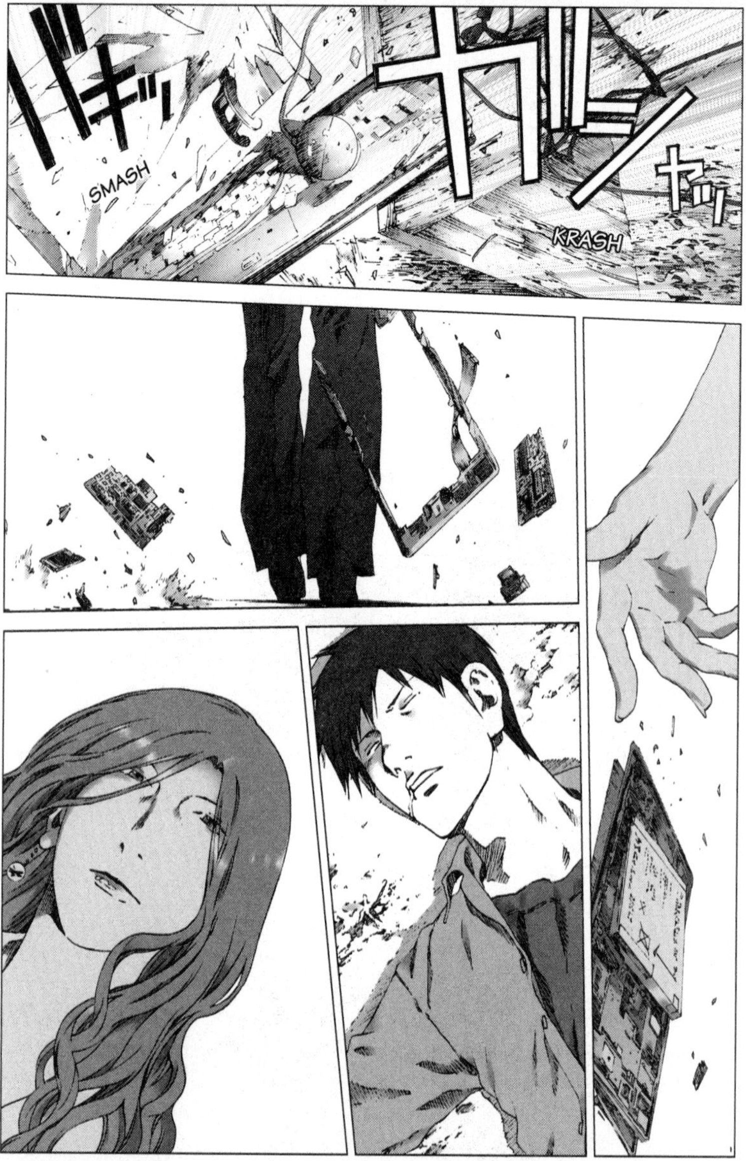
KRASH
SMASH

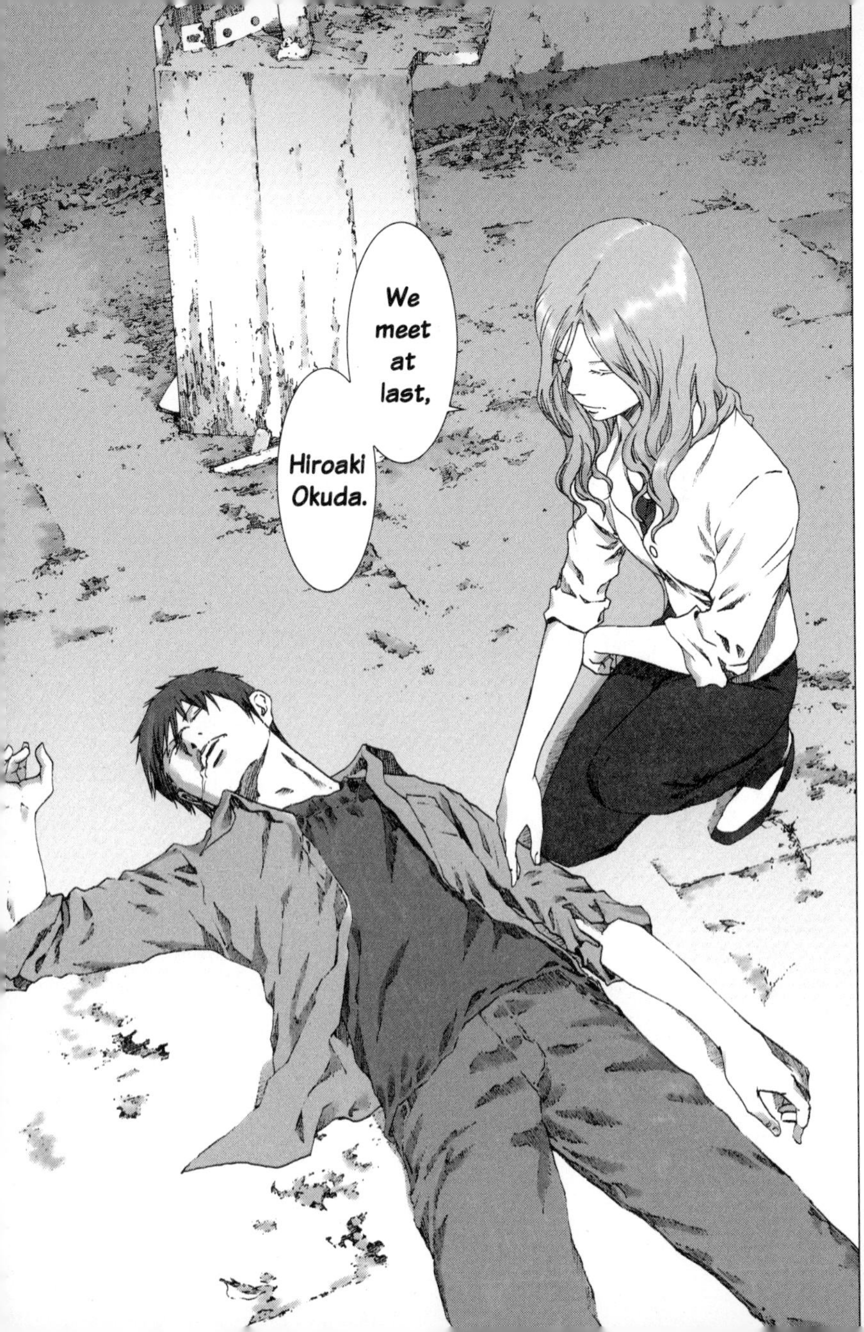
We meet at last,
Hiroaki Okuda.

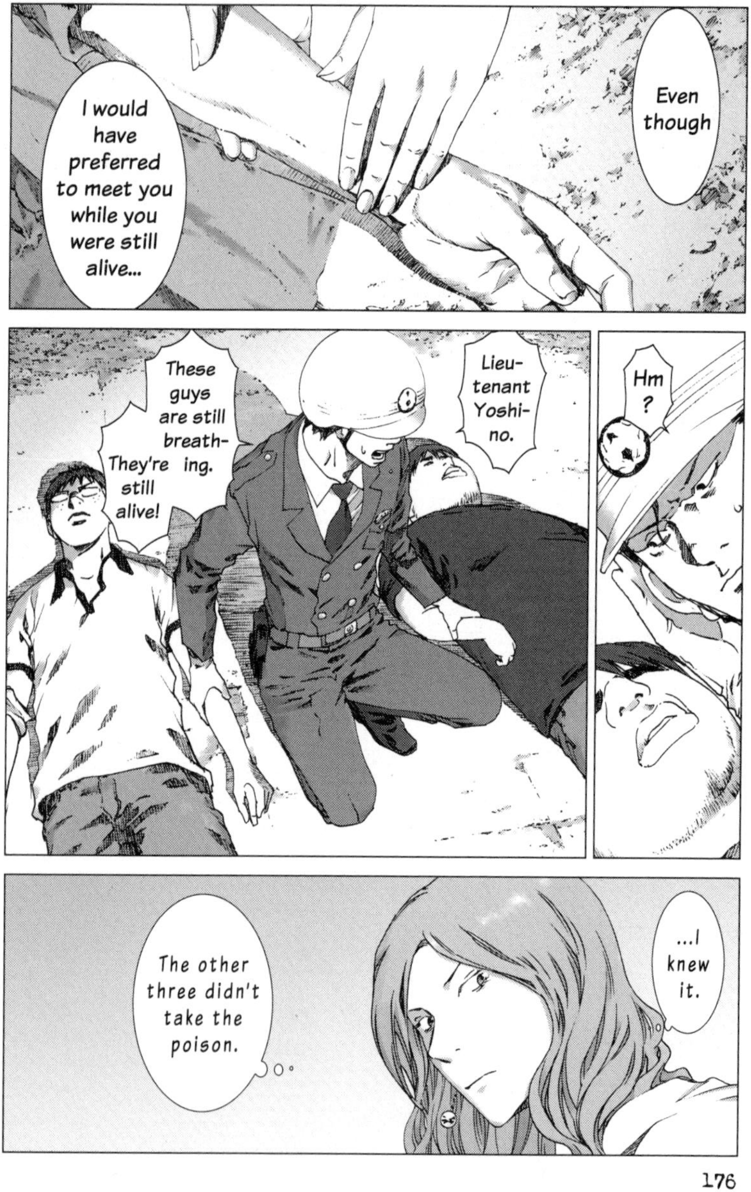
Even though
I would have preferred to meet you while you were still alive...
Hm?
Lieutenant Yoshino.
These guys are still breathing.
They're still alive!
...I knew it.
The other three didn't take the poison.

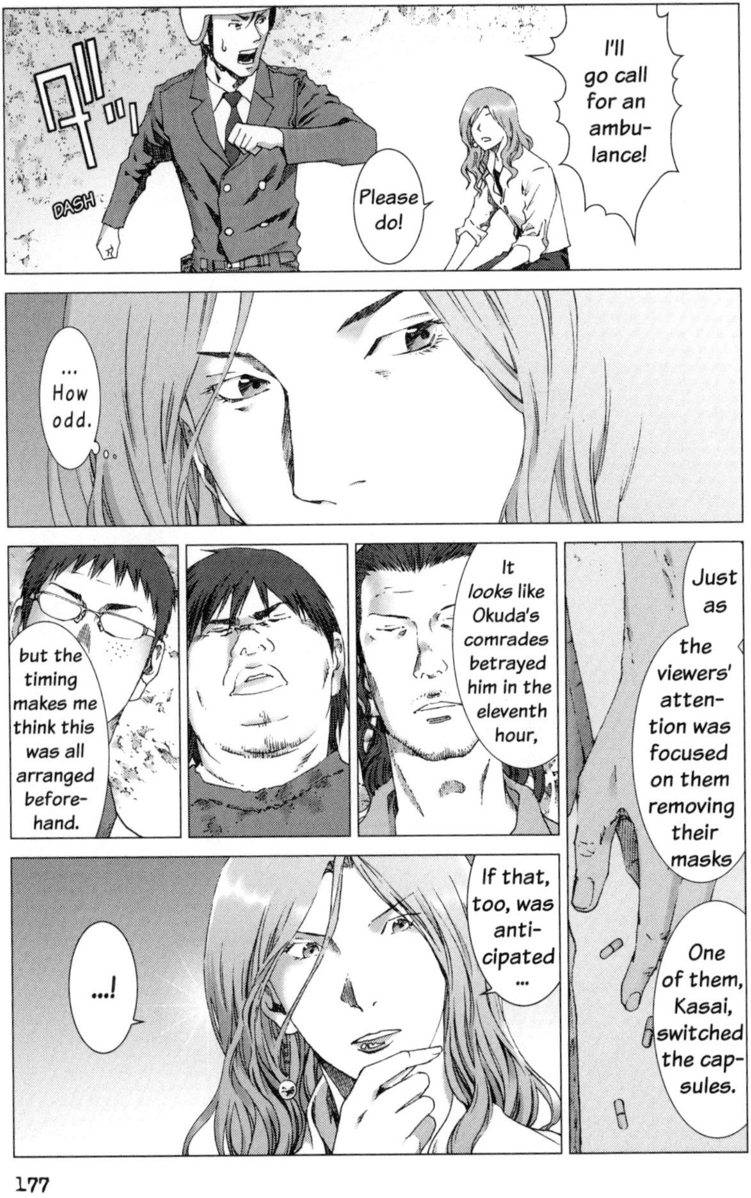
I'll go call for an ambulance!
Please do!
DASH
... How odd.
Just as the viewers' attention was focused on them removing their masks
One of them, Kasai, switched the capsules.
It looks like Okuda's comrades betrayed him in the eleventh hour,
but the timing makes me think this was all arranged beforehand.
If that, too, was anticipated ...
...!

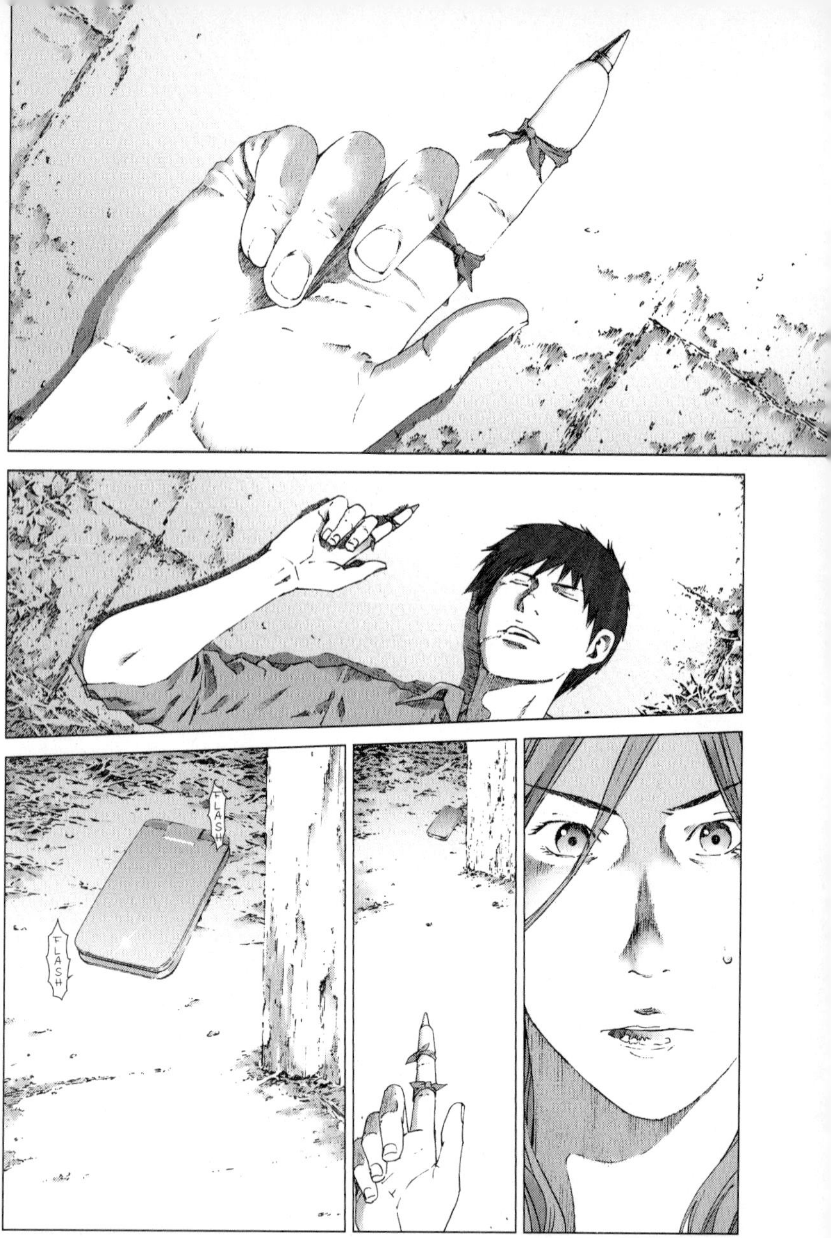
FLASH
FLASH

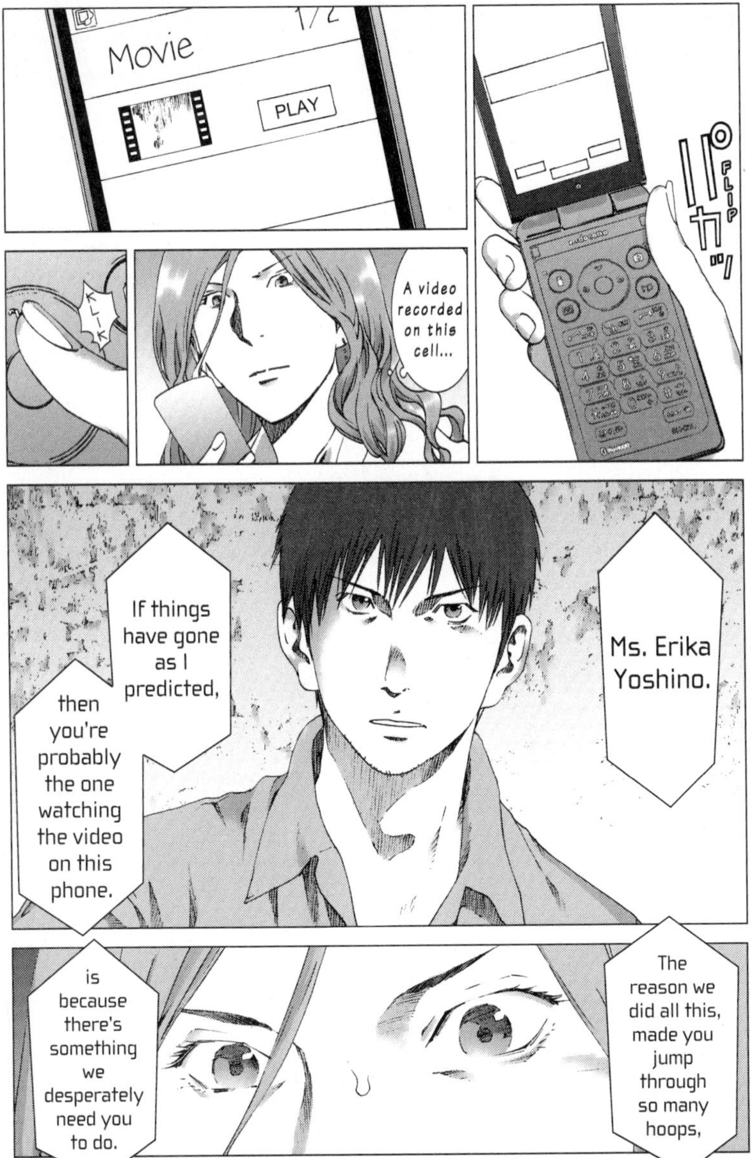
FLIP
1/2
Movie
PLAY
A video recorded on this cell...
KLIK
Ms. Erika Yoshino.
If things have gone as I predicted,
then you're probably the one watching the video on this phone.
The reason we did all this, made you jump through so many hoops,
is because there's something we desperately need you to do.

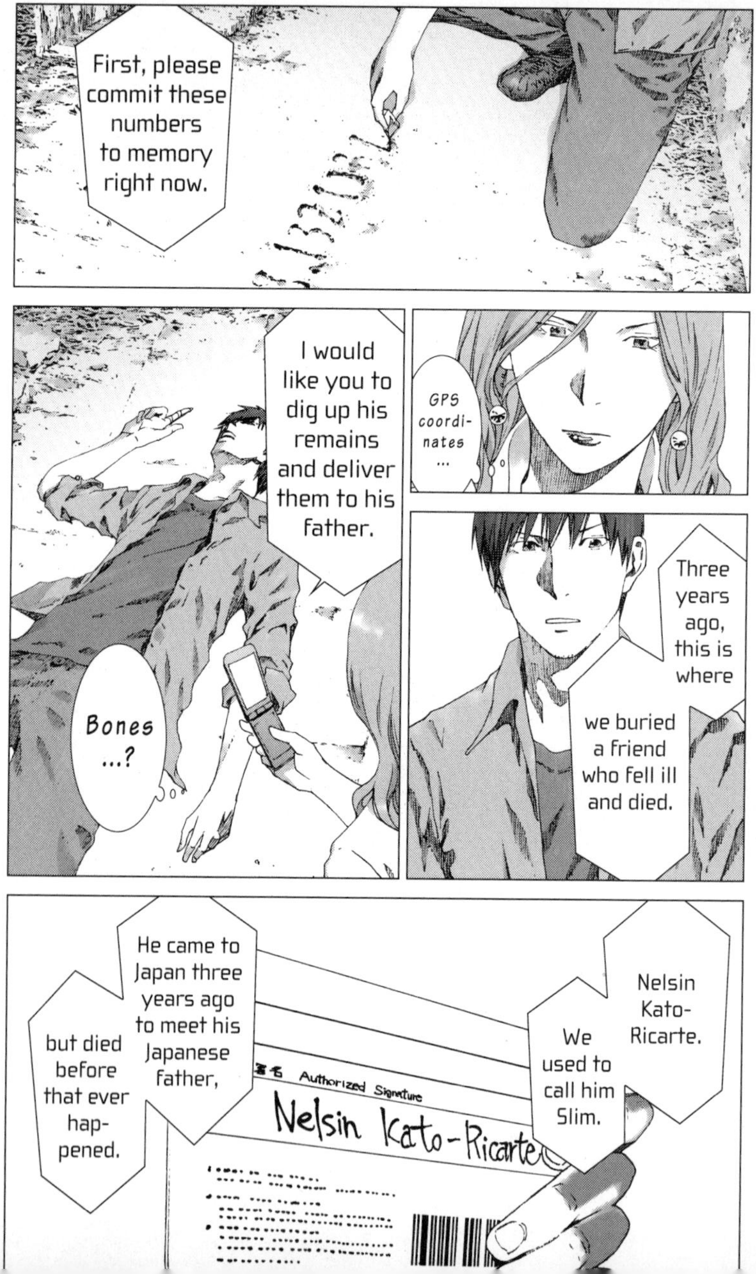
First, please commit these numbers to memory right now.
GPS coordinates ...
Three years ago, this is where
we buried a friend who fell ill and died.
I would like you to dig up his remains and deliver them to his father.
Bones ...?
Nelsin Kato-Ricarte.
We used to call him Slim.
He came to Japan three years ago to meet his Japanese father,
but died before that ever happened.
Authorized Signature
Nelsin Kato-Ricarte

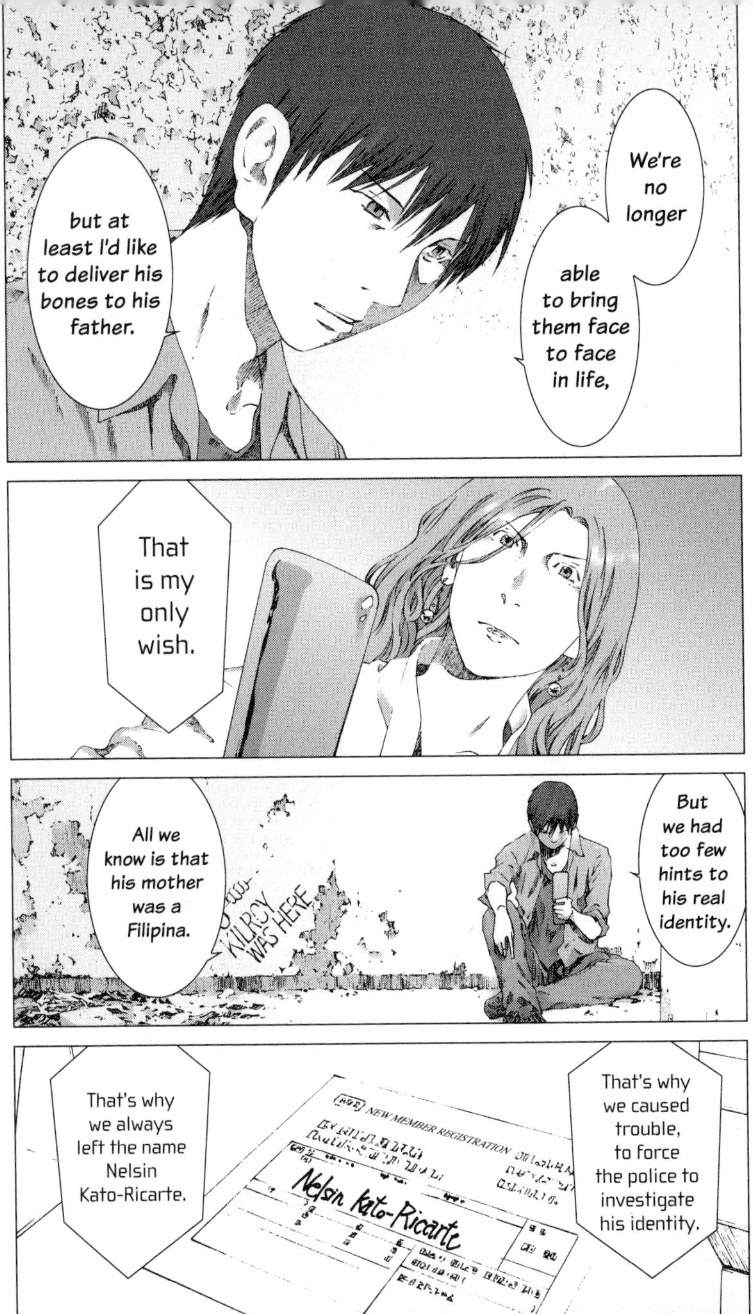
We're no longer
able to bring them face to face in life,
but at least I'd like to deliver his bones to his father.
That is my only wish.
But we had too few hints to his real identity.
All we know is that his mother was a Filipina.
KILROY WAS HERE
That's why we caused trouble, to force the police to investigate his identity.
That's why we always left the name Nelsin Kato-Ricarte.
NEW MEMBER REGISTRATION
Nelsin Kato-Ricarte

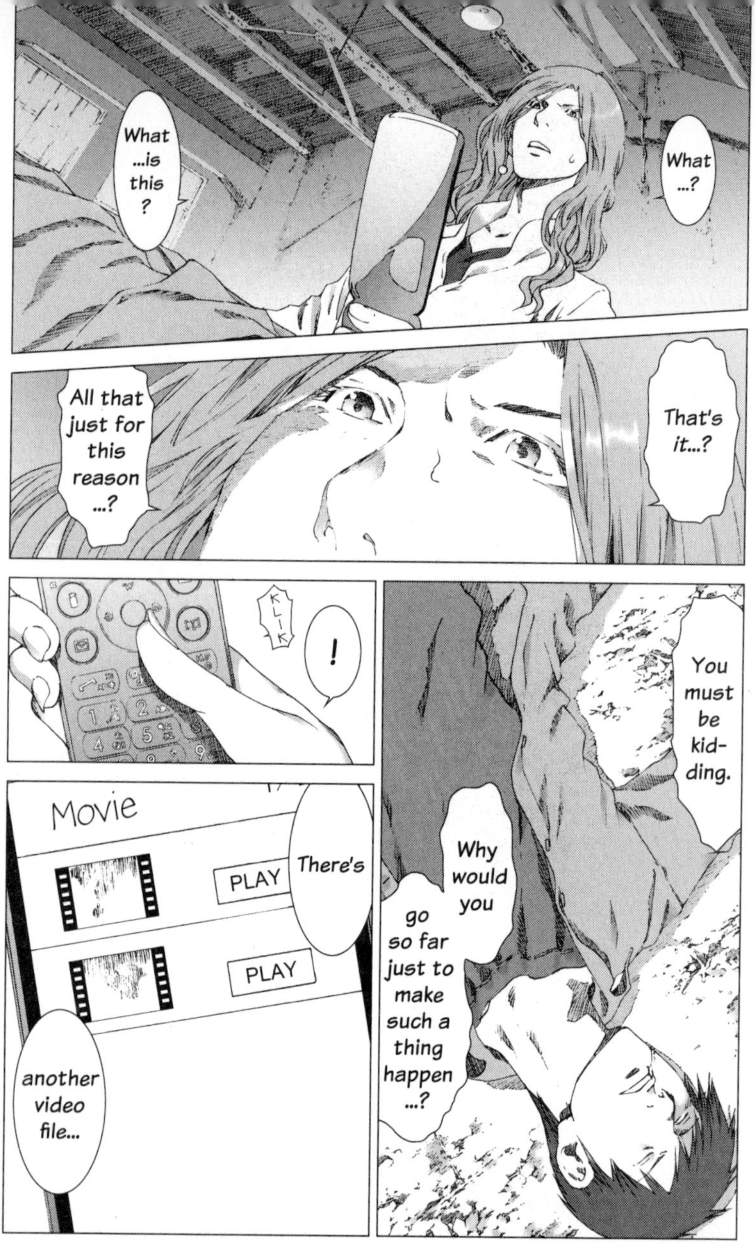
What ...?
What ...is this ?
That's it...?
All that just for this reason ...?
You must be kid-ding.
Why would you go so far just to make such a thing happen ...?
KLIK
!
Movie
PLAY
PLAY
There's
another video file...

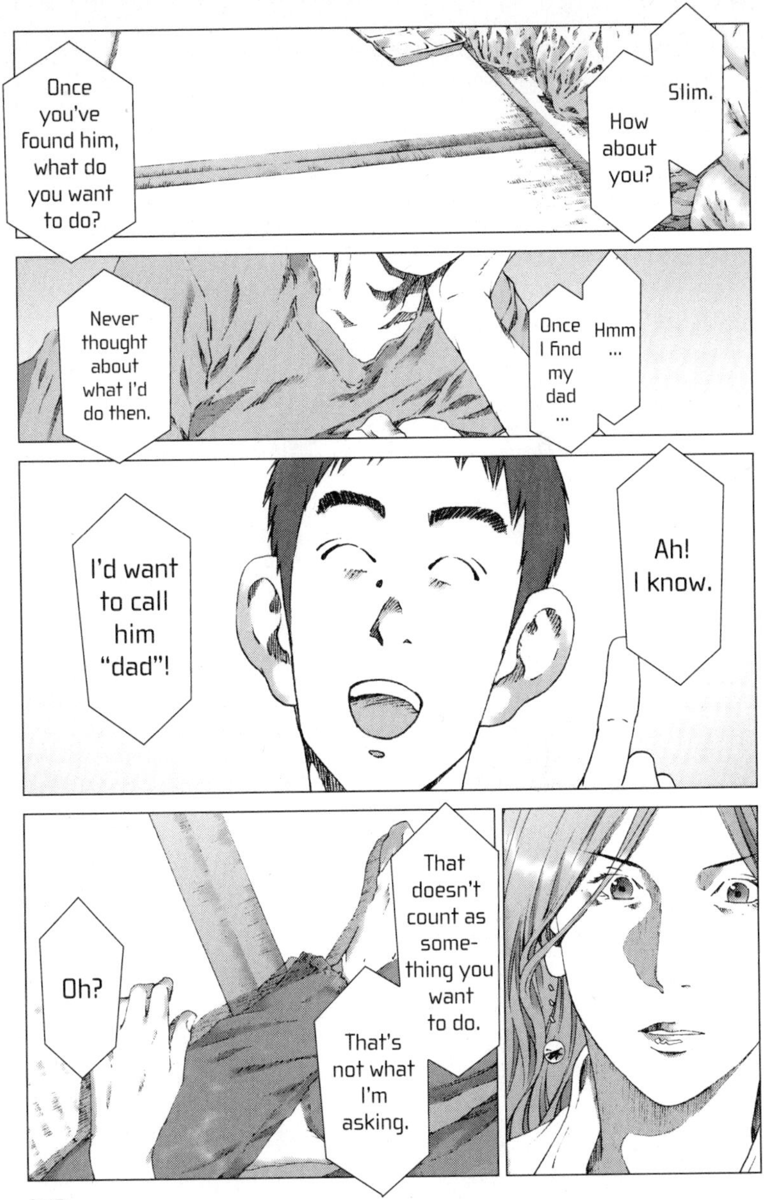
Slim.
How about you?
Once you've found him, what do you want to do?
Hmm ...
Once I find my dad ...
Never thought about what I'd do then.
Ah! I know.
I'd want to call him "dad"!
That doesn't count as some-thing you want to do.
That's not what I'm asking.
Oh?

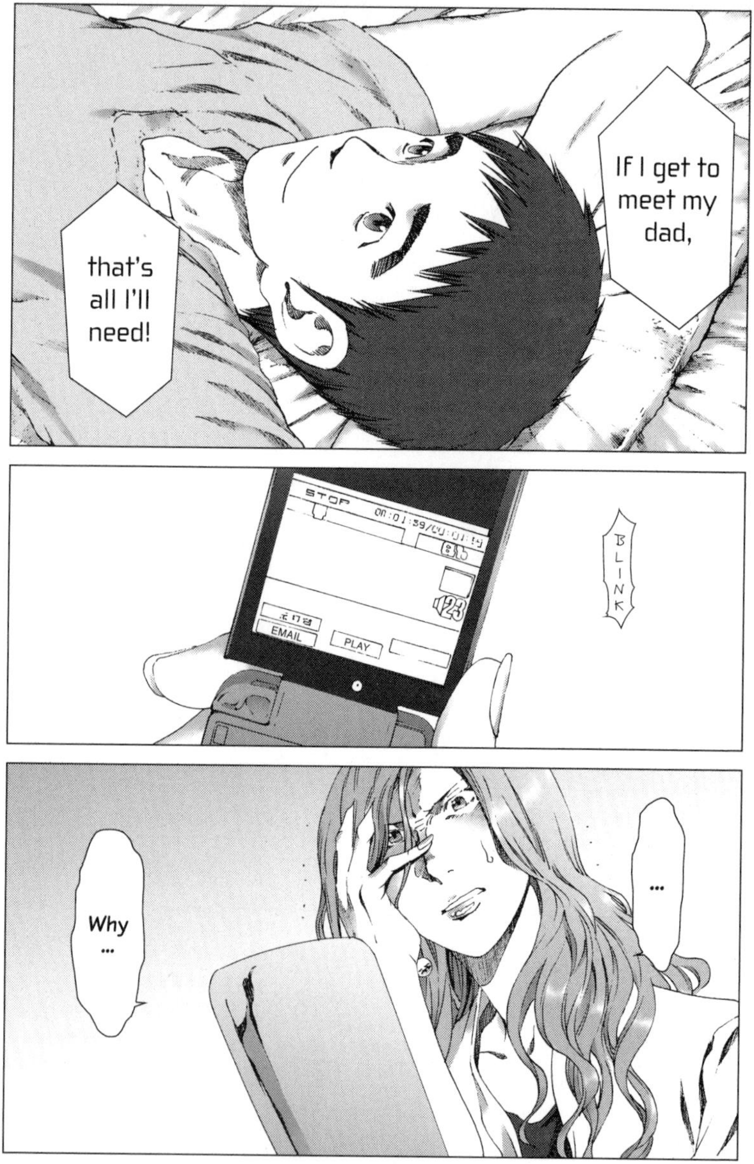
If I get to meet my dad,
that's all I'll need!
STOP
EMAIL
PLAY
BLINK
...
Why ...

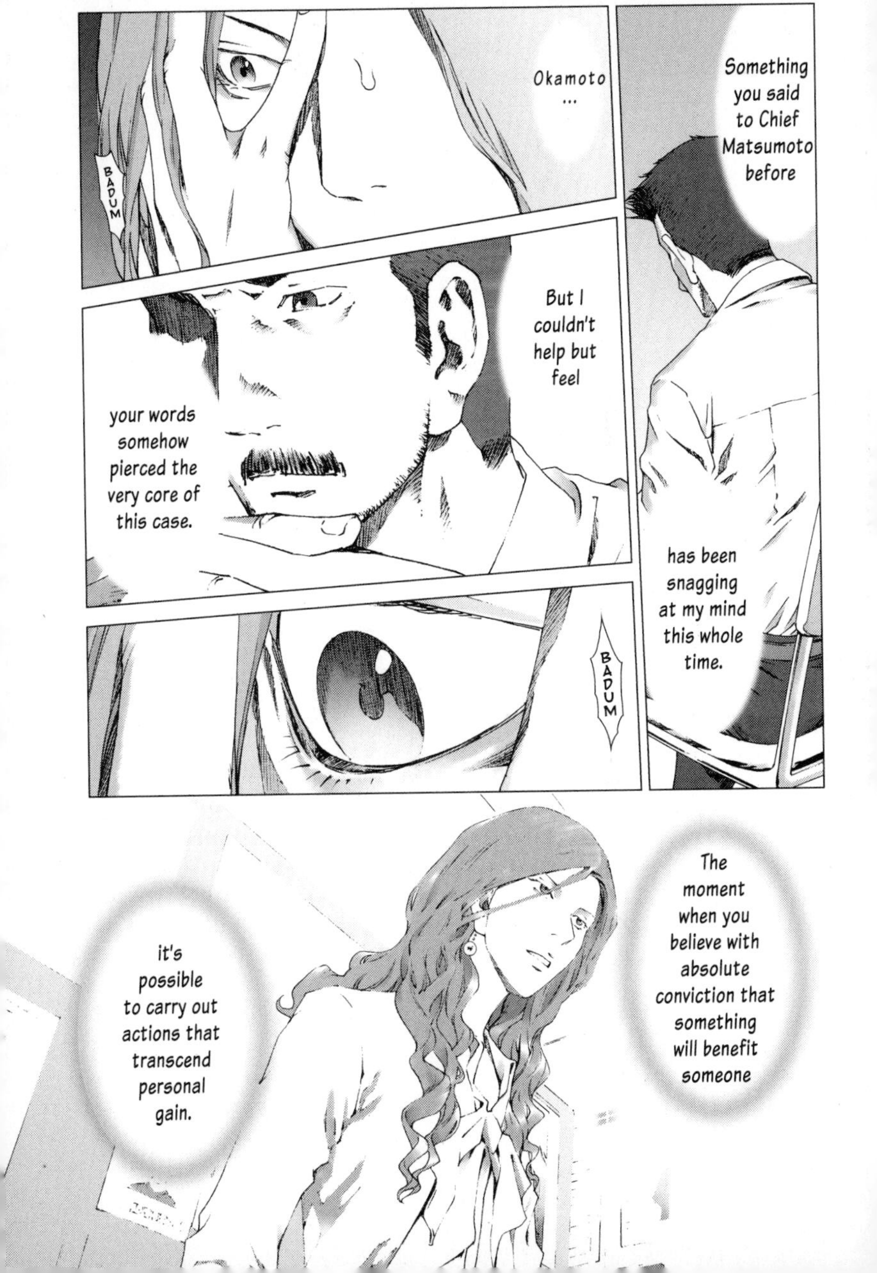
Something you said to Chief Matsumoto before
has been snagging at my mind this whole time.
Okamoto...
BADUM
But I couldn't help but feel
your words somehow pierced the very core of this case.
BADUM
The moment when you believe with absolute conviction that something will benefit someone
it's possible to carry out actions that transcend personal gain.

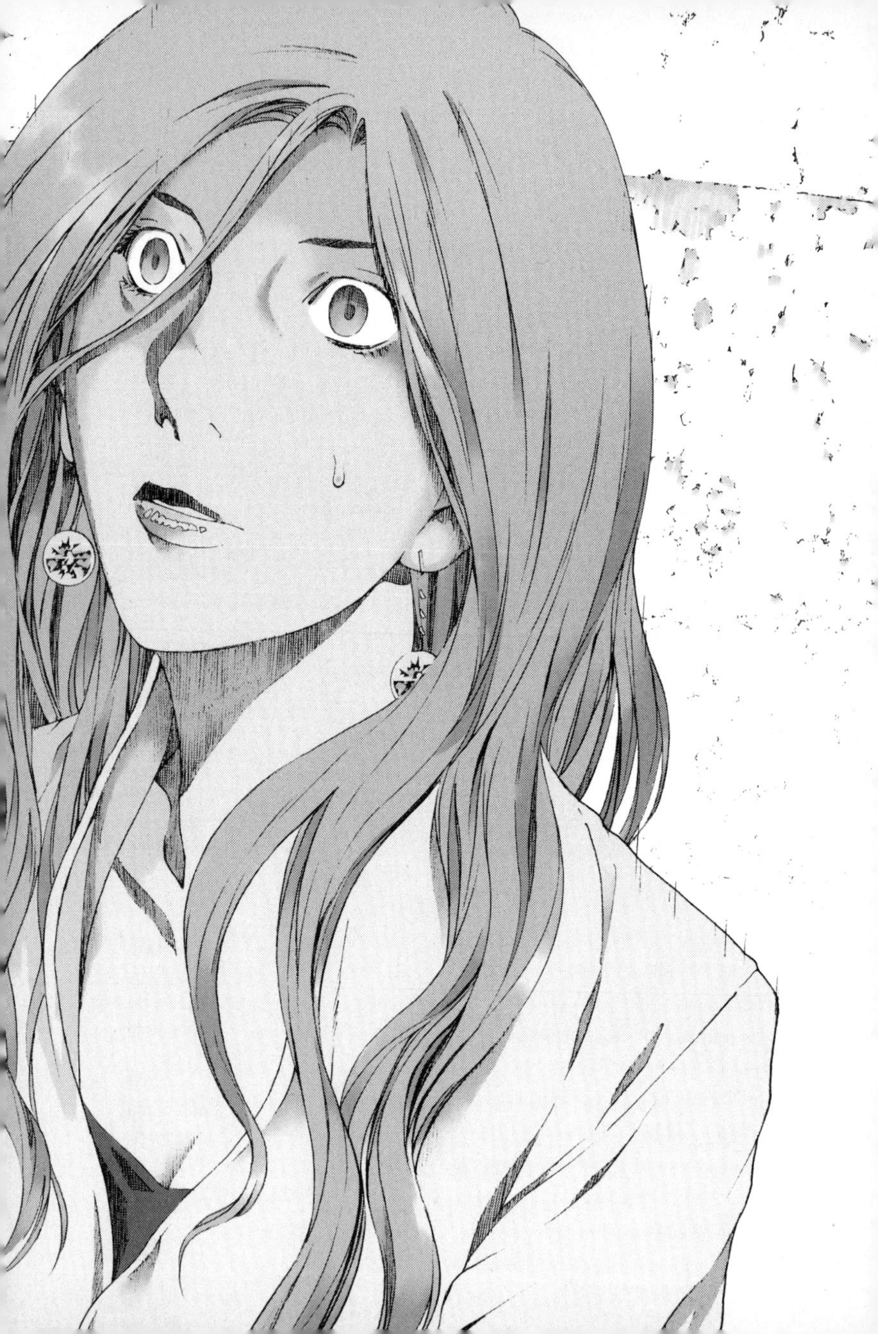

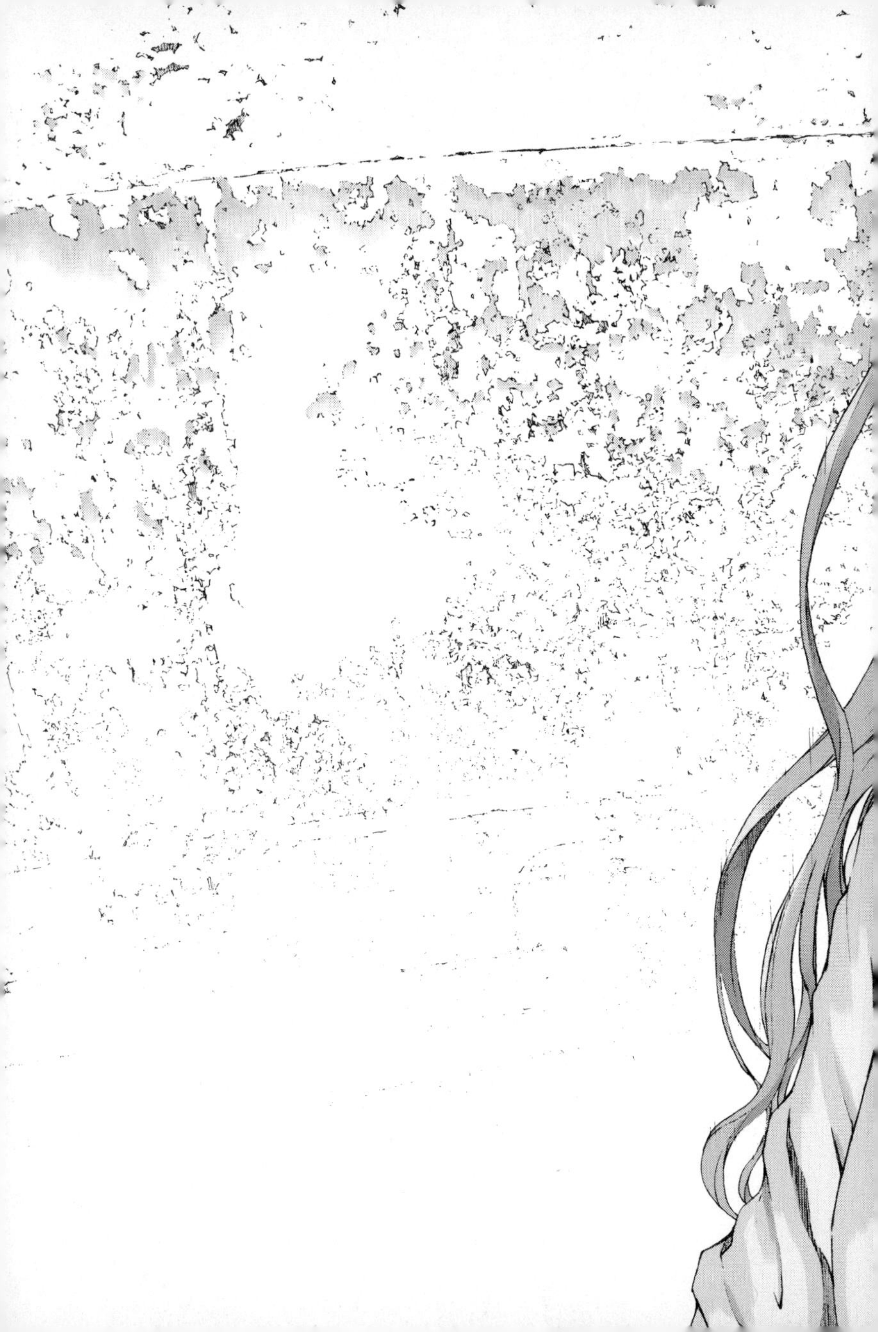

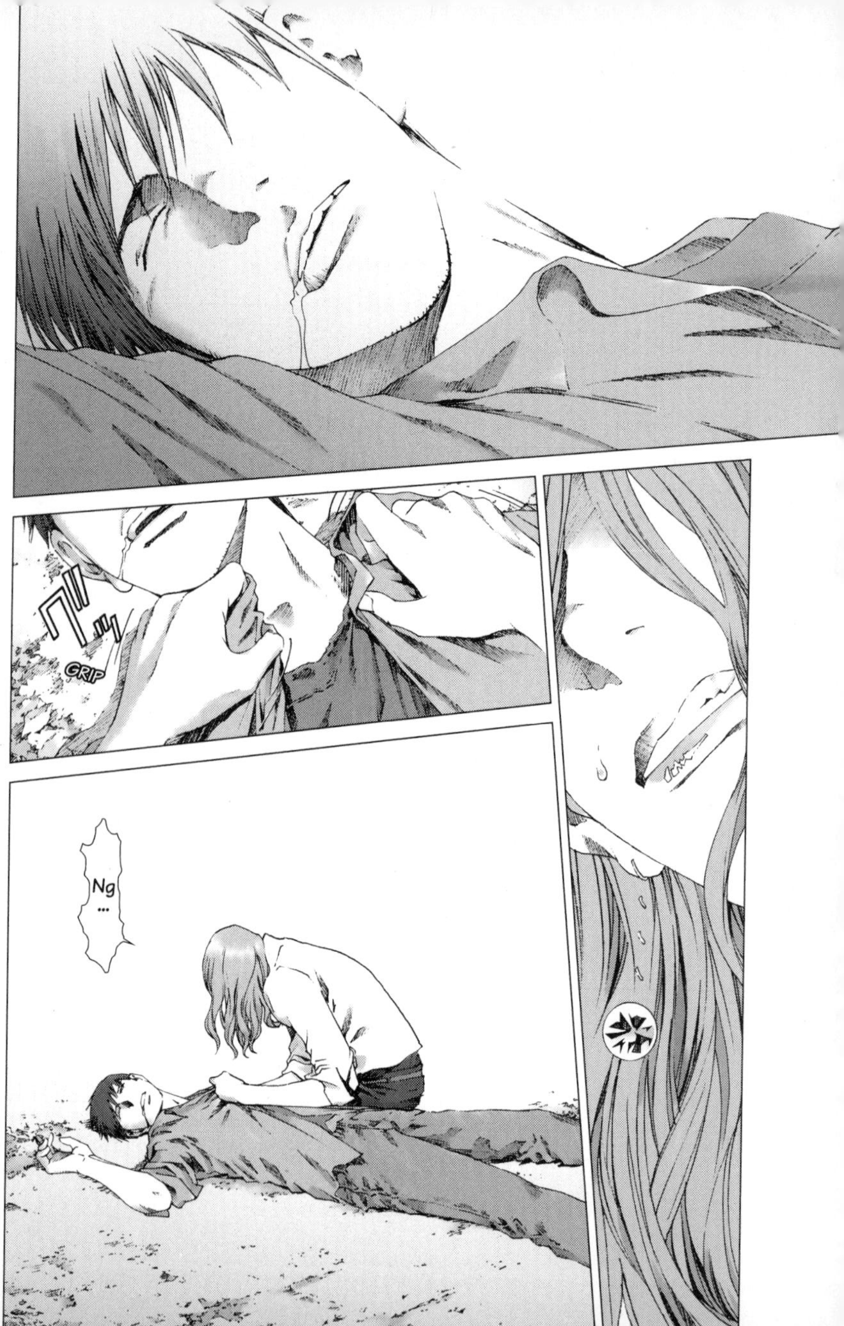
GRIP
Ng ...

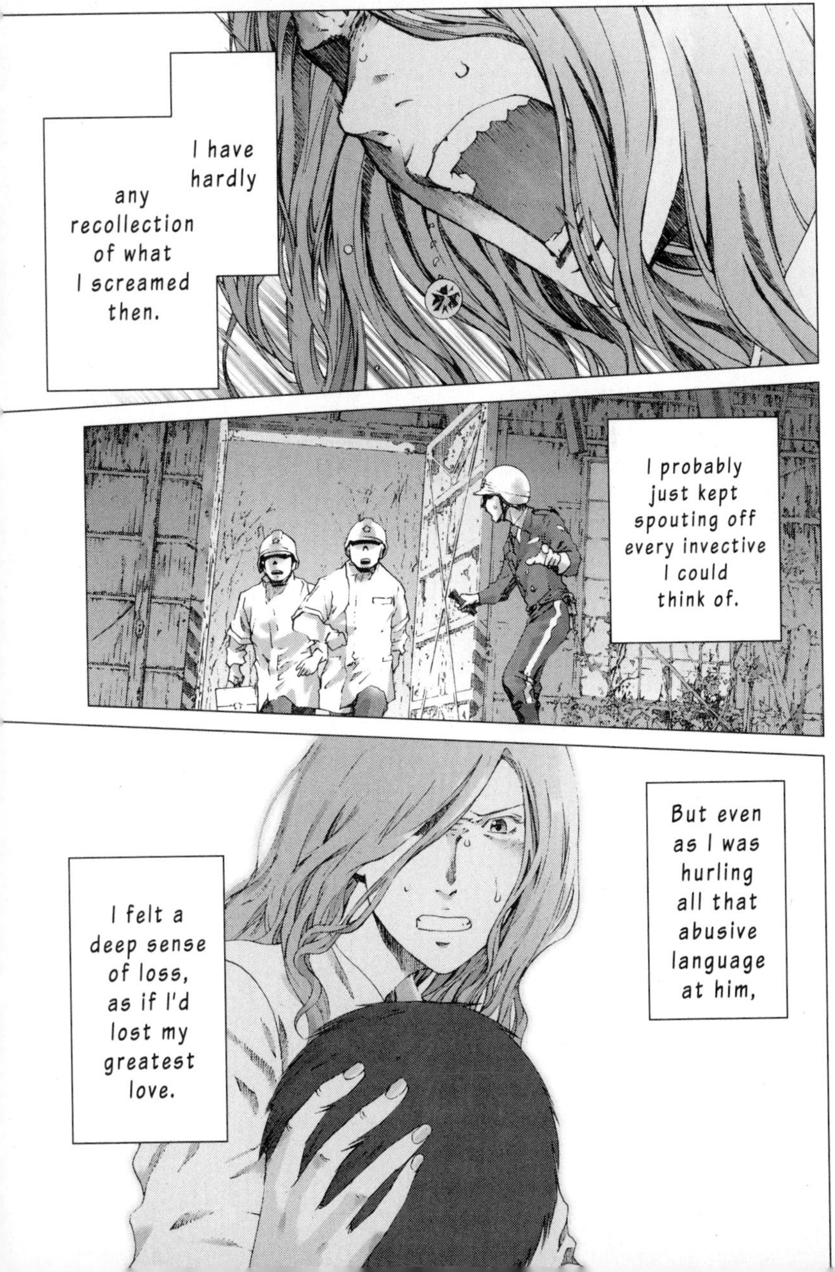
I have hardly any recollection of what I screamed then.
I probably just kept spouting off every invective I could think of.
But even as I was hurling all that abusive language at him,
I felt a deep sense of loss, as if I'd lost my greatest love.

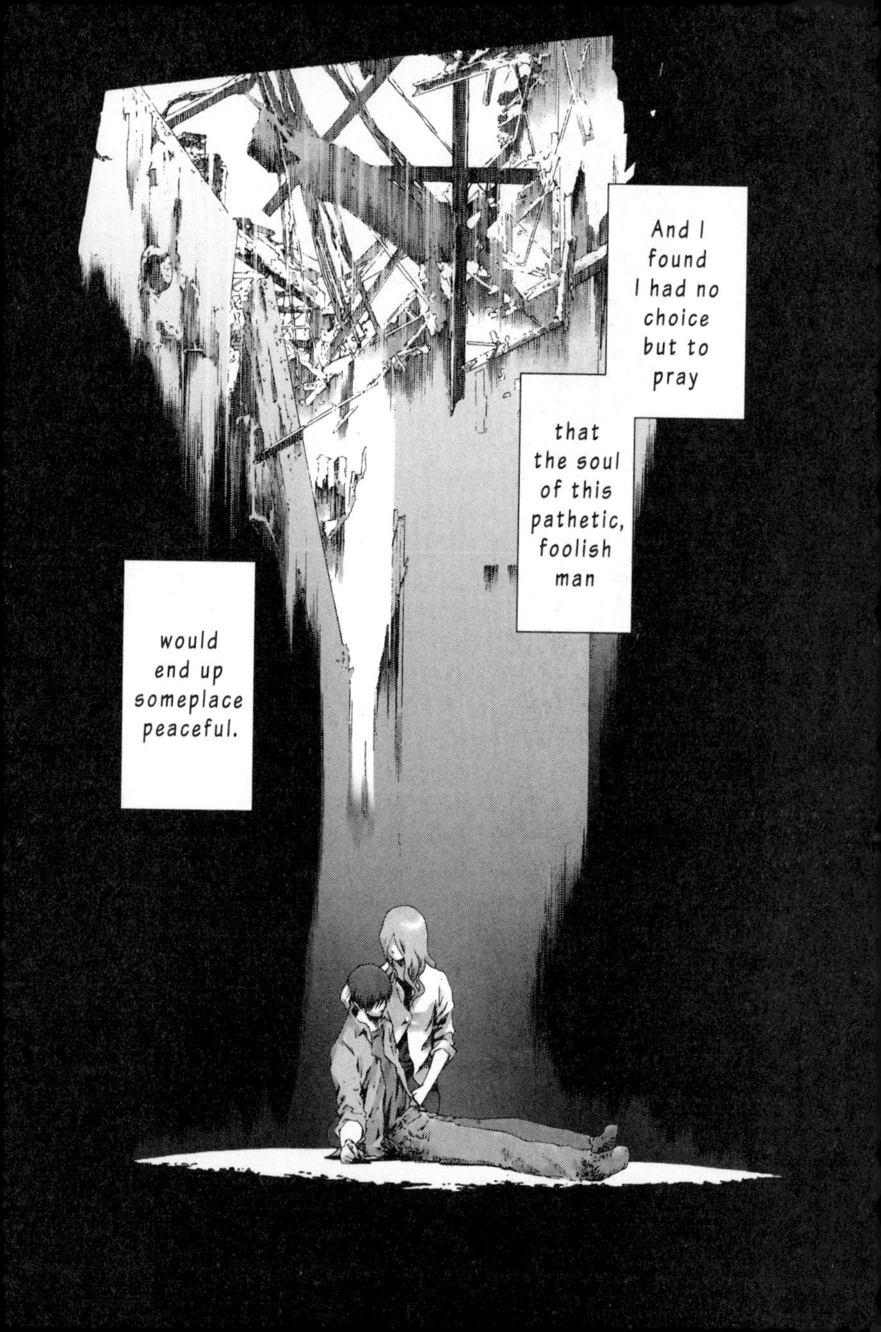
And I found I had no choice but to pray
that the soul of this pathetic, foolish man
would end up someplace peaceful.

PROPHECY

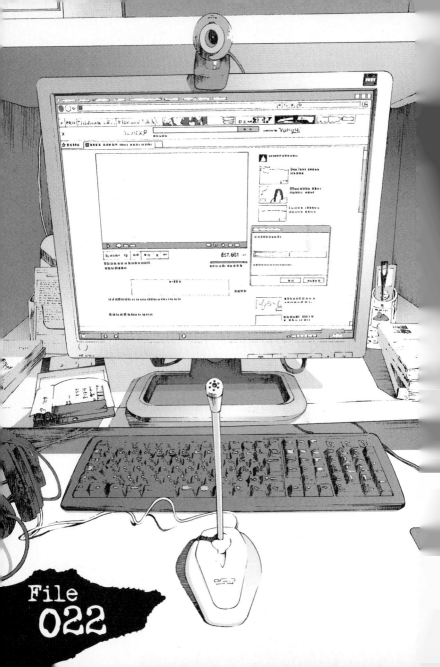

File
022

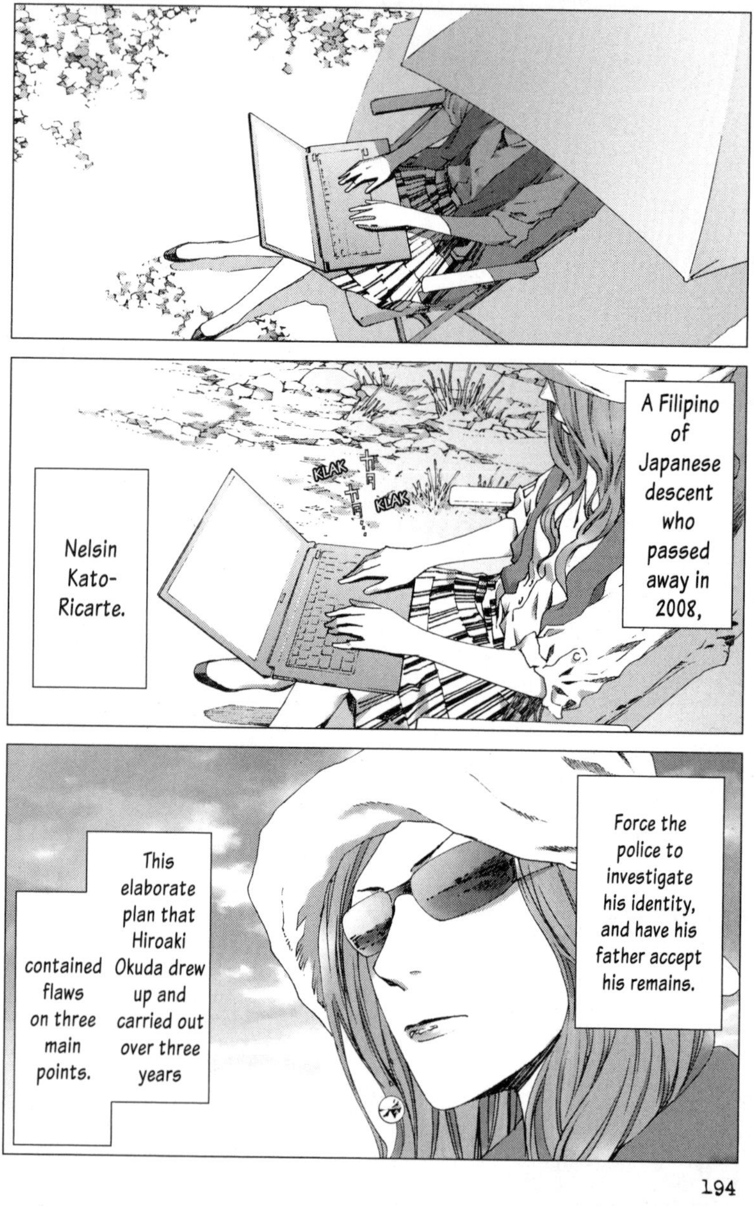
A Filipino of Japanese descent who passed away in 2008,
KLAK
KLAK
Nelsin Kato-Ricarte.
Force the police to investigate his identity, and have his father accept his remains.
This elaborate plan that Hiroaki Okuda drew up and carried out over three years
contained flaws on three main points.

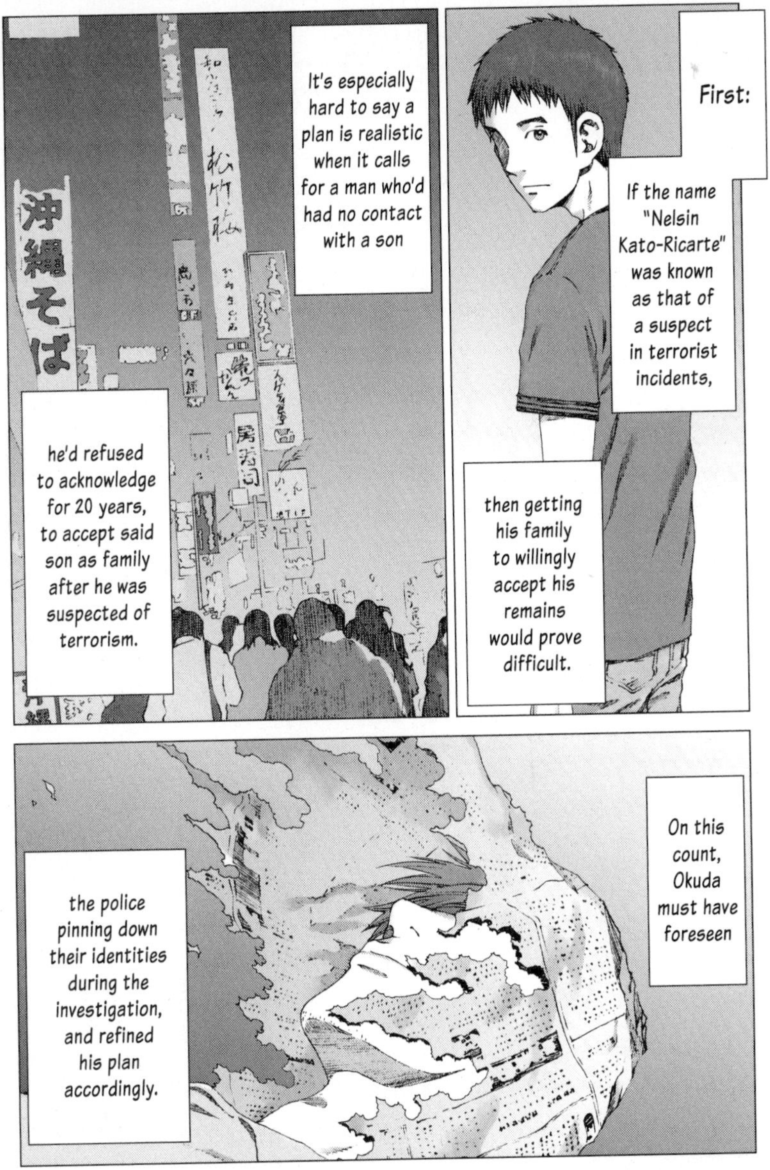
First:
If the name "Nelsin Kato-Ricarte" was known as that of a suspect in terrorist incidents,
then getting his family to willingly accept his remains would prove difficult.
It's especially hard to say a plan is realistic when it calls for a man who'd had no contact with a son
沖縄そば
he'd refused to acknowledge for 20 years, to accept said son as family after he was suspected of terrorism.
On this count, Okuda must have foreseen
the police pinning down their identities during the investigation, and refined his plan accordingly.

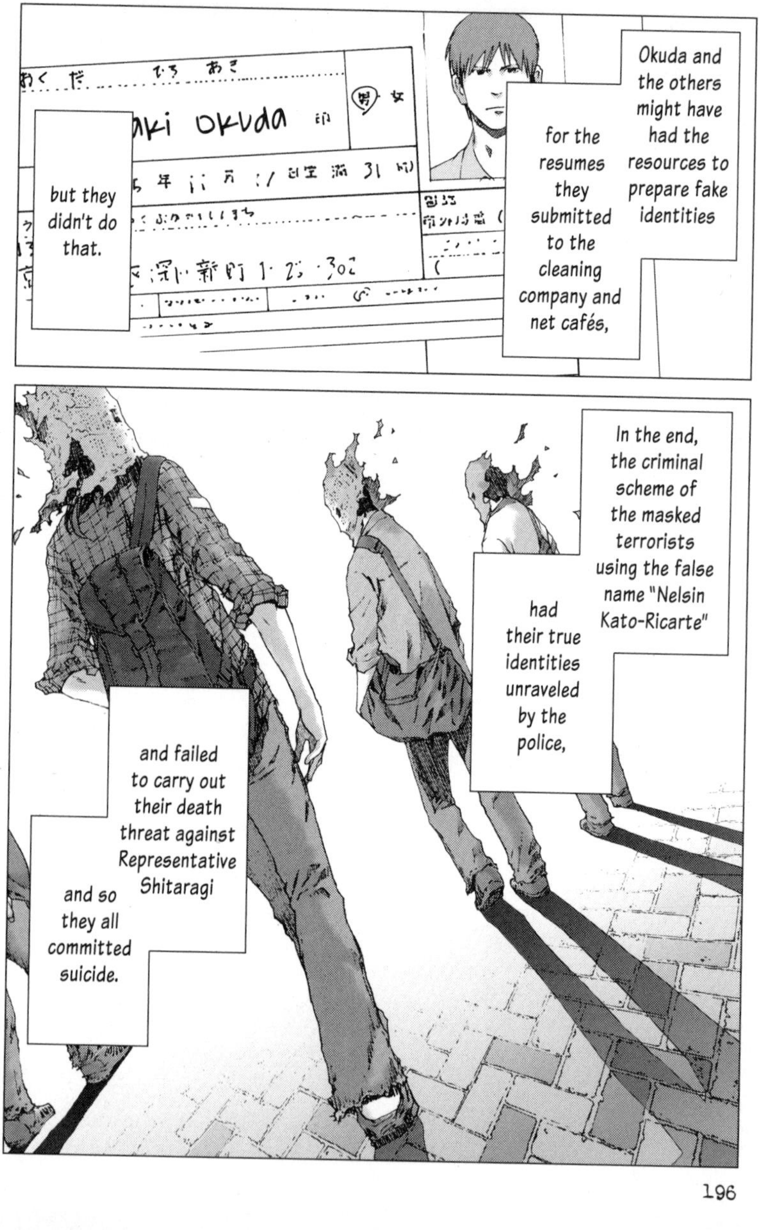
Okuda and the others might have had the resources to prepare fake identities
for the resumes they submitted to the cleaning company and net cafés,
but they didn't do that.
In the end, the criminal scheme of the masked terrorists using the false name "Nelsin Kato-Ricarte"
had their true identities unraveled by the police,
and failed to carry out their death threat against Representative Shitaragi
and so they all committed suicide.

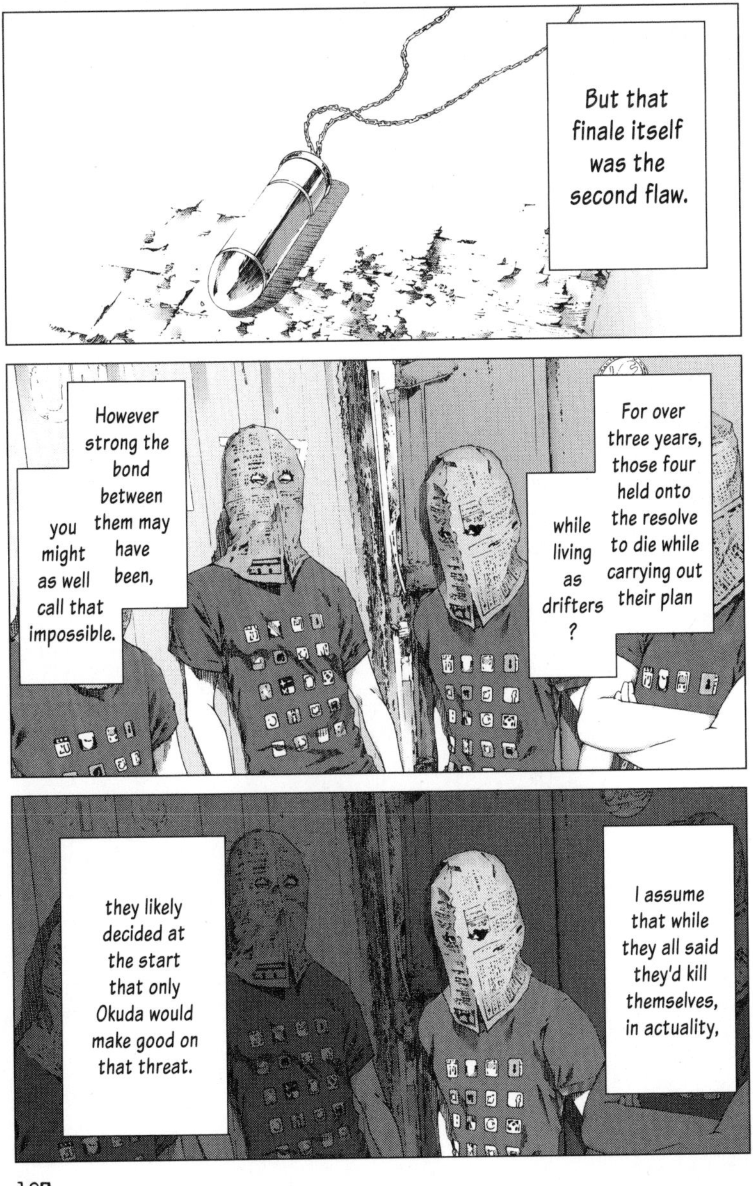
But that finale itself was the second flaw.
For over three years, those four held onto the resolve to die while carrying out their plan
while living as drifters ?
However strong the bond between them may have been,
you might as well call that impossible.
I assume that while they all said they'd kill themselves, in actuality,
they likely decided at the start that only Okuda would make good on that threat.

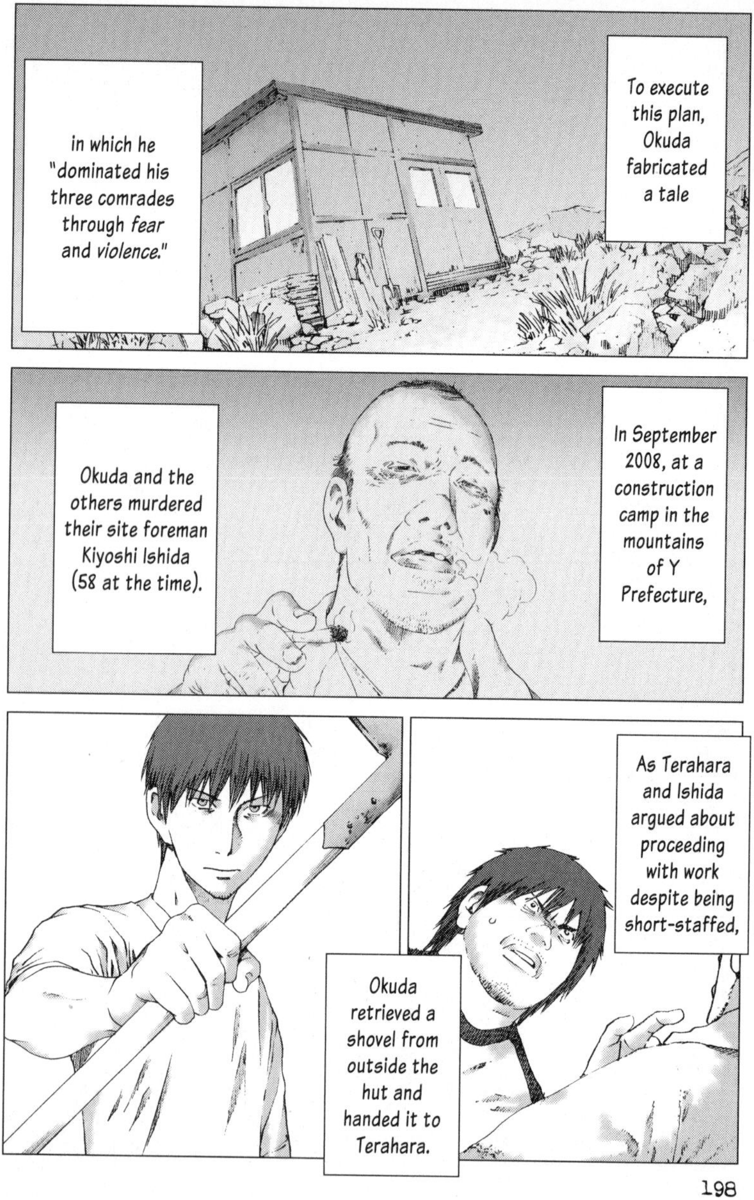
To execute this plan, Okuda fabricated a tale
in which he "dominated his three comrades through *fear* and *violence*."
In September 2008, at a construction camp in the mountains of Y Prefecture,
Okuda and the others murdered their site foreman Kiyoshi Ishida (58 at the time).
As Terahara and Ishida argued about proceeding with work despite being short-staffed,
Okuda retrieved a shovel from outside the hut and handed it to Terahara.

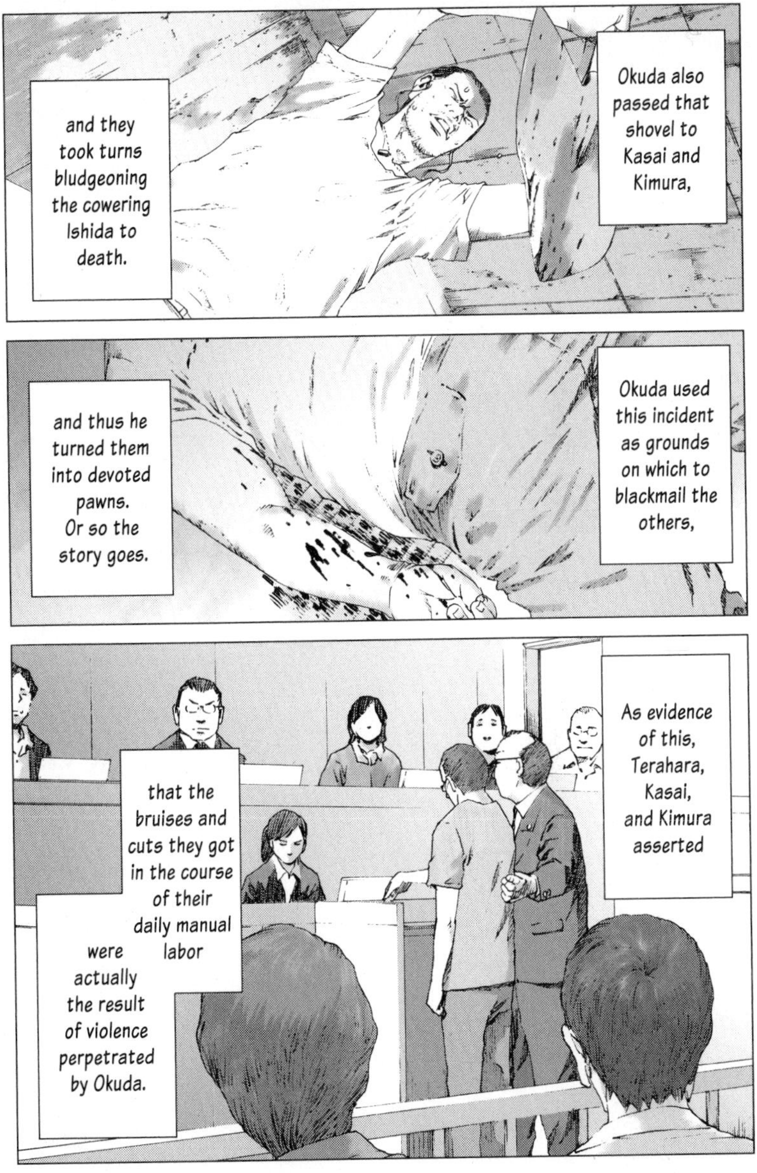
Okuda also passed that shovel to Kasai and Kimura,
and they took turns bludgeoning the cowering Ishida to death.
Okuda used this incident as grounds on which to blackmail the others,
and thus he turned them into devoted pawns. Or so the story goes.
As evidence of this, Terahara, Kasai, and Kimura asserted
that the bruises and cuts they got in the course of their daily manual labor
were actually the result of violence perpetrated by Okuda.

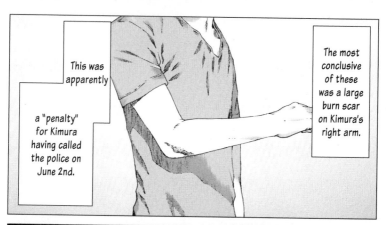

The most conclusive of these was a large burn scar on Kimura's right arm.

This was apparently

a "penalty" for Kimura having called the police on June 2nd.

A similar, smaller burn was also identified on Okuda's left forearm,

but according to the testimony of Kasai and the others, this, too, was a penalty

that Okuda inflicted on himself for carelessly causing a disturbance in Akihabara on May 30th.

While Kasai, Terahara and Kimura were all submissive to Okuda,

they all testified that they had watched and waited for a chance to escape his control.

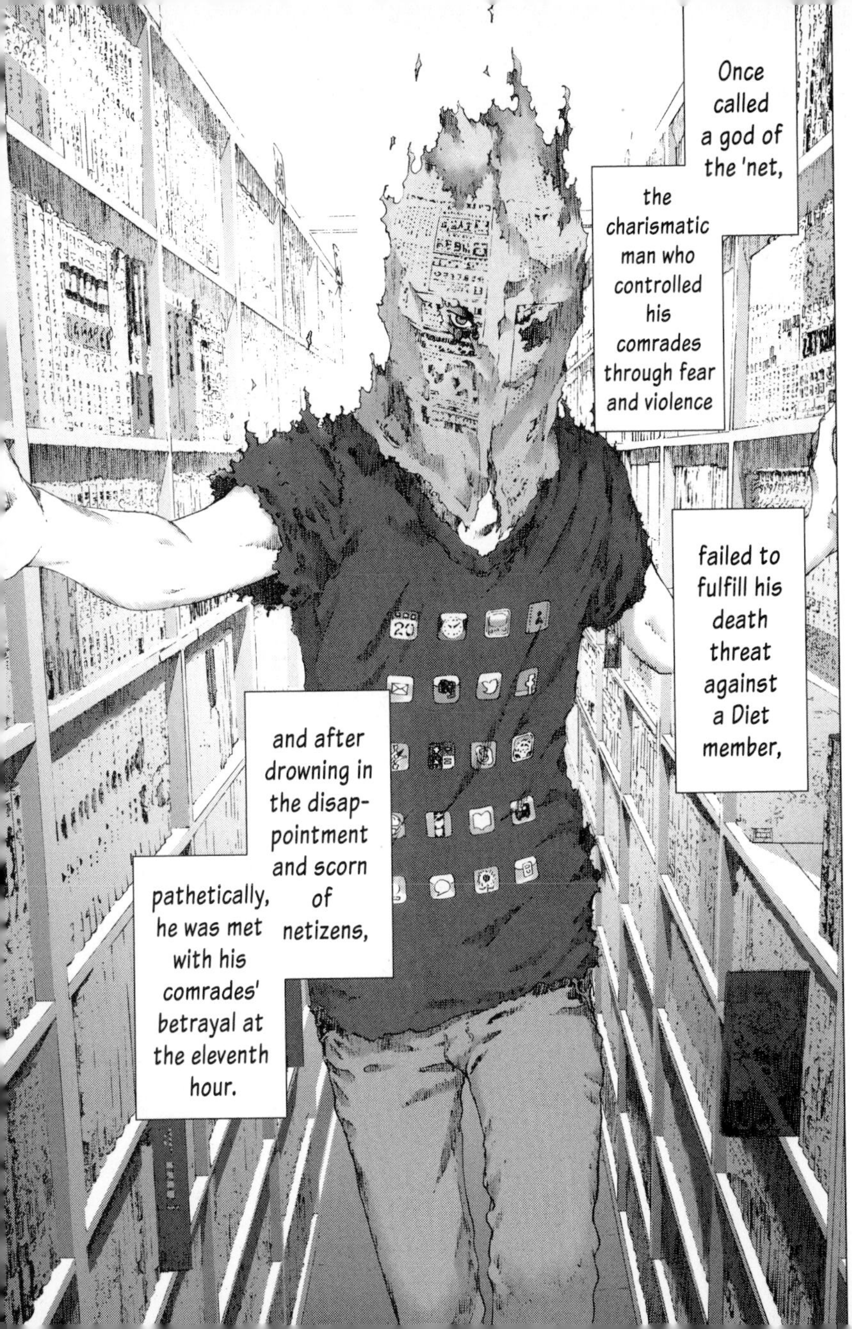
Once called a god of the 'net,
the charismatic man who controlled his comrades through fear and violence
failed to fulfill his death threat against a Diet member,
and after drowning in the disap-pointment and scorn of netizens,
pathetically, he was met with his comrades' betrayal at the eleventh hour.

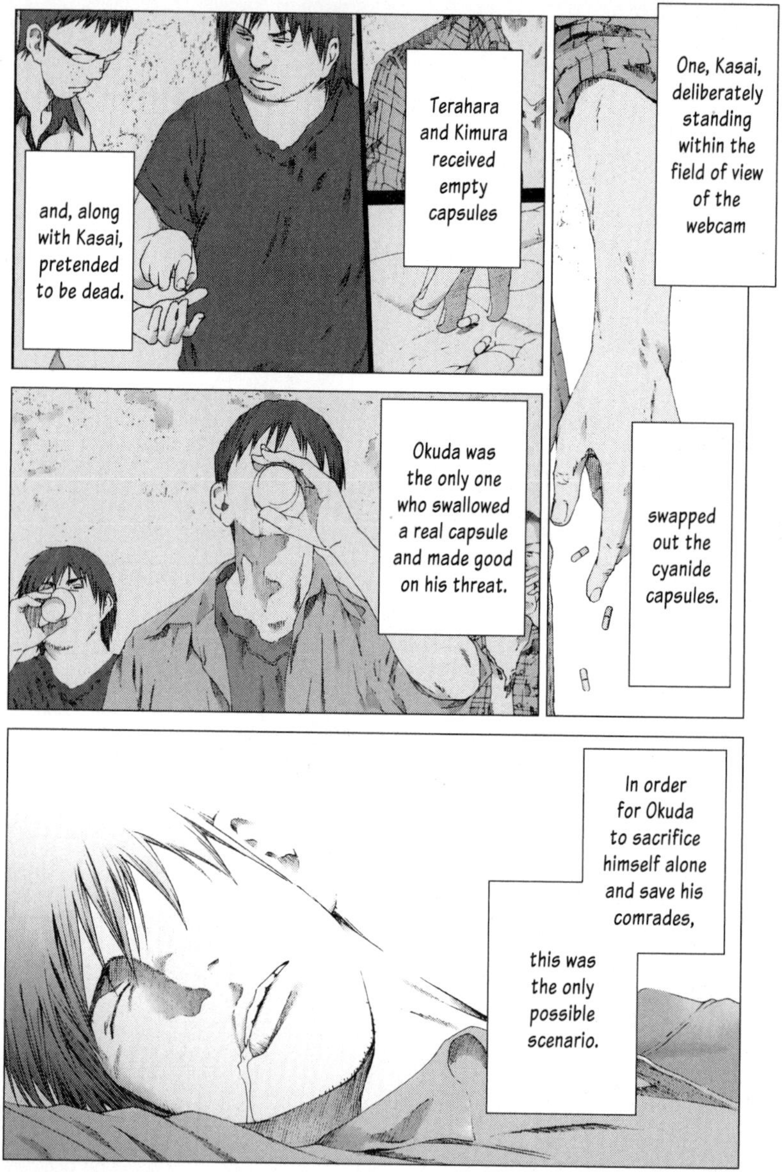
One, Kasai, deliberately standing within the field of view of the webcam
swapped out the cyanide capsules.
Terahara and Kimura received empty capsules
and, along with Kasai, pretended to be dead.
Okuda was the only one who swallowed a real capsule and made good on his threat.
In order for Okuda to sacrifice himself alone and save his comrades,
this was the only possible scenario.

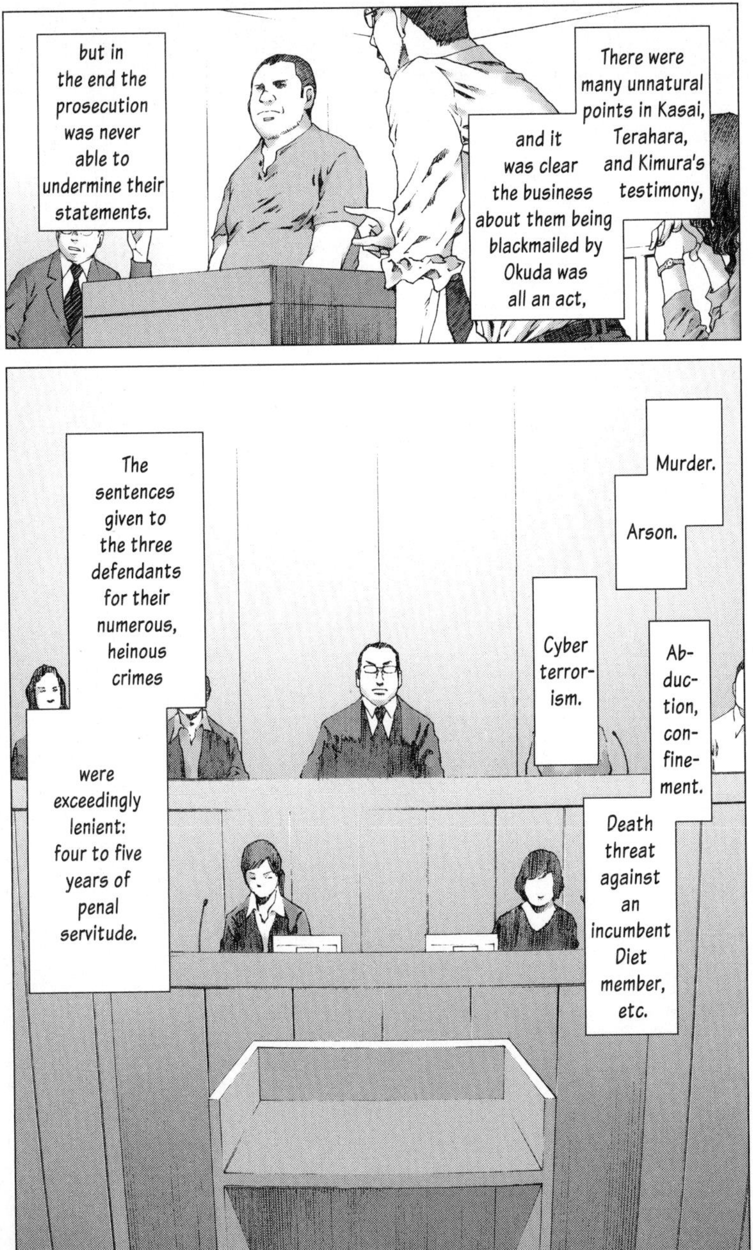
There were many unnatural points in Kasai, Terahara, and Kimura's testimony,
and it was clear the business about them being blackmailed by Okuda was all an act,
but in the end the prosecution was never able to undermine their statements.
Murder.
Arson.
Cyber terror-ism.
Ab-duc-tion, con-fine-ment.
Death threat against an incumbent Diet member, etc.
The sentences given to the three defendants for their numerous, heinous crimes
were exceedingly lenient: four to five years of penal servitude.

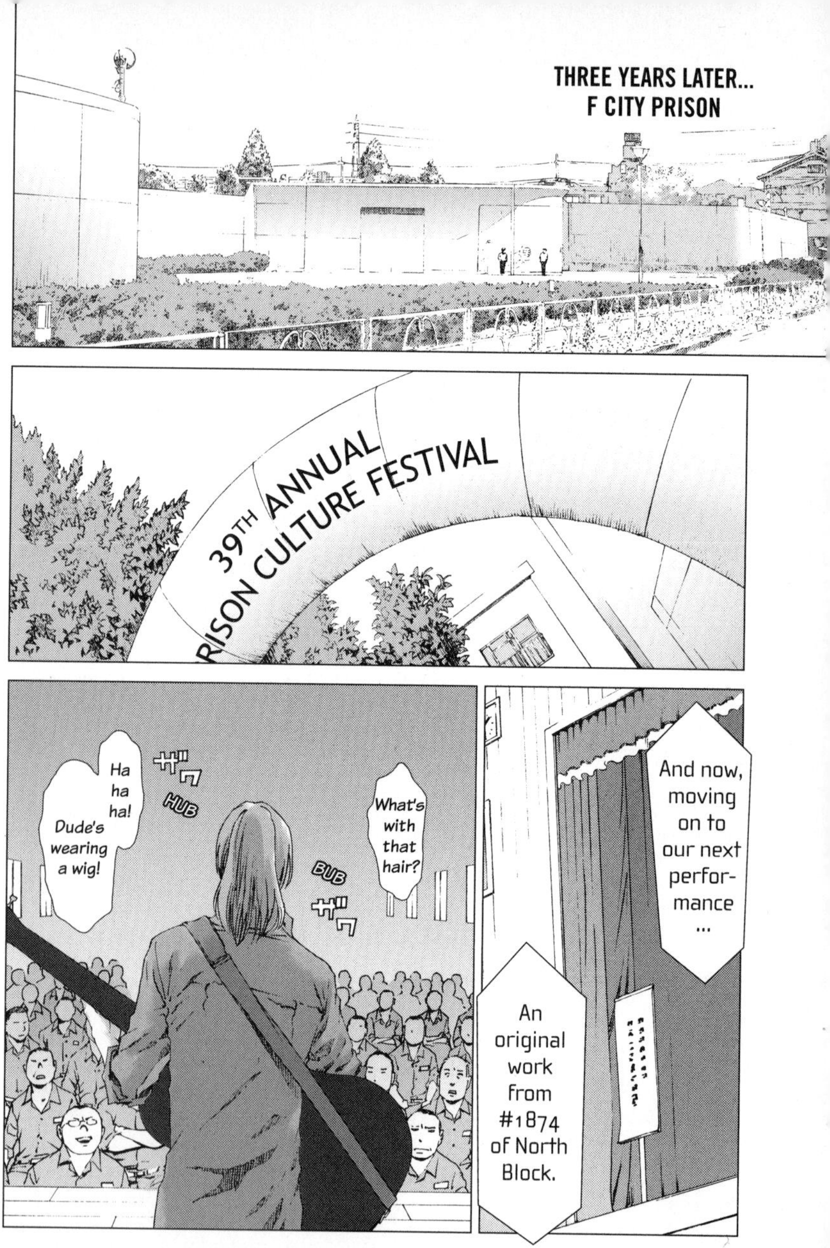
THREE YEARS LATER...
F CITY PRISON
39TH ANNUAL
PRISON CULTURE FESTIVAL
And now, moving on to our next performance...
An original work from #1874 of North Block.
What's with that hair?
ザワ
HUB
BUB
ザワ
Ha ha ha! Dude's wearing a wig!

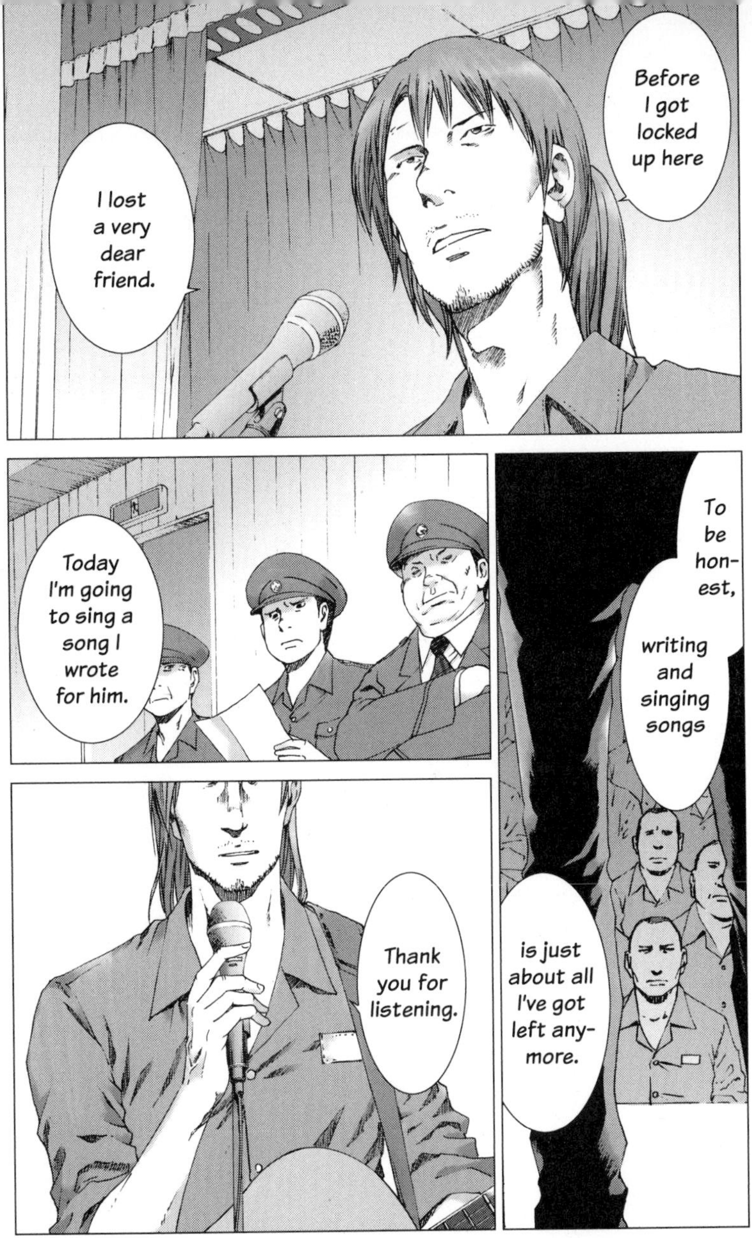
Before I got locked up here
I lost a very dear friend.
To be hon-est,
writing and singing songs
is just about all I've got left any-more.
Today I'm going to sing a song I wrote for him.
Thank you for listening.

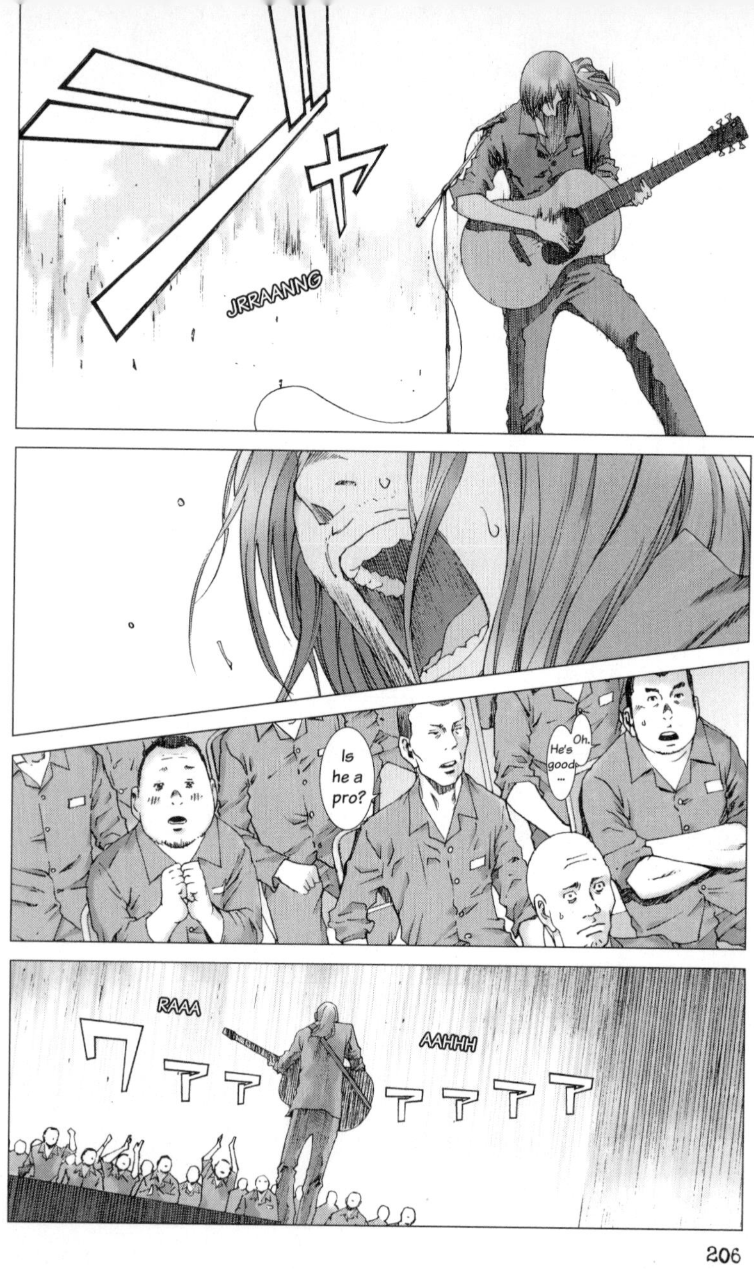
JRRAANNG
Oh. He's good...
Is he a pro?
RAAA
AAHHH

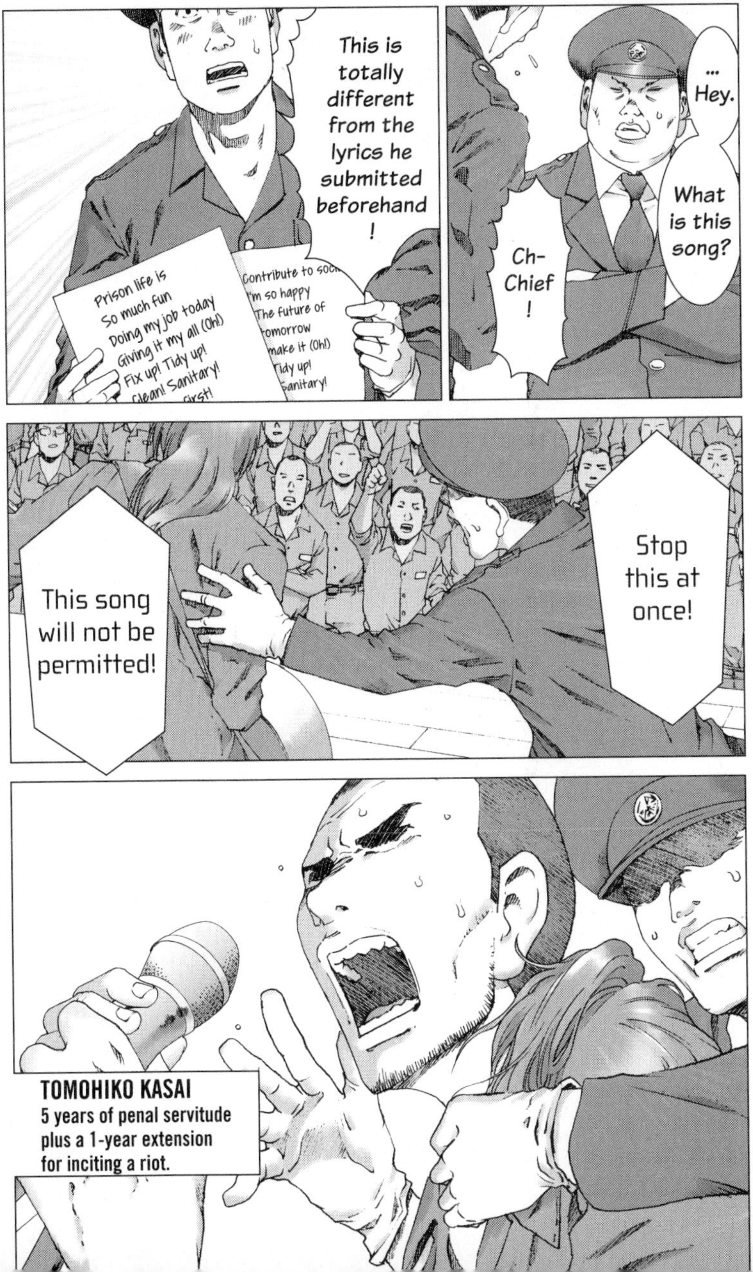
... Hey.
What is this song?
Ch- Chief!
This is totally different from the lyrics he submitted beforehand!
Contribute to soc
'm so happy
The future of
omorrow
make it (Oh!)
Tidy up!
Sanitary!
Prison life is
So much fun
Doing my job today
Giving it my all (Oh!)
Fix up! Tidy up!
Clean! Sanitary!
First!
Stop this at once!
This song will not be permitted!
TOMOHIKO KASAI
5 years of penal servitude plus a 1-year extension for inciting a riot.

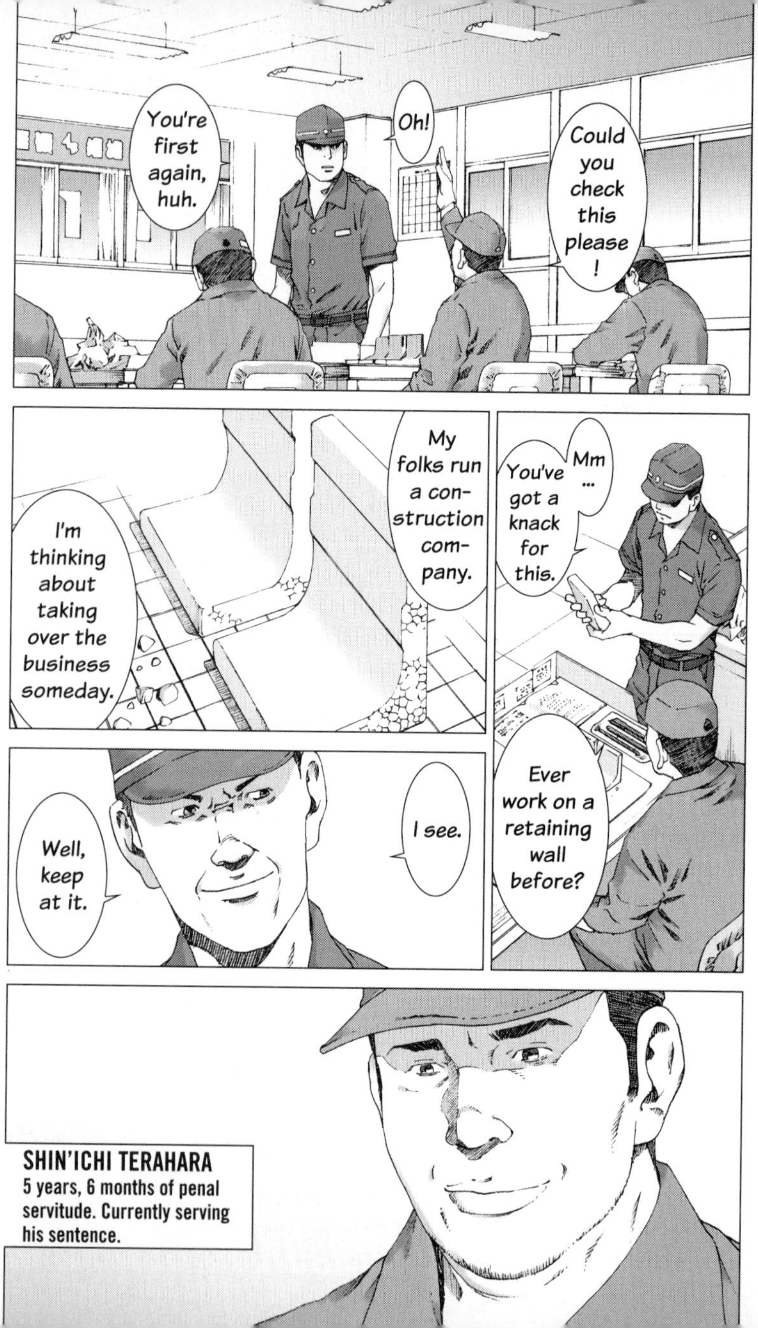
Could you check this please!
Oh!
You're first again, huh.
Mm...
You've got a knack for this.
Ever work on a retaining wall before?
My folks run a construction company.
I'm thinking about taking over the business someday.
I see.
Well, keep at it.
SHIN'ICHI TERAHARA
5 years, 6 months of penal servitude. Currently serving his sentence.

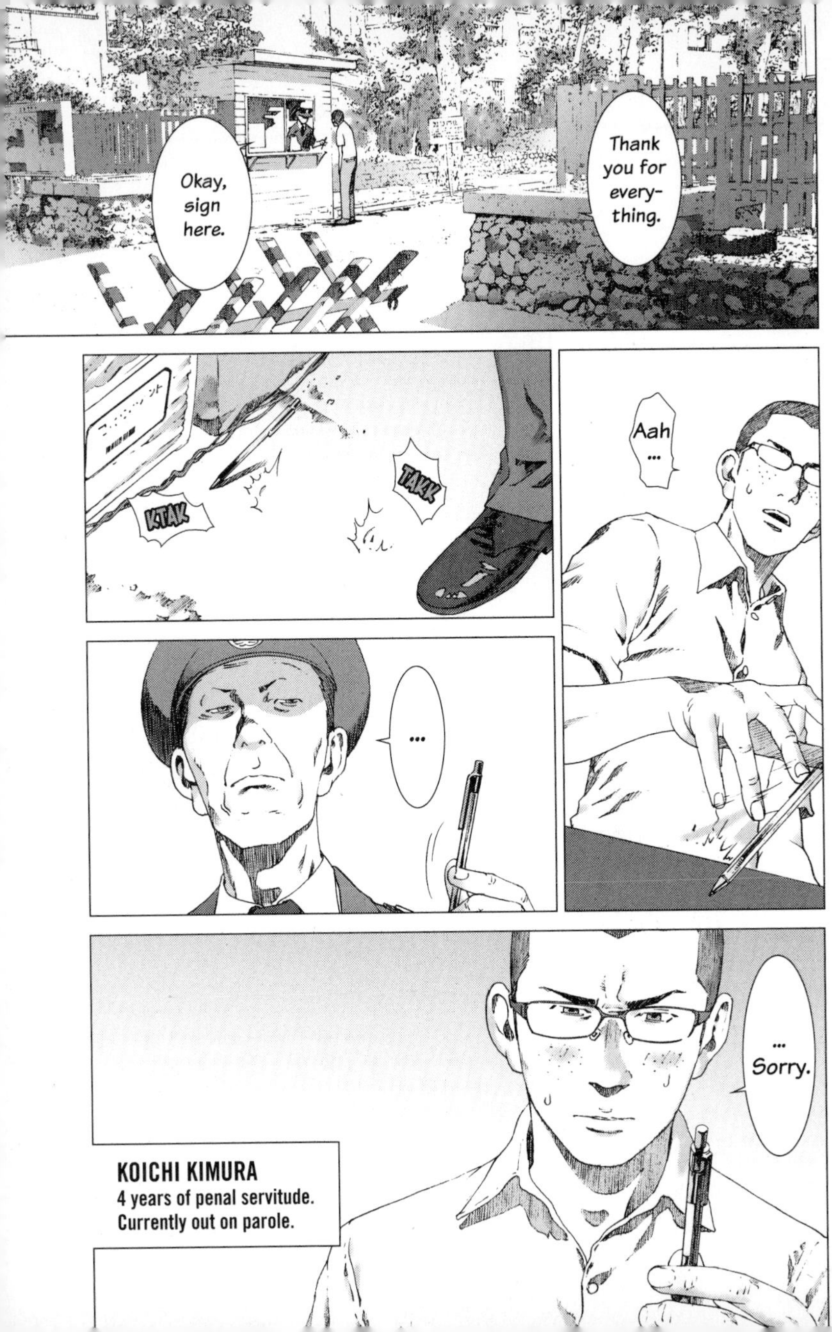
Thank you for everything.
Okay, sign here.
Aah ...
TAKK
KTAK
...
... Sorry.
KOICHI KIMURA
4 years of penal servitude.
Currently out on parole.

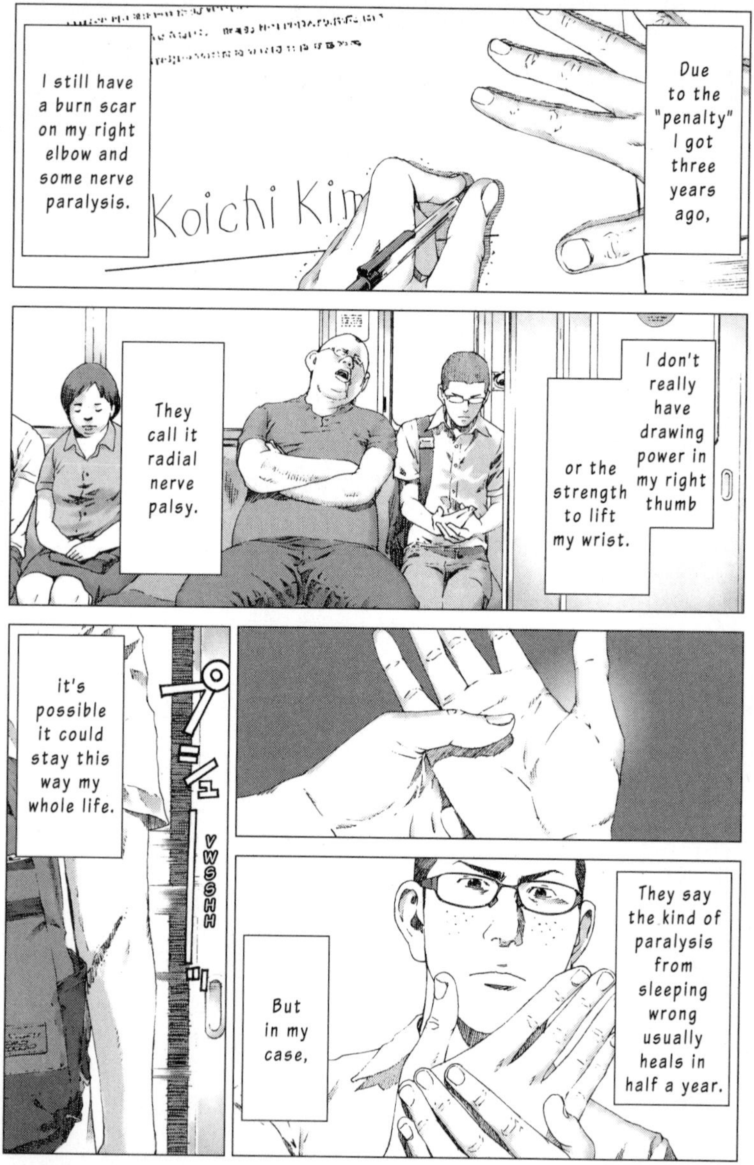
Due to the "penalty" I got three years ago,
I still have a burn scar on my right elbow and some nerve paralysis.
Koichi Kim
I don't really have drawing power in my right thumb
or the strength to lift my wrist.
They call it radial nerve palsy.
They say the kind of paralysis from sleeping wrong usually heals in half a year.
But in my case,
it's possible it could stay this way my whole life.
VWSSHH

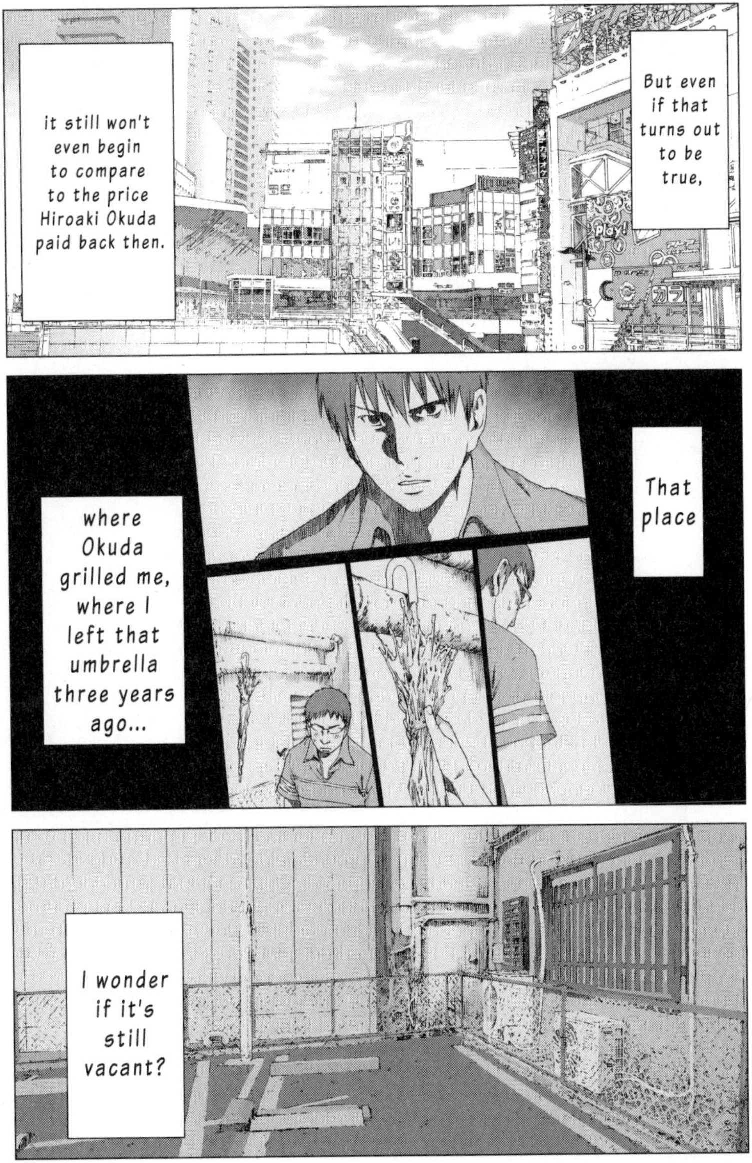
But even if that turns out to be true,
Play!
it still won't even begin to compare to the price Hiroaki Okuda paid back then.
That place
where Okuda grilled me, where I left that umbrella three years ago...
I wonder if it's still vacant?

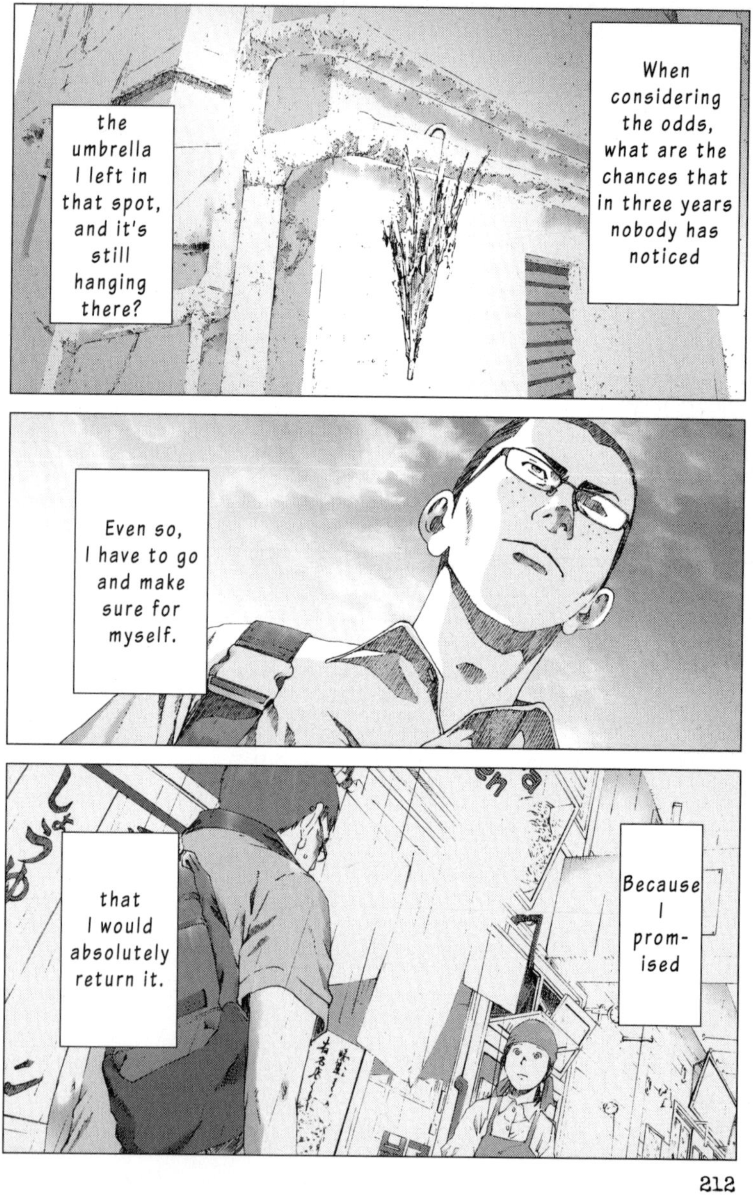
When considering the odds, what are the chances that in three years nobody has noticed
the umbrella I left in that spot, and it's still hanging there?
Even so, I have to go and make sure for myself.
Because I prom-ised
that I would absolutely return it.

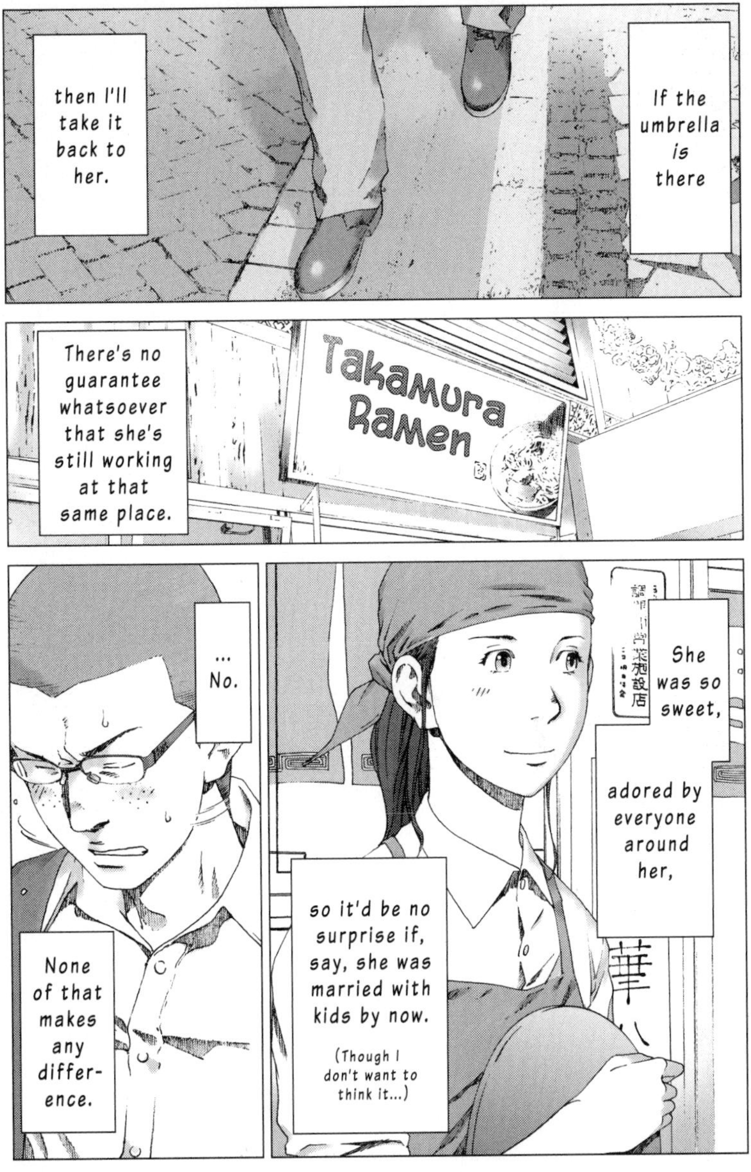

If the umbrella is there
then I'll take it back to her.
Takamura Ramen
There's no guarantee whatsoever that she's still working at that same place.
She was so sweet,
adored by everyone around her,
so it'd be no surprise if, say, she was married with kids by now.
(Though I don't want to think it...)
... No.
None of that makes any differ-ence.

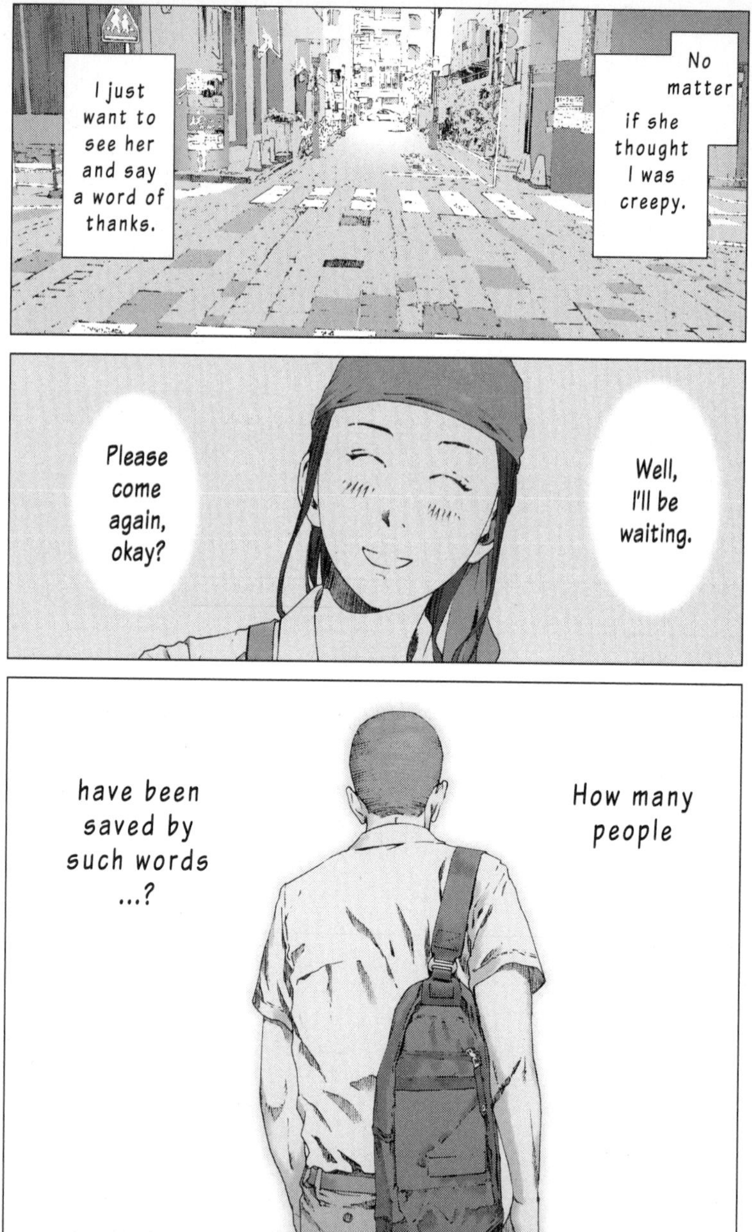
No matter if she thought I was creepy.
I just want to see her and say a word of thanks.
Well, I'll be waiting.
Please come again, okay?
How many people
have been saved by such words ...?

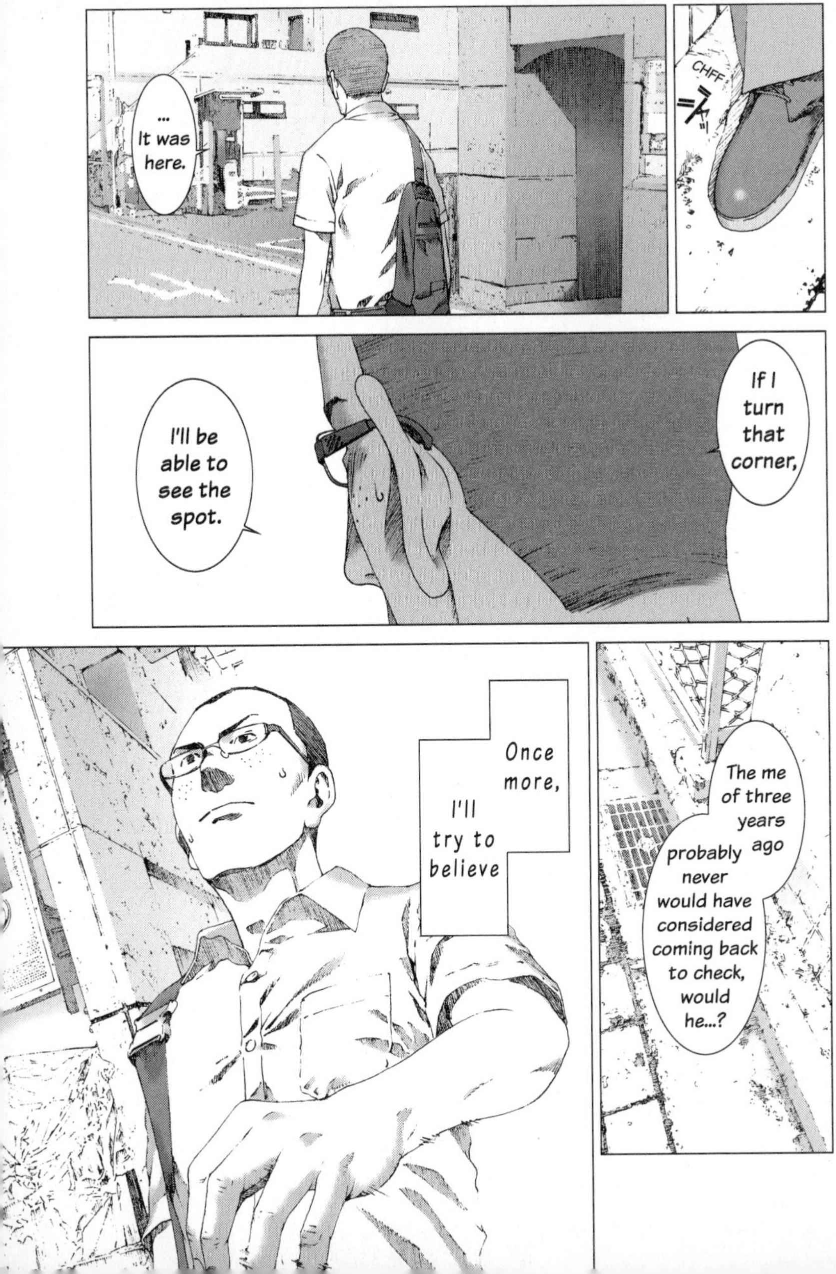
CHFF
... It was here.
If I turn that corner,
I'll be able to see the spot.
The me of three years ago probably never would have considered coming back to check, would he...?
Once more, I'll try to believe

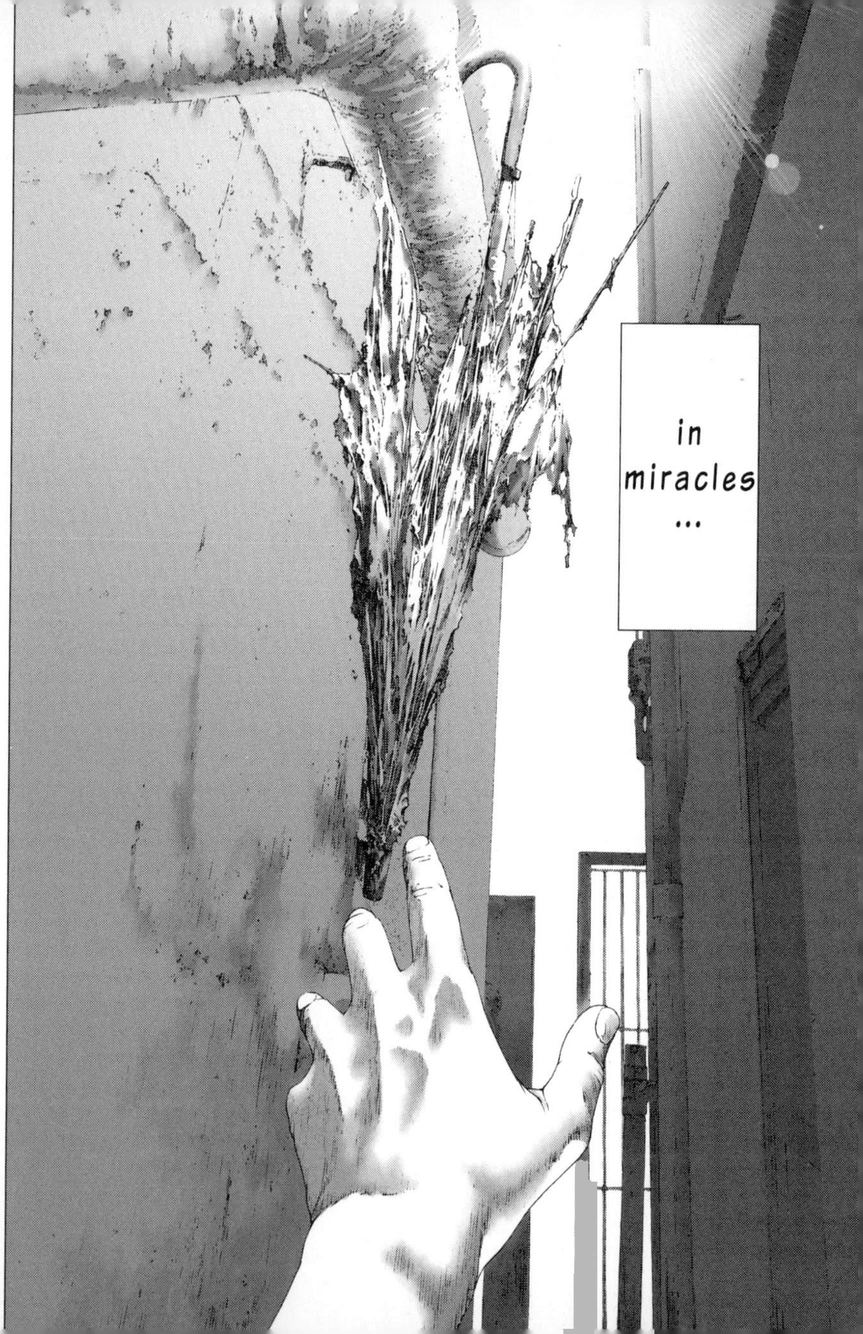
in miracles ...

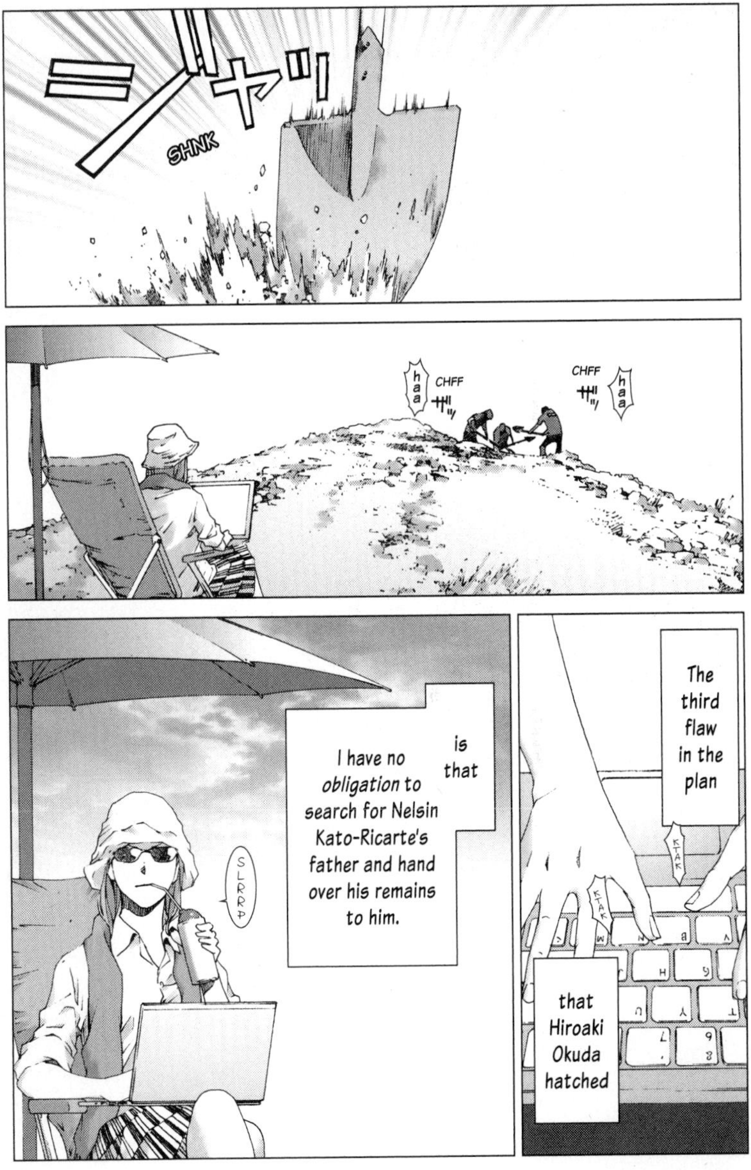
SHNK
haa
CHFF
haa
CHFF
The third flaw in the plan
KTAK
KTAK
that Hiroaki Okuda hatched
is that
I have no *obligation* to search for Nelsin Kato-Ricarte's father and hand over his remains to him.
SLRRP

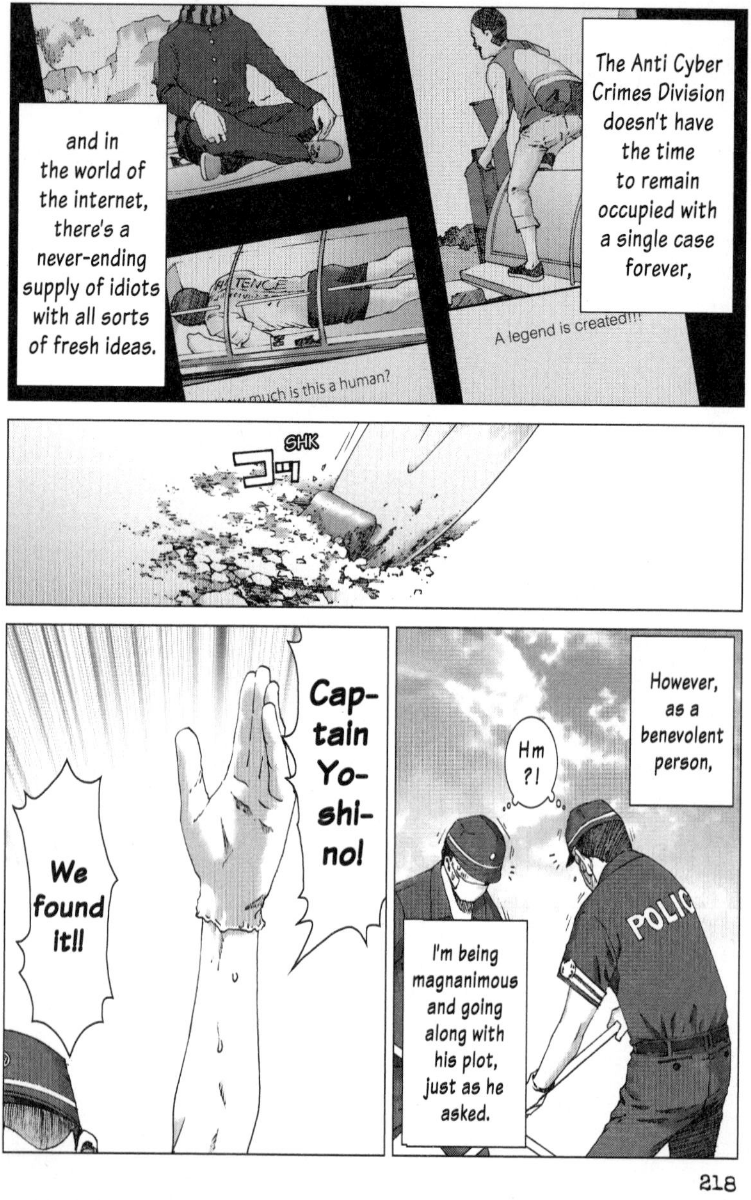

The Anti Cyber Crimes Division doesn't have the time to remain occupied with a single case forever,
A legend is created!!!
and in the world of the internet, there's a never-ending supply of idiots with all sorts of fresh ideas.
much is this a human?
SHK
However, as a benevolent person,
Hm ?!
I'm being magnanimous and going along with his plot, just as he asked.
POLIC
Cap-tain Yo-shi-no!
We found it!!

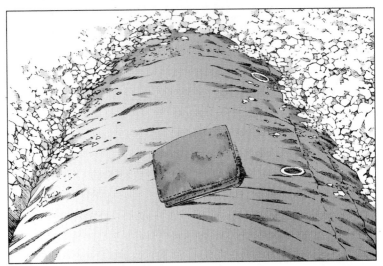

Hmf.

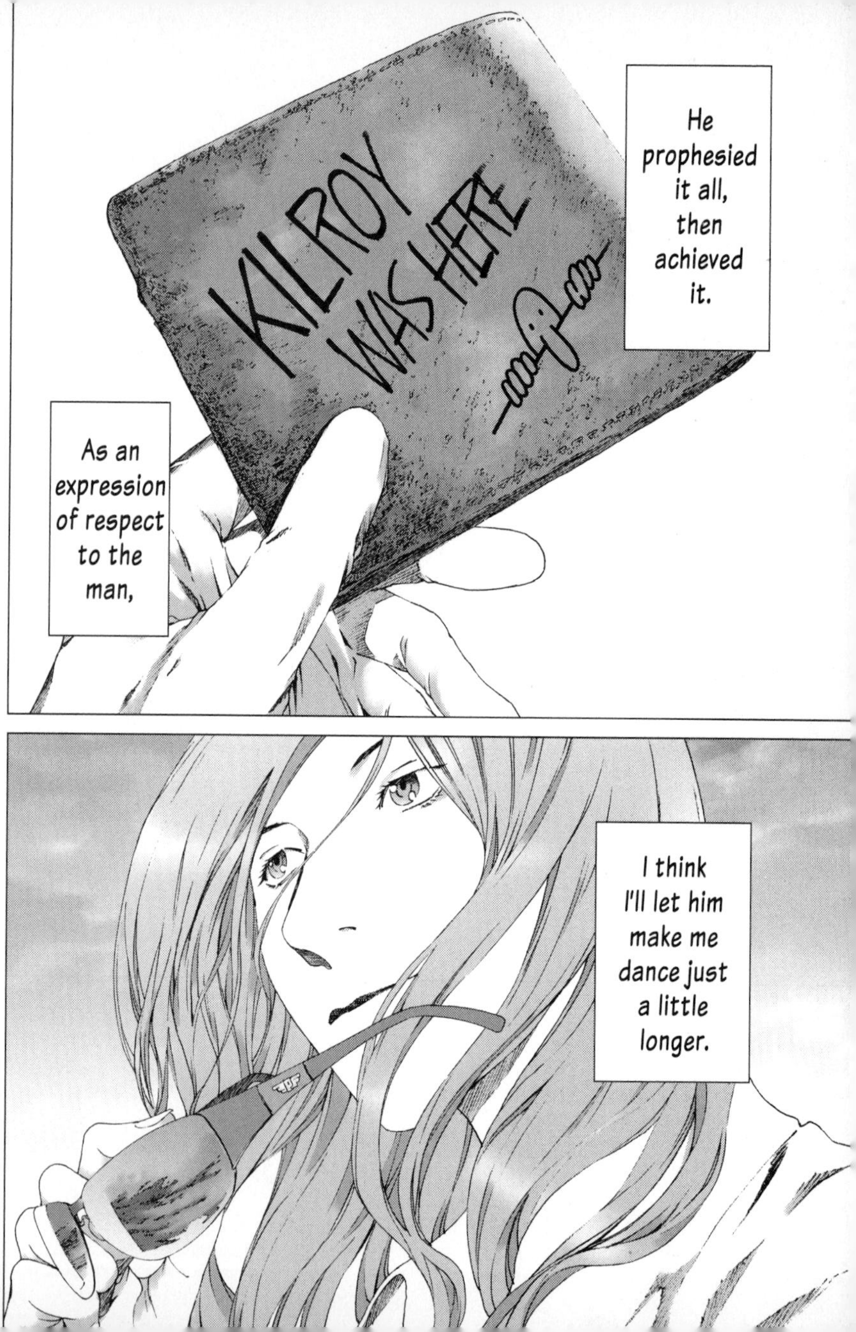
He prophesied it all, then achieved it.
KILROY WAS HERE
As an expression of respect to the man,
I think I'll let him make me dance just a little longer.

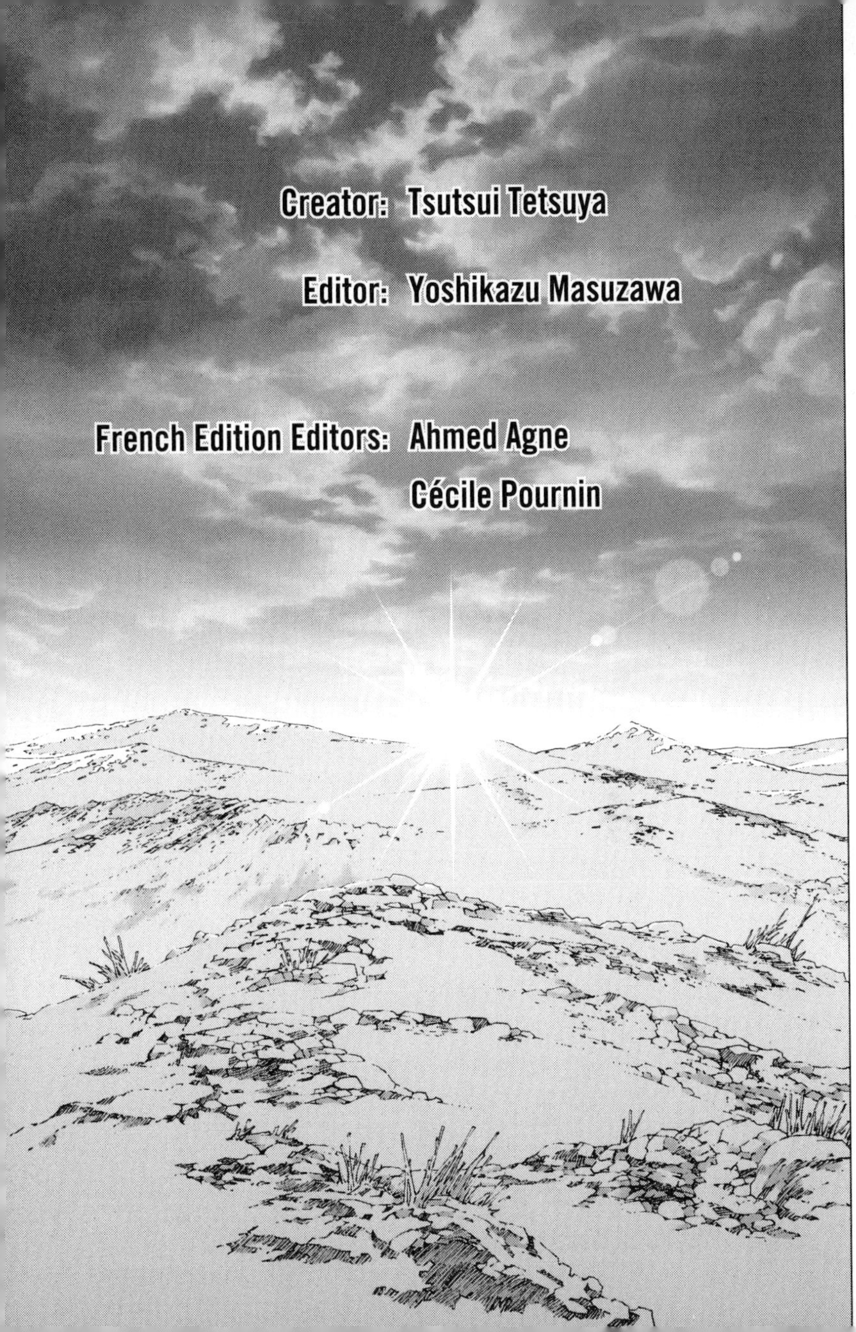

Creator: Tsutsui Tetsuya

Editor: Yoshikazu Masuzawa

French Edition Editors: Ahmed Agne

Cécile Pournin

PROPHECY

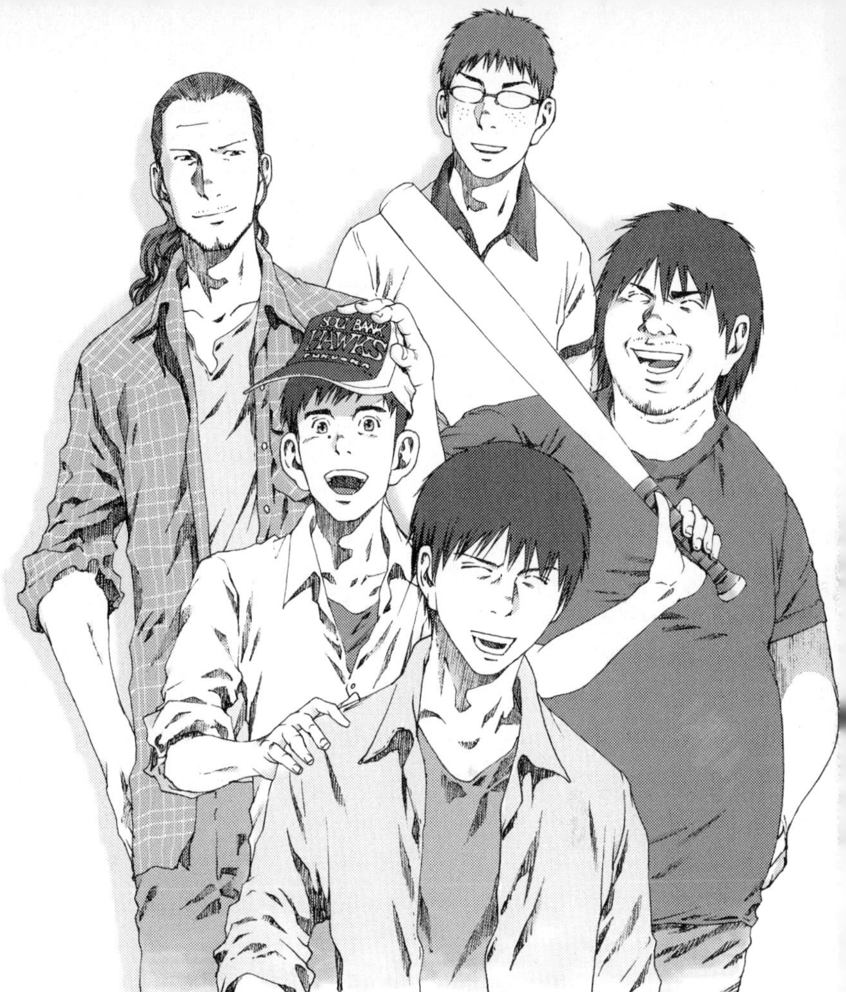
HAWKS

Thank you very much for reading!

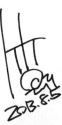

2013.8.5

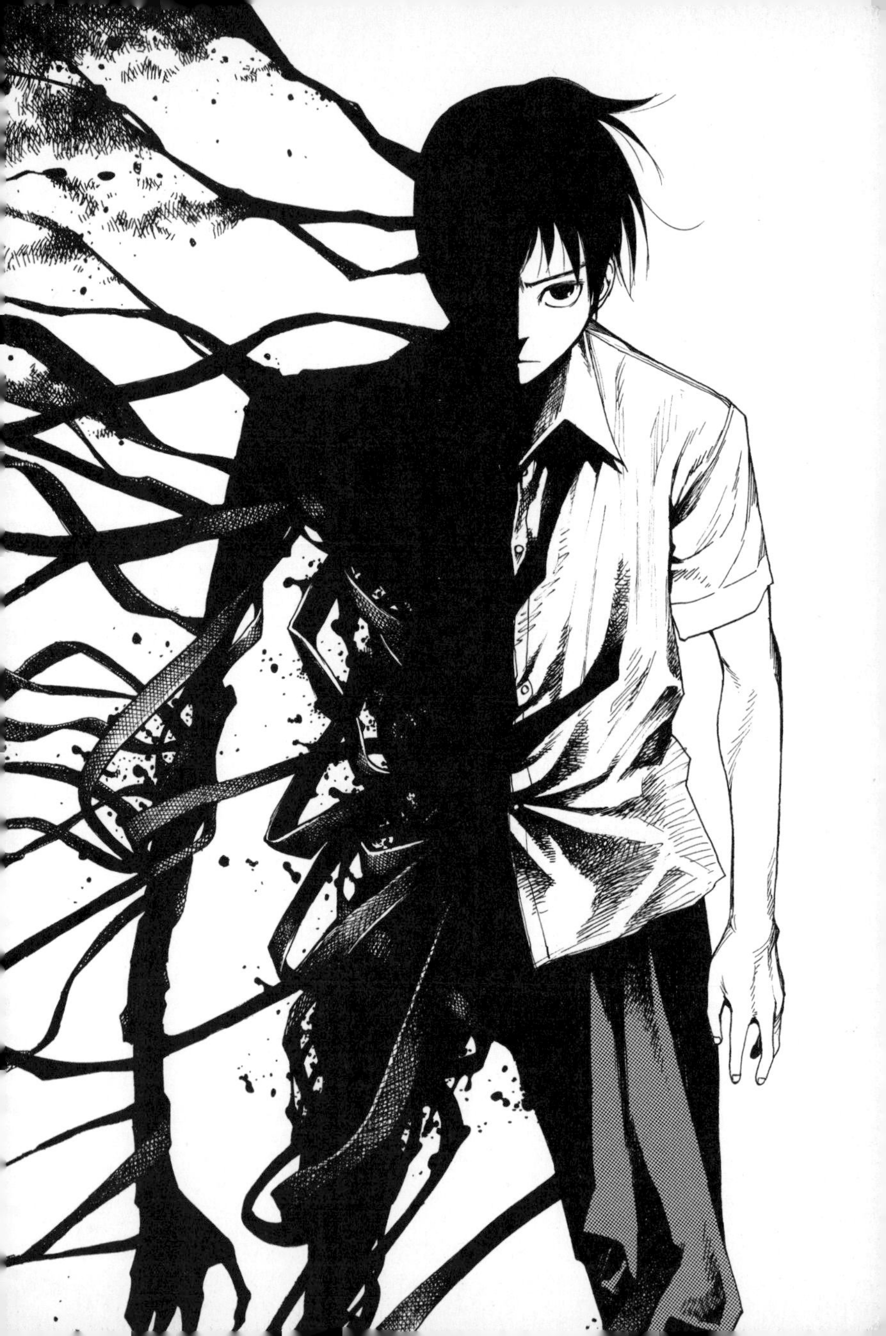

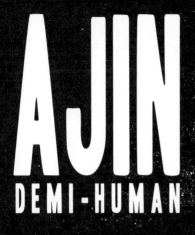

AJIN
DEMI-HUMAN

STORY: TSUINA MIURA
ART: GAMON SAKURAI

SAY YOU GET HIT BY A TRUCK AND DIE.
YOU COME BACK TO LIFE. GOOD OR BAD?

FOR HIGH SCHOOLER KEI—AND FOR AT LEAST FORTY-SIX OTHERS—
IMMORTALITY COMES AS THE NASTIEST SURPRISE EVER.

SADLY FOR KEI, BUT REFRESHINGLY FOR THE READER, SUCH A FEAT
DOESN'T MAKE HIM A SUPERHERO. IN THE EYES OF BOTH THE GENERAL
PUBLIC AND GOVERNMENTS, HE'S A RARE SPECIMEN WHO NEEDS TO BE
HUNTED DOWN AND HANDED OVER TO SCIENTISTS TO BE EXPERIMENTED
ON FOR LIFE—A DEMI-HUMAN WHO MUST DIE A THOUSAND DEATHS
FOR THE BENEFIT OF HUMANITY.

VOLUMES 1-3 AVAILABLE NOW!

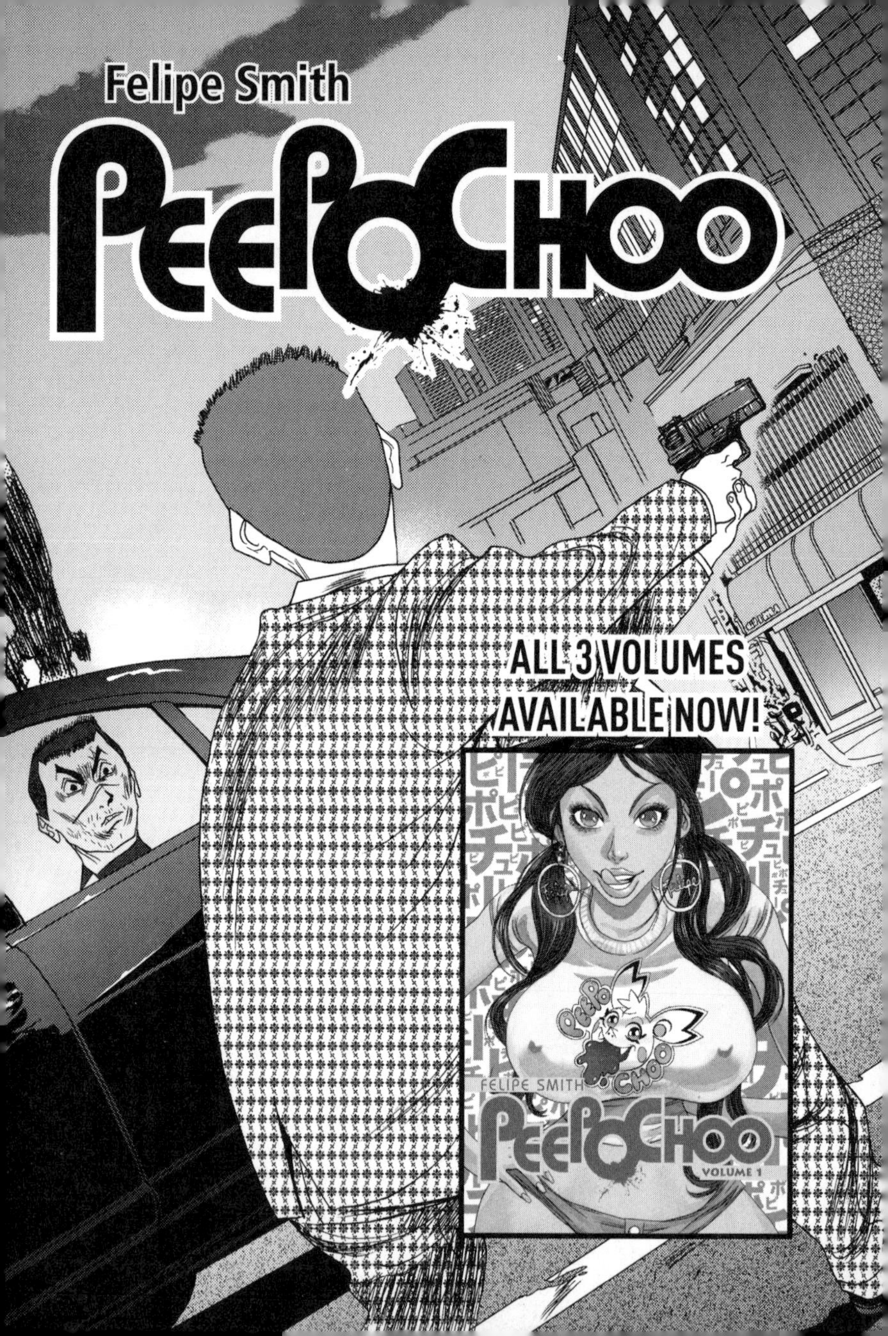
Felipe Smith
PEEPO CHOO
ALL 3 VOLUMES
AVAILABLE NOW!
FELIPE SMITH
PEEPO CHOO
VOLUME 1

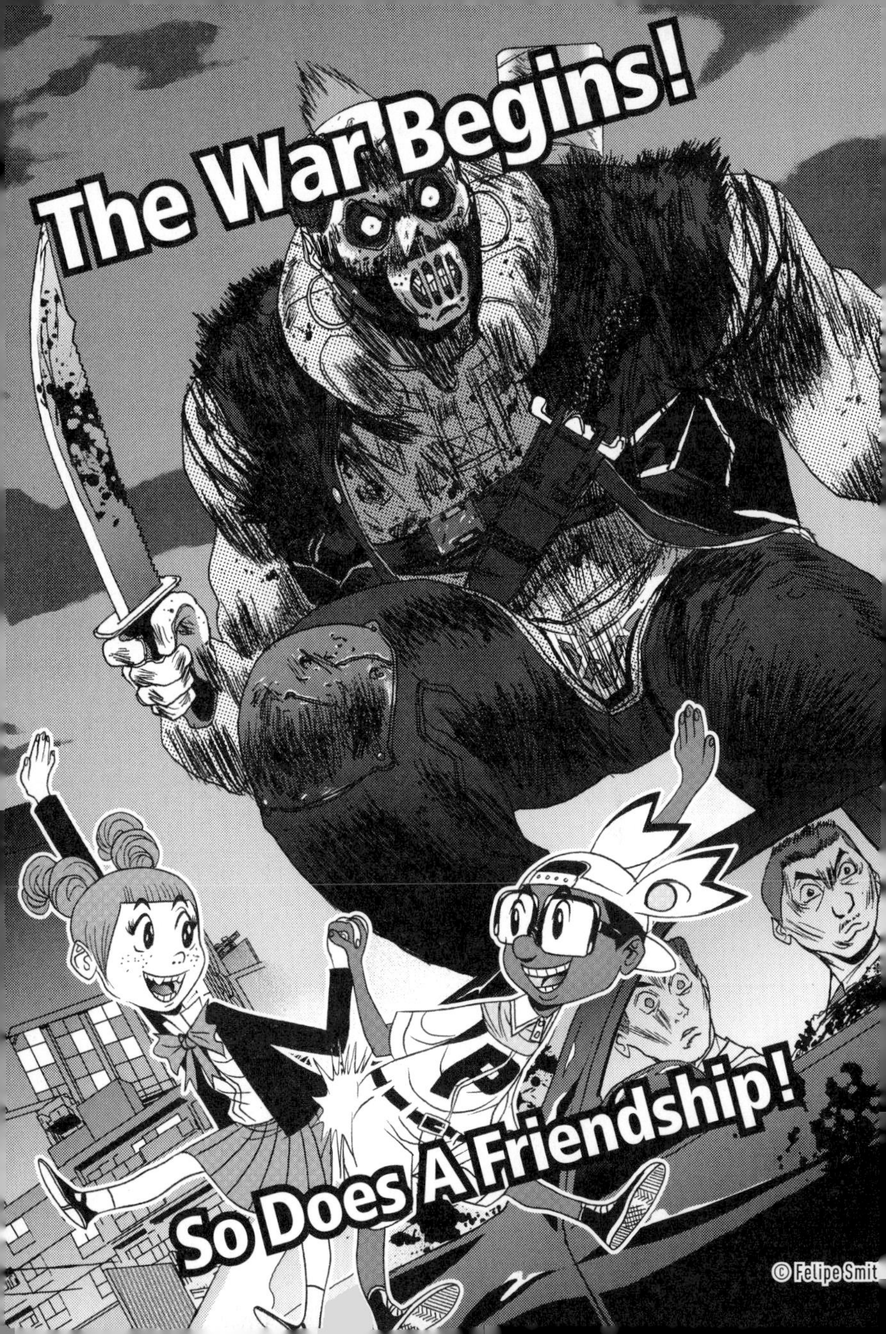
The War Begins!
So Does A Friendship!
© Felipe Smith

Prophecy, part 3

Translation: Kumar Sivasubramanian
Production: Grace Lu
Nicole Dochych
Anthony Quintessenza

First published in France in 2013 by Ki-oon, an imprint of AC Media Ltd.
English translation rights arranged through Tuttle-Mori Agency, Inc.
English language version produced by Vertical, Inc.

Translation provided by Vertical, Inc., 2015
Published by Vertical Comics, an imprint of Vertical, Inc., New York

This is a work of fiction.

ISBN: 978-1-939130-78-5

Manufactured in the United States of America

First Edition

Vertical, Inc.
451 Park Avenue South
7th Floor
New York, NY 10016
www.vertical-inc.com